Baptist
Battles

Baptist Battles

Social Change and Religious Conflict in the Southern Baptist Convention

by
Nancy Tatom Ammerman

Rutgers University Press
New Brunswick and London

Library of Congress Cataloging-in-Publication Data

Ammerman, Nancy Tatom, 1950–
    Baptist battles : social change and religious conflict in the
Southern Baptist Convention / Nancy Tatom Ammerman.
        p.   cm.
    Includes bibliographical references.
    ISBN 0-8135-1556-4 (cloth)   ISBN 0-8135-1557-2 (pbk.)
    1. Southern Baptist Convention—History—20th century.
2. Baptists—United States—History—20th century.
3. Fundamentalism.   4. Church controversies—Baptists—History—20th
century.   I. Title.
BX6462.3.A55   1990
286'.132—dc20 —dc20   89-48883
                                                              CIP

British Cataloging-in-Publication information available

for baptists

Contents

List of Figures and Tables

Preface

This book is a peculiar mixture of sociological curiosity and personal involvement. It is a scientific analysis of a denomination in conflict, and it is indirectly the story of my own religious odyssey. The story told here of consensus moving toward division is also the story of my own journey from unquestioning acceptance to alienation. The elements of systematic analysis and autobiography are not often brought together in scholarly work; indeed they can be a dangerous mix. All I can promise is that my own involvement may give passion and life to the story and that my sociological discipline may yield insight that my involvement alone would not have revealed.

My sociological curiosity has to do with the nature of religious conflict. In the early 1980s I complained that as a sociologist I wished *somebody* would study the Southern Baptists; to that my friend Walker Knight replied, "Why not you?" This, then, is a study examining why and how Southern Baptists differ among themselves and how that conflict can be understood within the context of other conflicts, other organizations, other times. It is a study offered to other sociologists and students of religion as a contribution toward our understanding of the role of religion in the lives of modern Americans.

My interest in studying this phenomenon began in part because I became convinced that our existing knowledge about religious conflict and schism was limited in two critical ways. First, accounts of conflict were always retrospective, told as an answer to the question "Why did this denomination split?" As such, they could never take adequate account of the process of division or of conflicts that did not result in division. Second, our theories about division seemed to come in two varieties, neither complete without the other. Either we tried to answer the cultural question of why social and religious differences arose within a once united group, or we tried to answer the organizational question of how one group gained dominance over another. It seemed to me that a theory of religious division would be incomplete without answers to both the cultural and the organizational questions.[1] What follows is not a theory of religious division, as such. It is rather an account of the process of conflict that is informed by theoretical questions. It is intended as a contribution toward the kind of data we need if a more adequate theory of religious conflict and division is to be developed.

But this is also a study I offer to the people about whom it is written. These are important people in my life, and I have shared with them in the griefs of these years. Many of the people about whom I care most deeply have been a part of the ministry of the Southern Baptist Convention (SBC). They are the people who have nurtured me—the congregations of which I have been a part; my parents, who have invested their lives in leading Southern Baptist churches; the teachers and chaplains at the small Baptist college I attended, who began to open up a bigger world to me; the community of faith and scholarship that surrounds the Southern Baptist Seminary, where my husband attended and where we both found lasting friendships and sustaining ideas. These people taught me to be "baptist." I share with them and with the others described in this book a deep commitment that has not been altered by my own movement away from being "Southern" baptist.

My involvement with the people I have studied has admittedly posed challenges to the task of objective and even-handed analysis. No analysis is ever completely objective—both we and our informants are after all subjects. This book is about subjects by a subject. It is about history, made by people, and of which I have sometimes been a part. So while it is not *objec*tive, I hope it is even-handed. From the beginning, I have imposed rules on myself as a way to minimize the risks. Most basically, the questions I would ask about this conflict would be informed by sociological theory, not by any desire to prove one side right or wrong. This book is not an analysis of who was right and who was wrong but an analysis of why each side came to view the other as wrong and what they did once that had been decided.

The rules I imposed on myself in gathering data were so basic as almost not to need stating: I would never betray the confidence of either side or provide either side with research reports that were not also available to the other. And I would never vote or otherwise support either side. Because I had much more natural access to informants among moderates, I intentionally spent most of my convention time with conservatives; and in the process I learned to appreciate their grievances. In the political battles, my ability to be evenhanded was probably aided by an early realization that my own long-term loyalty really did not belong to either side. I really did not have a stake in which side won. As the research has drawn to a close, however, I have realized that I do have a stake in the survival of the organization that has become known as the Southern Baptist Alliance. In writing on that group, I cannot claim the same detachment I claim for the rest of the book.

Along the way I have accumulated many debts, many partners who have made this project possible and who deserve at least the thanks I can give them in print. I am deeply grateful to the hundreds of Baptists who talked to us and the hundreds more who sent us their questionnaires. They opened their lives to us in a way that I hope is faithfully offered back in the pages that follow. Talking to researchers was especially risky for many of the people who were involved in the political struggles in the denomination, as well as for many who were working in the agencies. Their trust made this account possible, and I have tried to be worthy of it.

Three graduate students at Emory have served as primary research assistants in various phases of the work. Scott Thumma, Deborah Finn, and Arthur Farnsley have not only helped with questionnaire construction, mailing list management, transcript typing, and other mundane work; they have also been valued conversation partners and fellow learners. Throughout the writing of this manuscript I have benefited from the careful reading and responses offered by Arthur Farnsley and by Ray Norsworthy, who spent the spring of 1989 at Emory. In 1988 an ad hoc group of people who have written about Baptists offered valuable insight into the early chapters of the book. That group included James Mc-Clendon, Robison James, Sarah Frances Anders, Fisher Humphreys, William Rogers, Robert Moore, and Gary Mayfield. Historians Brooks Holifield and Walter Shurden offered critical comments on chapters 2 and 3. Sociologists Rodney Stark and Wade Clark Roof offered important help with chapters 4 and 5. And Larry McSwain, sociologist at the Southern Baptist Theological Seminary, gave chapters 6 through 8 a critical reading. Conversations with historians Bill Leonard, Ben Primer, and Samuel Hill have also helped to clarify my understanding of what was happening in this denomination. Political scientist James Guth, also engaged in the study of Southern Baptists, made available his questionnaires and research reports and offered many helpful suggestions. My Candler colleague William Johnson Everett read the entire manuscript and offered important insights about ways it might become better. I am also indebted to Karen Ivy, Terry Thomas Primer, and Walker Knight who helped me to make sure that this book would make sense to non-sociologists. And Paige Patterson has read much of what I have written, offering very helpful insight and critique. I am grateful to all of these who entered into the writing process with me. They are, of course, absolved of blame for the flaws that remain, but this is clearly a better book because of their involvement.

I am also indebted to people and organizations that made information available to me. Dr. Lynn May and the staff of the Southern Baptist Historical Commission run a very impressive operation. Pat Brown and Bill Sumners were especially helpful in providing materials and equipment whenever I needed them. I have also benefitted from the audio-visual archives at the library of the Southern Baptist Theological Seminary and appreciate the generous help of librarian Andy Rawls. Orrin Morris and the Research Division of the Home Mission Board made available the data and internal studies housed in their library. Martin Bradley's staff in the Research Services Department of the Sunday School Board created our random sample with great skill and dispatch. Wilmer C. Fields and then Al Shackleford, along with Dan Martin, Marv Knox, and the rest of the SBC newsroom staff were helpful above and beyond the call of duty. They did more than run the operation that provided the regular reporting I depended on for events I could not directly observe, they were also the people who filled in details, connected me with people I needed to know, and otherwise made my work during conventions pleasant and possible. Southern Baptist *Advocate* editor Russell Kaemmerling generously provided back issues, as did *SBC Today*. Walker Knight and Jack Harwell, editors of *SBC Today* during these years, have been of immeasurable assistance. They offered access to their files of *Baptist Press* releases, as well as to numerous other materials. Both have been extremely helpful in keeping me on top of events and filling in background I might not otherwise have had. I am grateful for the help and encouragement offered by all of these.

Money for the project—no small matter—has come from the Center for Religious Research at Candler School of Theology and from grants made by the Society for the Scientific Study of Religion and the Emory University Research Committee. The American Council of Learned Societies provided generous support for the preparation of this manuscript during a 1988–89 leave.

Getting out several thousand questionnaires and producing hundreds of pages of transcripts is not a task any one person could ever do. In getting out questionnaires, I have been aided not only by my primary research assistants, but also by Emory graduate students Christine Pohl, Laurel Kearns, and Fred Glennon, secretaries JoAnn Stone, Mary Lou McCrary, and Susan Johnson, and even my daughter Abbey. Christine also did the bulk of the transcribing, proving herself the kind of skilled and informed listener who can produce truly useful documents. Scott Thumma, Troy Workman, and Sam Porter have done data input. The Survey Research Center of the University of Kentucky handled data input from the 1988 questionnaires. My husband Jackie wrote the program that managed our mailing list. And the staff of the Emory University Computing Center answered questions about handling and analyzing this mass of data. For help with all of these necessary details, I am grateful.

I have been aided in the actual preparation of this manuscript by Juliana Smith, who assisted with the notes and bibliography, by Barbara Elwell who produced figures 4.1 and 6.1, and by Susan Johnson, Carol Wilson, and Linda Tatro who have formatted and printed disks and disks full of text.

I have said that this book really ought to be dedicated to Steve and Karen Ivy and their daughters Holyn and Krysten. I occupied their guest room whenever my work took me to Nashville, sometimes for as much as a week at a time, sometimes when they were not even there, but much more happily when they were. Theirs was my home away from home, not only a place to sleep, but a place to share the joys and sorrows of this work. I am grateful for their generosity and for the way this project provided an excuse for spending so many delightful hours with them.

Now I look forward to sharing some time of celebration with my family. They have been incredibly understanding of how important this project has been to me. This work is done, but the family that sustains me goes on.

*Baptist
Battles*

1. The Baptist Battle in Dallas

It was not yet 7:00 on that rainy Tuesday morning, but the dozens of Baptists who were staying in the suburban La Quinta motel outside of Dallas had already begun to make their way toward the center of town. My research assistant, Deborah Finn, and I gambled that we could avoid a $20 taxi fare that morning. We were right; a pastor and his wife offered us a ride. They listened to the local Christian radio station as we crept slowly along in the morning traffic. The cars around us also seemed to be full of Baptists, and as we rounded the corner approaching the Convention Center, a mass of umbrellas and buses outside its doors let us know we were certainly not the first to arrive.

In all the history of Southern Baptist Conventions, barely more than 22,000 people had ever come to one of these annual meetings. But when registration had closed the night before, more than 35,000 had already signed in for this one. By 9:00 Tuesday morning, the number would pass 40,000; and by the time the crucial presidential vote was taken that afternoon, 5,000 more would have picked up their ballots.

It was June 1985, and Southern Baptists had been embroiled for months in what one combatant had dubbed a "holy war." For six years, a conservative coalition led most visibly by Paige Patterson (president of Criswell Center for Biblical Studies in Dallas) and Paul Pressler (a Houston judge) had been victorious in the election of convention presidents. Their aim was to control the appointment process by which trustees are nominated so that, in turn, conservative trustees could purge the denomination of liberalism.

Other Baptists, more satisfied with the convention's trend toward progressive programs, had begun to call themselves "moderates." In 1985, they made a major effort to organize to stop the takeover. Agency heads and seminary presidents, joined by leading pastors, had spoken out to warn of the dangers of the conservative movement. The conservatives counter-organized, holding rallies and signing up riders for chartered buses. The results were now clear. Both sides had successfully gotten out their troops. Thousands of Baptists had come to Dallas—some angry, some determined, some just plain worried about the future of the largest Protestant denomination in the country.

They had come to cast their ballots for either Charles Stanley (the incumbent candidate of the fundamentalist party) or Winfred Moore, an equally conservative Texas preacher representing the moderate party.

3

What separated the two was not theology—both sides conceded that—but their views about the value and limits of diversity in an admittedly conservative denomination. Moore was convinced that differing views on scripture and its interpretation could be tolerated so long as cooperation on mission support was maintained. Stanley was equally convinced that such toleration was dangerous to the denomination's future.

The crowds had begun to gather in Dallas even before that Tuesday. On Saturday various specialty and professional groups as diverse as Southern Baptist Religious Educators, Southern Baptist Women in Ministry, and Associational (district) Directors of Missions began their meetings. By Sunday the crowds were turning into hoards. The legendary First Baptist, pastored by W. A. Criswell, father of the conservative movement, had Charles Stanley as guest of honor and treated their massive crowd of guests to a Texas barbeque after the services. Across town, Wilshire Baptist treated moderates to a service longer on formality and shorter on exhortation and food.

At 2:00 Sunday afternoon, the registration booths had opened for "messengers" to present their credentials, in most cases a card signed by their local church clerk certifying that the church was a "cooperating" Southern Baptist church and that this person had been elected to be their messenger to the meeting. If the church had given at least $2,250 to the convention's Cooperative Program (the central denominational budget) during the last year, they could send up to ten voting messengers. If they had given less, the number was less; but each of the denomination's 36,000 churches was entitled to at least one. Theoretically, 200,000 or more messengers could qualify to attend. In practice, many churches sent only the pastor, and possibly his wife, with most churches sending no one at all.

Once registered, messengers were given a pack of computer punch cards which would serve as ballots. The last card in the pack was colored pink and could be held aloft by messengers when votes were taken by show of hands. On Tuesday, the pack of ballots would also serve as proof of registration to the ushers who had been instructed to allow only registered messengers and press onto the convention floor.

But for Sunday and Monday, the business was less official. The smaller specialty groups continued to meet, and so did three larger convocations with more inspirational themes. In the Arena of the convention center four or five thousand women were gathered for the annual meeting of the Woman's Missionary Union (WMU). They would hear reports from around the world, see parades of missionaries in "native" costumes, and thrill to singing and preaching that urged them to do all they could to support missions.

In the main convention hall, up to 20,000 gathered for a ritual more of words than of sight. For several decades, the Pastors Conference had been a staple of the pre-convention schedule. Pastors came early to hear a dozen or more outstanding pulpiteers before business started. Since the 1970s, the Pastors Conference program had been dominated by the conservatives, offering only a choice between the more homespun revival styles of preachers like Bailey Smith and the more telegenic manner of Charles Stanley or James Kennedy. Their sermons almost always centered on conservative issues like biblical inerrancy, abortion and pornography, and the need for moral and spiritual revival in America. At the Dallas Conference, a huge American flag was stretched across the speaker's platform, and a message of greeting was read from President and Mrs. Reagan. These pastors had gathered not only to hone their craft (and add to their supply of preachable jokes) but also to express their concern for the dangers that threatened their convention and their nation.

People on the moderate side of the denomination had become increasingly dissatisfied with such Pastors Conference programs; and in 1983, they organized a reception as an alternative to the Monday evening Pastors Conference session. The next year, they expanded into an afternoon's program and an evening reception; and in Dallas, between 5,000 and 7,000 moderates heard five speakers of their own in a hall created out of the west end of the huge convention center. They called their program the Forum.

Here the emphasis was on the Baptist heritage of freedom and cooperation, with themes of social justice alongside spiritual renewal. They described their goal as translating the message of the Gospel for a contemporary society—and none of the speakers hesitated to condemn the means and the messages of the "fundamentalists" in the next room. Even their music contrasted with the offerings in the adjacent hall. Instead of thrilling to huge choirs and orchestras creating music of divine triumph, moderates listened to Darrell Adams, a 1960s-style folk singer whose music combined simple, old-fashioned hymns with gospel protest and peace songs. One moderate who had been suffering through Pastors Conferences for years later recalled how the music at the Forum that year moved him to tears. It gave him an overwhelming sense that he was "home" at last.

By the time Monday evening had arrived in Dallas, inspiration was running high on both sides, each renewed in the conviction that their cause was just. W. A. Criswell's closing sermon reminded the Pastors Conference crowd that the life or death of the denomination depended on affirming the inerrancy of the Bible. At the Forum, Atlanta pastor Bill Self had declared that afternoon that Baptists would lose their distinctiveness if they did not defend separation of church and state. Other

Forum speakers added "soul competency" and cooperation in missions to that list.

But people were more than inspired; they were also mobilized. Each side was busily checking registration figures and caucusing with state and local "precinct" captains. Conservatives somehow knew that the crowds were good news for them, but moderates were clinging to a desperate hope that the huge numbers arriving in Dallas meant that ordinary pastors and lay people had gotten their message. Then news began to circulate that Billy Graham had endorsed Charles Stanley, and the mood at the Forum reception turned decidedly glum. How could they possibly undermine the legitimacy of someone endorsed by Billy Graham? Still no one could say for sure what would happen on Tuesday.

What did happen on Tuesday was, among other things, a study in the kind of improvisation necessary when crowds far exceed expectations. The cavernous main hall was full by 8:00, nearly an hour before gavel time. Auxiliary halls were hastily wired for sight and sound, to accomodate the overflow.

There were not enough bathrooms, and desperate women and children finally began comandeering the relatively less-used men's rooms. Toilet paper everywhere was gone by noon. When the full press corps arrived for the afternoon voting, they discovered that their reserved chairs had been confiscated from the press section by irate messengers (who did not much like what the press had been saying about them anyway). No one wanted to risk losing a fought-for seat while out shopping for food, so many had brought lunch in coolers (which also doubled nicely as extra seating). When the lunch break came almost no one left, and the hall was turned into the world's largest "dinner on the grounds."

Since the hall was so big, only a relative few could actually see what was happening on the platform, but convention officials had dealt with that problem before. Using closed circuit television, they projected platform images onto three giant screens—right, center, and left. For business discussions, floor microphones were scattered throughout the hall, with yellow blinking lights to indicate that someone was waiting to speak. What they had not planned on was similar facilities for remote locations. As Monday night wore into Tuesday morning and printing presses were turning out more copies of the "Daily Bulletin," Tim Hedquist, in charge of convention arrangements for the SBC Executive Committee, scrambled to deal with the huge number of messengers who had come to Dallas.

As the crowds poured in that Tuesday morning, frantic ushers tried to monitor the flow, making sure that only messengers and press entered the hall. Their efforts proved irregular, however. One prominent pastor, expected on the platform to make an important motion, was turned back at the door for lack of ballots. But another Emory graduate student working with me, Scott Thumma, freely passed in and out, with neither a visible press badge (which he had) nor ballots (which he did not).

This ballots-or-press-badge rule had posed a problem for us as researchers. We were neither messengers nor press, but we needed access to the convention floor. I took the problem to W. C. Fields, in charge of public relations for the convention. I explained the nature of our work, and he graciously issued press credentials, not only giving us access to the floor, but also to the press room with its comfortable chairs, free soft drinks and coffee, and TV monitors piping in the events on the platform. It was a researcher's dream—access to both people and events and a place to escape for quick notetaking and recuperation. Except, of course, that we always had to explain to the people with whom we talked that we were not really press, that our "reporting" was of a different kind. The Center for Religious Research at Emory University, we said, was conducting a study of the Southern Baptist Convention.

By the spring of 1985, the idea of studying the Southern Baptist Convention had become too intriguing to ignore. I had recently completed a theoretical essay on religious schism, and I had realized that the literature on religious conflict consisted entirely of analyses constructed after the fact.[1] Here was a chance to study a major religious conflict as it happened. Whether the denomination split or not did not matter; empirical data about either survival or schism would be invaluable. Grant proposal deadlines had already passed, however, so I went to my dean, Jim Waits, who approved using money from the Center for Religious Research budget to get the project started. Soon thereafter, the Society for the Scientific Study of Religion also provided a small grant that made the first summer's research possible. Later funding would come from the Emory University Research Committee and the American Council of Learned Societies.

During the Spring, we had already observed meetings of Concerned Southern Baptists (the moderate group in Georgia) and had talked with a number of people identified to us as moderate or conservative organizers. When we arrived in Dallas, our plan was to observe the cultural, ideological, and organizational dimensions of this monumental controversy. We wanted to hear how both elites and ordinary folk described what was at stake, and see what they were willing to do about it. We wanted to discover how people on the two sides were different from each other, both in ideas and background, in values and style of life. We also wanted to observe the organizational strategy each side was adopting as a way to reach its goals. In short, we wanted to know why Baptists were fighting.

Because I had been a Southern Baptist all my life and had a network of friends from my husband's (and father's) pastoring days, I already knew a good many of the people I saw around me in Dallas. I had been a messenger at more than a half dozen conventions and knew what to expect. Scott and Deborah were new to Southern Baptist life. Scott was a member of a Baptist church, but had never been involved in convention activities; Deborah was Jewish. Both of them offered the kind of outsider objectivity that nicely matched my insider status.

Our strategy was to observe and ask questions. We worried less about exactly what happened on the platform than about how people responded. (What happened on the platform was video- and audio-taped, materials to which we would have access for supplementing our field notes.) I spent most of my time within ear and eye shot of the entrance to the platform area and the table where most agency executives were seated. Around me at the press tables were a number of editors of state Baptist newspapers, whose job it would be to interpret this convention for the people back home. Mine was the task of observing the official and unofficial activities of the "elites."

Deborah and Scott both spent time observing and talking to people who sought out the floor microphones for a chance to speak, people who were among the relative "activists" in the crowd. And all three of us spent time in the snack and exhibit areas observing and striking up conversations with ordinary folk. In between these unstructured observations were a number of arranged interviews with key players in the controversy. These were tape recorded and later transcribed, along with our reams of field notes, to form the first installment toward the four years of data on which this book is based.

The next installment was a nine-page questionnaire mailed to randomly selected samples of pastors and local lay church leaders. Over 1,000 people responded to our queries about their demographic histories, their political opinions, and their ideas about the controversy. Shorter follow-up surveys were done in the following three years, yielding a massive body of information about these local church leaders as they faced the changing realities of this critical period. A more complete discussion of methodology is found in appendix A.

What we observed during those three convention days in Dallas and in the numbers that accumulated from the questionnaires was a denomination coming to grips with the fact of its division. The mood in Dallas vacillated wildly from intense prayerful concern to raucous calls for "points of order," from hopeful signs of reconciliation to despair that any Peace Committee could heal the wounds. Late Tuesday afternoon it was announced that Charles Stanley had indeed won reelection. Conservatives sent up a cheer of victory, while the agency heads who had campaigned for his defeat sat silently by. A few minutes later, an ordinary messenger came to the platform to nominate the defeated Winfred Moore for first vice president (against the designated conservative candidate, Zig Ziglar). Stanley, who was presiding, asked if Moore would give his permission to be nominated. Moore, who had been in the midst of a television interview and did not know what was going on, asked innocently, "Charles, are *you* asking me to serve?" The house exploded in applause as the crowd sensed a potential reconciliation in the air. Perhaps if messengers elected both men, they could work together to bring peace.

Moore won the election easily, but by the end of the year, he would complain that his suggestions for key nominations were ignored (just as those of other moderate vice presidents had been ignored in the past). Indeed he would eventually resign from the place on the Peace Committee to which he fell heir by virtue of this election. Reconciliation was much more illusory than real in that moment in Dallas.

The Peace Committee was an effort by denominational loyalists to deal with the crisis. In the midst of the Holy War of the previous months a number of people had decided that a small group of trusted leaders should be convened to discuss the convention's problems and offer solutions. Such tactics had worked in the past; perhaps they would again. In the weeks before the meeting, feverish phone calls negotiated the composition of the group. It would not be the presumably-neutral state convention presidents, although they would present the proposal. Trades were made—I'll serve if you will; we'll accept X, if you'll accept Y. In its final form, the committee would be divided about evenly among aggressive conservatives, aggressive moderates, and people presumed to be neutral. In the first camp were Adrian Rogers and Jerry Vines; in the second, pastors Cecil Sherman and Bill Hull; and in the third, the venerable Herschel Hobbs (author of the 1963 statement of faith over which the two sides seemed now to be in disagreement) and retired convention executive Albert McClellan. There were twenty members as the recommendation went to the floor; but since all were men, organizers were persuaded that two women should be added—one representing each side. Stanley and Moore were added ex officio. No one could predict what effect the committee might have, but everyone thought they should at least try to find some grounds for reconciliation.

Throughout the convention, however, each side was still trying to outmaneuver the other. The conservatives presented their slate of nominees for the key Committee on Boards, the body that would nominate trustees for all the denomination's agencies.[2] As in every year since conservatives had begun their campaign, this Committee was populated with determined conservatives who would safeguard the rest of the nomination process. Moderates responded by proposing an alternative slate, composed of the convention president and WMU president from each state Baptist convention, people they trusted to be more representative of mainstream Baptists.

The minutes that followed that proposal on Wednesday morning were as near chaos as I have ever seen at a Southern Baptist Convention. There was rarely a moment without a shout of "point of order" coming from the floor. People stood at nearly every microphone, waiting to be recognized. At one microphone moderate activist Jim Strickland and conservative activist Robert Tenery literally jockeyed for position; and when they got to speak, each accused the other side of not playing fair. Frustrated messengers, anxious to break for lunch, just wanted to get on with business; but neither side could quite figure out how to do that without giving the other side an unwanted advantage. Could this alternative slate be considered, and if so how?

At first, Stanley and his parliamentarian, Wayne Allen, hoping to block the moderate move, ruled that substitute nominations could only be made one at a time (and with only a few minutes alotted in the order of business for this report, few substitutions were likely).[3] The frustrated James Slatton, maker of the moderate motion, at first began to comply, offering the first of over fifty individual names he would have to list for consideration. But soon, with prompting from the floor, he appealed the ruling of the chair. The show of hands on the ruling of the chair was too close to call, as was the try at a standing vote. Stanley wanted to call it in the chair's favor, but veteran vote-counter and recording secretary Lee Porter pled with him to "do the right thing" and call for a ballot on whether to support the chair. The ballots were punched and collected, and the assembly dismissed for the afternoon, with business to be resumed in the evening.

Before the seminary alumni luncheons (moderate strongholds) had concluded, word spread that moderates had won the ballot, overturning the ruling of the chair and clearing the way for a vote on an alternative committee slate. There was rejoicing in the land. But meanwhile, conservatives had gotten the word, too. At the Evangelists Conference (a conservative stronghold), Charles Stanley pled for everyone to return for the evening's business. He warned that if the power of nomination were taken away, everything would be lost. Reportedly, a Dallas Christian radio station also broadcast an appeal. Banks of telephones in the convention center were lined with workers calling local messengers back to the battle. Conservatives were worried that the bus-loads of their messengers who had left town after Tuesday's presidential vote had reduced their supporters below a majority. Moderates joked on Wednesday night that

173 buses had been ticketed that afternoon for making U-turns on the freeway. They seemed to have a sense that although they had won the vote, they would be out-foxed yet.

And they were right. When the business session opened on Wednesday evening, Charles Stanley immediately recognized at the main podium one of the state convention presidents to say that he had not been asked about serving on this key committee and would refuse to do so. He argued that the substitute slate violated Baptist polity by linking state and national organizations (thus making it "presbyterian"). Then Stanley reported that after consultation with his parliamentarian, it had been determined that the substitute motion had been out of order all along—that the convention had no choice but to accept or reject the slate offered by the Committee on Committees, without amendment or substitution of any kind. He then called for an immediate vote on that report, allowing no discussion and recognizing none of the frantic points of order being shouted from the floor.

The report passed, but the issue did not go away. On the following morning other business virtually ground to a halt as frustrated messengers kept calling for points of order regarding Wednesday's votes. Only when Winfred Moore came to the platform and pled for cooperation did the logjam finally break. And in the months that followed, a small group of messengers filed suit against Stanley for violation of their rights under the constitution and by-laws of the Convention. It was another sign that peace was not at hand.

The reconciliation that would eventually come to the Southern Baptist Convention was not any mutual effort at compromise or an arbitrated settlement. It was not reconciliation *between* but reconciliation *to*. When the Peace Committee presented its final report in 1987, conservatives declared that the war was over. "We have settled the issue of the Bible," they said. It was time to move on. They were right that the war was over. From 1985 on, it was clear that a conservative victory was assured and that the Southern Baptist Convention would take a more conservative direction. Those who wanted to remain a part of the denomination would have to accept that change in direction. Because the presidential appointment process takes three years to complete, the effects of any election are never immediate.[4] Those eventually elected as trustees of seminaries and agencies as a result of Charles Stanley's election in Dallas, would not take their places until 1988. And in that year, virtually every denominational board of trustees would come under the sway of a conservative majority. At that point, moderates were faced with the necessity of winning an equal string of presidential victories if they hoped to reverse what Paige Patterson, Paul Pressler, and their friends had accomplished.

Many moderates left Dallas hoping that just such an election strategy might be possible. Next year in Atlanta, they pledged. But next year and the next and the next would pass, with ever narrower margins of defeat, but with defeat nonetheless. The Southern Baptist Convention had reversed its direction. The moderately progressive trends of the 1960s and 1970s were replaced by strongly conservative policies in one agency and institution after another. Even if moderates were to win an election or two, the impact of this conservative resurgence would be lasting. Soon moderates would be wondering if any place would remain for them in this denomination they had once loved. They had been nurtured in its churches, programs, and institutions, but they were no longer welcome in positions of service or leadership. Few of them recognized as they left Dallas that their fate had already been decided. There would be no turning back from the conservative direction in which the Convention was headed. They would eventually have to decide whether to accommodate or leave.

The Plan of the Book

This book is the story of that Southern Baptist reversal in direction and of the battles that accompanied it. We will begin by looking at the history out of which Southern Baptists have come. Their religious ancestors emerged in the seventeenth century as radical reformers, insisting on churches composed only of believers and proposing that neither priest nor government should stand between those believers and God. But during the nineteenth century, Baptists in the U.S. south became the unofficial "established" religion of the region. They were transformed from a marginal sect into a religious defender of the region's status quo, maintaining that position for at least a century. But the region of which they are a part underwent rapid and fundamental change after World War II, change that dislodged Southern Baptists from their place at the center of the culture. It will be argued here that the division so evident in Dallas reflects deep cultural divisions separating people who have responded differently to that cultural change. Chapters 2 and 3, then, will establish the place of Southern Baptists in their culture and will show how that place changed over the past generation. This will begin to lay the foundation for an understanding of why divisions developed.

It will also be argued here that one cannot understand these Baptist battles without understanding the impressive organizational machinery that is the Southern Baptist Convention. Chapters 2 and 3 will also trace the development of the denomination's bureaucratic structure and show

how it supplemented southern culture as the glue that bound Southern Baptists together long after they might otherwise have fallen apart. Presumably no Baptist agency can control what individual Baptists believe or what individual churches choose to do, but the Southern Baptist denominational bureaucracy had become so pervasive as to make it the prize for which conservatives fought. An introduction to the agencies, their size, and their complexity is found in table 1.1. What cannot be seen so easily there is the vast extent to which local churches are linked to these national organizations. Those linkages will be described in chapter 3.

Having established the historical context of this struggle, chapters 4 and 5 will look at the shape of the differences that divided Southern Baptists on the left from those on the right and both from people in the middle. Religious divisions do not happen at random. People fight over religious beliefs and practices when those beliefs and practices represent real differences in the way they live their lives. We will trace the story of the emergence of a self-conscious fundamentalist movement in the Southern Baptist Convention. We will take a look at the people who found fundamentalist ideas attractive, trying to understand the concerns that motivated them. Likewise, we will look at those who took the label "moderate," examining the social forces that have pushed some Southern Baptists to the left from their old cultural center. Drawing on our survey of Southern Baptist pastors and lay church leaders, we will assess the array of opinions that exist in the denomination, and we will look for the issues that most clearly separate one side from the other. Likewise, drawing on interviews, sermons, and editorial opinions, we will assess what they think of each other. We will seek to determine the extent to which moderates and fundamentalists perceive each other as insiders or outsiders—potential brothers and sisters or alien invaders. And we will look here at the vast constituency caught in the middle, between the two camps—sometimes neutral, sometimes alternating between the two sides.

An answer to why Southern Baptists became divided is only part of the story, however. It is also important to examine the organizational structure that gives form to the differences people feel. Unhappy church members do not turn their unhappiness into schism unless they are able to mobilize sufficient organizational resources to accomplish that task. We will move, then, from a description of differences to a description of resources. To understand Southern Baptist battles and their outcome we must know both how people differ from each other and what efforts they have expended in organizing to support their cause. Again, survey responses, interviews, news reports, and four years of observation will

Table 1.1. The Southern Baptist Bureaucracy

Organization	Size	Tasks
Executive Committee	budget = $2.8 million staff = 9	plans, coordinates, budgets, and handles legal and public relations matters for the denomination as a whole
Annuity Board	budget = $953,000 assets = $1.6 billion staff = 50	handles retirement and health benefits for pastors, church staff and denominational workers
Home Mission Board	budget = $71.9 million 2,758 missionaries 877 pastors receiving aid staff = 141 + 22 external consultants	through state conventions and associations, supports varied ministries, endorses chaplains, helps start churches, etc.
Foreign Mission Board	budget = $170.2 million 3,197 missionaries staff = 101	supports overseas ministry and evangelism

Sunday School Board	budget = $171.6 million
	78.4 million pieces of literature
	staff = 52 executives +
	    375 writers/editors/
	    program coordinators
	83 at Broadman press
	137 in technical services
	26 in publishing/
	    broadcasting
		develops church programming, publishes support materials, provides support services, including 2 national conference centers, a satellite network, and 63 book stores

provide a base from which to assess, in chapter 6, why the fundamentalists won and the moderates lost.

But, these two organized camps were fighting about more than ideas or even lifestyle. They fought for control of the denominational bureaucracy; and if victory means anything, it should mean changes in the policies being put into place in the agencies. The concrete results of conservative victory will be examined in chapter 7. We will look for ways in which ideology is being put into action, as well as for ways in which bureaucratic structures themselves may blunt the effects of ideology. Given that the staffs and previous trustees of these agencies were overwhelmingly moderate in their sympathies, a conservative "course correction" (as the leaders liked to call their movement) amounted to a "hostile takeover." With legitimate power on their side, new conservative trustees brought in new goals and new personnel policies, hoping that those who disagreed would quietly move on to other jobs. Some did, but for several

Table 1.1. (*Continued*)

Organization	Size	Tasks
Commissions, etc.	budgets = $16.1 million staff = 92	9 separate entities with 20 program assignments, ranging from social issues to historical preservation

Seminaries			
Golden Gate	budget = $5.8 million* 24 faculty 15 administrators 1,011 total students**	Southeastern	budget = $6.3 million 37 faculty 20 administrators 1,620 total students
Midwestern	budget = $4.2 million 21 faculty 13 administrators 653 total students	Southern	budget = $11.2 million 89 faculty in 4 schools 61 administrators 3,524 total students
New Orleans	budget = $6.3 million 45 faculty 7 administrators 2,704 total students	Southwestern	budget = $17.7 million 97 faculty in 3 schools 36 administrators 5,070 total students

SOURCE: Compiled from the 1986 Southern Baptist Convention *Annual*.

*Seminary budgets include moneys from tuition and other sources beyond the Cooperative Program.

**"Total Students" is the total number enrolled in all programs and includes parttime and off-campus students.

years hiring and firing were a constant concern as the new management sought to shape the institutions by changing the composition of the work force.

Faced with the fact of this conservative victory, the rest of the denomination had to decide how to respond. Would all but the most radical fundamentalists leave? Or would the Convention's congregational polity make it possible for everyone to live happily under conservative leadership, each church finding its own organizational niche? Would denominational loyalty survive, or would various subgroups create their own new networks of cooperation and investment? By 1987, many moderates were feeling like outsiders and were seeking new places to feel at home. Some created the Southern Baptist Alliance, an organization that developed rapidly and laid the foundation for a long period of exile—and possibly for schism. Others created Baptists Committed to the SBC, an organization to formalize their efforts to win back the denomination's presidency. The balance among accommodation, the establishment of new organizations, and the possibility for schism will be examined in the final chapter.

We will look at who is staying and why and which disaffected moderates are choosing to be "loyal opposition" and which are choosing a more independent course. We will also look at the likelihood that most Southern Baptists may simply go on about their lives as if nothing important has happened.

A Word about Words

In the pages ahead, we will come to call those on the right wing of the Southern Baptist Convention "fundamentalists." That is a term most of their leaders detest. It seems to them to connote narrow, moralistic, backwoods rednecks, or perhaps even terrorist fanatics. Clearly for many people that is the image the word conveys. But fundamentalism will be used here in its historic sense, *not* with any pejorative intent. During the earlier part of this century, the term was coined by groups that chose to fight to defend their traditional understanding of the Bible against the onslaughts of liberalism and the social gospel. Earlier, in the nineteenth century, they had just been ordinary believers, but as various forces presented challenges to their faith, they became fundamentalists. They intentionally organized against a real threat to what they believed—the threat and the organization are what distinguish fundamentalists from ordinary believers or traditionalists.[5] Some Southern Baptist conservatives, it will be argued here, perceived a clear threat in their denomination, and they organized against it. For that reason they fall into the historical pattern established by earlier fundamentalists.

Use of this term is also necessary as a way to understand how Southern Baptists differ among themselves. It helps to distinguish the "conservatism" that characterizes the mainstream from the ideas and practices of people to the right of that conservative middle. Rather than calling those to the right of the middle "ultra-conservatives," I have chosen "fundamentalist" as the term that historically fits their concerns. It is also the term a significant number chose for themselves. In chapter 4, we will elaborate more thoroughly on the divisions and what to call them, but for now it is important simply to establish the sense in which this controversial term will be used.

It is just as difficult to choose words to describe the Convention's left wing. A tiny fraction might be considered "liberal" in the theological sense of that word. A slightly larger proportion might fit the term liberal as it is used in political and social contexts. A fairly large number are "neo-orthodox" in theology, but at least as many neatly fit no theological camp. Almost all of those on the left are committed evangelicals, believing that a life-changing encounter with Jesus Christ is necessary for salvation. They are a very diverse group, however—some are politically liberal, but some are conservative; many are supporters of women in ministry, but not all; some think the world was created in six days, and some take a more evolutionary view. What they share is a rejection of a *required* traditional orthodoxy and a general attitude that seeks to accommodate change (which makes them all "liberals" in the eyes of fundamentalists). Their faces are turned away from the past and toward the future. Theirs is not an uncritical acceptance of all that is new, but their desires for their denomination can safely be called "progressive."

As on the right wing, this helps us to distinguish those on the margin from the conservatives in the middle. Many who are to the left of the middle call themselves "moderates," and we will often use that term, especially in describing the movement that organized in opposition to fundamentalism. But when we are speaking of those who are consciously at odds with the traditionalism of the denomination, the term progressive will point out the tensions involved.

Terms, of course, are but one small aspect of what Southern Baptists fought about in the 1970s and 1980s. They brought to the battles almost four centuries of history as a sometimes-independent, sometimes-established, but always energetic and evangelistic religious movement. As they moved toward their fifth century, the Baptists who had established themselves as the religion of the South were struggling to determine just which strands of their history would guide them toward the future.

2. From English Dissent to Southern Establishment

The family tree on which today's Southern Baptists grow has its roots firmly in the soil of the Reformation. Those who became "Baptist" were among the most radical of the dissenters who objected to papal and state interference in matters of faith. That insistence on a free conscience and independence from outside authority has made for a stormy history, full of conflicts inside and out. The battles of the 1980s were not the first.

Both in England and in the United States, Baptists became distinctive for their insistence on adult baptism by immersion, their arguments for religious liberty, their egalitarian and democratic ethos, and their vigorous evangelistic and mission work. During much of the first two centuries of Baptist existence these ideas resulted in persecution and even death, but it was two centuries in which Baptist evangelists kept on preaching, with and without official approval. Emerging in England in the early seventeenth century as a scattered and persecuted minority, by the middle of the nineteenth century Baptists in the southern United States had been transformed into a dominating religio-cultural force. And in the move from minority to majority, the character of their battles changed.

Baptist Beginnings

During England's stormy sixteenth century, various dissenters arose, preaching the purification of the church and a return to a New Testament Christian model.[1] They directed their sermons first at the papacy and then at the Anglican bishops, charging that no officer outside the local church should have authority over a congregation and its pastor. One of the predominant ideas among these reformers was that the congregation was formed by a covenant between God and humanity that called for strict accountability on the part of members, accountability that could not be legislated from above nor bound by tradition, accountability that was possible only in the context of a local body of committed believers, relying on scripture as their sole guide. Such ideas earned their preachers reprimands, jail sentences, exile, and death. But underground congregations of believers kept alive the idea of a renewed church.

Some of these reformers wanted to purify the church from within, patiently waiting for change. Puritans, as they were called, wanted "liberty for self-expression in matters of religion, but not to the point where it would disrupt the decent order of the church."[2] Others felt compelled to separate themselves from "false worship in a false church," and, when a recalcitrant hierarchy refused their efforts at reform, many Puritans were eventually pushed to become separatists.

Out of the lineage of Separatist preachers came one John Smyth. Shortly after the turn of the seventeenth century, he took his small band of followers to Amsterdam to escape English persecution. There his writings continued the Separatist tradition, arguing that the church is "a company of faithful people separated from all uncleanness and joined together by a covenant of the Lord."[3] But Smyth went much further than previous separatists. He also began arguing that adult baptism was a necessary sign of participation in the covenant, and that adults baptized as infants ought to be rebaptized as a sign of their faith. He took this idea so seriously that in 1609 he rebaptized himself and several others. In that act, the first English Baptist church was born.

While in Amsterdam, Smyth sought out conversations with a community of Mennonites, but his congregation was never fully accepted by these believers from the continental Anabaptist tradition. Just how much influence they had on Smyth (or on any of the other radical Puritan dissenters) is the subject of much historical debate.[4] Perhaps the safest assertion is that made by historian Bryan White that "similarities between the forms of English Puritanism and continental Anabaptism seem to derive more from a similar type of appeal to the norm of the Church in apostolic times than to any observable sixteenth-century cross-fertilization."[5] It seems entirely plausible that during such a period of religious ferment many influences are present in the formation of new groups. Likewise, in such periods, nomenclature is likely to be much less precise than in periods of stability and institutionalization. We can be sure of the similarities between English radical separatists and continental Anabaptists, but less sure of their actual interaction with each other.

Both movements emerged out of similar circumstances and advocated similar programs. Like the English dissenters, Anabaptists had emerged in the early days of the Reformation. They were scattered in small bands throughout Germany, Switzerland, and the Netherlands. They got their name because they, too, rebaptized adult believers. Those who were led by Menno Simons (c. 1496–1561) were called Mennonites (or Brethren). In those early days, these widely dispersed and usually persecuted radical reformers were anything but uniform in their beliefs and practices, differing on details such as modes of baptism and relationships with the state. However, they shared in common an insistence that churches ought to be composed of regenerate persons, individuals who had made a conscious choice to be Christian and who accepted responsibility for their own souls' welfare.

In addition, as the Anabaptists came to see it, to have a regenerate membership implied democracy as the only appropriate form of church government. No distinctions between "clergy" and "laity" were recognized among them. Every member was "ordained," usually at the time of their baptism, to the work of daily witnessing and service. Smyth, too, can be described as an egalitarian, arguing that church leaders ought to be accountable to their congregations.[6] His ideas of a regenerate, rebaptized, congregation in covenant with God under the authority of scripture alone were remarkably similar to the ideas these continental dissenters had developed. But he never became a part of them (although a remnant of his congregation later did), and other evidence of direct influence is lacking.

Another new idea Smyth introduced to his congregation was the Arminian theology that was a hot topic of debate in Holland at that time. Unlike most of the Puritans back in England, who were strict Calvinists, Smyth came to teach the Arminian view that God's grace is available to all, not just to a predestined few. That is, although God may have known (and even chosen) the eternal destiny of each person before the beginning of time, the atoning, redeeming work of Christ is available to all. Individuals may choose to be saved. Because they saw the atonement (Christ's saving act) as "general" and not limited, Smyth's followers became General Baptists.

It appears that Smyth continued his quest for new ideas and church practices and eventually left his congregation behind. By 1611, he had lost favor, and his disciple Thomas Helwys, took up the mantle of leadership. Between 1611 and 1612, Helwys produced four volumes that became the first Baptist confession of faith. By 1612, he was back in England with a courageous band of followers. And within the year he had landed in Newgate prison for daring to say that kings are mortal and have no power over the immortal souls of their subjects. He wrote, "Let them be heretics, Turks, Jews, or whatsoever, it appertains not to the earthly power to punish them."[7]

In the early years of their existence in England, Baptists faced formidable odds, with few, if any, allies. Anglicans did not like any sect that separated from the official Church, and Puritan groups disagreed with Baptists on both the atonement and church practice. Within a generation, however, prison or no, this small band had found receptive ears for their message of religious liberty. By 1644, there were nearly fifty General Baptist churches in England, and in another fifteen years, that number had doubled again.[8] They were soon joined by other Baptists more strictly Calvinist in their teaching. Known as Particular Baptists, these posited a God who not only knew who would be redeemed, but limited redemption to those chosen ones. The Particular Baptists were, then, direct descendents of the English Puritan tradition and added to the strength and acceptability of the Baptist movement.

As these groups slowly coalesced, they were also working out the doctrines that would make them distinctive. They continued to study the scriptures on the matter of baptism, for instance, and some concluded that infants should not be baptized. As a result, they formed "antipedobaptist" congregations. They too were insistent on a regenerate church membership; and it appears to have been they who first began to distinguish themselves by insisting that the mode of believer's baptism should be immersion.[9] In the earlier part of the century, believer's baptism usually meant sprinkling or pouring; but in 1644, a group of Particular Baptist ministers signed a fifty-article London Confession of Faith that specified immersion as the only proper mode of baptism. This practice rapidly spread to General Baptists, as well, and the London Confession became another of the important milestones on the journey of Baptists into a distinct identity within the Protestant tradition.

Historian Robert Torbet argues that the common threads that bound these emerging groups together had to do with their radical insistence on the freedom (and responsibility) of the individual before God.[10] In advocating churches composed of regenerate members, they flew in the face of ecclesiastical and government authorities who claimed the power to baptize and excommunicate, to license preachers, and to tax everyone for the support of the established church. Beginning in England, but especially in eighteenth-century America, Baptists became the most prominent champions of the principle of religious liberty, the freedom of each individual conscience to approach God without interference from secular authority.[11] They were convinced that true religion must be voluntary to be valid.

They also gave flesh to the principle of the priesthood of all believers by their emphasis on corporate decision making and corporate responsibility. Just as each believer was free to approach God, so the body of believers was corporately responsible for its life together. Each believer, without distinction of office, was responsible for evangelizing, service, and mutual discipline. No priest could bear that responsibility for his flock.[12] And all of this took place within a movement that sought to return to the primitive church practices of the New Testament. These groups sought to strip away centuries of institution and tradition to return to a faith based solely on scripture. Theirs was an individual liberty constrained only by the Bible but disciplined by a congregation of fellow priests.

Despite this individual and congregational emphasis, however, early

Baptists were by no means isolationist. They immediately began to form associations of churches in their regions, primarily for the purposes of fellowship and evangelism.[13] They did not yet have any recognized Baptist creed, however. Even when a pastor was accused of heresy, members of his association were unwilling to apply a creedal test. As various Confessions began to emerge from associations and other bodies, no one confession was recognized as having the force of a creed.

By the end of the seventeenth century, the Act of Toleration was finally in place in England, establishing the right of dissenters to exist; but rather than experiencing growth due to the lack of repression, Baptists began to experience controversies within their own ranks. For sixty years surrounding the turn of the eighteenth century, General Baptists fought among themselves. It was partly a matter of disagreement over incarnation—whether Christ was both fully human and fully divine—and partly a dispute rooted in the varying origins and locations of the different churches.[14] Even then, theological disputes carried a heavy burden of social history. There were, for a time, two rival General Baptist denominations in England, each different both in doctrine and in constituency.

Baptists in America

While English Baptists were fighting to establish an identity, many of their number began to migrate west to America. At the same time, dissenters from the dominant Puritan tradition in New England, were replaying the struggles of their Old World counterparts. Among the most famous of these early American dissenters was, of course, Roger Williams. Williams came to Massachusetts in 1631 to escape religious persecution in England. He became a teacher in the church in Salem, but soon ran afoul of the Massachusetts Puritans for his idea that church and state ought to be separate. His expulsion from Massachusetts led to the founding of the Rhode Island Colony in 1636, a colony where from the beginning, religious liberty was guaranteed and where in 1639 Williams founded the First Baptist Church in America in Providence. Like Smyth before him, this Baptist pioneer soon proved too radical even for those who at first followed him. Williams became a Seeker, leaving the Baptist church he had helped to found.

Without his leadership, the church in Providence was less influential in the coming years than were churches founded soon thereafter. A similar congregation of dissenters led by John Clarke was located in Newport, Rhode Island. They were able to help Baptists spread into Connecticut, the middle colonies, and even back into Massachusetts. Clarke's first missionary visit to Boston resulted in his arrest, a fine, and imprisonment.

His colleague Obadiah Holmes was publicly whipped. They were not alone there in their Baptist sympathies, however. Henry Dunster, the first president of Harvard College, was enough influenced by Baptist teachings to refuse to have his child baptized. By 1665 even Boston would have a Baptist congregation.

Throughout the next half century, Baptists continued to arrive from England and separate from their Puritan neighbors; and they continued to be persecuted by those who thought everyone ought to baptize their infants, officially licence their preachers, and support official churches. They were, throughout the colonial period, "the pariahs of New England society. Known Baptists could not . . . vote or hold office. Their children were the butts of childish malevolence, their sons and daughters were considered unfit for marriage to the orthodox."[15] Nevertheless, they organized churches in the New England area; and by the end of the century a few Baptists were migrating to the more southern colonies.

In the mid-1690s William Screven, along with several relatives and friends, moved from Kittery, Maine, to the Charleston area in the Carolina colony. There, in 1696, the First Baptist Church of Charleston was established. Before that time, there had been "known Baptists" showing up among the settlers moving into the Carolinas. The Charleston church was followed shortly thereafter by churches in the surrounding area and in Virginia.

The place where Baptists really thrived in the early eighteenth century, however, was neither in the South nor in the Puritan New England colonies. Rather, Baptists gained their greatest foothold in the middle colonies of Pennsylvania and New Jersey. Here religious liberty was guaranteed, allowing Baptists (and other dissenters) fleeing persecution in England (or Massachusetts) a place to practice their religion without fear. In 1698, the First Baptist Church in Philadelphia was organized, followed nine years later by the Philadelphia association of five small area churches. This church and the association would play a central role in American Baptist life over the next century. Among its many influences was the establishment of the Calvinist Particular Baptist tradition as the dominant strand in American Baptist life. They so predominated at the time over General Baptists that Particular and Regular became synonymous in early colonial descriptions of Baptists. The adoption of the 1689 London Confession by the Philadelphia Association in 1742 made this emphasis official.[16]

The Philadelphia Association, while completely voluntary in membership, also exercised a good deal of influence over its member churches. It acted as an ordination council, examining candidates for ministry. It helped to settle disputes, and it served as a forum for the discussion of doctrinal matters. It also had the power to exclude from its fellowship churches it deemed to have departed from acceptable teaching and practice. Each year ministers or deacons from the churches gathered, bearing a letter giving their names, telling the condition of their church, and asking for needed advice. They returned from the meeting with a letter that contained both statistics on the association's progress and specific advice for their church.

By mid-eighteenth century, Baptist numbers in the north were growing, thanks in large part to the Great Awakening. Jonathan Edwards, George Whitefield, and their disciples in the 1740s set in motion a wave of revivals in which the experience of conversion was central. Assurance of salvation came from the heart, not the head; and no halfway covenant allowing church membership without regeneration was acceptable. As a result, "Separate" Congregational churches began to appear in New England, rejecting the compromises of their more established Congregational neighbors and insisting on a personal experience of regeneration as a test of membership. And in the process it sometimes happened that whole congregations, along with their ministers, accepted believer's baptism, as well. As in the earliest days of Baptists in England, the insistence of church purifiers on a regenerate membership often led to the rejection of infant baptism and finally toward a Baptist position, although not always, in this case, toward Baptist affiliation. And as in earlier English history, separatists were not treated kindly by the established churches they left.[17]

One of the ministers who underwent such an oddysey from Congregationalist to Baptist was a native of Boston and resident of Connecticut named Shubael Stearns. In 1755, after his conversion, he headed south with evangelistic motives, eventually settling in Sandy Creek, North Carolina. There a remarkable series of revivals over the next seventeen years led to the establishment of forty-two Baptist churches in the surrounding territory. These Separate Baptists insisted on an emotional conversion experience, baptism by immersion of the adult convert, and membership in a community to which one was held accountable.

There was a strong antiestablishment streak among these early Baptists in the south that included their refusal to adhere to the state's religious laws, their highly emotional services, and their inclusion of women among their preachers.[18] But their peculiar combination of community accountability and nontraditionalism provided just the right mix of order and stability on the new nation's frontier.[19] Here among the thousands of settlers streaming west from the coast, the message of individual regeneration and democratic responsibility preached by these Baptists found a receptive audience.

In the north from whence Stearns came, Separate Baptist churches were often composed of lower class, uneducated folk and were derided by outsiders in comparison to the more urbane Regular Baptists (who tended to value education and decorum at least as much as religious experience). Even when their ranks were being swelled by converts from the Great Awakening, these Regular Baptists were slow to embrace revival methods. Likewise, in the southern colonies, the Separates had their greatest success in the less civilized frontier regions. But the revivals were so strong in both regions as to begin to overcome these distinctions. Even the northern Regulars were inspired to evangelism during the Awakening, beginning many new churches. And the lines between southern General and Particular groups began to blur. By the end of the eighteenth century the Baptist cause was much strengthened and unified, with the adjectives dividing them largely gone.[20] In most places they were at least tolerated, although they had not yet truly gained a place for themselves in American society.

Meanwhile, of course, the new nation had been born. Baptists supported the Revolutionary War, at least in part because they saw it as a prelude to religious liberty.[21] The religious freedom enjoyed by Baptists in Philadelphia and the middle colonies had formed a marked contrast to the persecution suffered by their neighbors to the north and south. As late as the 1760s and 1770s, Virginia and Carolina Baptists were being beaten, jailed, run out of town, and otherwise harrassed. Their refusal to baptize their infants resulted in charges of cruelty to children, and their refusal to obtain official licences to preach resulted in charges of breach of peace. New England Baptists had long suffered similar legal and social ostracism. Both from their own experiences and from their convictions about the individual's need for a direct and unhindered relationship to God, Baptists throughout the nation took the lead in fighting for guarantees of religious freedom. Led by men such as John Leland and Isaac Backus, they argued that government had no business prescribing and regulating religious beliefs and practices. And their arguments finally took root in the soil plowed by the Revolution—first in Virginia, then in the new nation's Constitution, and finally in the Bill of Rights. Religious liberty became the law of the land.

From their lowly status as outcast dissenters, Baptists had quite naturally seen the wisdom in toleration. As McLoughlin argues in *New England Dissent*, their fight for liberty was also a fight for equality and acceptance, for the chance to function as equal partners in society. By the end of the eighteenth century, that fight for both liberty and equality was largely won. Baptists were an accepted part of the American religious landscape and were about to enter a very different era in their history.

Baptists Established and Organized, 1790–1845

Having secured liberty for themselves and others, Baptists in America turned to the task of expansion and organization. It was both domestic expansion born of frontier revivals and overseas expansion supported by missionary societies. Baptists were at the forefront of the movement that took American and European missionaries to the far corners of the earth, spreading the Christian way of life (and often a good deal more).

In 1792, English Baptist William Carey had set sail for India, beginning the modern missions movement. Within a few years, Baptists in New England began to organize themselves into societies for the purpose of supporting Carey and the others who were following him into India. Among the first of the American mission groups was the Boston Female Society for Missionary Purposes, organized by Mary Webb. She and hundreds of other women began to organize correspondence and fund-raising networks for the support of those who were spreading the Christian gospel in far-off lands.

These mission societies were important both for the work they supported and for the form of organization they fostered. Until that time, mission work had been supported by each local association largely within its own territory. Now new organizations were arising to support bigger causes. The mission societies had no official connection to local bodies, but rather brought together larger groups of Baptists around one specialized purpose. By adopting a cause bigger than any one locale, Baptists in America began to develop organizational structures that would soon transform them into a denomination.

It was out of a call to rally missionary support that the first national organization of Baptists in America was born. In 1812, Ann Hasseltine Judson and her husband Adoniram, along with Luther Rice, left Massachusetts to join the mission work in India. However, they soon found themselves in an awkward situation. They had been commissioned as missionaries by the Congregational mission board, but during their voyage to India, they had become convinced of Baptist teachings. They were baptized by immersion upon arrival in India, and sent their resignations to their sponsoring board. Rice then returned to America to seek aid for their Baptist mission work in India. In the next year, he traveled throughout the nation generating enthusiasm for a national organization to support missions.

So it was that in May 1814, a convention was called in Philadelphia for the purpose of organizing a national Baptist missionary society. Its members were to be delegates from state and local mission societies and other

Baptist bodies, and they called themselves the General Missionary Convention of the Baptist Denomination in the United States for Foreign Missions. Since they planned to meet every three years they became known more commonly as the Triennial Convention. They were truly national in scope, reflecting the expansive nationalism of those early days of the republic. Dr. Richard Furman, of Charleston, was elected president of the convention, and Dr. Thomas Baldwin, of Boston, was elected secretary.

The group quickly appointed the Judsons and Rice as their missionaries, and asked Rice to continue his fund-raising trips to churches throughout the land. By this time, there were nearly 200 Baptist mission societies in the nation—over half of them women's groups—and many of them sent representatives to the Triennial Convention.[22] By the time the Convention met again in 1817, the delegates were ready to expand their concerns toward domestic mission work and education. In 1824, the Baptist General Tract Society was formed to begin publishing educational materials, followed in 1832 by the American Baptist Home Mission Society. As Baptists were taking their place in the American religious mosaic, they were establishing the institutions that would help to perpetuate and spread their way of life.

Meanwhile, on the frontier in Kentucky and Tennessee, revival was breaking out again. Between 1800 and 1805, a series of "camp meetings" swept the region along the border between the two states. Beginning among the Presbyterians, but embraced most enthusiastically by Methodists and Baptists, these meetings laid the foundation for the domination of the South by those denominations and the evangelical religion they practiced. While they may at first have been spontaneous responses to a widespread feeling of need and expectation, camp meetings were soon institutionalized as a regular means for gaining new converts.[23] They were announced in area newspapers and carefully planned according to advice published in manuals on the subject. They were indeed highly emotional events, but the emotion seems to have been well-planned and carefully contained.[24] Campgrounds were systematically laid out around the preaching area, with each family building a tent for its shelter. At the foot of the pulpit was a special area into which those "under conviction" came to mourn their way toward conversion under the watchful eyes of exhorters and "good singers and praying persons." During the day, services consisted of testimonies from recent converts, spiritual singing, and one full-fledged sermon addressed to the doctrinal and moral concerns of believers. At night, the focus turned to exhorting sinners to salvation and observing the visible, physical signs of that conversion process. Since conversion was becoming the badge of membership in Southern evangelical society, the visible displays of the camp meeting clearly demonstrated one's right to enter and participate in the community.

Called protracted meetings, these gatherings were a natural form of organized religion in a frontier region of highly-scattered population. In addition to their religious functions, they also served a number of social functions. Almost always scheduled near harvest time, when farmers had nearly completed their work for the year, they provided a time of association in an otherwise scattered and lonely land. They were undoubtedly part of the structure of courting and family maintenance. And they brought comfort and assurance in uncertain times.

The message of individual salvation and piety heard at camp meetings made a special kind of sense in this uncivilized region. Historial Wayne Flynt writes, "In a world where the nearest neighbor might be miles away, where physicians were too remote to be of any practical use, where a family had to be self-contained by being its own architect, carpenter, herbdoctor, well-driller, furniture-builder, potter, and blacksmith, the individual had little choice but to rely upon [his] own wit and ingenuity."[25] A gospel of individual salvation and local church autonomy did well on the frontier, and the Baptist churches that preached those doctrines welcomed both revival converts and new settlers in the early years of the nineteenth century.

The number of Baptist churches was growing rapidly, as a result of both the Great Awakening and the Southern revivals. Baptist presence was spreading throughout the new nation, and Baptist organizations for the promotion of missions were gaining strength. Baptist churches were moving from their position as scattered, beleagured bands into the mainstream of American religion. Baptist mission societies took their place alongside the dozens of other voluntary societies that were springing up in the early decades of the nineteenth century. National groups promoting Sunday Schools, Bible distribution, peace, and charities of all sorts were the order of the day. The half century following the American Revolution was a time of developing national consciousness and expansiveness in most of the country, and other denominations were forming national organizations, as well. As the nation itself began to develop its identity, these religious organizations were uniting church people into a national network of which Baptists were now a part.

These new national organizations were barely formed, however, before opposition arose, especially on the frontier. "Anti-mission" movements began to take shape in the 1820s. Movements led by Daniel Parker, John Taylor, and Alexander Campbell, declared that organizations beyond the local church were unbiblical and that human efforts to save the heathen violated God's predestination of everyone's fate. Tennessee was especially affected, but from Alabama to Ohio and westward to Missouri, churches and associations fought battles over the propriety of raising money for missions.[26] Campbell's followers left to become the Disciples of Christ, and the followers of Parker and Taylor eventually formed numerous small sects and independent churches—many with designations like Primitive, Hardshell, or Anti-Missionary Baptist.

This fight over the way to do mission work reflected differences in interpretation of scripture and differences in the cultures in which various Baptists were located. Baptists in cities and in well-traveled areas found national organizing sensible. But fiercely independent pioneers, located in scattered settlements, found national fundraisers an unwanted intrusion into their lives. Even though this battle was won by the pro-missions forces, the strong resentment of outside fundraisers generated by these anti-mission movements remained with Baptists for a century. It was not unlike the resentment other representatives of national agencies (from carpetbaggers to revenuers) would later find.

Just how "national" Baptists would be, and how they would get their collective work done, was still being shaped during their first quarter century of organization. The polity chosen in these early years was a compromise between two competing methods. The associational method of organization brought together churches into a comprehensive structure that would do a variety of work on their behalf. It was defined by territory. It was modeled after local associations where fellowship, discipline, missions, education, and anything else concerning the Baptists in a district could be brought for the collective advice and support of other Baptists. The society structure was defined by a cause—missions or Bible publishing, for instance—and might have other local and state organizations as constituents, along with churches or individuals. Delegates to a society meeting might represent themselves, a state-level organization, or another society; but the society would concern itself only with its designated cause. During its early years the Baptist General Convention vacillated between these two poles. In its first decade it branched out into missionary and educational ventures under a centralized administration; but by 1826, advocates of decentralization (primarily from the north) had carried the day. From then on, throughout its national existence (and later as a northern body), the Triennial convention operated as a loosely connected network of independent societies, each funding and governing its own work.

Focus on organization, however, should not deflect attention from the remarkable growth experienced by Baptists in America during this period. Their evangelistic activity and strong appeal to ordinary folk brought growth in membership at almost three times the rate of population growth. Both Baptists and Methodists experienced explosive growth, especially in the South. And together with the Presbyterians, who also participated in the revivals spreading through that region, these denominations came to dominate Southern culture, establishing an evangelical ethos that continues until today. As historian Donald Matthews argues, evangelical "symbols, style of self-control, and rules of social decorum became dominant in the social system."[27]

Along with their growth in numbers came a new breadth in the evangelical social base. As the revivals spread, Baptist ranks came to include high status, as well as low. Between 1770 and 1820 evangelicals in the South moved from being a marginal sect of (often lower-class) dissenters to establishment status. And as the dominant religion of the land, dominant social classes joined their ranks. During colonial times Baptist simplicity and humility of style were often a conscious "rejection of the dominant values they did not have the wherewithal to emulate."[28] But after 1820, a community's First Baptist Church was likely to claim a fair share of the community's elite.

But this was a peculiar religious establishment. It was an establishment without apparent official support. There was no official church hierarchy to set legal norms for the region, yet the norms of conversion and pious living became the rule of life. The evangelical emphasis on individual salvation kept efforts at legal social reforms minimal, but the centrality of evangelical churches in the culture gave them impressive power in sanctioning individual and community behavior, facilitating reform if they so chose. The Baptist focus on the individual and on local congregations meant that what was established was more a religious culture than a religious community, an ethos more than an institutional structure.

That is not, however, to say that there was no institutional structure undergirding Baptists in the Southern cultural establishment. From the beginning Baptist churches had banded together into associations which established a certain uniformity of doctrine and practice within their districts. As the position of Baptists in Southern society became more central, they also took on the role of planning for the future protection of society through education. A number of academies and colleges began to be established, partly with doctrinal aims, partly with aims more clearly social and cultural.[29] The Baptist focus on foreign and home missions (including efforts in the vast western territories and the Native American populations) linked Southerners to a world-wide cause they began to perceive as commensurate with the spread of a pious Southern way of life. Associations, mission societies, and schools embodied both the Baptist concern for fellowship, evangelism, and discipleship and a growing

Southern regional consciousness. With evangelicalism at the center of the culture, Baptists in the South began to proclaim theirs as the best possible way for a Christian to live, a model for humanity.

That regional consciousness would, of course, eventually undo the national alliances Baptists had formed. Just as Baptists were discovering their national strengths in organized missions, publishing, and other activities, regional allegiances came to the fore. One of the most influential of the national movements in which Baptists became involved in the early nineteenth century was the movement to abolish slavery. By the 1830s, many Baptists in the North had embraced the abolitionist cause and were active in anti-slavery organizations. In the South, Baptists were becoming equally active in the effort to defend the institution that stood at the center of their social and economic order. Both sides were convinced that God smiled on their cause. Northerners were sure that God could not condone the treatment of one race as less than fully human. The doctrine of individual "soul competency" before God served abolitionists well. But Southerners were equally convinced that God meant for the races to be separate, each fulfilling unique foreordained functions of master and slave and living as individually pious persons, obedient to God's law.[30] With the national lines of argument so intertwined with the religious ones, it was inevitable that the issue of slavery would make its way into organized Baptist life—as it did in every other denomination with significant Southern membership.

As early as 1835, Southern states began to complain that they were not receiving their fair share of mission activity from the American Baptist Home Mission Society. Four years later, they organized a short-lived Southern society to make up the difference. But it was not mere lack of attention that would cause the eventual schism. By the early 1840s the battle lines were being drawn. Missionaries in India had formed a separate mission society so as to assure themselves separation from advocates of slavery. Meanwhile, on the other side of the issue, Baptists in Alabama were threatening to withhold their mission money unless the Board of Foreign Missions assured them that it was free of the influence of abolitionism. For several years, compromise was attempted by trying to keep the mission appointment process "slavery neutral."

But in the fall of 1844, the Home Mission Society got a test case from the Georgia Baptist Convention. Georgians sent James Reeves, a slaveholder, to the Society for appointment as a missionary to the Cherokee Indians. The board voted seven to five against his appointment, and the die was cast. Later that fall, the Alabama convention asked the Foreign Mission Board whether a slaveholder could be appointed. The reply was to the point, "If any one should offer himself as a missionary, having slaves, and should insist on retaining them as his property, we could not appoint him."[31]

By spring 1845, the Home Mission Society had decided that it should carry on its work in separate northern and southern divisions, and a call went out for Southerners to gather in May, in Augusta. There, 328 delegates from nine state conventions (and miscellaneous other Baptist organizations) in the South met to organize the Southern Baptist Convention. Two other states (Tennessee and the District of Columbia) were also represented, although they did not yet have state conventions. Before the war broke out, four more states would join, extending the new denomination's territory from Texas to Florida and from Virginia to Missouri.[32] It encompassed the region that would become the Confederacy.

Conflict, Defeat, and the Struggle for a Southern Identity, 1845–1877

Throughout the years surrounding the Civil War, the Southern Baptist Convention, like the region of which it was a part, struggled to define its identity apart from the North and to build institutions that would sustain it into the future. The battles Southern Baptists would fight during this generation would be against outsiders, not among themselves. They would be battles defined almost solely by culture, not battles for religious liberty or purity of doctrine.

At that initial 1845 meeting, Southern Baptist delegates formed Foreign and Domestic Mission Boards and invited existing Baptist missionaries to serve for the new Southern Boards. Although most of the churches in the South seemed happy to have a separate organization, they were often unwilling or unable to support the new denomination's work. During the first thirty-five years of its existence, the Southern Baptist Convention grew enormously in number of churches and number of members, but often languished as a central organization supporting missions and publications. Churches were sure they wanted to be "Southern" but not yet certain what that would mean.

In 1845, the delegates in Augusta represented a territory occupied by 4,000 Baptist churches with 350,000 members. By 1880, there were over 1.6 million members in over 13,000 churches. Yet, the vast majority of these churches were tiny, isolated, and served by untrained clergy. Typically they met for services only one or two times each month, with a pastor dividing his time among several congregations, none of which paid him more than a few dollars worth of farm goods. A small minority of the churches, however, was located in the towns and cities of the region, where Baptists were becoming the leading citizens.[33] The pastors of these churches were often well-educated and urbane, and it was they who dominated the leadership of the convention in these early years.

For almost all of these congregations, the association remained the most significant Baptist organization with which they were connected. It was local associations that settled doctrinal disputes and local associations that undertook mission projects in their own territories. With travel to state and Southwide meetings nearly impossible for most, this was the primary point of Baptist identification. And with resources severely limited, local mission efforts were often all that were possible.

In the decade following the organization of the SBC, the Landmark movement turned this tendency toward a local focus into a virtue. Led by J. R. Graves (later editor of the *Tennessee Baptist*), J. M. Pendleton, and A. C. Dayton, this movement sought to establish certain landmarks of the faith and declared that people missing such landmarks were not worthy of shared communion, of preaching in Baptist churches, or of administering baptism. Only a person properly baptized (immersed as a confessing adult) by someone who has been properly baptized was, as they saw it, truly a member of a Christian church, others merely held membership in religious societies. Only members of a proper Christian (Baptist, of course) church could partake of the Lord's Supper, and then only in their own local congregation. Further, the argument was that such proper churches and proper baptisms had existed since the first century in a kind of unbroken apostolic succession. Therefore, Baptists were not Protestants, Landmarkers argued, since Baptist churches had existed all along.[34]

These beliefs led to numerous controversies among Southern Baptists in the nineteenth century, and they continue to have heavy influence on Baptist life even today. The argument which most affected the new SBC was Landmarkism's insistence on radical local church autonomy, viewing any organization beyond the local association as unbiblical. Not only were baptism and communion to be administered in an exclusively local manner, but mission work was to be done only by local churches. Conventions and boards were simply not found in the New Testament and were thus not appropriate expressions of the Christian church. Where the anti-mission movements of a generation before had already plowed the ground, Landmarkism sowed the seeds that kept many Baptist churches from cooperating in the new Convention's mission endeavors.[35] Nearly a century later, almost half of the churches in Tennessee and Arkansas would still be giving nothing to national convention causes.[36]

Beyond that, the doctrinal issues raised by Landmarkism have persisted over the years. Alien immersion is the term Landmarkers used to designate any baptism not administered in a proper Baptist way. When an adult confessing Christian came to a Baptist church from any other church, the Landmark tendency was to quiz the person about their baptism. If they were immersed *after* they experienced conversion, and the minister who administered their baptism had also been properly baptized, the candidate could transfer membership. However, if any of those criteria were unmet, the earlier baptism was declared "alien" and the person was rebaptized. Beginning in the 1850s and continuing until the present, churches that accept such alien immersions risk the wrath of other churches in their associations who may still be influenced by Landmark teachings.[37]

The Landmark movement reached its height in the 1850s as the South was preparing to declare its political independence. Just as the region was forming a separate identity, declaring Southerners superior to outsiders, so many Southern Baptists were claiming a separate religious identity, declaring themselves superior to any other Christians.

The radical localism of the Landmark churches, however, was only one of the obstacles faced by those who wished to organize a Southwide denomination. The War and its aftermath left the region in disarray. During the War, the convention did little more than field chaplains for the Confederate Army. After the War, their Confederate dollars were worthless, and financial recovery took some time. The story of the denomination's Foreign and Domestic Mission Boards during this period is one of recurrent debt followed by determined solvency followed by another depression and more debt.

These financial woes helped to shape the way agency heads spent their time. They were called "corresponding secretaries," and correspond they did. When they were not sending written appeals to churches throughout the land, they were traveling the backroads to preach in scattered pulpits. Where the corresponding secretaries could not go, fund-raising agents went in their stead. Each agency had to raise its own support directly from the churches, and many churches were still hostile to sending their money off to distant causes. It is estimated that even by the end of the century, over half of all Southern Baptist churches gave nothing at all to missions (meaning that they were functionally disconnected from the denomination).[38] Most churches—even those without anti-mission sentiments—were simply too small and struggling to have money to spare.

In addition, competition from more established northern agencies also hampered Southern efforts at stability. Some associations and state conventions were simply accustomed to working with the American Baptist Home Mission Society and the Tract Society of the Triennial Convention. Even though they declared themselves Southern Baptist, they continued old working relationships rather than joining the new Southern Boards' efforts.

The mission efforts churches were being asked to support in those days consisted largely of a few dozen missionaries in China and Africa and ministries to American Indians and various other ethnic groups in the United States. The only publication of note during this era was *Kind Words*, a Sunday School tract. It did so poorly that in 1873 the first attempt at a Sunday School Board collapsed, and the Domestic Mission Board took over this lone publication.

Perhaps the most lively area of Baptist organizational growth during this period was in education. Up-and-coming Baptists were concerned about learning a proper heritage for the future, and such concern naturally led toward the formation of colleges. In nearly every Southern state, leading entrepreneurs joined hands with church people to establish Baptist secondary schools and colleges that would prepare a refined, Christian leadership for the future. They had a vague sense that the schools of the North were alien and godless, that only evangelicals (preferably Southern) could properly provide an education. At the very least they wanted schools of their own equal or better than the ones Northerners had established.[39] Like other Baptist organizations during this period, schools struggled to survive; but by late in the century, a firm Southern Baptist educational base was being built.

In addition, in 1859, Southern Baptists established their first seminary. In Greenville, South Carolina, the Southern Baptist Theological Seminary was formed with four members of the faculty and twenty-six students. It was not directly supported by the convention, but was closely tied in other ways. Leading churches sent their brightest young men and expected to be served by well-trained graduates of the seminary. Until the turn of the century, this was the only Southern Baptist Seminary, but even after it was joined by others, its graduates enjoyed a special prestige. For nearly a century, Southern Seminary's faculty and graduates would dominate convention leadership.

While Baptists in the South were struggling to establish an organizational identity, they were nevertheless firmly entrenched in their position at the heart of Southern culture. The evangelical revivals of the previous generations had achieved their greatest success in just the time that Southerners were establishing a regional identity. As a result, revivalist religion and pious Christian living became as much a part of Southernness as the South's "peculiar institution" of slavery. Southerners were thoroughly evangelical and Baptists were thoroughly Southern; culture and religion were inextricably linked.[40]

Yet, Southern Baptists hesitated to use their cultural power in the service of most legislation. As Baptists, they firmly held to their tradition of separation of church and state, arguing that the state (especially the national government) ought to keep out of the business of religion. However, during this period, a number of issues began to arise that pushed them toward increasing cooperation with local and state government. There were new sabbath observance laws and various laws against the vices of gambling and drinking, for instance. While a few diehard separationists pointed out that the state ought not to define and punish sin, most Baptists were only too eager to have the assistance of government in upholding the morals they saw as essential to the life of a Christian community.[41]

As the religious voice of Southern culture, however, Southern Baptists inevitably had to face harder questions than those of sabbath observance and personal vices. Questions of slavery, Confederacy, and segregation, faced them, and in each case, Southern Baptists provided enthusiastic religious support for the Southern cause. They helped to develop the religious justifications for slavery before the War and supported the Confederate cause in the fighting. Even after the War, they refused to see defeat as disgrace or as an indictment of their cause.[42] In 1865, the Virginia *Baptist Herald* editorialized, "We shall ever regard it as a most sacred duty to guard the reputation and cherish the memory of those noble men who laid down their lives in the Confederate service."[43] Nearly a generation later, when Jefferson Davis died in 1889, Baptist state papers were still full of tribute to his life and cause. Throughout the nineteenth century Southern Baptists legitimated and celebrated the domination of white Southerners over their black neighbors. What Kentucky Baptists stated in 1860 was little changed, even into the twentieth century.

> [A]mong the white race in the Southern States there is no difference of opinion upon this subject; all are united in opinion in reference to the political, intellectual and social inequality between the colored and the white races. And the people of our Commonwealth generally feel that the present condition of the colored race in this country accords both with the Word and the providence of God.[44]

After the Civil War, freed slaves began to withdraw from the Baptist churches in which they had worshipped in special sections (slave galleries) set aside for them. The Convention and its churches generally supported these moves, sometimes generously. In part, the support was altruistic, but Baptists also worried about the social mixing of free blacks and whites in integrated churches. With slavery gone, the distance between blacks and whites was even more carefully guarded. The Virginia

Baptist paper told its readers in 1866, "As for equality, either social or political, between the races, that cannot be, must not be . . . Let no man try to bring together what God has set so far asunder."[45] Baptist papers throughout the Southland argued vehemently against the 1875 Civil Rights Act and supported efforts in the years after Reconstruction to legalize the system of disenfranchisement that was taking shape informally.

During this same period, Northern Baptists were taking a lively interest in the education and welfare of blacks in the South. They sent a contingent of home missionaries into the South that was roughly three times the size of the entire Southern Baptist Domestic Mission force. These missionaries were primarily concerned with establishing Negro colleges and helping black churches get started. Their presence, however, was a major irritant to the struggling Southern Baptist mission agency, an irritant made the more galling because, as previously noted, some Southern churches and state bodies were still turning to the more-established northern Society for assistance in mission causes.

Throughout the period following the War, both the Southern Baptist Domestic Mission Board (the Home Mission Board after 1874) and the American Baptist Home Mission Society claimed all of North America as their territory. The Northern body wanted to return to its status as a national organization and for over ten years following the War's close sought to reunite with their Southern family. But their overtures were steadfastly resisted. The Southern Convention was convinced that it was better off as a separate body, and they resented Northern interference. As Reconstruction drew to a close, Southern Baptists—like the New South that was emerging—claimed their regional identity by ejecting Northern influences and replacing them with growing Southern institutions. In 1877, President Rutherford B. Hayes recalled federal troups from the South, and Reconstruction ended. In the period that followed, the region and its religious alter-ego began to thrive as a distinct subculture within American society. With Northern influences and competition gone, a monopoly of Southern influences was put in place.

Southern Baptists Thriving in the Southland, 1878–1917

After years of struggle, Southern Baptist institutions began to show impressive strength in the years following Reconstruction. In 1882, the Home Mission Board gained Dr. I. T. Tichenor as its head and moved from Marion, Alabama, to Atlanta.[46] Tichenor was a man tirelessly dedicated to placing his agency on firm, Southern footing. Over the next several years, he traveled to nearly every state convention meeting, urging the states to reject alliances with the (Northern) Home Mission Society and support the Southern Board. Within five years, "there was not a missionary to the white people of the South who did not bear a commission from either the Home Mission Board of the Southern Baptist Convention or one of [the] State Boards in alliance with it."[47] Although gifts never matched Tichenor's grand vision, the financial condition of the organization was soon to have a firm foundation. The climax of Tichenor's efforts came in 1894, at Fortress Monroe, Virginia. There a joint committee of Northern and Southern Baptists met and arrived at territorial agreements about the scope of their respective work. These "comity" agreements were often contested in later years, but for the next generation they established the Southern states as the exclusive territory of the Southern convention.

During the period following Reconstruction, both the Home and Foreign mission efforts of Southern Baptists grew at a rapid pace. In 1877, the two boards had fewer than fifty missionaries between them. By 1917, there were over 300 missionaries in 8 countries abroad and over 1,500 evangelists and other missionaries in the U.S. In addition to preaching and starting churches, they were establishing schools and hospitals wherever they went.

This concern for both spiritual and temporal needs also showed up in various social and political causes to which Baptists in the South gave attention during these years. Some rural preachers became convinced that the farm economy of the South needed drastic reform. They were attracted to the Populist cause in the 1890s, despite the protests of their urban cousins that preachers should stay out of politics. As small town economies became dominated by mills, most Baptist churches served the needs of the owners, but at least a few preachers spoke out against the injustices and abuses of the mill system, as well.[48]

But no cause rallied Baptist support like Prohibition. Like other evangelicals and like reformers in the Social Gospel movement, they became convinced that the banishment of alcohol was necessary for the redemption of society. Despite the growing Southern Baptist distaste for ecumenism, here they joined forces with other religious groups. In addition, the denomination formed its own committees to aid the cause. In 1913, a Social Service Commission was formed, the denomination's first effort to address issues beyond the church, an effort dominated for two decades by the crusade against liquor.[49]

This crusade grew naturally out of the continuing link in Southern Baptist minds between their religion and their virtuous behavior, their evangelical calling and their calling to spread their way of life. And as they saw it, white Southerners had preserved a faith and a way of life superior to any other and it was therefore worthy of imitation. When

V. I. Masters, head of the Home Mission Board's publicity department from 1909 to 1921, described the heart of the Board's work, he spoke of spreading the "Anglo-Saxon evangelical faith" uniquely preserved in Southern religion.[50]

With such clear convictions about Southern superiority, continued battles to establish Southern-controlled institutions were to be expected. Not only was the Home Mission Board establishing its own territory, but the battle for denominational identity was also being fought in the arena of publications to be used in the churches. The American Baptist Publication Society was well established as a supplier of Sunday School lessons and other materials for churches. And after 1873, Southern Baptists had no publication board at all. Tichenor's Home Mission Board was still publishing *Kind Words*, but Tichenor was convinced that a truly unified convention must have its own publications—"Southern literature for Southern churches."[51] He mentioned his idea to James M. Frost, a Richmond pastor. (Typical of Tichenor, his "mention" was a two-hour passionate appeal.) Frost took up the cause; and in 1891, a new Sunday School Board was formed, with Frost as its head.

The Board faced formidable odds. Many within the convention opposed it at first, and the Northern publication society was still very strong in the South. As in the field of Home Missions, the influence of the Northern body would have to be overcome before a Southern organization could thrive. The matter came to a head at the Convention meeting of 1897. The Northern society had multiple representatives at the meeting, one of whom made a speech critical of the new SBC Board. Such criticism from an outsider sparked immediate and passionate defense from the Southern messengers. From that day forward, the Southern Baptist Convention could increasingly count on Southern support for its own Sunday School publications.

Almost from the beginning, the Sunday School Board did much more than publish Sunday School lessons. It was this agency more than any other that introduced an internal uniformity of program to match the denomination's external uniformity in culture. To promote Sunday School, the Board sent "field workers" out to churches and state conventions to train local personnel. As a result, in the first generation of the Board's existence, the percentage of churches with Sunday Schools rose from thirty-eight to sixty-five. In addition, the Board quickly added programs in publishing church music and books, distributing church supplies, supporting church libraries, collecting research and statistics, and promoting church member training through Training Union and the Baptist Young People's Union.[52]

In each case, they began to work through the state conventions to encourage adoption of these programs in the churches. Many of the states had been undergoing a period of consolidation, uniting competing and fragmented societies into one state convention structure. Now they had even more incentive (and resources) to put their state organizations in order. The Sunday School Board now stood ready to aid their efforts. If a state convention could not afford to hire personnel as support staff for church Sunday Schools or Training Union, the Sunday School Board supplied the funds (and, of course, the materials to be purchased).

The Board's own publishing and distributing enterprises quickly grew into lucrative businesses that fueled program development and support activities. As churches bought materials from the Board, they also turned to Nashville for training in the use of those materials. The profits from materials sold paid the salaries of field workers to do the training. The more the Board sold, the more they were able to do; and the more they did, the more they sold. All the while, these programs and supplies were making the Southern Baptist Convention a strong and unified organization with an identity built in large part on its shared use of common materials.

Southern Baptists were also continuing in their task of providing Southern institutions of higher learning. The colleges of the previous generations, from Baylor in Texas to Mercer in Georgia, were now thriving. During the generation following Reconstruction, nearly a dozen more Southern Baptist colleges were founded. In 1877, the Southern Baptist Seminary had moved from Greenville, South Carolina to Louisville, Kentucky; and in 1909, it was joined by a second seminary, even further west, in Fort Worth, Texas, with a third added in 1918, in New Orleans. By that time, the faculty of Southern seminary had grown from four to twelve, and the student body grew to nearly 400, about one third of them women enrolled at the Woman's Missionary Union Training School which had opened on the campus in 1907.[53] Students in these institutions were not just gaining a theological education, they were also learning to administer the programs of the denomination as developed by its various Boards. By sponsoring lectureships and providing materials, the Sunday School Board ensured that the denomination's church leadership would support denominational programs.[54]

Establishing a firm denominational identity also depended on conquering the remains of the antimission movements from the earlier part of the century. The Landmark movement had its greatest impact during the 1850s in the initial disputes over mission support. It was interrupted by the War, but continued to gain followers for thirty years after the war in a broad area where Graves' publications circulated. From Tennessee to southern Kentucky and northern Alabama to Mississippi, Louisiana, Texas, and Arkansas, Landmark teachings made their way into the churches. Some of Graves' ideas became so pervasive that they could be resisted only at great peril. One of the few who tried to resist was William H. Whitsitt, professor of church history and president of the Southern Baptist Seminary. Not until the 1890s did he publish articles claiming that Baptists had their origins in the seventeenth century in England—not with John the Baptist as Landmarkers claimed. His careful historical documentation was no match for the furor of Baptists who had come to believe they descended in unbroken line from the first century. He was forced to resign in 1899.

Whitsitt's resignation, however, did not indicate any great strength for the Landmark notion that only local churches should be in the business of doing mission work. In the 1880s, the Foreign Mission Board had refused to adopt a plan for making each missionary dependent directly on local church support. And in 1905, when presented with an ultimatum from Arkansas Landmarkers, the convention again affirmed its own legitimacy as a body working beyond the local church. That group of Landmark dissenters promptly withdrew to form the American Baptist Association, a new denominational body. Graves had died in 1893, and with the departure of these Landmark leaders, the overt arguments against central funding died down.

The other major organizational development at the beginning of this new era was the institution of the Woman's Missionary Union, in 1888. There had been missionary societies for women from the beginning of organized Baptist life in America. Some women's societies had even been represented (by men) at the organizing meeting of the Southern Baptist Convention in Augusta. Over the years, hundreds of local women's groups were formed to support home and foreign mission efforts; and as these mission-minded women began to accompany their husbands to Southern Baptist Convention meetings, they organized their own women's meetings to hear news from the mission fields and talk about ways to support their missionaries.

In 1876, women began to form central committees in the states; and in 1885, their desire to organize got an ironic boost from the Convention's decision to formalize its "brethren only" attendance rule.[55] No women would be allowed to register as messengers, although a few apparently had in the past. In 1888, female representatives of twelve states gathered in Richmond to form a Southwide women's missionary body that would meet at the same time as the all-male annual Southern Baptist Convention.[56] From the beginning they were a formidable group. They helped to organize annual weeks of prayer and giving to missions, and within a generation they would be contributing over a quarter of a million dollars annually to the mission budget of the denomination.[57]

From the beginning, men in the convention feared that this financial and organizational prowess might siphon resources from the growing official programs. The women, however, chose to use their skills in the service of the denomination, while at the same time maintaining autonomy for their own body. Men gave the reports of the Union to the denomination's annual meetings, but women steadfastly refused to allow men a voice in their own internal affairs. The WMU was organized as an auxiliary to the Southern Baptist Convention, with its own decision-making and financial authority, but pledged to the exclusive support of Southern Baptist mission causes. It was a delicate balance that seemed to serve the interests of all concerned.

The annual Convention meetings were, in those days, a gentlemanly affair. Seminary professors and learned pastors delivered eloquent sermons (usually on short notice). Matters of business drew the messengers into long and passionate debates. Important issues might occupy them for half of a day, with speeches on each side running to twenty and thirty minutes each. An historian writing in 1894 observed,

> The Southern Baptist Convention has always been particularly happy in its choice of presiding officers. While other bodies have passed the office around in a complimentary way, without much regard to presiding ability, this body has been presided over by a succession of the ablest parliamentarians that the denomination has possessed, and has established the habit of continuing through a series of years presidents who have shown special fitness for the office. . . . It is probable that the Southern Baptist Convention is surpassed in the ability and eloquence of its members and in the dignity of its proceedings by no similar body of any denomination.[58]

Such gentlemanly harmony, however, was soon overtaken by the sheer success and growth of the Convention. In the years between 1876 and 1925, church membership tripled from 1.2 million to 3.6 million, while the number of churches (now somewhat larger on average) nearly doubled from 13,000 to 24,000. But with increasing prosperity and improved transportation, the size of the annual meetings increased not twice, but tenfold, from several hundred to several thousand. And as the work of the convention grew, the time available for each report or item of business decreased. By the turn of the century, it was already apparent that the structure of the convention would not accommodate the reality of its size and growing breadth of functions.

The problems posed by the breadth of the denomination's functions appeared not only when the convention met to hear reports, but also when the convention dispersed, leaving each agency to its own devices. Each was still raising and administering its own funds—a system increasingly unwieldy as the number of causes grew. Each was also setting its own policy, with no method for coordinating their work. Each agency's staff was directly responsible to whatever group of messengers arrived at any given annual meeting. They were even given mandates from time to time that reflected nothing more than the regional interests of the people nearest the convention meeting site (who obviously came in the largest numbers). Beginning at the turn of the century, the convention began establishing study committees aimed at finding a more efficient method of organization. The Southern Baptist Convention would soon learn to fight its battles in the committee room.

During that same period, there were also repeated calls for examination of the convention's methods of representation. Just how big should an annual meeting be, and who should be allowed to vote? At that point, state conventions, local associations, and individual churches could send representatives, with the latter allocated on the basis of one for each $250 given to the convention's mission boards (the same dollar amount still in use 100 years later). Many churches argued that such a large required amount effectively disenfranchised them. Others argued that because of the increasingly unwieldy size of the meeting, states and associations should not be allowed messengers. Landmarkers argued that only churches should be represented, since only churches, not any centralized board, could legitimately do mission work. It was a perennial argument, and no one seemed yet to know how to maintain the democratic ideals of a Baptist body in the midst of immense program and numerical growth.

From the end of Reconstruction to the time the nation entered World War I, the Southern Baptist Convention had been transformed from a vast scattered band of churches with little in common beyond their Southernness and their Baptist ethos into an even larger band of churches sharing both culture and program, training and mission. Their struggling regional institutions had grown into a burgeoning religious empire. No longer were Baptists the outcast dissenters fighting for the rights of minorities. No longer were they the lower classes attracted by the anti-establishment and democratic ethos of congregational autonomy. No longer were they even the independent frontier churches created by revivals. By the second decade of the twentieth century, Baptists in the South were a cultural establishment enforcing moral conformity and sustained by an institutional structure that reached into all areas of church life. And they were ready to reorganize their institutional empire into an efficiently-run Southwide religious system that for the next fifty years would make them proud.

3. Organization, Growth, and Change: The Seeds of Controversy

New forms of organization came rapidly to Southern Baptists in the years following World War I. During the period from 1917 to 1931, the organizational structures of today's denomination emerged. It was one of the most creative periods in the convention's history, despite recurrent financial crises and theological debates. The farm economy was already moving into depression in the 1920s, and Southern Baptist causes were affected deeply. The American religious world was in turmoil in fundamentalist versus modernist battles, and Southern Baptists spilled their share of ink (but very little blood) defending orthodoxy. But in those years, Baptist leaders helped their agencies to pay off crushing debts and kept the work alive. Baptist scholars articulated the faith in a way that affirmed tradition while defending the value of study. These leaders bridged the gap between the nineteenth century southern world of common consent evangelical piety and the later twentieth century world in which the Bible Belt would become the Sun Belt.

The first step in that organizational process came in 1917. After repeated efforts to form some sort of coordinating council, the Convention finally established its first Executive Committee. It was to be composed of seven men, representing the various territories of the convention. At first it was given only the duties of arranging for the convention meetings and acting for the Convention "ad interim on such matters as may arise pertaining to the general business of the Convention and not otherwise provided for. . . ."[1] It had no power over the existing agencies and Boards and no financial powers; but during the next decade, all that would change.

Two years later, in the midst of post-war exhilaration, the Convention decided to launch its first unified fundraising effort. The goal was $75 million to be raised over the following five years. In a great organizational flurry, pledges of over $92 million came in; but the growing financial crisis, especially in the farm economy, reduced actual receipts by the end of the period to $58 million. The shortfall wreaked havoc on the budgets of agencies that had counted on projected receipts. But this experience of unified fundraising laid the groundwork for what was to follow.

As the campaign drew to a close, a committee was appointed to study the Convention's future direction in financial affairs, and in 1925 their recommendation for the Co-Operative Program was adopted. They urged each Baptist to tithe and to give that money in a timely, regular fashion to their local churches. In turn, the churches that received those tithes were urged to set aside a regular portion of their moneys for the work of the Convention. They would send their contributions to their own state convention, which would, in turn, send a portion to a new Commission headquartered in Nashville. Two years later, that Commission was merged with an expanded Executive Committee to become the central fiscal and coordinating body for the denomination. Working through the states, it became the sole fundraiser and budgeter for all the Convention's agencies.[2]

Such systematic finance was, of course, the order of the day. The nation's economy had moved from its era of entrepreneurial capitalism into a period of regulation, consolidation, and emphasis on management and efficiency. Organized, bureaucratic structures were the wave of the future, and religious bodies did not want to be left behind.[3] Throughout the 1920s, many denominations in the United States were adopting plans of centralized finance and administrations that moved them beyond their own entrepreneurial days of independent fundraisers canvassing the churches for uncoordinated benevolent causes.[4]

Growing numbers of church members were moving from unpredictable farm incomes to regular salaries and wages. Systematic giving was now both more logical to them and more possible. As more laity became involved in the affairs of the Southern Baptist Convention, there were increasing demands that the church be no less efficient than the businesses they ran. With the adoption of the cooperative program, the Southern Baptist Convention became the business-like, efficient organization many of its leaders desired.

Having inaugurated new administrative and financial structures, the Convention turned, in 1931, to revisions in its constitution. It began to address the problems of representation that had plagued it from the beginning, but had become acute since the turn of the century. It had never been clear just who should come to the annual meeting and on what basis they should cast their ballots. The ideal of a pure democracy (on the order of a congregational meeting) had never quite meshed with the reality of large groups gathered from distant places and overseeing several distinct organizations. Finally, in 1931, the Convention resolved that its messengers would be solely from churches, not from associations, mission societies, or other entities. In doing so, it actually over turned the recommendation brought by its by-laws committee, opting for a substitute motion from the floor. Each cooperating church would be entitled to send at least one messenger, no matter how small or impoverished it might be, with additional messengers alotted according to the amount of contributions made to Convention causes.[5] Over the next several years, the

Convention continued to tinker with how many additional messengers would be allowed, finally settling on ten as the maximum. Between those limits, a church could send an additional messenger for each $250 given to Convention causes.[6] Later, church size was added as an alternative to contributions for calculating representation; for every 250 members, an additional messenger was added.

In 1931, very few of the Convention's nearly 24,000 churches would have qualified for more than one messenger. Indeed, if giving something to the Convention was the measure of cooperation, nearly one-third would have qualified for no representation at all.[7] In that depression year the average Southern Baptist church member gave less than $10 all year to his or her local church, and there was often little left over at the church to send to the state or to Nashville (and equally little opportunity to travel to annual Convention meetings). Few churches would have qualified for extra messengers on the basis of size, either. There were few enough large churches, in fact, to list all those with membership over 500 in the annual denominational *Handbook*. There were just over 1,000 such churches listed that year. The average church had 165 members, but that number masks the huge number of tiny churches at the low end of the scale since the average is raised by a few very large churches at the other end.

Depending on where the convention actually met, the size of the gathering was not reduced appreciably by the new rules. Over the next decade attendance varied between nearly 6,000 in Birmingham and Richmond and barely more than 2,000 in St. Petersburg. What the new formula had introduced was not reduction in size, but some clarity about the constituency being represented. The convention would still gather en masse once a year to try to do its business. And exactly who came to vote would still depend mostly on the ability to make the trip. Most Southern Baptists would still be unrepresented in the decision-making process.

That same constitutional reform, in 1931, also introduced a new system for doing the convention's business during the remainder of the year. Recognizing that four or five thousand people in open session could not effectively debate the policy decisions that faced several dozen agencies, Boards, and schools, a regular method for electing and rotating Boards of Trustees was created. What had previously been an ad hoc collection of committees, appointed to aid the agencies with various aspects of their work, now became a regularized feature of the denomination's decision-making structure. These new boards of trustees were small enough to deliberate effectively and were to be made up of people recognized as well-versed in the convention's affairs. The boards were to be more strictly representative than the annual conventions. Each state convention got a set number of representatives based on its size, and in later years there would be rules requiring a minimum proportion of lay representation. The Convention chose to balance the pure democracy of its annual meeting with this more republican arrangement. While the messengers might still overturn the work of the trustees, these groups of respected leaders were given the responsibility for direct oversight of the Convention's growing bureaucracy.[8]

Selection of trustees was entrusted to a consultative process that gradually grew more elaborate over the years. As the process was first set in place, the messengers would elect a president who would, before the convention meeting adjourned, appoint his Committee on Boards.[9] That body would nominate all agency trustees for approval at the next convention.[10] In 1946, the convention experimented with turning over the selection of the Committee on Boards to the messengers themselves, meeting in state caucuses.[11] That evidently proved cumbersome, and by 1950, the Convention had given the task of selecting a nominating committee to a presidentially-appointed Committee on Committees.[12] Figure 1 in chapter 6 outlines the election process that has been in place since 1950. Messengers get to vote on the nominees for the Committee on Boards (now Committee on Nominations) and again on the nominees for trustees, but the process hinges on the people the president chooses as consultants (the Committee on Committees). Each step of the nomination and election process assumes that natural leaders will emerge from the pastors and leading lay people of the denomination and that these natural leaders can represent everyone. The 1931 constitution writers saw no need to construct a system that would allow various subgroups in the denomination to be equitably represented. There simply did not seem to be any subgroups whose interests needed representing.

In deciding that it was churches who would send the messengers and states that would be represented on boards of trustees, the Convention was not thereby empowering those messengers or trustees to represent their churches and states. They were not delegates representing interests other than their own. Rather, the annual gathering was viewed as a calling out of individual Baptists from throughout the Southland to come and do the work of the denomination. It was assumed that people from one church were pretty much like people from any other.[13] Like the people meeting in an individual congregation or town, the culture, language, and beliefs they shared would provide the basis for their deliberations. They could debate and differ precisely because they had no need to question each other's membership in the body. It was assumed that each messenger or trustee had a right to belong; they were part of a common body bound together by culture, religion, and now by denominational program, as well.

For the very reason of that denominational and cultural homogeneity, the Southern Baptist Convention largely escaped the divisive effects of the fundamentalist-modernist controversies of the 1920s. There were simply not enough modernists around in the Convention to generate a good fight.[14] There was a good deal of rhetoric about modernism, evolution, the social gospel, and the need for orthodoxy; but the rhetoric never turned into insurrection. Leaders wrote pamphlets, preached sermons, and editorialized in Baptist state papers. But no significant split ever occurred. As James Thompson argues, "the establishment of a fundamentalist wing among Southern Baptists was a superfluous act."[15]

That, of course, did not deter the fiery J. Frank Norris, of Fort Worth, from his constant accusations against the Convention. He fought the $75 million campaign and all other efforts at centralization, accusing the Baptist "machine" of violating the autonomy of the local church.[16] He joined forces with Northern Baptist William Bell Riley of Minneapolis and Canadian Baptist T. T. Shields of Toronto to form the fundamentalist Baptist Bible Union; but he was never able to bring the Southern Convention into that cause. Norris worried about the same modernism that Northerners saw around them, but he was never able to convince many of his fellow Southerners that the threat was real.

In part, Southern Baptists were simply not willing to accept Norris' premillennialist vision of the world's doom. In the North, both the Social Gospel and premillennialism made sense. In the South, neither did. The Social Gospel spoke to the problems of cities and workers, of multiple nationalities and human dignity. Premillennialism spoke to the same urban problems, but interpreted them as signs of Christ's immanent return. Both movements assumed an urban, pluralistic, rapidly changing environment, and that environment simply did not exist in the South in the 1920s. "Except for Birmingham, Alabama, the South had none of the massive industrial centers that did so much to prod the Social Gospelers into action in the North. Manufacturing remained limited, and employed people with strong rural ties."[17] In the mid-1920s, less than 10 percent of Southern Baptist churches were located in places with more than 2,500 in population, and nearly three-quarters of all Southern Baptist church members lived in traditional small communities. Neither at the grassroots level nor in the denomination's institutions were cries of decay and destruction believable.

Whatever evidence there was, of course, Norris found it. In Texas, Norris sought to expose and dispell the teaching of evolution in the classrooms of Baylor University (forcing eight faculty members to resign), but he could find no convincing liberals in the denomination's seminaries. In reality, more than anything, he despised his fellow Texans (and rivals for leadership) George Truett (pastor of First Baptist Dallas) and Lee Scarborough (president of the Southwestern Baptist Theological Seminary). At one point, after months of vicious attacks on their integrity, he offered them an opportunity to use his radio station for a reply. After they spent hours slinging mud back at him, he demurely offered a prayer for their forgiveness and preached an evangelistic sermon. His performance won him a number of followers, but his bitter power struggles and attacks eventually resulted in his defeat. In 1930, he led his First Baptist Church of Fort Worth out of the Convention.[18]

Fundamentalism was not only unsuccessful in disrupting a decade of Southern Baptist organizational development, it also brought the Convention new churches and new territory as by-products of the controversies outside the South. The first development came in 1910, when disgruntled conservatives in southern Illinois, in protest over the liberalism of the (Northern Baptist) Divinity School at the University of Chicago, sought union with the Southern Baptist Convention. Similar splits of Northern Baptists in New Mexico and Arizona resulted in separate conventions in those states seeking alignment with the Southern body, as well. In each case, the dissidents were often of Southern origin themselves and had existed in uneasy alliance with the agencies of the Northern Convention. The pattern in each case was the formation of a schismatic conservative group at odds with the Northern Convention, followed within a few years by their request to join Southern Baptists.[19]

It was the request of the Arizona group in 1928 that precipitated the Convention's move to regularize its procedures for determining state affiliation and representation on trustee boards. It was also that move that hinted at the broad territorial growth that was ahead. Northern Baptists protested bitterly that a Southern Baptist state convention in Arizona violated the territorial agreements arrived at a generation before. They saw this as a threatening move by the Southern Convention. The Southern Baptists, however, did not yet see it that way. They were merely opening their doors to believers of like mind, they said, believers who sought to cooperate in the Southern Convention's mission efforts.

The other visible result in the South of the decade's Northern controversies was the adoption of Southern Baptists' first official statement of faith. Since Baptist polity has never allowed any organization to prescribe a creed for the individual believer, this statement was more a guideline than an enforceable document. But some Baptists were concerned that a clear statement of their fundamentals was necessary, if only as a precautionary measure. In its preamble, the statement mentioned the teaching of "naturalism" as a reason to reaffirm what Baptists believe; but it did not contain the antievolution clause that a few activists wanted.[20] Rather, E. Y. Mullins, president of Southern Seminary, led the convention to adopt an adaptation of the 1833 New Hampshire Confession. They titled it A Statement of the Baptist Faith and Message.

As the 1920s moved into the 1930s, Southern Baptists were formalizing their life together in a number of ways. Where a faith of common consent had been enough, now an official statement took its place. Where there had been miscellaneous agencies, raising miscellaneous funds, voted on by miscellaneous messengers, and overseen by miscellaneous committees, now there were clear guidelines and procedures. The Executive Committee was to raise and disperse the funds through the Cooperative Program, and decision-making procedures in both agencies and annual meetings had been set in place. Like the modern culture of the nation around them, Baptist culture had taken into itself the drive to rationalize its structures. Procedures were put in writing; hierarchies and chains of command were created.[21]

The drive to put modern structures in place did not, however, indicate that the culture of which Southern Baptists were a part had changed appreciably from its traditional forms. Both religion and culture were still rooted in the traditions of the region. Religion was still pervasive, and few structures of the society were genuinely secularized. Most Southern Baptists still lived in small towns or on farms, and their expectations about leadership had not yet changed to match the new structures. While the structures Baptists created demanded that staff office holders be selected on the basis of rationally evaluated credentials, the reality of Southern life was that leaders still emerged through a strong combination of tradition and charisma. They were the great preachers, the holders of historic pulpits, the motivators and inspirers of mission work. They embodied the ideals to which everyone aspired. These were the people who rose to elective office and who filled the board rooms and fledgling bureaucracies in the 1930s. The denomination had adopted the structure of a corporation, but it still had the culture of a small town. As the Baptists of the South struggled through the dark days of the depression, they did it as a giant extended family, revering their paternal leaders and sacrificing together for the good of the family. In those days of struggle, few could have imagined the revolution that lay ahead.

Explosion Outward, 1942–1960

During the Depression, Southerners had been leaving their homes in record numbers. Hundreds of thousands left behind desolate farms from

Georgia to Oklahoma, traveling north and west in search of a better life. If they began looking for a church when they arrived in Ohio or California or Michigan they often found none to their liking. Churches that wore the name Baptist did not feel much like home to these Southern migrants. The Northern Baptist Churches usually offered a more formal style of worship and a more learned ministry than rural Southern Baptists had been used to. Few of the familiar hymns and none of the SBC programs were present, and Southerners strongly suspected that the people in these churches were too liberal for Southern tastes.[22] This was especially true if the Southerners in question had been influenced by Landmarkism and therefore believed that communion and baptism and church membership ought to be strictly controlled. Northern Baptist churches were entirely too tolerant on such matters to pass Landmark tests. All in all, Southerners simply found themselves in alien territory.

But they were not alone. Soon enclaves of expatriates found each other and began to form congregations. Sometimes they labeled these churches "missionary" Baptist or "independent." Often they started in homes and were pastored by men who worked alongside their parishioners in the factories.[23] But there was little doubt where their denominational sympathies lay. So it was that in the late 1930s, fourteen churches had been formed in central and southern California. And in 1940, they organized themselves into the Southern Baptist General Convention of California. The next year, they petitioned for recognition by the SBC; and in 1942, the convention voted to admit them.

At the time, Southern Baptists recognized that this was a major break with the past. California was far outside the territorial limits set at Fort Monroe nearly fifty years earlier. These were not disgruntled former Northern Baptists. These were people who went into a new territory and started Southern Baptist churches. Some of the Convention's most respected leaders argued that accepting such churches into the fold would be an insult to the Northern Convention that was seeking to minister in that area. But they were overruled by the expansive mood of Baptists who had become convinced that Northern Baptists were no longer true to the gospel.

This simple acceptance of fourteen churches was a move that heralded incredible expansion to follow, and Northern Baptists were furious. For several years, the Southern Convention tried to maintain the last vestiges of the old territorial agreements by refusing to send missionaries into new territories, working only with churches after they had formed on their own. However, by 1950, when the Northern Convention adopted the name American Baptist, the Southern Convention dropped all pretense of territorial civility. The entire nation would be official Southern Baptist territory.

During the twenty-five years following the seating of California messengers, nine new state conventions were formed, raising the total entitled to representation on Boards of Trustees from nineteen to twenty-eight. Six more conventions joined in the next twenty years, with every state except Iowa organized into an official state or regional body. By sometime in the 1960s, there were Southern Baptist churches in every state. Usually a core of former Southerners led the way into these new territories, but nearby state conventions often sent missionaries, as well. Californians helped start churches in Oregon and Washington. Arizonans worked in Utah and Nevada. Kentuckians helped in Ohio, and so the story went throughout the nation. While official policy was to avoid starting new churches where Baptist ones already existed, overzealous "pioneers" often violated that rule, looking for prospects wherever they could find them.

Enthusiastic preachers and lay people were convinced that they could "win the nation for the Lord" and that no one could do it better than Southern Baptists. They often talked of their expansion outward in pioneer terms, echoing the language of manifest destiny that had characterized the nation in the previous century.[24] It was a time when church attendance was booming, but Southern Baptists out-boomed everyone else, growing in the twenty years from 1941 to 1961 from 5 million members in 25,000 churches to 10 million in over 32,000 churches (see table 3.1). By the 1960s, Southern Baptists had so thoroughly spread over the

Table 3.1. Southern Baptist Convention Growth, 1931–1986

Year	Number of Churches	Numbers of Members (in millions)	Number of States in Conventions	Number of Messengers	Amount of CP Giving (in millions)
1931	23,800	3.9	19	3,200	$5.8
1936	24,700	4.5	19	3,700	$5.0
1941	25,600	5.2	19	5,900	$7.8
1946	26,400	6.1	22	7,900	$21.2
1951	28,300	7.4	25	6,500	$37.3
1956	30,800	8.7	27	12,200	$65.0
1961	32,600	9.9	29	11,100	$84.4
1966	33,900	10.9	31	10,400	$115.2
1971	34,400	11.8	41	13,700	$160.5
1976	35,100	12.9	41	18,600	$262.4
1981	36,100	13.8	43	13,500	$441.4
1986	37,100	14.6	50*	40,900	$635.4

SOURCE: Compiled from *The Quarterly Review: Handbook Issue* 48(4), 1988, pp. 70–71, 95.

*Includes the District of Columbia. Iowa churches were still appended to the Missouri convention.

Table 3.2. The Declining Rural Base of the SBC

Year	% South's Population Rural*	% SBC's Churches Rural	% SBC's Members Rural
1926	—	92.0	72.0
1931	65.9	—	—
1936	—	86.7	62.1
1941	63.3	—	—
1951	51.4	68.7	39.3
1961	41.5	61.3	32.9
1971	35.2	54.7	27.5
1981	33.1	50.1	25.3

SOURCES: For the percent of the population that is rural, "Urban and Rural population: Earliest Census to 1980." (U.S. Bureau of the Census, 1983). For the 1926 and 1936 figures for churches and membership, *Census of Religious Bodies: 1926* (U.S. Bureau of the Census, 1929) and *Census of Religious Bodies: 1936* (U.S. Bureau of the Census, 1941). Note that SBC data are incomplete for 1936. Percentage is based on available data. For 1951 through 1981 figures on churches and membership, *The SBC Handbook* (1952); *The Quarterly Review* 22(3), 1961, pp. 14, 18; *The Quarterly Review: Handbook Issue* 32(4), 1971, pp. 10, 12; and *The Quarterly Review: Handbook Issue* 42(4), 1981, pp. 10, 12.

*Rural refers to churches and persons located in places of less than 2,500 population.

nation that they were second only to Catholics and Methodists in the number of counties containing at least one congregation.[25]

Such growth did not come without change. Not only was the Convention changing its territorial base, it was also changing the type of population it served. Almost all these new churches were being established in towns and cities. By 1978 the number of rural Southern Baptist churches was no greater than it had been in 1922; the number of urban churches, however, had increased fourfold.[26] Table 3.2 charts the declining rural base of the South's population, along with the shrinking percentage of the Southern Baptist Convention's churches and members who belonged to rural churches. By 1980, less than half of the Convention's churches were rural, and they accounted for less than one quarter of the total membership. The average rural church had, by 1985, slightly over 200 members (with at least 30 percent of those being nonresident), compared to their urban counterparts with an average of nearly 650 members.[27] By the 1950s, rural churches had simply lost their position of dominance in Convention affairs. They sent messengers to conventions less often than urban churches, contributed less money, and received fewer services from the growing national agencies. The typical Southern Baptist church had moved to the suburbs.

This migration to cities was simply a reflection of what was happening to Southern society. The South was changing in very fundamental ways. The years following World War II saw the kind of rapid industrialization and urbanization other regions had experienced earlier. In the 1940s, the South was nearly two-thirds rural; by 1960, that percentage had dropped to under fifty. In the 1940s, one third of the South's workers were in agricultural occupations; by 1960, only 10 percent worked on farms. In the 1940s, Southerners earned 52¢ to every non-South dollar; by 1968, they earned 69 percent of what non-Southerners earned. On a variety of educational measures, as well, Southerners were slowly catching up with the rest of the nation.[28]

In addition, patterns of migration were changing in the United States. Instead of streams of Southerners heading north, the tide reversed after 1960. The Sun Belt was born, attracting non-Southerners into the region in greater numbers than ever before. By 1980, over 10 percent of the South's population was born outside the region, with that number considerably higher in urban areas.[29]

By the mid-1960s, historian Samuel Hill would write, "Change—dramatic, basic, overarching change—is today's ranking fact. Everywhere old moorings are breaking loose, deeply entrenched attitudes are being shaken, traditional patterns of social life are gradually giving way and being replaced by new."[30] Over ten years later, sociologist John Shelton Reed would concur, even while arguing that "Southernness" persists. "[T]hese changes have had momentous consequences for Southerners: not just for their standard of living and for the setting in which they make and do that living, but for the South's culture, for its politics, its patterns of race relations and family life, the nature of its towns and cities, and much else besides."[31] The South would simply never be the same again.

Such change could hardly happen without affecting the churches that have called the South home. When patterns of residence and economy and culture change, religious patterns are likely to change, as well. And indeed that is the case here. Part of what had made the South distinctive had been its religious ethos, fostered by the relative concentration of church members into a few distinctively Southern denominations. Indeed, some migrants who move into the South are likely to increase their religious commitment in response to the region's norms.[32] But equally, as the Yankees move in, Southern norms in church going apparently change in response to their presence. Social geographer Roger Stump has demonstrated that the proportion of non-Southern-born people in the populations of Southern counties is negatively related to overall church membership rates and to membership in Southern denominations.[33] The more Yankees there are, the fewer church members there are, and the less likely it is that they will be Baptist, Methodist, or Presbyterian. Having more non-Southerners in the population also introduces greater overall denominational heterogeneity. There are simply more churches to choose from. And all of this is especially true in urban areas.

As migration brought diverse people into the South, and as urbanization pulled them away from small towns, norms for church going—and for which church to choose—became less strong. Although the South certainly remained religiously distinctive, Baptists and Methodists could no longer claim an unchallenged place at the center of Southern culture. Church affiliation became increasingly irrelevant to establishing one's place in the community. Indeed in urban areas churches could no longer set and regulate community standards. Southern evangelicalism—while still pervasive—had been disestablished.

Sociologists since Troeltsch and Weber have been accustomed to describing established religions as "church-like," in contrast to voluntary religious groups on the margins of society that were described as "sects."[34] That distinction presumed a stable society dominated by one over-arching official religion. It predicted that the "church" would adopt all those within its borders as its rightful members and would ostracize any group that challenged its authority. "Sects" would then gather up the misfits. While southern evangelicalism was never officially established, it enjoyed a privileged church-like status in Southern law and society. Blue laws established rules for Sunday conduct, and vice laws (including prohibition) gave evangelical morals legal force. Pastors routinely served as school chaplains, and Sunday School teachers populated the classrooms. No one ever seemed to complain about the prayer and Bible reading students did in school. There was enough religious homogeneity that people could act as if a consensus existed, disregarding the rules of civility that apply in more pluralistic settings and giving the region its appearance of pervasive religiosity.[35] There had always been Episcopalians and a few Lutherans scattered throughout the region, but most other mainline denominations were absent.[36] The absence of Catholics and Jews from most locations in the south was related as both cause and effect to the region's anti-Catholicism and anti-Semitism. By both effort and default, then, evangelical Baptists, Methodists, and Presbyterians occupied the mainstream, acting as the region's "church." Black Baptists and Methodists served a separate churchly function for the region's African-American population. This establishment was effectively challenged only from below. During the early twentieth century pentecostal groups had mobilized the south's lower classes into a sectarian protest movement, leaving evangelicals as representative of the working, middle, and upper classes.[37] At least until World War II, then, the south's mainstream evangelicals and its marginal pentecostals nicely fit the model of church and sect postulated by early sociologists.

But following the War, that would no longer be the case. Like the rest of American society, Southern society would be characterized by too much pluralism for any one group (or coalition) to claim church-like status. All the South's religions were becoming "denominations."[38] Each would have to recognize that the others existed and would have to treat rival groups with at least some civility. And no one group could assume that its norms would guide the community. The taken-for-granted ties between church and local government, between evangelicalism and culture, were being irrevocably loosened.

Those ties were also being loosened because Southern Baptists themselves were changing. Southern Baptists were not only moving to cities; they were also making more money and becoming less concerned about traditional moral prohibitions. Unwritten rules about observance of the Sabbath, the avoidance of card playing, and proper women's attire all began to disappear in the face of urban norms. Even divorce was becoming less taboo. Middle class norms that prescribed moderation rather than abstinence were making clear inroads even among Baptists.[39] Throughout Southern religion traditional rules against movies, dancing, and other "worldly activities" were falling into disfavor.[40] Being a respectable Southerner was less often being defined by adherence to "thou shalt nots."

Southern Baptists were adopting middle class norms because they were, in fact, becoming middle class. Farmers who had struggled through the depression were seeing their children go to college, get good jobs, and move to a new subdivision. The typical Southern Baptist church had not only moved to the suburbs, but it had some money to spare. As Baptists made more money, they shared more with their churches. Per capita giving rose from $16.79 per year in 1945 to $108.93 in 1975, a figure that represents a substantial gain even when adjusted for inflation. Those increased dollars going into local church coffers meant bigger buildings, more church staff members and more programs. They also translated into more money for the Cooperative Program, for missions and for national church programming (see table 3.1).[41]

Taking advantage of its new wealth, the denomination engaged in rapid institutional expansion.[42] Three new seminaries were started in the 1950s, in San Francisco, Kansas City, and Wake Forest, North Carolina. The Sunday School and Home Mission Boards also expanded their staffs and programs. In 1941, the Home Mission Board listed seven professional staff members, with half a dozen clerical support workers. In 1961, they had over fifty professional staff members and did not list their support staff anymore. The Sunday School Board started the period with fewer than forty on its staff, including field workers. By 1961, the *Annual* listed over 190 professionals in multiple departments.[43] In 1941, "The Baptist Hour" debuted on radio across the nation, featuring Southern Baptists' premier preachers. In 1953, the agency sponsoring that broadcast became the Radio and Television Commission and received a greatly expanded mandate. It was an era of more missionaries in more countries, more programs for more people.

The institutions and people of the Southern Baptist Convention began to think in terms that were greatly expanded in scale and more national in scope. They began to recognize themselves as part of the national religious scene in the United States. Credentials of all sorts were beginning to be defined in terms beyond traditional Southern boundaries. In the years following World War II, an increasing number of the denomination's "best and brightest" would go on from seminary to the nation's preiminent graduate schools, while others would choose top-ranked national seminaries for their basic pastoral training. Chaplains were now officially credentialed, as well. At the beginning of World War II, Southern Baptists had joined other groups in providing endorsement for those who would wear the SBC label.

Social issues and methods of addressing them were also being defined more broadly. In 1947, the Social Service Commission (later Christian Life Commission) was elevated to fulltime status and given a broad mandate that ranged from international affairs to race relations to family problems.[44] The Commission had existed since 1913, but had never been given enough resources to do more than issue an annual exhortation to the Convention gathering. After 1947, there would be at least some official recognition of the individual and collective role of Baptists in their society. In just the year before, the Convention had also formalized its participation in what became the Baptist Joint Committee on Public Affairs. Working with Northern and National (black) Baptists, Southern Baptists sought to influence national and international situations in which religious liberty was at stake.[45] Meanwhile, the Home Mission Board had also adopted a variety of new social service programs and educational efforts. The Southern Baptist Convention was, for the first time, acting like a national body, placing itself squarely in the midst of the problems of the day.[46] In the process, organizational links with the non-Southern world were being forged.

That did not, however, mean that the Convention ceased being Southern. Even into the 1980s, no more than 15 percent of all Southern Baptists were located outside the southeastern region, and nearly half of those were in the midwestern states of Illinois and Missouri where Southern connections have always been strong (see Table 3.3). Although the number

Table 3.3. Geographic Distribution of Southern Baptists, 1987

Regions & States	State Convention & Date of Founding	Number of Members (in thousands)	Percent of Total
Old Eastern Seaboard			25.8
South Carolina	South Carolina (1821)	699.6	
Georgia	Georgia (1822)	1,214.2	
Virginia	Virginia (1823)	599.9	
North Carolina	North Carolina (1830)	1,163.9	
Maryland	Maryland/Delaware (1836)	97.0	
Delaware*	"		
District of Columbia	District of Columbia (1877)	30.0	
Nineteenth-Century Frontier			30.2
Alabama	Alabama (1823)	1,031.1	
Mississippi	Mississippi (1836)	658.1	
Kentucky	Kentucky (1837)	738.3	
Florida	Florida (1854)	918.9	
Tennessee	Tennessee (1874)	1,068.7	
Across the Mississippi			33.2
Missouri	Missouri (1834)	621.8	
Louisiana	Louisiana (1848)	575.1	
Texas	Texas (1848)	2,460.9	
Arkansas	Arkansas (1848)	479.6	
Oklahoma	Oklahoma (1906)	746.4	

EXPANSION STATES

Regions & States	State Convention & Date of Founding	Number of Members (in thousands)	Percent of Total
Great Lakes and Great Plains			4.3
Illinois	Illinois (1907)	231.9	
Kansas	Kansas/Nebraska (1946)	82.6	
Nebraska	"		
Ohio	Ohio (1954)	144.3	
Michigan	Michigan (1957)	50.0	
Indiana	Indiana (1958)	89.2	
South Dakota	Northern Plains (1968)	17.3	
North Dakota	"		
Montana	"		
Minnesota	Minnesota/Wisconsin (1983)	12.3	
Wisconsin	"		
Iowa	Iowa Fellowship	10.8	
Northeast			0.6
New York	New York (includes North Jersey) (1969)	24.6	
West Virginia	West Virginia (1970)	27.6	
Pennsylvania	Pennsylvania/South Jersey (1970)	20.2	
New Jersey	"		
Connecticut	New England (1983)	17.9	
Massachusetts	"		
New Hampshire	"		

Table 3.3. (*Continued*)

Regions & States	State Convention & Date of Founding	Number of Members (in thousands)	Percent of Total
Vermont	"		
Maine	"		
West			5.8
New Mexico	New Mexico (1912)	119.8	
Arizona	Arizona (1928)	120.4	
California	California (1940)	394.4	
Hawaii	Hawaii (1943)	13.7	
Alaska	Alaska (1946)	20.2	
Oregon	Northwest (1948)	76.3	
Washington	"		
Colorado	Colorado (1956)	64.0	
Utah	Utah/Idaho (1964)	18.3	
Idaho	"		
Nevada	Nevada (1978)	20.6	
Wyoming	Wyoming (1984)	13.2	
TOTAL		14,723.2	100.0

SOURCE: Compiled from *The Quarterly Review* 48(4), 1988, pp. 12, 95.

*Delaware was not part of the original Maryland convention, but was added in 1982.

of churches and members in non-Southern areas was growing at a rapid rate, that number was growing from a base of zero, compared to the slow, steady growth of their much more numerous Southern cousins.[47] The population base changed markedly, but membership remained disproportionately Southern.[48] In the process, however, the denomination's territorial consciousness changed, a change symbolized by a gradual dropping of the adjective "Southwide" from the ecclesiastical vocabulary.

People began to expect to find (or start) Southern Baptist churches wherever they went. A vacationer could travel from coast to coast never missing a Sunday or Wednesday service in a Southern Baptist church. And, no matter where they were, the churches had a familiar feel of home. That comfortable feeling came in part from the Southern accents that might be heard; in part from the familiar biblical and evangelistic themes touched on in sermons and the warm, expressive character of the service; and in part it had to do with an assumption that because these people were Southern Baptist, they were brothers and sisters in the faith. Even as the regional base for family-feeling was disappearing, Southern Baptists still felt like a family.

And the Southern Baptist family was one in which a strong sense of ritual prevailed. The worship styles of SBC churches were in fact so routine that only the hymn numbers might change from Sunday to Sunday or place to place. Services varied mostly in the degree of polish and formality given to them in churches of varying sizes and resources. An organ (Hammonds and Wurlitzers were popular) played familiar hymn tunes as the congregation gathered and again later as they dispersed. A period of congregational singing and prayers opened the service, followed by an offering (usually taken up by deacons). There was a special number from the choir or a soloist, a sermon of about thirty minutes, and an invitation hymn—often "Just As I Am" or "Softly and Tenderly"—when sinners were exhorted to be saved and new members were encouraged to join. Both sermon and invitation focused the attention of listeners on the importance of making a personal decision to accept Christ. The service closed with a spontaneous prayer from someone in the congregation. Then everyone would file past the preacher at the door, heading home for a special meal, or perhaps to the local cafeteria (just in time to beat the Methodists whose liturgy often took a bit longer). Although Southern Baptists vigorously claimed to be a "nonliturgical" denomination, there was a liturgy as predictable as in any church with a prayer book. Like the Latin Mass, it provided a universalizing experience for those who participated in it.

But even more important than a common liturgy, the home-like feeling visitors experienced as they moved from place to place had to do with the many programs and materials the churches were likely to share. On Saturday night a traveler could read a Sunday school lesson for the next day, confident that the town's church would be studying the same lesson. The church's usher would hand out a Baptist Bulletin Service bulletin printed with a lovely inspirational color picture on the front and a story about the denomination's missionaries and other workers on the back. The hymnals in the pew racks would almost certainly be the official Baptist Hymnal, and the choir would probably sing a special number they had learned from *The Church Musician* (a Sunday School Board monthly) in robes they had ordered from their local Baptist Book Store. If the pastor had a college or seminary education, it was almost certainly from a Southern Baptist school. The church itself might have been designed by architects in Nashville, and it was perhaps financed with loans underwritten by the Home Mission Board. The visitor's card the traveler would fill out was probably printed by Convention Press (another Sunday School Board affiliate), and the church might be observing some special emphasis designated for this Sunday on the denominational calendar.

The visitor would note in the listing of the week's activities that people would be coming back on Sunday night for Training Union and another preaching service. On Wednesday night they would have prayer meeting, and at various times there would be choirs for all ages. The children would have Sunbeams, with the older girls in Girls Auxiliary and the boys in Royal Ambassadors. Perhaps Tuesday morning, the Woman's Missionary Society circles would meet, with a Thursday night all-church visitation of prospects. If it happened to be October, there might be an associational missions conference underway, with Southern Baptist missionaries on furlough speaking in area churches each night. In January, people would come every night to study a book of the Bible during January Bible Study. In March, the church might be having a week-long study course on Home Missions. In December, the study was Foreign Missions; and following each study, the church would raise money for a special missions offering, perhaps lighting a Christmas tree light or coloring in a map section for each $25 raised toward their goal.

In each case, for each organization or special program, materials were supplied by Southern Baptist agencies, and leaders were trained by state or associational personnel. Local church workers who studied Sunday School Board study course books about doing their church jobs got special certificates recognizing their competence. And during the summer, a contingent from the church might travel to Ridgecrest, North Carolina, or Glorieta, New Mexico, for a week in a resort setting to study better ways to do the work of the church. What people experienced in the local churches was a wealth of programs and resources to meet their every need or desire. There was simply a Southern Baptist way to do everything.

That plethora of programs was made possible by the continued expansion and increased efficiency of the denomination's bureaucracy. In 1948, the Calendar Committee began planning for several years at a time, projecting the emphases they hoped the churches would adopt. In 1956, an extra layer of coordination was added at the national level in the form of an Inter-Agency Council. This body consisted of representatives from the staffs of all the boards and agencies and was charged with coordinating programs and settling management territorial disputes.

In the mid 1950s, a major management study was undertaken at the Sunday School Board with the guidance of Booz, Allen, and Hamilton, a professional consulting firm.[49] All departments were urged to establish clear goals, procedures, and measurable criteria for success. Each job description contained the expected credentials for its holder, and almost all required a seminary education, preferably from a Southern Baptist institution. In 1955, Sunday School Board chief James L. Sullivan described his reorganization goals in his annual report to the convention.

The new organization attempts to define responsibilities of divisions and departments, to prevent overlapping of functions and duplication of effort, to unify editorial and educational activities in purpose, direction, and administration, to provide adequate supervisory personnel with sufficient delegation of responsibility to insure a smooth flow of work, and to make use of the best business and merchandising procedures.[50]

By 1960, all agencies were required to have organizational manuals detailing their program assignments, lines of authority, internal procedures, and relationships with state and local bodies. Yearly reports to the denomination contained columns of numbers reporting each agency's progress toward its assigned mission. The denominational bureaucracy had become a well-oiled machine producing impressive growth and a broad-based program of church support.

Sometimes this bureaucracy was a bit like an uncontrollable giant, not realizing its own strength. When a mission lesson for children suggested writing a missionary or sending helpful supplies, the result might be bags and bags of mail arriving on the doorstep of some unsuspecting missionary, each letter full of questions from eager children, each box of supplies demanding a place to be stored.[51] The annual Christmas in August ritual of sending supplies to missionaries in August for their use at Christmas (evidently begun when packages had to be transported by steamer) sometimes became an ordeal for those on the receiving end. One inner city pastor in New England received his shipments by truck when his mail carrier refused to continue delivering the onslaught on foot. Both the resources and the organizational efficiency of Southern Baptists had increased to sometimes monumental proportions.

At the same time, there were still elements of charisma in the system. In the early 1950s, nearly every major leadership position in the Convention changed hands, and a group of revered leaders took the reins of SBC agencies. In 1953, Courts Redford assumed office at the Home Mission Board, Sullivan at the Sunday School Board, and Paul Stevens at the Radio and Television Commission. Baker James Cauthen became head of the Foreign Mission Board in 1954. Duke McCall had become president of Southern Baptist Theological Seminary in 1951, and was succeeded in his former post as head of the Executive Committee by Porter Routh. For a decade, these men symbolized the agencies they led. They were respected as fine Southern gentlemen, looked up to as outstanding pulpiteers, depended on for the inspiration that kept missionaries volunteering and support money flowing. All of them served long terms, extending well into the 1960s as a team. When they spoke to local churches, state meetings, Ridgecrest and Glorieta assemblies, and in annual reports to the convention, people were stirred to response, and Baptists were reassured of God's presence in their work.[52] Both the personalities of these men and their messages evoked the days when the denomination was led by great Southern gentlemen and bound together by its common cultural traditions and evangelistic goals.

The agencies they headed and the reports they brought were shaped by the most modern, efficient, and rational of procedures. The work they reported was successful as measured by the criteria of management. And an increasingly urban, middle-class constituency wanted to hear the goals and the numbers that demonstrated their denomination's success. What that generation of leaders accomplished was a remarkable bridge between the world of past and present, between the efficiency of the bureaucracy and the inspiration of the pulpit. It was a bridge that bound together an increasingly unwieldy and disparate constituency.[53]

And as the 1960s approached, it began to be apparent just how disparate and unwieldy the denomination had become. During the 1950s, enormous changes had begun, and during the next decade and a half, controversy began to surface. In these initial skirmishes the fault lines of future divisions appeared.

Controversy Contained, 1961–1978

As Southern Baptists had moved increasingly into the mainstream of American religious culture, Southern Baptist scholars began to appropriate the methods and ideas of that larger culture. The Bible became more than a source of inspiration and sermons; it was studied in its historical and literary context. Scholars and other educated folk alike learned in school that the earth was probably several million years old and that life in earlier ages differed substantially from what we know today. With little fanfare, Southern Baptist scholars joined the conversations among their peers about the nature and essence of the biblical stories, especially those found in Genesis. They rarely thought of themselves as doubting the texts they studied—only finding new ways to understand their truth.

Nevertheless, the people in many Southern Baptist pews were unwilling to accept interpretations other than the old ones. More importantly, a new generation of pastors was becoming aware of the many threats to faith that existed in this new world in which Southern Baptists lived. They looked at the seeming chaos of the cities and the apparent impotence of liberal denominations, and they perceived a coming disaster if Southern Baptists did not remain vigilant. If Southern Baptists did not remain true to the Bible and committed to evangelism, they might end up like the liberal mainline churches and the unchurched millions that surrounded them. For many Southern Baptists, maintaining the truth of the Bible was a matter of spiritual survival in a sometimes alien land.

The first sign that alien ideas might have found their way inside the gates came in 1961, and the reaction was swift and passionate. Ralph Elliott, a professor at Midwestern Seminary in Kansas City, published (with Broadman Press, the denominational publisher) *The Message of Genesis*. In it, he placed the early stories of Genesis in their middle eastern historical context and offered the opinion that they tell us more about Who created than about how exactly that creation took place.[54] He further claimed that no specific author or date can be given for the book, since it depends heavily on several oral traditions. Such claims were so commonplace in the scholarly community as to be unremarkable—similar ideas had even been appearing in earlier Southern Baptist sources.[55] But books by seminary professors, published by the denominational press, have an air of doctrinal authority; and this was doctrine some Southern Baptists were unwilling to accept.

When the convention gathered in San Francisco in 1962, the floor was hot with debate. Conservative pastors, led by K. Owen White of First Baptist in Houston, wanted Elliott fired. The Convention establishment did not want anything so disruptive. The compromise was the passage of two resolutions that spoke to the issue, but not the person. They affirmed the entire Bible as authentic, authoritative, and infallible. They also decried any views that undermined the historical accuracy of the Bible. More substantively, a committee was appointed that year to review and redraft the Convention's statement of faith. The committee consisted of all the state convention presidents and was chaired by SBC president Herschel Hobbs. After passing resolutions declaring its faith in the Bible, the convention entrusted the handling of this controversy to a committee of trusted leaders and to the trustees of the institution where Elliott taught.

The trustees acted first. When Elliott refused to withdraw the book from reprinting by a new publisher, he was dismissed for insubordination.[56] On the surface, worried conservatives had a victory—Elliott was gone. But in other ways, they felt defeated. In a direct confrontation with heresy, the Convention had taken a backdoor route toward resolution.

At the next convention, in Kansas City, the committee headed by Hobbs presented its report. Debate was again lively, but the new statement of faith passed. It kept the 1925 language about the Bible, describing it as "having truth without any mixture of error for its matter." It added a statement, however, indicating that the standard for interpretation of scripture is to be Jesus Christ, and the preface reasserted that no Baptist statement of faith can be made binding on the individual conscience. Again the conservatives seemed to have a victory in a statement that seemed to them to endorse the view of scripture they called inerrancy. But it would soon become apparent that "truth without any mixture of error" could be interpreted in a number of ways that did not please conservatives.[57] In the years ahead, scholars would continue to teach views other than inerrancy, and denominational literature would occasionally hint at interpretations some considered suspect. It was beginning to be clear that Baptists did not all agree on what the Bible meant or on how to use and interpret it.

But more than doctrinal disagreement was brewing in the Southern Baptist Convention. Southern Baptists were again having to face the question of race. Since 1954, it had become apparent that integration was inevitable; and Convention leaders, at least since the 1940s, had sought to support that move. Early in that decade dissertations began appearing from Southern Baptist ethicists setting out the mandate for racial justice.[58] Many of the students who studied outside the denomination, along with those inside the official seminaries, began to formulate a passionate commitment to change the way Southern society treated blacks. In 1947, the convention adopted a Charter of Principles on Race Relations; and when *Brown v. Board of Education* was decided, various agency heads issued official endorsements.[59] In the years that followed, further direct statements were rare. The tactic in Nashville was rarely direct confrontation, but it was a quiet denominational emphasis on human equality before God.[60]

Change would not come easily—to the South as a region or to the denomination that had been its religious establishment. The years of the civil rights struggle were tumultuous for Southern Baptists. Just as surely as there were Southerners who saw the justice of integration, there were many more who reacted with determined, deeply-felt, opposition to what seemed like outside tampering with Southern ways of living. One Louisiana lay leader spoke for many when he warned the SBC that if it did "not cease its sinister maneuvers against Southern traditions, we can repeal them at the local level by being less cooperative with their cooperative program."[61] For every church that opened its doors to blacks, many more enacted new membership and seating rules designed to prevent any breach of segregation. In some cases churches split over the issue, with a small minority of integrationists either forming a new fellowship or being left with a virtually empty church.[62] For many Southern whites it was time to reassert the fundamental rightness of the "anglo-saxon evangelical faith."

The battles between integrationists and segregationists in the South were fought in thousands of public and private arenas. Sometimes they were precipitated by an invitation to an African American to speak in chapel, or to attend a Friday night student group. But each event caused soul-searching, argument, compromise, or confrontation. Sometimes public protest was involved, but more often behind-the-scenes negotiation averted public scenes.[63] Individual Southern Baptists changed their own minds and sometimes the minds of their friends. But just as often, the courageous ministers and teachers who welcomed blacks into homes and churches were subject to abuse and alienation, even threats of death, at the hands of their fellow Baptists.

Those who stood for the change they had come to believe to be right would never forget the price they paid. They would recount their stories from this crusade in the years to come and remember those who had opposed them. There would be an unspoken bond among these crusaders, a conviction that the churches that had nurtured them into the Christian faith had also been terribly wrong. Many, for the sake of conscience, would not remain in the denomination of their birth. Some of the brightest and most committed of the denomination's young leaders of the 1950s would put their talents to use in the service of others. And some of the activists who stayed would move out to the very fringes of the denomination.

Other younger Baptists of the 1960s and 1970s continued to be nurtured in their commitments to progressive change within the denomination. They made the Baptist Student Union their home or found an outlet for their energies in programs of the Home Mission Board. The BSU, a campus-based ministry of the Sunday School Board, provided the influx of baby-boom college students with a place to air their doubts and work out a faith that made sense of the intellectual and social world in which they lived. BSU students in the 1960s challenged all the assumptions under which they had been raised, and materials and leadership from Nashville offered resources for their journeys.

In 1968, students took their concerns about the Vietnam War directly to the convention in the form of a silent protest. In that same year, the convention adopted a Statement Concerning the Crisis in Our Nation, calling for "vigorous Christian response" and the "redemption of the whole of life." The Home Mission Board took this as a mandate for increased attention to Christian Social Ministries of all kinds, and students often became involved in those efforts. Some college students spent summer vacations working in inner city missions, while others gave two years after college as US-2 workers or overseas missionary Journeymen. They were often sent to places where their comfortable Southern notions about how to be a church were challenged by poverty and cultural differences. They often came back hopeful that their denomination could tackle all sorts of new problems, moving past its previous failures and into an exciting new future.[64] In the years following 1968, students were even heard from the platform of the convention, offering their vision of the denomination's future.

Students, Baptist and otherwise, were on the leading edge of changes that were rocking all of American culture. They were protesting the Vietnam War, revolutionizing relationships between men and women, challenging authority and institutions. The 1960s were a decade of change throughout the nation, and the South was no exception. As a new generation of Southern Baptists emerged from colleges and seminaries in the 1960s, many were dreaming dreams of equality and progress in their church and in their world.

But the students' vision was not shared by all. For many others the most relevant issues were not race, social justice, and sexual equality but the truth of the Bible. They looked at the changes of the 1960s as the sort of chaos one might expect when biblical rules are discarded. Their concerns re-surfaced in the SBC in 1970, and again the issue was Genesis.[65] This time the offending book was the first volume in a new series of Bible commentaries to be published by Broadman. Like Elliott, British scholar G. Henton Davies adopted a nonliteral reading of the early stories, suggesting among other things that Abraham might have been mistaken about thinking God had commanded him to sacrifice Isaac. Staff at the Sunday School Board evidently thought that Southern Baptists had changed over the last decade—and they may have been right—but concerned conservative leaders were quick to take on this new threat to orthodoxy.

Southern Baptists were having their annual meeting in Denver that year, and they would be presided over by W. A. Criswell, long-time pastor of First Baptist in Dallas and outspoken critic of liberalism. During the previous year, Broadman Press had published his book, *Why I Preach That the Bible Is Literally True*. Before the convention convened, thousands gathered for a conservative-organized conference called Affirming the Bible. By the time the official convention sessions began, the crowd was ready to do battle. A messenger from California moved that volume I be withdrawn and rewritten from a conservative point of view. Staff representatives of the Sunday School Board argued that there was room in the SBC for a diversity of opinion about the Bible, but the crowd would have none of it. The motion passed by a wide margin.

The Board of Trustees of the Sunday School Board did not, however, perceive that they were obligated to do exactly as the messengers instructed. They did not share the same conservative sentiment that had been expressed on the convention floor. Instead of starting from scratch, they asked the original authors of the commentaries on Genesis and Exodus (Davies and seminary professor Roy Honeycutt) to revise their work.

When the conservatives pressed the issue at the 1971 convention, the Board finally reassigned the Genesis commentary to Clyde Francisco. Even Francisco, however, made clear that he did not repudiate Davies' work; and the Board made arrangements to sell its stock of the original volume through a British publisher. Conservatives had succeeded in getting a new volume, but not in destroying the old one. Conservative author James Hefley, looking back on the episode, writes, "Conservatives could only look back over the past decade in frustration. They had won almost every vote on the Bible issue at the Southern Baptist Convention, but it seemed little had been accomplished with the agencies, particularly the Sunday School Board and Midwestern Seminary."[66] It was becoming clear to conservatives that winning votes at annual convention meetings—even votes directly addressing the work of the agencies—was not enough to derail what they perceived as a dangerous slide toward liberalism being fostered by professional staffs and allowed by complacent or sympathetic boards of trustees.

For the progressive leaders of the establishment it had been no less a frustrating decade. The Christian Life Commission routinely planned its annual seminars around controversial topics designed to educate and inspire the progressives in Southern Baptist ranks. But just as routinely, Commission head Foy Valentine was chastised by messengers denouncing his programs and materials. The 1970 seminar in Atlanta (which had included a representative from *Playboy* in a debate on "situation ethics") particularly infuriated conservatives, and they came to the Denver convention determined to stamp out liberalism at the CLC, as well as in the Broadman commentary series. Only a petition from four prominent and respected pastors averted moves to dismantle the agency entirely. These men (including Herschel Hobbs) acknowledged that there were differences in the Convention over whether such programs ought to be held, and they pled for future restraint in CLC programming, but they also asked opponents to "forgive and forget." Their tactic succeeded, and all five motions that had been brought against the agency were tabled indefinitely.[67] Trusted leaders had come to the rescue of an embattled progressive agency with a compromise in what was becoming a tug-of-war between the trustees who guided the agencies and the messengers who thought *they* should have the last word.

The year before, in 1969, the Sunday School Board was less lucky. They had planned to announce a revised version of their Sunday night church member training program. The old Training Union was to give way to the new "Quest." It was an unfortunate choice of names. In part it seemed to signal a progressive, changing view of truth—sought after, but not finally found. But more importantly, it turned out that a toiletries firm had beaten Baptists to the name. A feminine hygiene deodorant spray was just coming on the market with the same name. It was more than the messengers were willing to buy. With cartons of Quest materials sitting on loading docks awaiting shipment, the messengers told their Board to dump the program. Looking back nearly twenty years later, a conservative convention messenger recalled to us her anger over that episode. "They're going to dictate to you what you're going to receive," she said. She recalled that event as one of the first signs that people needed to try to regain control of a bureaucracy that did not respect their wishes. They did not yet, however, know how to do it, she said.

There was indeed a growing sense that it was time for conservatives to act, and in moving toward action, concerned SBC conservatives took up the mantle of fundamentalism. Having perceived a dangerous drift away from orthodoxy, they resolved to fight for the truth. Like the fundamentalists of half a century earlier, these believers insisted on an unwavering faith in the Bible. A literal creation, a literal fish to swallow Jonah, literal miracles, and a literal virgin birth became their tests of true orthodoxy. And like their Northern predecessors, they were willing to "do battle royal" for the beliefs they saw threatened by the changes around them.[68] Their first step was to call a meeting of fundamentalist pastors, to be held at the First Baptist Church of Atlanta, where Charles Stanley was pastor. They voted there to start their own publication, *The Southern Baptist Journal*, to be edited by Bill Powell; and they took the name "Baptist Faith and Message Fellowship."

The first issue of the *Journal* was published a few months later. Its logo was a picture of the globe, with an open Bible superimposed over it. The banner across the Bible read "INFALLIBLE." The masthead also carried the disclaimer "This is not an official publication of the Southern Baptist Convention." Official it was not, but the *Journal* gave a national voice to fundamentalist discontent. Powell published accusations against seminary and agency "liberals," often quoting passages from their works. He also offered a forum for other fundamentalist complaints. After the 1974 convention, at which Owen Cooper had presided, for instance, writer Robert Tenery complained that Cooper had presided more "by whim" than by the letter of the law. Obviously unhappy with the treatment fundamentalists had received, Tenery wrote, "It is not unthinkable that we could some day find some action of the Convention challenged in a court of law and have a judge overturn actions of the Convention simply because we did not follow our own legally adopted constitution during the course of our deliberations."[69]

Beyond its role as critic, the *Journal* also offered a showcase for fundamentalist leaders and for programs effectively marginalized by the denominational establishment. It lauded loyal fundamentalists as the backbone of the Convention, printing their sermons and stories about their ministries. And there was also attention to religious and national issues—from abortion to the ordination of women—about which fundamentalists were becoming concerned. A reader of those early issues wrote to Powell,

> Thank you for permitting us to join hands with others who are deeply concerned with the inroads that the liberals have made and are making in our loved Southern Missionary Baptist life. We do trust that in joining together the voice and vote of the Southern Baptist men who still hold the truths of the Baptist Faith and Message, will be listened to, and felt as they prayerfully assert themselves.[70]

There was also plenty of news to report on the fundamentalist front. In 1972, fundamentalist Southern Baptists, despairing of the official six seminaries, had organized Mid-America Baptist Seminary. They began in Little Rock, with eighty-five students, but soon moved to Memphis, to property adjacent to Bellevue Baptist Church, where Adrian Rogers was pastor. In 1970, the First Baptist Church of Dallas had also voted to start a fundamentalist alternative to the seminaries. Their Criswell Biblical Studies Center began evening classes in 1971 and a full schedule two years later. These two institutions joined Luther Rice Seminary in Jacksonville, Florida, as training grounds for Southern Baptist inerrantists. Luther Rice, which offered extensive off-campus (correspondence) programs, had been established in the 1960s to serve the needs of southeastern churches, especially the ones that found the official Southeastern Baptist Seminary, in Wake Forest, too liberal. None of the fundamentalist schools had accreditation from the official Association of Theological Schools or sanction from the denomination, but they had the approval of fundamentalists who trusted them to produce orthodox graduates.

In 1977, the *Journal* also reported to its readers that an International Council on Inerrancy had been formed. Among its founders was W. A. Criswell, who was joined there by Robert Preus, new head of the Lutheran Church Missouri Synod. The paper had reported approvingly in earlier issues how conservative Lutherans had taken over their church. The ICE now provided an interdenominational forum where concerned conservatives could share information and strategy, along with their biblical scholarship.

Fundamentalists were rapidly building an institutional infrastructure in which their views were dominant.[71] They had means of communication—in numerous conferences around the country, as well as in the

Journal—and schools for training leaders. There was an increasing constituency of informed and committed inerrantists in Southern Baptist churches and a core of nationally recognized leaders: Adrain Rogers, W. A. Criswell, Jerry Vines, Fred Wolfe, Robert Tenery, and others. In addition, Judge Paul Pressler began to appear in the inner circles, speaking at conferences where fundamentalists gathered. A fundamentalist movement was clearly underway.

The question in the 1970s for the fundamentalists, however, was which way their movement would take them. Fundamentalists had always had a tendency toward division, preferring a small, pure group over large, cooperative, and probably impure ones. In the *Journal's* lead article for April 1976, author Charles Blair wondered in print about viable options for "orthodox believers." He noted that they could stay in the denomination and keep quiet in order to get along and not cause trouble. They could become independent, like so many of their fundamentalist cousins. Or they could stay in the SBC and persistently make their views known. He advised the third option.

In the 1970s Fundamentalist churches seemed to be resigned to maintaining a stance of loyal opposition. They were actively making their views known, but were confined to operating at the margins of the Convention and cooperating with a variety of alternative institutions. They gave minimal amounts to the Cooperative Program and directed most of their mission money elsewhere. They rejoiced when various victories were won on the convention floor, but they had not yet discovered that they had the power to control and change the institutions they were criticizing and avoiding.

Sometime in the late 1970s, politician Paul Pressler put two and two together: he figured out that the denomination's machinery could be wrested from the hands of its progressive (he would say liberal) bureaucratic leaders. His discovery changed the course of this fundamentalist movement and focused its energies inside the denomination. Within ten years, the Southern Baptist Convention would be transformed.

The story of how and why that happened—and how the rest of the denomination responded—is to be told in the chapters that follow.

4. Drawing the Battle Lines: Issues Separating Fundamentalists and Moderates

B y the 1980s, Southern Baptists were already a divided denomination. While a strong traditional conservatism occupied the vast middle of the denomination, distinct right and left wings had developed that were vastly different from each other and from middle-of-the-road Southern Baptists. While those in the middle were basking in the continued growth of Southern Baptist programs, membership, and mission work, those on the left were anxious to see rapid change that would bring their denomination out of its provincial southern enclaves and into the mainstream of American religious life. Such a movement into the mainstream was precisely what those on the right feared; they saw a clear threat to Southern Baptist orthodoxy in the changes that were afoot. What progressives wanted, fundamentalists sought to resist. The stage was set for a colossal tug-of-war for the hearts and minds of ordinary Southern Baptists. The prize was the denomination's impressive organizational infrastructure—and all the influence those organizations could wield within and beyond the nation's largest Protestant group.

The existence of a left wing in the denomination must, of course, be seen in context. These were not people who were ready to deny the resurrection of Christ or label the Bible merely a book of wise sayings. They granted the Bible ultimate authority in their lives and studied it with great diligence. In any larger scheme of things, these were no liberals. On basic Christian beliefs (the deity of Christ, the resurrection, and the like), there remained very little differentiation among Southern Baptists.

But the progressives still looked and sounded different, especially when placed alongside traditional Southern Baptists. When fundamentalists began to read the books progressives wrote, listen to their lectures, and visit their churches, the theological world encountered there seemed vastly different from the traditional beliefs fundamentalists were ready to defend. On beliefs about proper forms of worship, the place of women, ministries of peace and justice, the nature of scripture, the details of the Second Coming of Christ, and a host of other points, the Convention's left wing had developed positions that stretched the boundaries of Southern Baptist traditionalism. Like many evangelicals elsewhere in the nation, Southern Baptist progressives had been pushed by the forces of change to positions left of the old center. While retaining their evangelical base, they were adopting new social and political views and giving their theology an intellectual foundation.[1] They were adapting to the modern world in some ways and seeking to change that world in other ways.[2]

Similarly, fundamentalists were stretching the old boundaries in their own ways. They, too, had developed distinctive traits that distinguished them from the traditional mainstream. After a couple of decades of building institutions of their own and supporting the schools and publications of other fundamentalists, the Southern Baptist right wing was relatively independent of Convention programs and networks. Some were in small country churches that had always been isolated from the denomination. Others were in huge "mega-churches" that were almost denominations in themselves. Their structural independence facilitated (and was facilitated by) their growing criticism of Southern Baptist schools and materials. They spoke as outsiders and were perceived as such by many loyal Southern Baptists. They were described by mainstream Southern Baptists as "independent."

The mainstream of the denomination—against which both groups stood out—was dominated by loyalty to programs and institutions. Traditional Southern Baptists were proud of what they had accomplished, of the fine southwide institutions they had created and of their missions and expansion beyond Southern borders. Criticizing those institutions, accusing them of heresy, felt to mainstream Baptists like disloyalty to the family—whether those criticisms came from left or right. Traditional Southern Baptists, like traditional Southerners, sought to keep their disagreements quiet, to be "nice" no matter what. They were confident that the vast majority of their fellow church members were conservative enough to please anyone. Fundamentalist cries of alarm were as foreign to many as was the progressives' agitation for change.

These three broad strands of Southern Baptist life had, by the 1980s, become identifiable in the thinking and speaking of people in the denomination. Although most of the rhetoric presumed that there were two parties in the arena, each side tacitly recognized that there was a middle, a middle they wished to claim for themselves. This chapter will explore how we define left and right and how these wings are different from the body in the middle.

A Theological Definition of the Parties

The terms of this Baptist battle are theological. It has obvious social, cultural, and organizational dimensions that are the concern of this book; but the terms used by the contenders have to do with what they believe. On at least some matters, Southern Baptists do differ rather widely in what they believe. To take some measure of the religious beliefs of this enormous denomination, the surveys conducted by the Center for Religious Research included among other things, a number of items on beliefs about the Bible, positions on lifestyle, and ideas about the nature and mission of the church.[3] If the denomination is indeed divided in its beliefs, then both variation in responses and consistent patterns among various parties ought to be apparent.

The most obvious question over which Southern Baptists have been fighting is "hermeneutics," that is, the proper methods for interpreting scripture. The 1925 and 1963 Southern Baptist Statements of Faith began with a statement on scripture that included the phrase "truth, without any mixture of error, for its matter." Thus inerrancy became the rallying cry for fundamentalists. For them, scripture was to be seen as without mistakes of any kind; it was, after all, written by God. Any attempt to place the Bible in a more human context was to be resisted. Just what might constitute an "error" had, of course, long been in contention. Even within fundamentalist circles there were lively debates on how to harmonize the events described in the Gospels. And among those on the left, debates ranged from whether Jonah was really swallowed by a whale to just how long creation really took. Neither side would say that the Bible was wrong on anything really important, but they differed widely on what they considered important. Fundamentalists were willing to insist that the Bible was accurate in its history and science, as well as in its religious and moral prescriptions. Moderates saw biblical history and science as conditioned by the times in which it was written—only its religious truths were really without error.

The word "inerrancy" became, then, a synonym for Southern Baptist orthodoxy, and only the most determined nontraditionalists refused to use the word. By 1985, when we first surveyed Southern Baptist pastors and lay church leaders, 85 percent of them agreed or strongly agreed that "the scriptures are the inerrant Word of God, accurate in every detail." However, the wide variation that is represented within that majority of "inerrantists" became apparent in how they responded to a second question about the Bible. Our statement was, "The Genesis creation stories are there more to tell us about God's involvement than to give us a precise how and when." It was just such a nonliteralist reading of Genesis that had gotten Ralph Elliott in trouble two decades before. Given the overwhelming endorsement of inerrancy among Southern Baptists, we might have expected overwhelming rejection of this statement. However, over half of our respondents agreed that Genesis is not primarily a "how and when" book. Only a little more than a third (38 percent) disagreed or strongly disagreed. In fact, even among inerrantists, less than half (44 percent) insisted on a literal interpretation. Whatever Southern Baptists mean by inerrancy, then, not all of them mean that Genesis is to be read as history or science. The number of Southern Baptists who insist on such a reading of the creation stories is well under half.

While inerrancy may be the dominant view in Southern Baptist life, then, literalism is not. The presence of diverse modes of interpreting scripture is reflected in these answers. A small minority (about 15 percent) is self-consciously nontraditional, rejecting the idea of inerrancy and accepting a nonliteral Genesis. A larger minority (just under 40 percent) on the opposite side is self-consciously literalist, insisting that Genesis is an historical account. And not quite half find themselves between the two—using the orthodox word, but accepting nonliteral interpretations.

Further evidence of the diversity present among these Baptists is found in what they say about whether the Bible is an all-sufficient source of knowledge. To say that "God recorded in the Bible everything He wants us to know" is to make a bold assertion about the ultimate superiority of biblical knowledge over other kinds. Nevertheless, 63 percent of the pastors and lay church leaders who responded to our survey agreed or strongly agreed with that statement. The remaining minority left the door open for knowledge that supplements the information found in scripture.

A similar number (59 percent) of our respondents agreed or strongly agreed that "The Bible clearly teaches a premillennial view of history and the future." They were willing to claim not only that the Bible is inerrant, but that it speaks clearly and precisely about the history of the world from creation to the end of time. That is certainly the position of the denomination's fundamentalist leaders, and it has been the position of most fundamentalists since the movement began.[4] During the 1985 Pastors Conference, fundamentalist pastor Morris Chapman declared, "The Bible gives us the greatest prophetic statement in the world in I Thessalonians, chapter 4, 'For the Lord himself shall descend from heaven, and the dead in Christ shall rise first.' Could it be any plainer than that? . . . When the trumpet shall sound, Jesus will come again." The next year, evangelist Eugene Ridley voiced similar confidence. "Someone said to me just the other day . . . 'Preacher Ridley, a lot of things are new that you are preaching, like this premillennialism . . . Isn't that new? None of your old timey preachers were premillennial.' I said, 'What about Daniel? Amen? Pretty old timey. What about Zephaniah, John the Baptist, Jesus, and John the revelator?' " And in the same 1986 Pastors Conference, future SBC president Jerry Vines lent his voice to the chorus of support for a premillennial interpretation.

The details of Jesus' return are given in language that cannot be denied. It is couched in the language of literality. It is impossible to take these words in a figurative, existential sense. It is a literal event which the Bible is teaching at this point. . . . It's all of one piece. If there be no literal return, there was no literal ascension; if there was no literal ascension, there was no literal resurrection. If there was no literal resurrection, there was no literal incarnation; and the whole Christian faith goes down the tubes if it's not what the Bible plainly says it's going to be.

For Vines and others, a literal premillennial Second Coming is an essential part of believing the Bible to be literally true.

But not all Southern Baptists are so sure that the Bible can be interpreted with such precision. Nearly one fourth (24 percent) claim to be unsure about premillennialism, while nearly that many more (17 percent) disagree or strongly disagree that this doctrine is taught in scripture. Baptists are slightly more sure that the Rapture will "take believers out of this world to heaven." Only 18 percent are unsure, and 13 percent disagree with that statement. There is less overall certainty about the Second Coming than about almost any other area of theology. Many people simply do not know what they believe, and some are not sure they *can* know.[5]

Across a number of measures Southern Baptists have a clear conservative majority, but not unanimity. On various views of the scripture and ideas about eschatology, majorities of varying sizes affirm a conservative, even fundamentalist position. But can all these Southern Baptists be called fundamentalists? Taking a number of items together, a scale of agreement with fundamentalist beliefs was constructed. It contains the items on inerrancy and on interpretation of creation discussed above, along with the item asserting that God put everything in the Bible we need to know. It also contains the statement about premillennialism and one asserting that Christians should "avoid worldly practices like drinking and dancing."[6] In each case, the most conservative response received the high score, with the highest total representing complete, enthusiastic (strongly agree) support for all five beliefs. Slightly more than one-third have scores that average higher than agree, indicating at least some strongly agree responses, and no disagreement. These are people we can safely label "fundamentalist," based on their beliefs. The bulk of the denomination (47 percent) is in the next range. They agree with most fundamentalist ideas, but may disagree with some, as well. They are less likely to say they strongly agree, so their average on the five items falls between "unsure" and "agree." We will call these Baptists conservative, on the basis of their beliefs. The remaining minority (18 percent) scored from the midpoint on the scale down. This group included both the ambivalent and those who clearly disagree with fundamentalist beliefs. We

Figure 4.1.   Beliefs and Identity in the Southern Baptist Convention

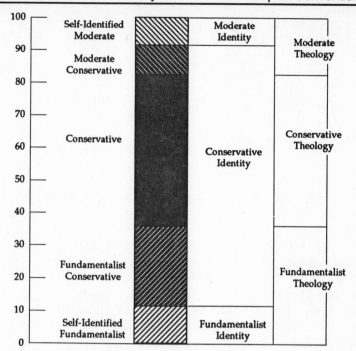

will call these theological dissidents moderate in theology. Again, the picture is of a denomination with a thriving right wing, a smaller left wing, and about half its local leaders solidly conservative and caught between the two. This theological division is represented in the outer brackets of figure 4.1.

We also asked our respondents to identify themselves theologically as fundamentalist, conservative, moderate, or liberal. Twenty percent identified themselves as fundamentalist; 58 percent chose conservative; 21 percent chose moderate; and a mere 1 percent chose liberal. These eleven persons who called themselves liberal were not, however, more liberal in actual beliefs than those who called themselves moderate. For that reason, and because of their small numbers, they will be considered in this study as moderates. Taking beliefs as the primary categories, but adding self-identification, the range of Southern Baptist theological positions begins to emerge (see fig. 4.1). (In addition to the 58 percent who chose to call themselves conservative, we will include with conservative identifiers those who chose other labels, but whose beliefs place them in the middle, bringing the total in that mainstream identity to 80 percent.)

Even those whose beliefs placed them at the margins often preferred to identify with the middle. People with fundamentalist beliefs preferred to be called conservative by a 2 to 1 margin. On the other side, almost half of those who rejected fundamentalist beliefs also chose to be called conservative. People who chose the conservative label, in fact, represent the entire theological spectrum of the denomination. People who call themselves conservative may be either in full agreement with fundamentalist beliefs, in complete disagreement, or somewhere in between. Choosing the conservative label seemed to represent not a description of theological beliefs, but a description of relationship to the Southern Baptist mainstream. It appears to be an identification with what is ordinary, normal, and expected for Southern Baptists, regardless on one's actual theological position.

Claiming either the moderate or the fundamentalist identity, on the other hand, is an equally conscious statement of differentiation from the majority. To call oneself "fundamentalist" may have represented either ignorance of the devalued status of that label in the denomination or defiance of a mainstream that valued cooperation over purity. Moderate, was an equally defiant label; it was a term invented to describe those who were willing to oppose the fundamentalists. As such, it carried clear political implications. One was not simply moderate in theology, but moderate in opposition to a fundamentalist direction for the Convention.

Actual beliefs and self-chosen identification are essential in locating the full range of positions taken by Southern Baptists. Those who have the same beliefs, but chose different labels for themselves were different in their orientation to the denomination. The three broad strands—fundamentalist right wing, moderate/liberal left wing, and conservative middle—can primarily be identified by how people answer questions about beliefs. But two important subgroups are defined by those whose beliefs and identity were at odds. Their beliefs placed them with either the right or left, but their identity was with the conservative middle. The range of Southern Baptist belief and self-definition, then, looks like this:

> *Self-identified fundamentalists.* Eleven percent held strong fundamentalist beliefs and identified themselves by that term. Super-church pastors, the members of the Baptist Faith and Message Fellowship, and most of the movement leadership belong here, even if they have learned for public relations' sake not to use the term fundamentalist.

> *Fundamentalist conservatives.*[7] Twenty-two percent held strong fundamentalist beliefs, but chose some other term to describe them-

selves—most often conservative. Men like Richard Jackson and Winfred Moore may belong here. They are inerrantists in theology, but strongly identify with the denomination.

Conservatives. Fifty percent held conservative beliefs and most often choose to call themselves that. Denominational statesman Herschel Hobbs perhaps belongs here. While quite conservative in theology, he is not in full agreement with fundamentalists; and he is fully committed to the conservative denomination he has always known.

Moderate conservatives. Eight percent held moderate beliefs, rejecting most of the fundamentalist way of understanding scripture— but they still chose to call themselves conservative. Much of the denominational establishment could probably be placed in this category. They refused to concede the label "conservative" to people they sometimes saw as "radical" in their departure from Baptist traditions.

Self-identified moderates. Nine percent held moderate beliefs and called themselves moderates. People like Texas pastor Cecil Sherman or Seminary President Roy Honeycutt might be placed in this category. They did not share the fundamentalists' beliefs about the Bible, and they did not hesitate to say that they thought the fundamentalist way of doing things was wrong.

Self-identified fundamentalists, on average, strongly agreed that they were looking for the Rapture, that premillennialism is what the Bible teaches, and that the Bible contains everything God wants us to know. Not one was even unsure about the inerrancy of scripture, and 71 percent fell into the literalist camp, insisting that Genesis is a how and when account. Self-identified moderates, on the other hand, disagreed, on average, with all those statements about the Bible and the Second Coming. Eighty-two percent of them rejected both a literal reading of Genesis and the claim of scriptural inerrancy. The two groups on the extremes held very different views of what the Bible says and how it should be interpreted—they did not even read the same translation of the Bible. Eighty percent of self-identified fundamentalists said they prefer the King James Version, and none of the few who chose an alternative preferred the Revised Standard or New English. On the opposite side, only 16 percent of self-identified moderates preferred King James, and nearly half (43 percent) chose the two translations rejected by fundamentalists. The left wing group was defined, in part then, by its nontraditional view and use of scripture, while the right wing was defined by its strict (King James) literalism. Those in the middle, by contrast, were defined by their acceptance of inerrancy, but an inerrancy modified by a nonliteral approach to scripture and use of a fairly wide range of translations.

These five categories identified both the ideological poles of the denomination and the range of variation between them. At each pole there is a relatively small, cohesive party, in the middle traditional conservatives defined more by loyalty than by ideology, and between the middle and the extremes were groups trying to bridge the gap by calling themselves conservative when theologically they were not. These lines of belief and identity form the contours of the battle lines Southern Baptists drew among themselves.

Biblical Authority

Among fundamentalists, the issue at stake in this Baptist battle is very clear: the truth of the Bible. Those who do not believe the Bible is true should not be teaching in Southern Baptist schools or writing Southern Baptist literature or serving in any other leadership capacity in the denomination. In 1986, future SBC President Jerry Vines told us, "Our Baptist Faith and Message says that the Bible is truth without any mixture of error. The view that the Bible contains error is worth fighting against. That's the first domino to fall. Then you move into areas like the resurrection of Christ, the deity of Christ, soteriology, the whole works—all stem from your view of scripture." Similarly, when interviewed by Bill Moyers, Paul Pressler insisted that the fight was about one thing and one thing only—beliefs about the Bible. A messenger to the 1986 convention told us that the present "confusion" is caused by people "who claim to be Baptist without holding to a true Baptist faith." When asked what constituted a true faith, he began with the inspiration of the Bible, included belief in Christ and concluded with the belief that "the Word of God is inerrant." Virtually all the self-identified fundamentalists we surveyed would have agreed; 95 percent said that the most important criterion for choosing SBC leaders was their "doctrinal soundness." Being doctrinally correct meant, for the denomination's right wing, believing the Bible.

Perhaps the most eloquent preacher who gave voice to these conservative concerns about the Bible was W. A. Criswell, longtime pastor of First Baptist Church in Dallas. At the climax of the 1985 SBC Pastors Conference in his home city, Criswell came to the pulpit to speak on Whether We Live or Die. It was at least his thirtieth Pastors Conference sermon, but he counted this as his most important, he said. He began by describing the "pattern of death for a denomination," taking the British

Baptists as his first model. Beginning in precise, lecture-like fashion, Criswell cited the ideas of Darwin and of German higher criticism as the beginnings of problems in Baptist life. Only the heroic British preacher Charles Haddon Spurgeon sought to defend the faith against such corrosive influences. British Baptist leaders, on the other hand, claimed that Baptists ought to be allowed to interpret scripture individually, according to the principle of the priesthood of the believer. They censured Spurgeon, signaling their acceptance of higher criticism, and from then on, Criswell declared, the Baptist witness in Britain began to die. "Church attendance fell off, prayer meetings ceased, miracles of conversion were witnessed less and less, the number of baptisms began to decline, and . . . the numerical graph of British Baptists since the halcyon days of Spurgeon, their mighty champion, is down and ever down." Criswell continued, with passionate intensity, "My brother, if the higher critical approach to scriptures dominates our institutions and our denomination, *there will be no missionaries to hurt. They will cease!*" The audience responded with raucous applause. He concluded his first point, "As with the Baptists of Great Britain, whether we continue to live or ultimately die lies in our dedication to the infallible Word of God."

Criswell then recounted the death of religious institutions, taking the Northern Baptists' Divinity School at the University of Chicago as his example. It was established to train preachers to spread the gospel, he said, "but then the infiltration began, the curse, the rot, the virus, the corruption of the higher critical approach to the gospel began to work." He then quoted a variety of writings from that school that represented a "massacre of Christian orthodoxy." Telling the story of a young graduate of the school who did not believe the Bible, Criswell quoted with approving fervor the advice of a friend to the young man, "I think if you don't believe the Bible, you ought to quit the ministry." Again his audience responded with shouts of approval and applause. He emphasized that such loss of institutions was not only in the North, "but in the South, where we live, in the South we are beginning to witness the same thing." When he described neo-orthodoxy as a parasite growing on institutions already built, he was interrupted by applause again. "No minister who ·has embraced the higher critical approach to the gospel has ever built a great church, ever held a mighty revival, or ever won a city to the Lord. The message they preach and think is modern is as old as the first lie." The applause was coming more often now, the audience revelling in his condemnation of their enemies.

Finally, Criswell began to bring the message even closer to home, recounting the dismissal of Crawford H. Toy from the faculty of the

Southern Baptist Seminary in the nineteenth century. Toy went on to become a renowned scholar teaching at Harvard, but a Unitarian whose spiritual life, according to Criswell, was dead. In a recent issue of the *Review and Expositor*, the theological journal of the Southern Baptist Seminary, Criswell said, an article gave Toy lavish praise and said that Toy was merely ahead of his time. "That is, if he lived and taught today, his higher critical, destructive approach to the Word of God would be perfectly acceptable, condoned, and defended. . . . If we are to survive as a people of God, we must wage a war against this disease that more than any other will ruin our missionary, evangelistic, and soul-winning commitment."

It is not too late, Criswell said. God is still in the business of doing ever bigger and better things, and God's Spirit is in us for "power, for conquest, for glory." America stands under judgment for her "secularistic, hedonistic, humanistic, materialistic" ways, but revival is still possible. Cooperation among believers is needed, but it must be based on the infallible Word of God. "If we deliver the message of the inerrant Word of God, God will rise to meet us. . . . No battle was ever won by retreat or submission or surrender. . . . 'We shall not cease from battle strife, nor shall the sword sleep in our hand, till we have built Jerusalem in this fair and pleasant land.' God grant it!"

Few could match Criswell's eloquence or passion or his single-minded devotion to the dangers of "higher criticism." He influenced and trained many of the leaders of the Convention's fundamentalist wing, and his power in the pulpit was awesome. Those who listened became convinced (if they were not already) that the Bible must be either completely accurate or completely wrong; and without the Bible, all other beliefs were in danger. Denying it is starting down the "slippery slope" toward liberalism. James Draper, one of Criswell's disciples and SBC president from 1982 to 1984 wrote, "There are people among us today, teaching in our institutions, laboring in our denomination, pastoring in our churches, who have not departed all that far from classic biblical doctrine. . . . But, they do not believe that everything in Scripture is necessarily accurate and without error. They have started over the edge. They have abandoned divine revelation as their final basis of authority."[8]

A prominent fundamentalist pastor told us about "one of the truly liberal Southern Baptist pastors" who claims that a certain incident in Samuel "is not historical because God would not act that way." He continued, "That man is picking and choosing what to believe in scripture." He and other conservatives believe that neither troublesome events nor puzzling happenings may be ignored. They believe that people were really healed, the Red Sea really became dry land, and Jonah really spent three days in the belly of a great fish. Jerry Vines used a modern analogy to explain his view of miracles.

> I'll tell you what I believe. If these fellows with their television cameras had been on that mountain that day they would have seen Jesus leave from a literal mountain, on a literal cloud, through a literal sky, in a literal body, going back to a literal heaven, to sit down on a literal throne. And in a literal body he's coming again. Literally. I really believe it.

The most important miracles were those, like the resurrection, that were associated with the life of Jesus. Among the other fundamentals essential to most Southern Baptists, for instance, was the virgin birth. Preaching to the 1986 Pastors Conference in Atlanta, Adrian Rogers proclaimed that the virgin birth is a "literal Bible truth" without which "there is no hope for humanity and the house of Christianity will collapse like a house of cards." To loud applause he added, "I wouldn't give you half a hallelujah for your chance of heaven if you don't believe in the virgin birth of Jesus Christ." His reasoning was "No virgin birth, no deity; no deity, no sinlessness; no sinlessness, no atonement; no atonement, no hope." (As we saw, Jerry Vines used a similar domino theory to defend his belief in inerrancy.)

Not surprisingly, creation is also important. During the 1986 Atlanta convention, I asked a messenger why he was supporting Rogers for president. He pulled out a *Christian Family* magazine and pointed to an article that claimed that evolution was being taught in Baptist schools. "That's just not right," the man said. He hoped that Adrian Rogers would make sure evolution was kept out of Baptist schools. This is a theme they had heard from the pulpit that convention year. In his sermon on the virgin birth (as in many of his other sermons), Adrian Rogers proclaimed that he rejects "with all the unction, function, and emotion of my soul that monkey mythology that tells us that man evolved. I believe in the direct creation of Adam and Eve." Like Rogers, Criswell was unimpressed with "modern pseudoscientific theories and postulates and hypotheses." In his 1988 Pastors Conference address, Criswell declared that any admission of scientific error in the Bible is "blasphemy."

> My brother, if the Bible is not also scientifically accurate, it is not, to me at least, the Word of God. I have a very plain reason for that. The Lord God who made this world and all the scientific marvels which we are now discovering in it—that same Lord God knew all these things from the beginning. . . . Now if the Bible is the Word

of God, and if God inspired it, then it cannot contain any scientific mistakes because God knew every truth and fact of science from the beginning."

The Bible's accounts of history and cosmology, then, are perfectly true, and those who believe otherwise are infidels. According to Criswell they represent the curse of liberalism. They may call themselves moderates, he said, "but a skunk by any other name still stinks." Paul Pressler agreed, "Those who believe that the original text of scripture can or does contain error" are theological liberals, even if they try "to call themselves biblical conservatives, moderates, all sorts of things. But they are liberal, because they don't believe the complete accuracy and complete truth of scripture."[9]

Moderates found such rhetoric frustrating and misleading. They argued that they were never quite sure how inerrancy was going to be defined, and they were quite sure that it was not a word they found very useful. Many suspected that its meaning was more political than theological. One pastor told us, "They make it sound like I'm liberal. That isn't true by any normative standard. But I don't use inerrancy. I think it's false. I think it's not a good way to go. I think there are very good literary, historical, factual reasons not to use it. That translates to the average Southern Baptist as 'You don't believe the Bible.' Simple as that." Seminary president and Old Testament scholar Roy Honeycutt was even more specific about his complaints. After reading the notes in the Criswell Study Bible, he observed, "He takes even stronger nonliteral views than I do. [His notes] say that the rod turning into a serpent is a case of Egyptian hypnotism. I say that and they say that I am either uninformed or lying, but Wally Amos [Criswell] can say it!"

Even when moderates considered the possible theological merits of inerrancy, they found it lacking. They disliked the way inerrantists sought to harmonize the scripture's discrepancies, forcing different stories into a single account or explaining differences away. They also disliked what they saw as a selective literalism—some sections were conveniently not required to be literal. Passages thought to be prophetic were taken by premillennialists as symbolic, and passages about women covering their heads or Christians owning slaves were explained as no longer applicable. Moderates were quite willing to agree that scripture must be interpreted in cultural context, and they wanted fundamentalists to admit that their interpretations were not so literal and culture-free after all.

One moderate author went so far as to call inerrancy "heresy." University of Richmond religion professor Robison James was among the most active moderates in seeking to argue against inerrancy as a flawed method of interpretation. In a 1985 article in *SBC Today*, the moderate news-paper, James argued that inerrancy distorts the Bible into conformity with a predetermined creedal understanding of what it must say. He said that "an inerrantist will repeatedly conform the Bible *to* his inerrantist belief. In his hands the Bible is not free—it does not have elbow room—to be anything for him, or to say anything to him, which is different from what he has declared the Bible to be."[10] James argued in his book *The Unfet-tered Word* that biblical criticism (that "destructive" method so feared by fundamentalists) is essential for keeping people open to God's message in the scripture.[11] He and other moderates criticized fundamentalists for presuming to interpret scripture perfectly when they cannot even read the Greek and Hebrew in which the text was written. In this view, edu-cation and critical interpretation can be important aids to one's faith, not destroyers of it.

The moderate argument with fundamentalists went beyond *how* to in-terpret scripture, however. They also differed on the place of the Bible in the Christian life. Ultimate commitment, they said, should be to a per-son, Jesus Christ, not to a book. They pointed out that The Word that was with God in the beginning (John 1) was Christ, not the Bible. They spoke of the fundamentalist view of the Bible as "bibliolatry." According to the moderates, fundamentalists simply miss the point of the gospel by focus-ing on the book, instead of the message and the person revealed in the book. They claimed that people's ultimate needs do not have to do with right doctrine, but with alienation from themselves, each other, and God. People who are hungry and hurting and lonely do not come saying, "Help me understand the doctrines of the virgin birth, direct creation, and ver-bal plenary inspiration." They come seeking the grace and comfort that moderates believed could be found in Jesus' life, death, and resurrection. Roy Honeycutt put it this way, "We read and understand the Bible, but we are transformed only by the gospel of the risen Lord."[12] The test of any interpretation of any scripture was whether it spoke clearly of God's love, as finally revealed in Jesus.

Likewise, the test of any doctrine about scripture was whether it was lived. Moderates claimed that there were more important things in life than getting every biblical interpretation right, that arguing over doctrine gets in the way of evangelism and service. They turned to scripture for inspiration and guidance in their service to the world. Preaching from II Timothy 2:15, Richmond pastor James Flamming told the 1986 Forum that "the scripture was not given us to shackle the mind, it was given us to equip us for service. It was not given us to debate about, but to profit from. It was not given us for the purpose of choosing sides, but to be completed for the great task of serving a world God loves." He added that "we will be judged on faith—on the way we treat the last, the lost, the least, and the lonely. . . . There is no final judgment on being doctrinally correct."

Moderates, then, affirmed the human role in the writing, transmission, and canonization of the scripture, but were convinced that its message is no less divine. Seminary professor Wayne Ward wrote, "Just as God used all the gifts, knowledge, and experience of the biblical writers to accomplish the task of writing the scriptural text, so He uses all the linguistic, archaeological, historical, and hermeneutical skills of the interpreter to bring that biblical Word into the lives of believers today."[13] The Bible moderates read was one in which the overall message of God's redeeming love was more important than the details of historical events. Whether there were real people named Adam and Eve was far less important than an affirmation of God's role in creating the universe. And whether miracles really happened the way they are described in the Bible was less important than affirming God's continuing activity in the world—then and now. They readily claimed that the science and history found in scripture reflect the understandings of ancient peoples, not timeless error-free truth.

With an emphasis on the overall message of scripture, they sought to "let God be God," remaining open to new understanding and interpretation. Midwestern Baptist Seminary president Milton Ferguson told his students in 1985 that such openness does not "mean being shallow or permissive, believing any old thing. Quite the contrary, it means betting your life on the fact that God was in Christ, reconciling the world unto himself."[14] Such openness means that there will be no simple answers— about what the Bible means or about anything else. Ferguson acknowledged, "All of us are confronted with insecurity in this life. We don't have all the answers; we are finite and limited; we are partial in our knowledge and understanding. All of us find it difficult to cope with this fact. Each of us wants to be right, to be secure; all of us are afraid to be wrong." But by moving beyond simplistic answers, a deeper faith is possible.

Moderates believe that forcing simple answers on the Bible is wrongheaded and dangerous. They claimed that a clear and infallible book would not be possible without an infallible interpreter. Only if one person establishes what the Bible "really" says can there be a text free from "error." Noting the Apostle Paul's reference to seeing the truth "through a glass darkly," (I Corinthians 13) James Flamming told his 1986 Forum audience,

> Since we are men and not God, we can never see the whole. For
> that reason, we do well, said our forefathers, to insist on beginning

with the scripture, but then allowing for individual freedom of interpretation. Let anyone who insists that they see through a glass
clearly realize that they are in obvious violation of scripture. This
person, whoever he or she might be, says in essence, that they are
more intelligent, a better interpreter, and more visionary than the
apostle Paul himself.

Setting oneself up as having such a clear vision of the Bible's meaning
sounded to moderates like an authorized "priesthood" Baptists long ago
chose to reject. They feared that any infallible interpreter must eventually claim the prerogatives of a pope, and they often referred to prominent fundamentalist pastors in just those terms. Moderates saw the desire
for clear simple answers as closely linked with a desire for a strong authority who would provide those answers.

Pastoral Authority

Even though the two sides meant very different things by it, they both
claimed that the Bible was their ultimate authority. However, even the
rhetoric was divergent when it came to the question of the pastor's authority in the local church. On one side the emphasis was on the priesthood of every believer, while the other side emphasized the rightful
authority of the pastor. One side responded positively to denominational
emphases on shared ministry, while the other was furious at another intrusion of misguided doctrines coming from Nashville.

It was, in fact, denominational programs on shared ministry that
touched off, in the mid-1980s, a rhetorical battle over the nature of pastoral authority. Responding to recent Sunday School Board emphases
during the 1986 "School of the Prophets" in his own First Baptist Dallas,
W. A. Criswell countered, "The pastor is the ruler of the church. There
is no other thing than that in the Bible." [15] Robert Tenery, editor of the
conservative *Southern Baptist Advocate*, joined the fray by calling the
emphasis on servant leadership and lay involvement part of "a rising tide
of anti-Pastor sentiment." [16] Paige Patterson addressed conservative students at the Southern Baptist Seminary on the "priesthood of the believer," emphasizing that pastors are "charged with the oversight of the
church." [17] And Nashville pastor Jerry Sutton argued that the pastor's authority is like the authority "which the head of a family exercises on his
household." [18] A clear hierarchy of husband over wife, pastor over laity, is
the way of the Bible, according to these principles. Just as the wife should
ask her husband for instruction (rather than speaking up in church) so
church women should be instructed by their pastors. Richard Land

wrote, ". . . who is in charge? The answer is that Christ is in charge and that He has left us a pattern of authority in every area of our lives, be it the state, the home, or the church."[19]

That view was made official in 1988, when the convention passed its controversial Resolution No. 5: On the Priesthood of the Believer. It stated, in part,

> WHEREAS, The Priesthood of the Believer is a term which is subject to both misunderstanding and abuse; and
> WHEREAS, The doctrine of the Priesthood of the Believer has been used to justify wrongly the attitude that a Christian may believe whatever he so chooses and still be considered a loyal Southern Baptist; and
> WHEREAS, The doctrine of the Priesthood of the Believer can be used to justify the undermining of pastoral authority in the local church,
> Be it therefore RESOLVED, That the Southern Baptist Convention . . . affirm its belief in the biblical doctrine of the Priesthood of the Believer (I Peter 2:9 and Revelation 1:6); and
> Be it further RESOLVED, That we affirm that this doctrine in no way gives license to misinterpret, explain away, demythologize, or extrapolate out elements of the supernatural from the Bible; and
> Be it further RESOLVED, That the doctrine of the Priesthood of the Believer in no way contradicts the biblical understanding of the role, responsibility, and authority of the pastor which is seen in the command to the local church in Hebrews 13:17, "Obey your leaders, and submit to them; for they keep watch over your souls, as those who will give an account," and
> Be it finally RESOLVED, That we affirm the truth that elders, or pastors, are called of God to lead the local church (Acts 20:28).

The resolution was seen as an indirect condemnation of Convention programs on lay leadership, but it was also seen as a forthright statement of the fundamentalists' belief that pastors really do "rule" their local churches.

The resolution spawned a storm of protest among moderates. The afternoon after it was passed a group marched from the convention center to the Alamo, singing "We Shall Overcome." They saw the morning's resolution as an endorsement of patriarchal pastoral dominance no less oppressive than slavery or the segregation many of them had helped to protest two decades before. When they reached the Alamo, they symbolically tore their copies of the resolution to bits, while singing Martin Luther's Reformation Hymn, "A Mighty Fortress is Our God." They could hardly believe that a Baptist body had just chosen to interpret "priesthood of the believer" to mean obeying the pastor. Such a view seemed to moderates to fly in the face of one of Baptists' most cherished principles. While in practice pastors might wield a great deal of influence, Baptists had rarely talked about obeying their pastors or granting them authority over either correct biblical interpretations or church affairs.

Just how foreign this idea of pastoral authority was in Southern Baptist life is seen in the fact that 81 percent of our respondents (even 70 percent of the fundamentalists) rejected the statement that pastors should have the final authority in the local church. Not surprisingly, that idea is more popular among fundamentalist clergy (34 percent agree) than among fundamentalist laity (15 percent agree). On the other side of the theological fence, virtually every moderate we surveyed disagreed with the idea, the majority of them strongly. Most Baptists were not ready to accept the rule of pastors in the local church. On this issue, moderates could claim a clear majority on their side.[20] While most Southern Baptists might describe the Bible as inerrant, they would not describe their pastor as their ruler.

Yet a minority had become convinced that pastors must rule. As Criswell put it, "A laity-led, layman-led, deacon-led church will be a weak church anywhere on God's earth."[21] Fundamentalist pastors expected to make decisions on their own or in consultation with a small inner circle of deacons. Town-meeting democracy in the congregation was not their style. A man from Charles Stanley's church expressed some mystification at the demands made on Stanley in Dallas. Stanley had rarely had to use parliamentary procedure because, the man said, "When we have a business meeting, it is just a formality."[22]

Fundamentalists, then, had become convinced that the Bible contains clear principles of hierarchy. Following those principles would lead to God's blessing, while flaunting them could only lead to disaster. Women are to submit to their husbands, and members are to submit to their pastor. That the pastor might be a woman was, of course, unthinkable.

Women in Ministry

But women serving as pastors was not unthinkable for others in the denomination. By 1988, over 500 women had been ordained by local Southern Baptist churches. Perhaps a dozen of them were serving as senior ministers, with the rest serving in other church staff positions, or as campus ministers, chaplains, or pastoral counselors.[23] For most of these women, the decision to become a minister had been agonizing; but they—and the churches that supported them—were convinced that God's call to ministry could not be limited by gender, that apparent biblical prohibitions on this matter were as culturally conditioned as biblical support for slavery.

Among Southern Baptists, it is the local church (usually in consultation with its association) that ordains. Most often it is the person's home church. Once a person has become convinced that he or she has been "called" and gifted for ministry, if the church agrees, it convenes an "ordination council." Ministers from that church and from the surrounding area question the candidate about his or her beliefs, abilities, and calling. In recent years this has usually followed the receipt of a seminary degree, but there are no formal requirements for education. In earlier times, and in some places today, education is more a hindrance than a help. If the council approves, a service of ordination is scheduled, in which other ordained persons ceremonially endorse the new minister in the "laying on of hands."

The person being ordained has usually preached several sermons already, often including a trial sermon before ordination. Since Baptists are a nonsacramental group, in the free church tradition, ordination theoretically implies little. There are no sacred elements or rituals forbidden to laity. But among most Baptists ordination is, in practice, quasisacramental. In most churches only other ordained persons participate in laying on of hands, and only ordained persons may marry and bury, baptize and serve communion. But in no Baptist church, does ordination guarantee a job. Even as more churches became willing to ordain women, few were willing to hire them.

So why would a Southern Baptist woman *want* to be ordained? In the 1960s, Baptist women, like all other women, had begun to rethink their roles in church, as well as in society. Baptist women were moving into the labor force, and young Baptist women were thinking about careers and callings no less than their male counterparts. They were being educated beyond high school in unprecedented numbers, staying single longer, delaying their child-bearing, and doing all the other things that were transforming the lives of women in all of American culture. Once in their careers, they experienced the independence and sense of competence working can afford. They were unlikely to go to church unchanged by their experiences.

Many of these young Baptist women had been active in their churches throughout their lives. They had especially benefited from years of experience in Girls Auxiliary, the branch of the Woman's Missionary Union aimed at girls from fourth grade through high school. In their G.A. groups, they had memorized scripture, prayed daily for missionaries, learned to name and locate every country in which Southern Baptists had missionaries, even learned the locations and executives of all the denomination's Boards. As they got older, they participated in service projects and wrote essays on theological topics. And at each stage of their childhood, girls were urged to listen for God's call to them. Perhaps God wanted them for some "special service." Their progression through G.A. "steps" (a bit like scouting badges) was recognized in church "coronation" ceremonies, complete with long white dresses and crowns. The highest step was to become a Queen Regent in Service. In these high sacred moments, the dreams of Southern Baptist girls were shaped by the ideals of an organization that instilled in them piety, a desire to serve, and denominational loyalty—and they kept listening for God's call.

While they were growing up, few of them would have dreamed that their call would be to pastor, rather than to the mission field; but that is just what happened. As they went off to college in the late 1960s and 1970s, their sense of God's call began to change. They watched women elsewhere begin to step into pulpits and wondered if they could, too. Some of them were invited to speak for Student Night at Christmas when they came home from college. Others worked as summer missionaries or as church interns. Without anyone making much of a fuss, the first Southern Baptist women began to imagine themselves as local church pastors. The fuss came when they began to act on their dreams.

On August 9, 1964, in Durham, North Carolina, Addie Davis was ordained to the ministry, the first Southern Baptist woman to take such a step. In the years that followed, a trickle of other women joined her. Davis never found a Southern church to pastor and went North. Others were entering positions on college campuses, in counseling, and in various chaplaincies in which they were unhindered by the reluctance of local Southern Baptist churches. Ten years later, the new *Southern Baptist Journal* began reporting regularly and disapprovingly on ordinations of women. By then, they estimated that the number had grown to fifteen.[24]

Most of the women who were ordained in the 1970s still went into nonparish ministries because so few Southern Baptist parishes would hire them. Like women in other denominations, they faced fears and prejudices from local members.[25] People were afraid that hiring a woman would divide the church or that she simply could not do the job. Even many members who personally favored hiring a woman held back out of deference to what they perceived other members to believe. Late in the decade, a few women entered church staffs as associates, and a few others took on small country churches no one else apparently wanted. But women pastors were still very rare indeed.

During the 1970s, however, people in Southern Baptist schools and agencies began to catch on to the trend. Schools realized that women were coming to them to be educated for the ministry. Instead of enrolling in religious education and music programs, women were enrolling as religion majors and in Master of Divinity programs. Seminary presidents began reporting to the annual Convention meeting that they were "preparing men and women for ministry." Writers in Nashville realized that some of their female readers might be considering a pastoral vocation, and in subtle ways that recognition worked its way into the materials they produced. No one announced one day that the denomination's officials would support women in ministry, but in a few key locations—especially the Student Ministries Department in Nashville, Southern Seminary, and Southeastern Seminary—the role of women was acknowledged and nurtured. And if a woman's home church would not ordain her, a growing number of churches, especially surrounding college and seminary campuses, would acknowledge her call and grant her official recognition.

In 1982, *Folio,* a newsletter for Southern Baptist women ministers, was begun. After 1983, women were added to the faculties of the theology schools at Southern and Southeastern. In that same year, an informal gathering of "Women in Ministry" preceded the meeting of the Southern Baptist Convention. They organized and continued to offer a program each year after that for crowds that varied from 200 to 500 or more. In the fall of 1984, Southern Seminary held a major conference on the role of women in church and society, and Southeastern followed with a similar event the next spring. Women in the Southern Baptist Convention were following their sisters in other denominations into the pulpit and into organizations for mutual support and encouragement.

It was perhaps only natural that Woman's Missionary Union should take an interest in this trend. It was in WMU that women had made and kept their own history for the previous 100 years. In the nineteenth century WMU had worked to open doors for women as missionaries, but recently they had watched a precipitous drop in the number of single women going overseas. WMU leaders in Birmingham recognized that women were channeling their energies into other work and service now that other opportunities were available. With a keen interest in keeping women involved in serving the church, they began to sponsor special dinners for women ministers during the annual WMU convention. Eventually the women wanted more time and their own space, and WMU helped again. And from this WMU encouragement, Southern Baptist Women in Ministry was born.

Likewise it was natural that those working with youth should be most attuned to changes in the ways those young men and women were shaping their lives. In February, 1985, an entire issue of *The Student,* the official Baptist student magazine, was devoted to women in ministry. Ordained (and unordained) women ministers told their stories. An historian wrote of "Sister Saints" in Christian history. There was a major article examining the Bible's teaching on women, concluding that "our churches could wisely ordain anyone, male or female, who had a special call of God."[26] In Christ, the author emphasized, there is "neither Jew nor Greek, slave nor free, male nor female." (Galatians 3:28). Female submission should be taken no more literally than should the admonition that slaves should submit to their masters. Other articles in the same issue assessed the status of women in the SBC and weighed the question of whether and when to seek ordination. In some sections of the denomination, this forthright treatment of the subject was welcome. Dozens, perhaps hundreds of young Baptist women celebrated that their callings were being recognized.

But even louder than the rejoicing was the uproar that came from the denomination's right wing. Within a year, the editor of *The Student* had been relieved of his editorial duties. Fundamentalists perceived that national agencies were actively promoting a cause that was plainly contradicted in scripture, and they wanted it stopped. Fundamentalists argued that they did not want their Cooperative Program dollars going to support women ministers. They added that it was only fair that agencies do what the majority of Southern Baptists wanted, and they were sure that 99 percent of Southern Baptists opposed women pastors.

They buttressed their arguments with their own reading of scripture. When the Bible says that a pastor must be "the husband of one wife," they claimed, it obviously rules women out. And when it says that women should be silent in church and submissive to their husbands, God's intentions are made all the more clear. No matter how a woman feels, the Bible says she cannot really be called by God to become a pastor. Moderates might counter with their own biblical exegesis, but fundamentalists were sure that women in the pulpit represented a dangerous disregard for clear biblical principles.

By the early 1980s, Southern Baptist women ministers were facing more than routine obstacles. They had become symbolic of the division facing the convention. When fundamentalists claimed that moderates did not really believe the Bible, they were likely to point to women pastors as the perfect example of defying God's Word. And when moderates wanted to contrast their tolerance and open-mindedness with fundamentalist oppressiveness, they pointed to their acceptance of women as proof. When a fundamentalist seminary student wanted to peg the stance of a professor, he might ask (as one Midwestern student often did), "Do you believe in the ordination of women and homosexuals?" (They were apparently equally abhorrent to him.) And on the other side of the theological fence, when moderates talked about how they might visibly identify their churches, they joked that perhaps their church signs should read, "Women ordained here." Every time the convention passed a resolution or a Board adopted a policy against women, a defiant surge of new ordinations took place in moderate churches. Positions on women became a litmus test on both sides. Over half of our survey respondents (52 percent) agreed that the ordination of women was a "major issue" in the denomination, and there was no variation in that response among people of different theological persuasions. A Southern Baptist woman pastor could even become a national celebrity of sorts—as Nancy Hastings Sehested discovered when she accepted the 1988 call to pastor Prescott Memorial Baptist Church, in Adrain Rogers' hometown of Memphis. The church was disfellowshipped from the Shelby County Baptist Association— barred from local meetings, but not necessarily from state and national affairs.

The question was not simply one of women in ministry. Baptists also ordain deacons, and many churches began to reexamine the role of women in this area, as well. Deacons sometimes serve as lay ministers, in both ceremonial and caring capacities; and they often function as the executive council of the church, with powerful decision-making roles. Many Baptist laywomen were no longer content to serve only submissively. A growing number of churches carefully studied the matter and found ample biblical precedent for women deacons. But when they followed through on their study, they often received wide attention and opposition, including motions to unseat their messengers at state conventions or local associational meetings.

At annual meetings, motions and resolutions against women in ministry were often on the agenda. In addition to this overt opposition, women had to face routine exclusion and invisibility, along with occasional jokes and hostile remarks. There were often jokes about inclusiveness (One trustee laughed that a "balanced" committee would have to include a "Jew, a woman, and a cripple"); and there were sarcastic references at the Pastors Conference to the "other" meetings and "other" people who let women preach. At the 1988 annual convention meeting several routine proposals came to the floor containing all male pronouns. Moves were made to amend them, altering the language to include "he or she." Those moves, however, were met with boo's and cat calls, and the votes were so close and rancorous that the chair finally suggested making such editorial changes by the common consent of those bringing the motion. When a woman pastor made a motion that a woman be invited to preach at a future convention, she was booed so vehemently that the chair had to quiet the crowd in order for her to finish presenting her motion. Sometimes women were an afterthought, as with the two women added to the Peace Committee's twenty men to represent the denomination's females. More commonly, women were simply invisible in this official world. The language used was so uniformly male in gender that even moderate women sometimes did not notice that they were referred to as "gentle-men" all day.

That does not, of course, mean that women were completely excluded from important positions. The number of women on Convention boards of directors dropped significantly in the 1980s, but those being elected were sometimes strong and visible. Several had cut their political teeth in the anti-ERA and Right to Life movements and were skilled tacticians and forceful speakers. They were vehemently antifeminist, but certainly did not wait for men to speak in their behalf. Fundamentalist leaders sometimes chuckled about watching "liberal" women messengers vote for a woman over a man, not knowing that the woman they voted for stood against everything the liberal women held dear. Some of the new women elected to agency boards, on the other hand, were less aggressive, more content to let the men do the business. In one meeting, the husband of a fundamentalist woman member did more speaking from the gallery than the woman herself did at the conference table. These new women trust-ees were a curious mix of submissive and aggressive, but they were all firmly opposed to women serving in ordained ministerial roles.

The clash between these new female leaders and the more moderate women of the older regime was most poignantly symbolized in the Home Mission Board meeting of October 1987. The issue of funding women pastors was again before the body, and a committee had composed an explanation for their new policy that cited both majority opinion and the 1984 resolution on women as justification for women not being funded. Beth McGhee, a moderate member of the board, rose to make a quiet, but passionate appeal for a modification in the statement. She pleaded with the board not to offend those who do not interpret scripture as they do. In the name of peace, she asked that the Board not presume to know what the majority of Southern Baptists wanted. When she sat down, a fundamentalist woman, Linda Principe, began to speak, gesturing with her Bible, as she argued that the Board must abide by what the Bible says and not allow the feelings of a few people to influence it. Quoting I Tim-othy 3, she continued to testify that women must not preach. But as she spoke, not ten feet away, Beth McGhee had collapsed in her seat. She had suffered a heart attack and would be pronounced dead on arrival at a nearby hospital. Her friends reported that she had not felt well that morn-ing, but had strong convictions about the business before the board. Said one, "She was not an avid feminist, she was not a women's libber. She was a person who believed that the Lord died for women, too."[27] Her plea for toleration was her final act.

Beth McGhee had asked her fellow Board members how they knew what the majority of Southern Baptists believed about ordaining women. They replied that they just assumed that most people would not want a woman pastor.[28] Depending on what they meant by "most," they were right about that. Fundamentalists could rightfully claim that a majority of Southern Baptists agreed with them about women pastors (see table 4.1). They were not quite correct, however, in claiming that the size of the majority was 90 to 95 percent. In fact, nearly half (45 percent) of the respondents to our 1986 survey claimed that they would support the hiring of a "qualified ordained woman" to their church staff. Many wrote in the margins that they would not support her as pastor, but that in other positions it would be alright. Among the local church leaders we surveyed in 1985, 26 percent said that they themselves think women may be ordained as pastors, although only 11 percent reported that their church supports that practice. Thirty seven percent of our respondents said they approve of women deacons, although again, less than half that many (17 percent) reported that their church permits women to serve, and less than half of those (7 percent of all the churches) reported any women actually elected and serving. Apparently only a small minority of Southern Baptist churches had accepted the leadership of women in practice. But a much larger minority of churches had policies and leadership in support of ordaining women.

Given the volatility of this issue, it is not surprising that there were vast differences in how people of differing theological positions responded to our questions on women in ministry (see again table 4.1). Among fundamentalists, almost everyone was opposed, even to women as deacons. Most would also like to censure those who do ordain women. Among moderates, the vast majority approved of ordaining women, almost no one wanted censure, and nearly everyone said they would support hiring an ordained woman. Reports of what their churches endorse and what those churches have actually done reflected considerably less acceptance for women, but the distance between moderates and fundamentalists was long indeed. Conservatives, the "half" in the middle that represents the mainstream of the denomination, were ambivalent. They did not support the idea of women pastors in any great numbers, although a fair number would not mind having an ordained woman on their staff. A significant minority favored women as deacons, and the majority opposed measures against either agencies or churches that disagree with them on this issue. This conservative middle seems to represent the slow change and relative tolerance of divergent practices that characterized Southern Baptists before this issue became symbolic of the fight between fundamentalists and moderates.

If fundamentalists in general were unenthusiastic about ordaining women, clergy in that camp were even more so. Almost all of the few fundamentalists who approved of ordaining women as deacons or pastors

Table 4.1. Support for Women in Ministry by Theological Parties

Position	% Self-Identified Moderates	% Moderate Conservatives	% Conservatives	% Fundamentalist Conservatives	% Self-Identified Fundamentalists
I think women may be ordained as pastors *(average = 26% N = 944)*	87	64	22	8	2
My church approves ordaining women ministers *(average = 11% N = 310)*	36	21	9	3	3
My church *has* ordained a woman minister *(average = 2% N = 322)*	6	3	2	0	0
I would support hiring an ordained woman *(average = 45% N = 360)*	90	81	43	26	20
I think women may be ordained as deacons *(average = 37% N = 944)*	96	71	36	16	9
My church approves ordaining women deacons *(average = 17% N = 317)*	45	31	14	6	5
My church *has* women deacons serving *(average = 7% N = 327)*	14	9	9	0	3
Churches that ordain women should be disfellowshipped *(average = 28% N = 948)*	0	3	25	44	59
Schools and agencies that support women's ordination should be censured *(average = 45% N = 939)*	2	14	42	66	78

NOTE: Number of cases varies depending on the year in which the question was asked. All differences between parties are statistically significant at p < .05.

were laity and not clergy. Whereas more than 95 percent of fundamentalist clergy believed women should never be ordained, only 77 percent of fundamentalist laity agreed. As with ideas about the pastor's authority, fundamentalist clergy were again more conservative than theologically like-minded laity.

The disparity between fundamentalist clergy and laity was even wider when it came to questions of what to do about those who support the ordination of women. Seventy four percent of self-identified fundamentalist clergy favored disfellowshipping churches that ordain women, but only 41 percent of similar laity agreed. When it came to the actions of a national agency or school, rather than a nearby church, fundamentalist clergy were even more adamant. Ninety-two percent of self-identified fundamentalist clergy thought such institutions ought to be punished for supporting women ministers, but only 62 percent of laity in the same category agreed.

There were also differences on this issue between self-identified fundamentalists and the fundamentalists who call themselves conservatives. While there is little difference between the two on what they believe about ordaining women, there are fairly substantial differences—averaging nearly 15 percentage points—in how they respond to others who do. By definition, calling oneself fundamentalist seems to mean both an opposition to women pastors and a greater willingness to disfellowship churches or censure agencies that support the ordination of women. Clergy who called themselves fundamentalist were willing to fight for what they believed.

On the left side of the denomination, moderates had staked out a place as defenders of women. Some progressives were so convinced of the importance of women ministers that they saw in them a kind of renaissance force, capable of transforming those willing to be transformed. One moderate man recalled sitting in a Women in Ministry conference and forcing himself to "shut up and listen." The result was a conviction that these women represented a "tidal wave that cannot be stopped." Their ideas about service, about power, about family and work, even about God were in fact quite different from those heard anywhere else in the Convention. Theirs were meetings in which inclusion of all sorts was a primary virtue. In her 1988 sermon to the group, Jann Clanton spoke of a day when the deacons greeting Baptist worshippers might be both black and white, men and women, a day when men's and women's voices might blend in the pulpit as well as in the choir, and when women would take their places in SBC board rooms as servant leaders of the denomination. At Women in Ministry meetings, business was done by consensus. Language was inclusive, and worship incorporated a variety of nontraditional styles, including liturgical dance. Even God could be spoken of in feminine terms. Here women were giving voice to a vision of church life intimately connected with their roots, but with branches far wider than anything else being envisioned in Southern Baptist circles. When he saw their 1988 program, fundamentalist Robert Tenery wrote, "Liturgical dancing in worship services is about as far away from Southern Baptists as you can get. Is this where the so-called Southern Baptist Women in Ministry organization is trying to lead us?"[29] Indeed the distance between these Southern Baptist women and the Baptists who read the *Advocate* was "about as far away as you can get."

A Social and Political Agenda

In all likelihood, the members of Southern Baptist Women in Ministry and the men at the Pastors Conference across town were also separated by how they voted in the last national election. While fellow Southern Baptist Jimmy Carter got a large majority of Baptist votes in 1976, he lost many of them in 1980. By then, conservatives had become disillusioned with his version of religion and politics. One fundamentalist leader told us that Carter talked about being born again, but "then quoted Reinhold Niebuhr, so we knew that he wasn't reading the right things." He was also a social drinker, and that was taboo. And his policies were too much like the New Deal and Great Society to please newly-awakening conservatives. By 1980, the gap between the conservatism of the Moral Majority and the progressivism of Carter was also present within Carter's Southern Baptist Convention.

During the 1960s and 1970s, Carter's kind of progressivism had been embodied in the denomination at the Christian Life Commission and the Baptist Joint Committee on Public Affairs. These were "new evangelicals" of the variety seen nationally in *Sojourners* or *The Other Side*. Foy Valentine had led the Christian Life Commission in producing materials and hosting conferences that touted peace, hunger relief, and economic justice alongside traditional concerns about alcohol, gambling, and pornography. Having led the Convention through the racial crises of the 1960s, Valentine and his agency continued to pursue the causes of justice. He had a loyal following of people who regularly attended the CLC seminars, but he also had dedicated opponents who were equally regular in calling for his ouster.

James Dunn came to his job as director of the Baptist Joint Committee from the Texas Christian Life Commission. In Washington, at the nine-denomination Baptist Joint Committee, he pursued an aggressive defense of church/state separation that often found him siding with the ACLU. When conservatives argued for prayer in schools, he reminded them that Baptists had historically said that government was not supposed to be in the business of promoting religion. In his witty, sometimes biting, down-home style, he called such proposals for "state sponsored religion in public schools" a Baptist heresy; and at one point he described President Reagan's involvement in the issue as "despicable demagoguery." When the SBC passed a resolution in 1982 supporting a school prayer amendment, Dunn and the BJCPA cited the eight previous SBC resolutions supporting the Supreme Court's 1963 ruling and went on opposing the school prayer amendment.[30]

Dunn also warned against mixing the particularity of conservative religious traditions with the power of the state. He noted that he did not want to "worship at someone else's altar." Nor did he want a "diluted 'religion in general'. We do not need," he said, "a sort of happy-face, 'we're number one' orgy of Americanism, with God as the national mascot. . . . That's blasphemous."[31] When he joined People for the American Way (and served a term on its board of directors), in opposition to the Moral Majority, his opponents saw this as the perfect proof that he was a bona fide, "card carrying" liberal pushing his liberal agenda with Southern Baptist dollars. As one prominent pastor said, "When you get associated with something that's against the conservative movement in the denomination, then that's just kind of thumbing your nose [at us]. . . . James Dunn does not represent mainstream Southern Baptists, and we will never get the representation from him on moral or First Amendment issues that we as mainstream Southern Baptists desire."

The vast majority of the Southern Baptists we surveyed agreed with Dunn, however, that separation of church and state is "an important Baptist distinctive" (see table 4.2). Over ninety percent agreed or strongly agreed with that statement. Even among fundamentalists, dissenters were only a small minority (15 percent), but they stood in contrast to nearly complete unanimity on the moderate side. The fundamentalists we surveyed who did reject church-state separation may have been responding to statements by leaders like W. A. Criswell or James Kennedy. Criswell had been quoted as claiming that "separation of church and state was an idea invented by an agnostic." And in his 1985 Pastors Conference address, Kennedy asserted that the only country where separation of church and state is in the constitution is Russia. Not many Baptists, even fundamentalist ones, agreed with them, but they had more supporters on the SBC's right wing than on the left.

On that right wing, a strong conservative consensus had evolved, especially around family-related issues. Among self-identified fundamentalists, the vast majority (83 percent) opposed the Equal Rights Amendment, and they were unanimous that the husband is the head of the household (see again table 4.2). But the most volatile issue was abortion. Almost no one (1 percent) among fundamentalists favored leaving abortion to individual choice. Nearly two-thirds (63 percent) would make abortion even more restricted than it was before *Roe v. Wade*—limiting it to cases where the mother's life is threatened. Indeed, one third of fundamentalists would never allow abortion under any circumstances.

For these pro-life adherents, the stance of the Christian Life Commission was not nearly strong enough. The CLC's material counseled that abortion was sometimes the lesser evil, especially in cases of rape, incest, and danger to the mother. Until 1980, that had been the position taken in various Convention resolutions. But since 1980, resolutions had changed. New statements further limited the range of abortions Baptists would sanction, and activists offered regular motions requesting Convention agencies to promote pro-life issues. Abortion was also a regular topic in Pastors Conference sermons. In 1987, former SBC president Bailey Smith told of a nurse who was forced to let an aborted fetus die. "Folks," he said, "I want to say to every supreme court justice, I want to say to every compromise lily-livered congressman, I want to say to every liberal pulpit in America, you'll stand before almighty God and answer for the deaths of those little babies!" Adrian Rogers also spoke out regularly in the pro-life crusade. He could be as passionate about abortion as about the virgin birth, declaring the "slaughter of millions of innocent lives" to be "wrong, wrong, wrong!" There was little doubt that the Convention's right wing opposed abortion and that abortion was a practice against which they were willing to fight.

Equally wrong, in their view was the sin of homosexuality. When faced with the statement "Even if homosexuality is wrong, the civil rights of gays should be protected," 77 percent of our fundamentalist respondents disagreed or strongly disagreed. In 1986, Charles Stanley, then president of the Convention, said, "I believe that AIDS is God indicating his displeasure and his attitude toward that form of lifestyle, which we in this country are about to accept."[32] Homosexuality, like abortion, was a recurrent theme in the sermons heard at the Pastors Conference. It was one of the problems cited as evidence of the world's sad state. In 1987, Pastor E. W. McCall told his fellow pastors, "we as a people, as a Convention, need to let the world know that any kind of lifestyle won't do. For I believe that the Bible is right. . . . The God that I serve, and the one that I preach about, made Adam and Eve and not Adam and Steve." On each of these family-related issues, a large majority of fundamentalists in the SBC took a position in favor of the "traditional" family.

The traditional family got only mixed support on the moderate side, however. Nearly two-thirds (69 percent) of self-identified moderates took the traditional position that "husbands have the God given responsibility to lead their households." But not all of them translated that belief into opposition to the ERA. Self-identified moderates were the only faction

Table 4.2. Positions on Social and Political Issues by Theological Parties

Position	% Self-Identified Moderates	% Moderate Conservatives	% Conservatives	% Fundamentalist Conservatives	% Self-Identified Fundamentalists
Separation of church & state is important Baptist distinctive (DISAGREE) *(average = 4% N = 964)*	2	2	3	4	11
Husband should be household leader *(average = 94% N = 979)*	69	87	96	99	100
Favor the Equal Rights Amendment (DISAGREE) *(average = 69% N = 963)*	43	57	68	80	83
Allow abortion never or only to save mother *(average = 42% N = 970)*	13	27	39	55	63
Rights of gays should be protected (DISAGREE) *(average = 58% N = 966)*	31	50	55	70	77
America should protect weak nations from communism *(average = 74% N = 972)*	39	55	73	86	95
The "bloated" defense budget is a major problem (DISAGREE) *(average = 48% N = 974)*	34	38	46	53	69

within the SBC that gave the ERA majority support (57 percent). While their positions on women in ministry seemed to indicate an openness to female equality, moderates were apparently not completely convinced that the Equal Rights Amendment was the right way to achieve it. Their positions on abortion were also mixed. Over one third (36 percent) of the moderates we surveyed were pro-choice on abortion, and only 13 percent would limit it to saving the mother's life. The majority (just over 50 percent) would allow abortions, but under fairly tight restrictions, such as in situations of rape or incest, as well as when the mother's life is threatened. These proportions among moderates are very similar to proportions reported in a 1989 poll of the population in twelve southern states.[33] Moderate Southern Baptists seemed to reflect the dominant conservatism of their region, while fundamentalists and SBC conservatives were consid-

Table 4.2. (*Continued*)

Position	% Self-Identified Moderates	% Moderate Conservatives	% Conservatives	% Fundamentalist Conservatives	% Self-Identified Fundamentalists
People on welfare don't want to work (average = 43% N = 337)	20	29	47	41	63
Civil Rights movement led in the right direction (Unsure or disagree) (average = 34% N = 335)	10	27	33	51	55
My church emphasizes patriotism (average = 81% N = 971)	57	73	82	89	85
Identify as conservative Republican (average = 27% N = 946)	7	17	25	36	36
Groups like Moral Majority are good (average = 61% N = 971)	15	42	59	79	89
My church emphasizes social change* (average = 23% N = 963)	15	21	18	30	38

NOTE: Percentages, unless otherwise noted, combine Disagree and Strongly disagree responses or Agree and Strongly agree responses. Number of cases varies depending on the year in which the question was asked. See questionnaires in appendix C for exact wordings of items.

*This difference between parties statistically significant at $p < .05$. All other differences significant at $p < .001$.

erably more opposed to abortion than average southerners.

Moderates are not unanimous on any of these political issues. There were both political liberals and political conservatives in their ranks, and moderate gatherings could generate lively debate. Over two thirds (69 percent) would protect the civil rights of gays, for instance, even if they did not agree with the homosexual way of life; but that meant that a substantial minority among moderates opposed gay rights. There were, in fact, substantial conservative minorities on all of these family-related issues. While a majority of moderates supported the goals of gender equality and choice that have characterized the sexual and family revolutions of the 1960s and 1970s, they were not the unanimous voting bloc that fundamentalists were on the other side.

On the civil rights revolution, however, there was unanimity on the moderate side. When compared to self-identified fundamentalists, self-identified moderates were almost twice as likely (87 percent versus 47 percent) to agree or strongly agree that "the civil rights movement led this country in the right direction." Even more revealing was the proportion of self-identified moderates who *strongly* agreed with this statement (37 percent) compared to the small number of all fundamentalists (2 percent) who had such strong feelings. Even moderate conservatives expressed strong approval at only an 8 percent rate. This difference between moderates with the same beliefs, but different identities points to this issue as a crucial one in defining the moderate identity. Those who claimed the moderate identity for themselves were often people who passionately supported the changes brought by the civil rights movement.

Fundamentalists were also politically conservative on the issue of welfare. Almost half of all fundamentalists thought that "people on welfare could work if they wanted to," while less than a quarter of all moderates agreed or strongly agreed with that assessment. Fundamentalists seemed to see welfare as a waste of money, while moderates were more convinced that it was necessary. On defense spending, however, the positions were reversed. Almost half of all moderates agreed or strongly agreed that "the bloated defense budget is one of the biggest problems facing this country," while only about a quarter of fundamentalists agreed.

On related issues, we again found Southern Baptist fundamentalists charting a conservative course. Nearly all (95 percent) agreed that "America must protect weak nations from communism so we can continue to spread the gospel." They stood in marked contrast to the moderate camp, where barely over a third (39 percent) would want to "protect weak nations from communism." Combined with positions on defense spending, the picture is one of a contrast between moderate caution and fundamentalist enthusiasm for America's role in the world. That fundamentalists were simply more "pro-American" is reflected in the large majority (85 percent versus 57 percent of self-identified moderates) who said their church "puts a lot of emphasis on being loyal, patriotic citizens."

What is striking about the figures in table 4.2 is both the wide distance between the two sides and the relatively even distribution between the two poles. Neither fundamentalists nor moderates could claim a clear majority of the mainstream on most of these issues. In many cases, the theologically conservative middle is split nearly evenly between political conservatism and political liberalism. Conservatives were very sure that husbands should be the head of the household and that their churches do emphasize patriotism, and they were only somewhat less sure that they oppose the ERA and that America should fight communism. On most other issues, however, they were positioned about halfway between the two sides, and the denomination thus had no clear grassroots consensus on its political direction. The perception that all Southern Baptists had taken a giant turn to the right in the 1980s is not reflected here.[34]

There were, however, signs that many Southern Baptists, especially the denomination's new leaders, were seeking new political alignments. The majority of our respondents (52 percent) described their parents as "conservative Democrats," hardly a surprise for a group that overwhelmingly grew up in the South. However, less than half that number (23 percent) described their own current position in the same terms. Comparing their descriptions of their parents to their descriptions of themselves, the biggest change has been in the number of respondents who described themselves as conservative Republicans (27 percent) compared to the number who described their parents in those terms (18 percent). Indeed, this movement from the conservative side of the Democratic party to the conservative side of the Republican fold may be quite recent.[35] Even Paul Pressler only became a Republican in 1988.[36] Almost exactly half of our respondents placed themselves somewhere on the Republican side of the ledger, compared to about a quarter of their parents. Not surprisingly the people most likely to identify themselves as "conservative Republican" were the fundamentalists, and the least likely were the moderates. Fundamentalists were most likely to label themselves "independent" or "conservative" on both sides of the party line. Less than 3 percent of self-identified fundamentalists chose either of the "moderate to liberal" (Democrat or Republican) labels. Almost half the self-identified moderates (43 per cent), on the other hand, chose one of those "moderate to liberal" categories. Identification with one of the SBC's "parties" appears to be related to national party identification, as well.

Fundamentalists and moderates differed politically, then, on both issues and organization. They especially differed on whether they thought groups like the Moral Majority were a good thing. Eighty-nine percent of self-identified fundamentalists agreed or strongly agreed that "it is good that groups like the Moral Majority are taking a stand for Christian principles." Among self-identified moderates, the proportions were almost exactly reversed. Only 15 percent approved of the Moral Majority's brand of political involvement. Jerry Falwell was the incarnation of all that moderates opposed. They feared that the SBC was being molded into a branch of Thomas Road Baptist Church and that Falwell wanted to become the "Baptist pope." It was not uncommon to hear moderates remark that the day Falwell joined, they would leave.

Among fundamentalists, however, Falwell was a hero, standing up for the cause of righteousness. Jerry Vines said that he liked Falwell so much that if he lived in Virginia he would go to Thomas Road. (Since Thomas Road is not a Southern Baptist church, Vines, then SBC president, had some explaining to do.)[37] Falwell returning the compliment, assured the 1989 Evangelists Conference that the SBC "is the hope of Bible-believing Christians everywhere." Fundamentalist SBC leaders worked alongside Falwell in the Moral Majority, and he worked alongside them in evangelism conferences. He was a friend and col league in a common cause.

The cause they shared was a concern for the moral well-being of America. Many of the SBC's fundamentalist leaders were also active in national conservative causes and organizations, and because of this they were often accused by moderates of using the SBC for political purposes.[38] They responded, however, that "what is sauce for the goose is sauce for the gander." Paige Patterson, for instance, argued that James Dunn himself had written that Christians should be involved in politics. "We have taken him at his word and have become involved. What [they] do not appreciate is the fact that it is no longer the left involved in isolation, but now conservatives who are involved."[39]

So, Southern Baptists differed almost as much on political issues as on theological ones. Their divergent positions on the Bible not only gave them differing ideas about the Second Coming or women in ministry, but also about defense spending and civil rights. While conservatives were caught in the middle, both the political right and the political left had found receptive audiences in the right and left wings of the Southern Baptist Convention; and each now distrusted the other. Bailey Smith said that he liked Falwell because Falwell had the right enemies. And among Falwell's most vehement enemies were progressive Southern Baptists. Indeed in the person of Falwell, the battle lines were again drawn between fundamentalist and moderate Southern Baptists. They not only did not share the same enemies, they sometimes *were* each other's enemies.

The Christian Life

Fundamentalists and moderates clearly differed on issues of public policy, but they differed on issues of private morality, as well. In a number of ways, moderates had begun to declare their independence from the "do's and don'ts" of traditional southern—and Southern Baptist—life. When asked if it "is important that Christians avoid worldly practices such as drinking and dancing," moderates, on average, were unsure. They were split almost evenly between those who agreed and those who disagreed. Among fundamentalists, on the other hand, there was no such ambivalence. Not a single person disagreed, and 93 percent agreed strongly that such "separation" is part of the Christian life.

Table 4.3. Practices Christians Should Avoid Reported by Theological Parties

Practices to Avoid	% Self-Identified Moderates	% Moderate Conservatives	% Conservatives	% Fundamentalist Conservatives	% Self-Identified Fundamentalists	Average
Swearing	75	89	97	96	100	94%
Drinking alcoholic beverages	63	86	95	96	97	91%
Smoking	36	52	68	79	82	67%
Social dancing	6	19	46	66	78	46%
Going to movies (not G-rated)	7	23	48	64	69	46%
Card playing	7	14	33	54	76	36%
(Number of Cases)	(42)	(32)	(156)	(75)	(32)	(337)

NOTE: All differences between parties are statistically significant at p < .001.

We discovered, however, that such a blanket statement about "worldly practices" masks a great deal of variation in which practices are actually condemned. Many people wrote in the margins of our questionnaire that drinking should be avoided, but dancing was okay. As a result, the 1987 questionnaire offered them a more precise way to respond. We asked, "When you think about what makes a Christian's life different from a non-believer's, which of these practices do you think should *not* be a part of the Christian's life?" Their responses are shown in table 4.3. Indeed, almost twice as many condemned drinking as dancing.

The practices we asked about were the traditional "don'ts" of southern culture, the moral questions about which southerners had traditionally been concerned.[40] With the exception of swearing, none is directly prohibited in scripture, but all have been condemned by southern Protestants as evidences of a degenerate life. Dancing could only lead to sexual impropriety, young people were told. Movies touted sinful lifestyles and put evil thoughts in the minds of their viewers. Smoking was harmful to the body, which is the "temple of the Holy Spirit" (I Corinthians 6:19). Card playing was taboo both because of the gambling often associated with it and because the cards themselves were believed to be profane representations of Jesus, Mary, and God. And alcohol was an evil of monumental proportions. Long after national prohibition had been repealed, many southern counties remained dry. Attempts to change that status were consistently met with a solid wall of Baptist and Methodist opposition. At the Pastors Conference in 1986, Jerry Vines admonished his hearers that "if our Southern Baptist people believed in the return of Jesus the way they ought to, some of them would get that Budweiser out of their refrigerators." He was applauded enthusiastically by an audience that deplored the slipping moral standards represented by Baptists who drink. They, like most Southern Protestants before them, were so convinced that alcohol was ungodly that they were pretty sure Jesus' miracle at the wedding of Cana was the turning of water into grape juice, not wine.

A prohibition against swearing ("taking the Lord's name in vain") is part of the Ten Commandments, and 94 percent of our Southern Baptist respondents agreed that Christians should not swear. This even edged out drinking as the most condemned practice. Among all but the most liberal, drinking and swearing were about equally condemned with almost everyone agreeing that Christians should do neither. However, among self-identified moderates, even these condemned practices got mixed reviews. A large majority (75 percent) thought Christians ought to avoid swearing, but the majority was much smaller (63 percent) on the question of drinking. And on both these practices, self-identified moderates were much more lenient than any other group, even those with similar moderate beliefs who called themselves conservative.

The tension between moderate lifestyles and the practices of their more conservative brothers and sisters was apparent at some moderate gatherings. The use of an occasional four-letter word seemed a kind of defiant badge of liberation for some. I have never heard a moderate use God's name in a profane way, nor have I heard any sexually explicit language, but other "four-letter" words can be heard on occasion. (However, if they were not entirely sure who was listening, the words were likely to be spoken in hushed tones or through clenched teeth.) Likewise, a glass of wine with dinner was not uncommon among moderates. But they would surely take care that they were unnoticed. Room service was heavily used in Southern Baptist Convention hotels. While moderates wanted to proclaim their liberation from puritanical standards, their freedom to express themselves fully or to drink in moderation was hampered by their knowledge that most of their Southern Baptist brothers and sisters did not approve. These matters of lifestyle were another of the ways in which the left wing of the denomination was self-consciously different.

Smoking was not the same sort of issue, however. Although only a third of self-identified moderates said that a Christian should not smoke, few moderates did, in fact, smoke. Here they seemed to be expressing their endorsement of freedom, not their own lifestyle preferences. Moderate leanings toward toleration were also seen in their response to the much more controversial issue of homosexuality. It was not that they were willing to endorse homosexuality as a "viable Christian alternative." Only about 2 percent of all our respondents, regardless of theological position, agreed or strongly agreed with that statement. However, self-identified moderates were much more likely to say they were unsure (11 percent versus 4 percent for everyone else) and much less likely to say they *strongly* disagreed (56 percent versus 77 percent of all others). Among all other Southern Baptists, the opposition to homosexuality was clear and strong. On the Convention's left wing, there was some room for doubt. It is unlikely that there were any more or less gay moderates than gay fundamentalists. It is not that moderates wish to practice homosexuality; their marginally greater tolerance appeared to be more a statement of principle than preference.

Dancing, movies, and card-playing—traditional "don'ts" of southern culture—were simply no longer taboo among the majority of the Southern Baptists we surveyed. They were widely practiced among everyone to the left of center. Here the traditions of southern Protestantism were clearly losing their hold. Virtually no self-identified moderates, and very few moderate conservatives saw such pastimes as outside the range of possibility for Christians. Even in the conservative middle, the house was divided almost evenly on dancing and movies, with fully two-thirds accepting card-playing.

Only among fundamentalists did majorities still disapprove of these practices. On dancing and card-playing the differences between self-identified fundamentalists and fundamentalist conservatives were great enough to flag these practices as part of the fundamentalist identity. Those who chose that label meant to communicate that they were strict moralists, observers of strict rules for Christian living. Those with the same beliefs about the Bible who called themselves conservative instead were evidently communicating that they were a bit less straight-laced. Self-identified fundamentalists not only condemned drinking, swearing, and homosexuality—as did almost all other Southern Baptists—but they also condemn smoking, dancing, movies, and card-playing, prohibitions on which a majority in the denomination did not agree.

On these issues of lifestyle and Christian practice, the gap between the Southern Baptist Convention's right and left wings was again very wide. On the right, all deviation from traditional southern norms was condemned. On the left, some taboos were completely gone, while others were widely contested and changing rapidly. In the middle, drinking, swearing, and homosexuality were still uniformly prohibited, but dancing, movies, cards (and to a lesser extent smoking) were accepted by enough people to keep them from being the taboos they once were. For those on each side of the middle, the lines were clear—either acceptance or rejection of southern norms—but in the middle, no such consensus existed. The conservative Southern Baptist middle half was caught between the strict moralists on its right and the changing times embraced by those on its left.

Evangelism and Cooperation

Fundamentalists were interested in strict moral standards at least in part because they wanted unsaved people to notice their distinctive Christian life. They wanted to be able to tell others that Christ really does make a difference. This kind of personal soul-winning was another of the practices on which fundamentalists and moderates differed.

Fundamentalists were convinced that people who do not believe the Bible and do not live a disciplined Christian life could not possibly be very interested in evangelism and missions. In his analysis of the SBC controversy, conservative author James Hefley asserted, "conservative pastors are generally more aggressive, energetic, and evangelistic at the local level than moderates. The result is seen in baptisms." As proof he listed the top twenty-five churches in baptisms in 1984, many of them pastored by the leaders of the SBC's right wing.[41] Our data also reflect that churches whose pastors or lay leaders are fundamentalist tend, on average, to report more baptisms than churches whose pastors or lay leaders are moderate. However, such figures on total baptisms mask one very important factor—the bigger the church, the more baptisms it is likely to have, and church size (as we will see in chapter 5) is related to theological position. Since we knew the sizes of the churches represented in our study, we could compare churches of similar sizes whose leaders differed in theological orientation. When we did that, we found no difference attributable to theology. Among churches of similar size, fundamentalists were more likely to have a large number of baptisms (fifty or more), but they were also more likely to have none at all. The fundamentalist average represents the mid-point between those two extremes. Moderates reported a consistently average number of baptisms in all church sizes.

That does not, however, mean that the perceived differences in evangelism were not present. One clear difference between fundamentalists and moderates was the practice of rebaptizing adults who became convinced that their earlier decision to be saved was invalid. One fourth of the conservatives and fundamentalists reported that at least some of their churchs' baptisms in 1987 would be of rebaptized adults. However, only 11 percent of self-identified moderates anticipated any rebaptisms. Moderates were more likely to see faith as a developmental process. Its character was expected to change at various stages in life, and rebaptism to recognize those changes was irrelevant. Fundamentalists, however, insisted on a strict conversionist model of faith. Either one is saved or not saved. Those who are seeking new or renewed commitments must be undergoing a conversion and therefore need to be baptized. This practice became common enough in fundamentalist churches in the 1980s to become the butt of jokes among moderates. They laughed knowingly about fundamentalist church members who were baptized so often they stayed wrinkled from the water.

Perhaps the most dramatic difference between fundamentalist and moderate practices, however, was the fundamentalist enthusiasm for soul winning. When asked if their church "puts a lot of emphasis on evangelism and soul winning," over three quarters (77 percent) of self-identified fundamentalists said that was very true, and another 17 percent said it was somewhat true. Only 6 percent disagreed or were unsure. Self-identified moderates, on the other hand, were more ambivalent. Only 14 percent said it was *very* true, while 61 percent chose somewhat true, and 25 percent disagreed or were unsure. Similarly, when asked about their own personal soul-winning practices, fundamentalists outscored moderates. Nearly three fourths (74 percent) of fundamentalists said it was very true that they "share the plan of salvation whenever [they] get a chance." Less than a quarter (18 percent) of moderates were so sure. Twenty-four percent either disagreed with that statement or were unsure, compared to 4 percent of fundamentalists. Again, most moderates said it was somewhat true.

The differences here were between fundamentalists who were overwhelmingly and enthusiastically committed to soul winning as their form of evangelism and moderates who were more ambivalent—the difference between very true and somewhat true. Many moderates were uncomfortable with the rhetoric of winning souls. Others practiced a more gradual and nurturing approach, especially with their children. They still managed to baptize roughly equivalent numbers, but they chose different words to describe what was happening in people's lives. Fundamentalists, on the other hand knew exactly what to do and which words to use. Evangelism meant seeking individual, life-changing, once-and-for-all decisions by whatever means possible.

Therefore, it made no sense to fundamentalists to talk about cooperating with moderates to do missions. They were convinced that moderates had neither the missionary zeal nor the commitment to scripture that was necessary for missions to succeed. If the gospel being preached came from a flawed Bible, it was no gospel at all. Fundamentalists did not believe that, "If we can agree on what we want to *do* together, we do not need to worry about agreeing on what we believe." Eighty four percent of self-identified fundamentalists disagreed with that statement. For them, believing must come before doing. Said one fundamentalist pastor, "A body of people working together need a common ground. It's not enough to just say 'let's love each other.' . . . The virgin birth, atonement, resurrection, and second coming of Jesus—these keep Southern Baptists together." In contrast, only about a fourth (28 percent) of the self-identified moderates said that belief is more important than common goals.

That disagreement over the virtues and grounds of cooperation was borne out when fundamentalists and moderates came together on the Convention's Peace Committee. Moderates and others on the committee soon discovered that their fundamentalist counterparts valued their vision of truth far more than they valued peace. In their view, it was simply not possible for truth to compromise with error, for preachers of the gospel to cooperate with "skunks." On the Bible (and by deduction on missions) there could be no pluralism or diversity.

Freedom and Toleration

The theme that runs through all these differences is the theme of individual freedom versus strict codes of belief and conduct. Fundamentalists argued that lines must be drawn, and moderates argued that there must be greater freedom. Fundamentalists accused them of bowing to the pressures of modern times, but moderates replied that toleration is not a new idea for Baptists. Priesthood of the believer meant, for them, not only limits on pastoral authority but also limits on the ability of one Baptist to impose interpretation on another. For moderates, this was the root issue over which they were fighting. Just as surely as fundamentalists would point to an error-free Bible as the crucial criterion by which everything else must be decided, so moderates claimed that the Baptist principle of "soul competency" was the first principle on which they would build their identity. Speaking to the 1986 Forum, Georgia businessman Norman Cavender declared,

> It is the call of liberty, more than any other concept, that Baptists have seized and proclaimed, have honored and practiced. Baptist bells have always been the bells of liberty. All that we are as Baptists can be summed up in that word—liberty. It is what we cherish; it is what we preach. The song of liberty is the sound of the living out of the Baptist faith.

That freedom was the real issue, not theology, was proved in moderate minds by the results of the 1985–1988 presidential races. The two men who carried the moderate banner in those years were avowed inerrantists. Even the strictest fundamentalist could not argue that theology was the reason people should oppose either Winfred Moore or Richard Jackson. They were opposed by fundamentalists because they would include moderates among their appointees and nominees. They would not support the fundamentalist plan for "restoring balance" on the boards. As one moderate told us, "I wouldn't give you a nickel for the difference between Moore's theology and Stanley's theology, but Moore's the more reasonable man. He's fairer. He wants balance, and he isn't afraid of diversity." Moore himself put it this way to us, "I doubt that there's a thin dime's worth of difference between where we [Stanley and I] stand theologically. . . . The difference is political, a different philosophy about how we as Southern Baptists should do our mission work." Moore and other moderates thought that mission work should be done cooperatively, even if there were differences over theology. Cooperation is a necessary corollary to toleration.

And toleration was central to how they defined what it meant to be Baptist. Cavender, Moore, and other moderates read Baptist history as a crusade on behalf of individual religious choice. They remembered the early English and German and American Baptists who were persecuted for refusing to allow the state to make their religious choices for them. They cited revered twentieth century Baptists E. Y. Mullins, Herschel Hobbs, and George W. Truett as supporters of the idea that "soul competency is the distinctive Baptist contribution to religion." Without individual soul competency, conversion, believers' baptism, and all the other Baptist distinctives make no sense. Standing on this historical and theological ground, church history professor Walter Shurden said, "I am opposed to every form of ecclesiastical imperialism and theological totalitarianism, and I am opposed to it even when advocated by Southern Baptists."

In 1986, we asked our survey panel to respond to the statement, "Baptists should have the individual freedom to interpret the Bible for themselves and be tolerant of differing interpretations." Forty five percent strongly agreed; 41 percent agreed, and the remaining 14 percent were unsure or disagreed.[42] The idea of toleration is clearly valued among these Baptists. But its value varied depending on the theological position of the person responding. Agreement was nearly unanimous among moderates. Only 7 percent of moderate conservatives, and not a single self-identified moderate was unsure or disagreed with this statement. Virtually all those who disagreed were in the fundamentalist and conservative camps. More tellingly, however, there were differences in whether people strongly agreed. Thirty seven percent of fundamentalists, 39 percent of conservatives, and 73 percent of moderates said they strongly agreed with this statement. Just as fundamentalists responded with strength of agreement to statements about soul winning, so moderates responded passionately to statements about freedom and toleration. In each case the two groups agreed in substance, but disagreed in emphasis.

When they were most true to these principles of toleration, moderates even embraced fundamentalists. They spoke of needing the diversity fundamentalists represented. Moderate leader Cecil Sherman told us, "It's fine with me if they say they're inerrantists, if they believe this or that; that's not my problem. In our polity, a measure of freedom for the individual is allowed." As difficult as it sometimes was, he and other leaders urged moderates to be inclusive, to invite fundamentalists to speak, to sit with them in decision-making groups, to listen to their concerns. However, they also became convinced that fundamentalists were not willing to afford them the same inclusion.

Shurden, Sherman, and other moderates became convinced that the fundamentalist leaders of their denomination did indeed represent "ecclesiastical imperialism and theological totalitarianism." They saw in the fundamentalist concern for doctrine the threat of creedalism and conformity. Sherman told us that the fundamentalist answer to the threat of liberalism is conformity, "giving you a correct way to believe. Some of us are resisting that," he said. "We see the denomination as beginning to insist on conformity." Moderates pointed out that even the Baptist Faith and Message statement does not presume to be a creed for all Baptists. In their view, no creed could ever be imposed on true Baptists who respect their own liberty. Yet they feared that just such creedalism was growing in the denomination. They saw people wanting to pin down exactly what should be believed, precisely what constituted correct Baptist doctrine.

Moderates were especially disturbed at the way teachers were being hampered in the classroom. Moderate presidential candidate Winfred Moore told us, "Our professors are under a cloud of suspicion, afraid to write anything, because things will be taken out of context, xeroxed, and widely distributed." Others echoed his concern that scholars were unable to exercise their scholarship. Southern Baptist professors had long known they had to write for a very conservative audience, but since 1979, their writing and teaching had slowly been pushed toward ideas that could be explained in terms acceptable to fundamentalists. Even if they did not sign a creed, a more narrow theology was shaping their work.[43]

Fundamentalists, of course, disagreed vigorously about what was happening in Southern Baptist classrooms. They were convinced that liberalism was being taught and that those teaching it ought to be fired. Charles Stanley asserted that "some seminary professors have written enough to indict them." Over eighty percent of fundamentalists agreed or strongly agreed that "There are people teaching in Southern Baptist colleges and seminaries who do not believe what Baptists ought to believe." And 77 percent of fundamentalists agreed that people on the convention payroll ought to teach what most Baptists believe. Stanley worried when professors at one seminary would not answer his doctrinal questions. "I don't believe any Southern Baptist would say I don't have a right to ask. . . . If he's teaching my son, he's accountable to me, if I'm paying his salary." Stanley said that students at Southeastern had told him that not "a man on this faculty . . . believes in the historical validity of the first 11 chapters of Genesis."[44] Soon after he was elected to the SBC presidency for the second time, Adrian Rogers added his voice to the calls for seminary conformity to Southern Baptist majority opinion. He explained that if most Baptists believed that pickles had souls, Southern Baptist professors ought to teach that pickles had souls. With a kind of gallows humor, one seminary professor responded by bringing a large jar of kosher dills to class—just in case they needed to learn theology.

The gesture did not, however, indicate that professor's acceptance of Rogers' ideas about limiting freedom. Most moderates were first of all unconvinced that heresy was being taught, but also less insistent that majority beliefs should define the boundaries of seminary curricula. Barely one fourth of self-identified moderates concurred about the presence of heresy, and some of them wrote in the margins that schools should be diverse. Nearly half (42 percent), on the other hand, agreed with the large majority of conservatives and fundamentalists who wanted majority views reflected in the classroom. On that question, moderate agreement was distinct from conservative and fundamentalist opinion only by being less overwhelming. However, since moderates did not think current teaching was out of bounds, their willingness to insist that employees stay inside majority opinion may also reflect their broader definition of what those majority opinions were.

For fundamentalists, the question of boundaries was twofold. First, the problem was where to draw them—a question to which we will return. Second was the question of who was affected by them. Since the idea of believer priests makes it difficult for one Baptist to tell another what to believe, any drawing of lines is problematic. But when professors objected that their individual freedom to interpret scripture was being infringed upon by the limits of majority opinion, fundamentalist leaders replied that they may think anything they like; but they may not teach it if they expect to be paid by Southern Baptists. Said a leading fundamentalist pastor of a hypothetical professor who cannot teach inerrancy, "He should say, 'I recognize that that is the idea upon which this seminary was founded, and I can't operate within those parameters. So I'll find me a place where I can operate within the parameters.'" The issue of individual freedom of conscience was not relevant here, according to the leaders of the Convention's right wing. The relevant issue was whether Southern Baptists have to pay people to teach things Baptists do not believe.

Cecil Sherman found such logic ironic. As a local pastor, he would be unaffected by fundamentalist restrictions. "Interestingly, they say they don't want individuals to conform, but only those who work for the denomination. I can be a heretic if I want to! Of course, they think that the conformity of those who write our literature, etc., will solve our problems." Indeed, fundamentalist leaders were willing to work for the kind of gradual change that would be effected by a fundamentalist denominational bureaucracy. They believed that when professors and writers were all working within acceptable boundaries, the rest of the denomination would naturally follow.

Where those acceptable boundaries could be drawn was the other problem. Speaking to the 1988 Inerrancy Conference, former SBC president James T. Draper proposed an "irreducible minimum theology." "I know of no one in the Southern Baptist Convention who is seeking lock-step conformity in every area of biblical interpretation," he said. "Southern Baptists, and Bible-believing Christians in general, have long differed on many things." The question, however, is "How much diversity in biblical interpretation can we accommodate?" He acknowledged that drawing the line would be difficult, but made a proposal of the doctrines he thought essential: "The deity and humanity of Jesus Christ; the penal, substitutionary atonement of Christ . . . ; the literal bodily resurrection, ascension and return of Christ; justification by God's grace through faith alone."[45] Reminiscent of the Fundamentals proposed in an earlier era, these beliefs were proposed as the boundary beyond which Baptists could not go.

He and others were unafraid of the idea of boundaries. Fundamentalist pastor Ed Young complained to the Pastors Conference, "If we are committed to theological pluralism . . . then we have no biblical base to stand on." Another fundamentalist pastor told us that he and others "want to be as broadminded as Jesus, who said 'narrow is the way.'" Concrete limits would have to wait for the slow working out of new institutional policies (the subject of chapter 7), but fundamentalists were not afraid to face the limits of freedom.

Those who were less firmly committed to fundamentalism, however, found it much more difficult to decide exactly what the Bible teaches and thus where the limits should be. Even moderates sometimes admitted that *some* boundaries were needed, although they did not agree with Draper on where they should be. They supported the idea that a Baptist school ought to be distinctive in some ways. But they were neither willing to draw the line so precisely nor so willing to draw lines at all. One moderate leader said that he recognized the need for church-related schools to have some boundaries, but he did not want to be the one to tell those professors what they could not teach. Whether out of indecision or humility, moderates were simply less willing to make proposals about the limits of freedom. One Baptist state paper editor put it this way, "People can believe a lot of things and be Baptist. They cannot believe some things and still be Baptist. But there is no way they can be Baptist without believing in freedom."[46]

Who Are We and Who Are They?

With such widespread differences in theology, lifestyle, and church practice, it is little surprise that fundamentalists and moderates in the Southern Baptist Convention came to view each other as outsiders and enemies. When moderates met in the Forum and fundamentalists spoke at the Pastors Conference, each referred to the other gathering as "they" and their own as "we." People on both sides commented about how good it was to "be among friends" in a place where "we all feel the same way." The publications on each side painted the other as at best misguided and amusing, and at worst, heretical and non-Baptist.

Each side had distinct ideas about what made someone a true Baptist. Fundamentalists looked first and foremost to doctrine: correct ideas about the Bible, the virgin birth, the Second Coming, and related issues. True Baptists are also evangelistic, caring more about the salvation of souls than about any other condition of humanity. The evidence of a Bible-believing, Bible-preaching Baptist church was the number of people it baptized and whether it was growing. And true Baptists certainly would not dabble in unbiblical ideas about "servant leadership" or, especially, women becoming pastors. A Baptist church that is doing what it ought to do would offer clear teaching on who has ultimate authority and how Christians should live.

A messenger to the 1986 Atlanta convention told us about searching for a new church when he moved. He noted the contrast between moderate churches and the fundamentalist ones he liked.

> I sort of had been wondering why I couldn't find a church that was more evangelical, teaching the Word the way it should be, not the Social Gospel, a church where people were being saved, being

taught to live the Christian life. . . . I picked the best church I could find at the time. The church I'm going to now has a dynamic pastor, and the church is growing at a phenomenal rate. The people there have a sweet spirit and have dedication to the Lord—they're interested in doing His work and not ashamed that they are evangelical type Christians. And they are living the Christian life.

He liked a "dynamic" pastor, correct teaching of the Word, and being taught to live the Christian life; and he did not see those things happening in the moderate churches he visited. He was willing to cast his vote in Atlanta to make sure that his vision of Baptist life prevailed.

Another messenger to that convention noted all the intangible, but obvious things he looked for in a good church:

The Sunday School, the type of teachers they have, the messages you get on Sunday morning, the type on Sunday night, the music program, the spirit of the music. . . . You feel a warmth there; you leave feeling you have worshipped. You leave wanting to live the Christian life, instead of just denying the fact that you are a Baptist or a Christian and feeling ashamed that you are a member of a church that is not doing what it needs to be doing.

Those feelings of warmth and real worship are tied to hundreds of small details no one notices until they are missing. They are as pervasive as which hymns are sung and the decor of the church auditorium (and whether it is called that or a sanctuary). The definition of a "good church" is tied to which translation of scripture is used and what the church does on Wednesday night. Those less tangible matters of taste and habit are sometimes as important in creating perceptions and identities as are matters of ideology and morality. People simply know that they are "at home" in some churches and not in others.

And it was often those very matters of style that other Southern Baptists found offensive. Moderates did not like listening to triumphant music about the Second Coming and scripture readings from the King James Version. They "really worshipped" when the service was planned, dignified, and highly literate. They did not like passionate sermons that "dangled sinners over the fires of hell." Among many moderate Southern Baptists, "home" included creative liturgy and a rhetoric of community involvement and individual growth.

But moderate Southern Baptists would be unlikely to say that any one doctrine or practice made a church more or less "Baptist." A true Baptist, as they see it, is too committed to freedom to impose such matters of taste—or even conscience—on someone else. For moderates, "being Baptist means freedom."[47] It means freedom for individual interpretation of scripture and individual accountability to God in salvation. It means freedom for laity and clergy to work together as partners. It means freedom for the local church to direct its own affairs. It means the kind of toleration that makes cooperation possible. And it means that the church must remain free from interference by the state.

Alongside freedom, moderate Baptists placed cooperation as the hallmark of their denomination. One moderate leader told us that there are

> a couple of things that I think are important about our Baptist heritage, maybe some contributions that we've made on the way. One is this thing of religious liberty. That's very important. Fundamentalists play that down, and that's where the rubber hits the road. [That is] where Baptists were born. Our Baptist ancestors were considered radical protesters. . . . [But] Southern Baptists have added something at least for our purposes that's very important. . . . That is this spirit of cooperation. The idea of religious liberty leads one to almost independence, without relationship with anyone else. I'm not there either. We have this spirit of cooperation which we have within the form of a program of missions that we call the Cooperative Program. I am free to think, and so are you. Even though we disagree, we still work together.

Retired Sunday School Board president Grady Cothen spoke of "togetherness, diversity and synthesis" in describing the Southern Baptist heritage. He told an audience at the Southern Baptist Seminary that the "modern cry for conformity violates the basis for Southern Baptist cooperation." He affirmed the centrality of scripture, but called for "theological unity, not uniformity." Creeds, he said, are alien to the Baptist way of thinking.[48] He and others had come to fear that required conservative doctrines—premillennialism, inerrancy, abortion, opposition to ordained women, and more—would become litmus tests for employees and uniform guidelines for programs. They feared both the idea of conformity and the ideas to which they would have to conform.

In a number of ways, moderates came to resent and deride fundamentalist leaders. They were characterized as unqualified interlopers—people who had neither paid their denominational dues nor adequately prepared themselves for leadership. Moderates pointed out that many of the "Dr.'s" in the fundamentalist camp got those degrees by correspondence or as honorary awards from unaccredited fundamentalist schools. They also pointed out that many fundamentalist churches gave only token amounts to the denomination's Cooperative Program. Indeed, compared to moderates, the churches of our fundamentalist respondents were four times as likely (22 percent versus 5 percent), to give less than 5 percent of their budget to CP. And they were less than half as likely (23 percent versus 57 percent), compared to moderates, to give more than 10 percent to the denomination.[49] It did not seem right to moderates that people who did not give to the Convention should be sitting on boards of directors making decisions about the money moderates gave.

They also pointed out that some fundamentalist leaders and nominees were unknown to the Baptist establishment in their own cities and states.[50] Without ever having served on associational or state committees, people were being elevated to national denominational positions. Moderates were not sure they could trust people who had not already proven themselves in denominational service. It seemed to moderates that fundamentalists did not know enough about the system or its history to make good decisions. A moderate leader told us, "I think its sad when a man says 'I love you' to his wife but knows nothing about her past, has no appreciation for her heritage, who she is, what she can do. . . . We are now seeing leaders in our convention who say they love the SBC, but who know nothing about its heritage, who we really are." Fundamentalists, of course, quickly pointed out that they had been shut out of such service in the past, that they considered the approval of the denominational establishment a liability not an asset, and that they had previously withheld their dollars on grounds of conscience. Nevertheless, they seemed to moderates like outsiders who did not deserve to run institutions they had not previously supported.

It frustrated moderates that fundamentalists were not willing to take their complaints through the existing system. They argued that if there were problems, the system could handle them; there was no need to change it. Southwestern Seminary president Russell Dilday told Charles Stanley that if his charges of liberalism were true, "we ought to deal with them. It is my position that we have a way within our convention of doing that." Stanley's son replied to Dilday, "The traditional method doesn't work." His father added, "We kept saying, 'There's a problem, there's a problem.' After a while what do you have to do? We've been by the process."[51]

It seemed to moderates that fundamentalists were simply unwilling to compromise or to cooperate. Once gaining majority status, fundamentalists felt no compulsion to listen to a minority they considered wrong. Winfred Moore, Don Wideman, and Henry Huff, moderate Convention vice presidents, all complained publicly that Charles Stanley took few, if any, of their suggestions for key committee appointments. Stanley listened, but had his own list in mind. On the Peace Committee, moderates discovered that there was a fundamentalist agenda, and compromise was unlikely. One moderate member told us, "The Peace Committee is just another place for the fundamentalists to win. Our meetings are war, not peace." Another member agreed, "They want to win and they want you to lose. They want to win totally. . . . One-third says there is no middle ground. We have to win, you have to lose." Because fundamentalists do have a clear agenda and a strong commitment to it, they embraced the role of dissenter, sometimes proudly calling themselves "troublemakers from way back." Compromise and cooperation were in fact no virtues for fundamentalists, and moderates could only respond with frustration and anger. A moderate board member, in his last term of office, complained that "fundamentalists are mean. We conservatives can live with their theology, but they can't live with ours. And we *can't* live with their methodology, which is judgmental, authoritarian, and legalistic. [Under them] Southern Baptists will become twentieth century Pharisees—narrow and anti-Baptistic."

Behind the frustration, for many moderates, was a deep cynical distrust. They wondered where fundamentalist money came from and who was involved behind the scenes. They sometimes speculated about the personal and political motives of fundamentalist leaders. They discovered that some classroom lectures and phone conversations were being secretly taped and sent to Dallas and soon envisioned the practice to be all-pervasive.[52] They began to assume that every strategy meeting would be reported to fundamentalist leaders.

Moderates also wondered if they were losing elections fair and square. They knew that fundamentalists sometimes baptized very young children, making those children full church members. Moderates often told tales of seeing five-year-olds with official messenger badges and ballots, and they wondered just how many preteens were extending the voting power of fundamentalist fathers. In Dallas, stories were rampant that local fundamentalist churches brought busloads to the convention on Wednesday night and gave them packs of ballots left behind by other messengers who had come and gone. Even when Convention officials investigated and determined the stories not true, moderates were still not sure. Some moderates even tried not to sit in recognizable blocks so as to prevent buckets of moderate ballots from disappearing on the way to the counting room. After the disaster in Dallas, moderates were thoroughly convinced that both parliamentary rulings and access to microphones were being used by the chair to prevent the moderate message from being heard. Moderates were positive that fundamentalists were master organizers and ruthless politicians; they could not help suspecting that they might also be willing to break a few rules for a good cause.

At the very least, moderates came to feel that fundamentalists were using their legitimate power to unfair advantage. Ninety percent of self-identified moderates (and 74 percent of moderate conservatives) agreed that "It is not fair for fundamentalists in the SBC to appoint only other fundamentalists to agency and seminary boards." Using the appointive power of the president to exclude loyal, nonfundamentalist Southern Baptists from boards seemed unfair and abusive to moderates.

But the most blatant of the abuse moderates perceived was the parliamentarians' ruling in Dallas that prevented a moderate challenge to fundamentalist nominees.[53] About a third of the messengers we surveyed saw this as a mistake, but an honest one. Another third did not object, trusting that the judgment of the parliamentarians was right. But the third on the left saw the whole thing as unfair manipulation. As usual, fundamentalists and moderates differed widely in their perceptions of what happened. Almost none (9 percent) of the fundamentalists saw it as manipulation, and most (63 percent) saw it as the right decision. Almost none (4 percent) of the moderates saw it as the right decision, and a large majority (74 percent) saw it as manipulation.

A majority (52 percent) of even the conservatives in the middle were critical of the presiding they saw in Dallas. They were about equally divided on whether that year's breakdown in order came from lack of skill or deliberate design. Fundamentalists, on the other hand, were almost uniformly (75 percent) supportive of the "strong" presiding represented by Charles Stanley, while moderates were even more uniformly (84 percent) critical. The next year in Atlanta, their fury with Stanley was intensified when he delivered his presidential address just hours before his successor would be chosen. One moderate in the audience summed up his message as: "If you don't vote for Rogers, you are going to hell." Another fumed, "Did you hear Stanley's speech—yeah speech—that wasn't a sermon. And he says he isn't political!" By using his sermon time to tout the fundamentalist agenda—and indirectly Adrian Rogers' candidacy— moderates felt that Stanley had again taken unfair advantage of his power. It was another evidence of the abuse of power moderates perceived in the new fundamentalist Convention leadership.

Fundamentalists, of course, would quickly respond that moderates were only getting back what they used to dish out. Fundamentalists were shut out of positions of power, kept from speaking, and labeled troublemakers. Said one fundamentalist pastor, "Up until ten years ago . . . I never got the opportunity to be in any place of leadership, because the winners 'took all' and I wasn't part of their group." Moderates caucused backstage and controlled how issues were presented. They controlled the press, the institutions, and usually the presidency. Fundamentalists perceived that moderates had been trying to impose their agenda on Southern Baptists for years. It was only right, said fundamentalists, that they have a chance now. While moderates might admit that they had excluded fundamentalists in the past, they saw it as a kind of natural selection process. People who went to school together, stuck together. As one moderate told us, "They [fundamentalists] just weren't in the crowd; they didn't go to Southern together. They weren't part of the brotherhood." But he went on, "What the fundamentalists are doing is very intentional, without that innocence. Ethically that is different." The old moderate exclusion, they argued, was different in kind from the new fundamentalist campaign.

This clash of perspectives took human form in a 1987 interchange between Lynn Clayton, moderate editor of the Louisiana *Baptist Message* and outgoing member of the Christian Life Commission's board of directors, and Paige Patterson, president of Criswell College and leader of the fundamentalist movement. Clayton had wanted to speak during the debate on the Peace Committee report and had waited patiently at a microphone while the debate meandered through amendments and substitute motions. He never got to speak because time ran out and the question was called. He walked down from the platform and confronted Patterson with the unfair use of power he perceived. He complained that it was unconscionable to keep people from expressing themselves, to silence even a minority. Patterson looked him straight in the eye and said, "Now you know how I felt for twenty-five years."

Another fundamentalist leader recounted how his questions to the Baylor board of trustees were met with suspicion and hostility. He was treated as a troublemaker. He became convinced that the institutions his church was supporting through the Cooperative Program were unresponsive to his concerns. "You get tired of buying bullets for somebody else to shoot at you," he told us. One of his fellow pastors agreed that trustee boards had been "stacked with people who were more loyal to the denomination than to the scriptures." They were rubber stamps who did whatever the bureaucracy asked them to do. What was needed, both thought, was a thorough housecleaning, a "course correction." In support of that, every president since 1979 had appointed solid inerrantists and would continue to do so until balance was restored.

Fundamentalists were particularly concerned to have strong trustees because they saw the agencies and schools as dominated by a hidden liberal agenda. Even if the persons on the boards had been personally conservative, they were being duped into trusting officials who were systematically promoting liberalism. Therefore, it was crucial to have a president who realized the danger and would make the right kind of appointments. In 1985, Paige Patterson made this point about his objection to Winfred Moore. "I don't think he's a liberal," Patterson said, "but he's being used by them."[54] Another fundamentalist leader agreed that Moore had the misguided attitude that those in power should be trusted. This was not a good time for going along with whoever is in charge, he said. He and others were deeply suspicious that those in charge would lead the denomination toward liberalism. Only 13 percent of the self-identified fundamentalists we surveyed said they were "very confident" that the denomination's schools and agencies were "doctrinally sound." This compared to 68 percent of self-identified moderates who had full confidence in their institutions. An even smaller 8 percent of fundamentalists were very confident that the institutions were "responsive to ordinary Southern Baptists." Again, 52 percent of self-identified moderates disagreed, claiming that the agencies were responsive. For those reasons, fundamentalists thought exclusive fundamentalist appointments are necessary, not unfair. Sixty-five percent of self-identified fundamentalists disagreed or strongly disagreed with the statement that appointing only fundamentalists is unfair.

They disagreed most of all because they did not want their denomination to fall to liberalism. They were convinced that a real danger existed. They pointed to questionable teaching in the seminaries, books published by Broadman Press, and materials from the Sunday School Board. They also pointed to the programs and materials of the Christian Life Commission and the Baptist Joint Committee on Public Affairs as evidence that a liberal social agenda was influencing Southern Baptist life. They feared that liberalism would destroy Baptist faith in the Bible and the denomination's evangelistic and mission fervor. They did not want to become like the liberal, mainline denominations—cold, dead, and losing members. Therefore, they were determined to fight. They would oppose both the liberals themselves and those who refused to see the danger they posed.

Needless to say, then, fundamentalists perceived the political struggles of the denomination differently from moderates. What fundamentalists did was necessary; what moderates did was mean and power-hungry. In his interview with Gary North, Judge Pressler detailed the devious tactics he thought moderates had used in the 1985 campaign. He claimed that seminary presidents Lolley, Honeycutt, and Dilday had used "every means at their disposal to try to defeat Dr. Stanley, the incumbent president, including the alumni lists, the publications of their schools, their personnel at their schools." He asserted that they had also used WATS lines to drum up support for Winfred Moore, and he labeled the campaign a "vicious, vitriolic attack." Having denominational officials take public positions in the battle seemed to fundamentalists completely unfair. They were sure that vast institutional resources were being rallied against them—and with money they had given to those institutions through the Cooperative Program.

Even the events in Dallas were perceived differently by fundamentalists. They saw the attempt to substitute an entire slate of moderate candidates as a blatant slap in the face. It represented divisiveness, not a
desire for peace. Charles Stanley told the Evangelists Conference that
afternoon that "we have extended the loving warm hand of love and cooperation" and have gotten this trouble in return. But it was not just
peace he was worried about. He urged his hearers to return and vote that
night because these appointments determine the direction of the Convention. "If they—and I say 'they' because it is they—if they are able to
totally replace committee on committees, then friends we've got real
trouble." He had already lost a key vote in that battle. This committee
represented the core of power (the "jugular"), and losing the ability to
place committed fundamentalists on it would represent a crucial loss of
power. As we have already seen, he won that vote, and a large majority
of fundamentalists supported both his intent and his methods in doing so.

The fundamentalists in the Southern Baptist Convention were very
clear that they had an enemy: liberalism and all its allies. And moderates
in the Convention were equally clear that they had an enemy: narrow
creedal conformity. The lines of battle had been drawn, and people on
each side felt the pain of exclusion and alienation from the other. The two
sides differed dramatically on what they considered important about being a Baptist, what they believed about the Bible, what the role of women
should be, what kind of life a Christian should lead, even on national
political issues. They often could not even worship in each other's
churches. While the majority of Southern Baptists were caught in the
middle, two distinct parties had emerged on their flanks. People in the
middle found some affinity with people on each side, but the people on
the two sides lived in worlds apart.

5. The Social Sources of Division

S outhern Baptists were certainly not the first religious group to become bitterly divided. Other people, in other times and places, have also found themselves on opposite sides of a developing religious chasm. A description of the "Hicksite" separation among early nineteenth century Pennsylvania Friends (Quakers) is in fact strangely reminiscent of Baptists in Dallas.

> In the months before Philadelphia Yearly Meeting of 1827, Friends were apprehensive. The discord which had troubled the Society for several years had been particularly bitter. . . . Yearly Meeting was unusually crowded when it opened. The very first session confirmed the suspicions of each faction about the other. Orthodox Friends thought the Hicksites were trying to pack the house, and Hicksites felt that the Orthodox were seeking to postpone important business until the delegates became too tired to engage in debate. . . . Disorder strengthened [the] already strong belief that Friends could no longer sit together in peace.[1]

In the late 1980s, it was not yet clear whether Baptists would be able to "sit together in peace." The denomination had not formally divided, but informally the divisions were very real.

How did such a situation come about? Were there processes at work that have appeared in religious movements before? How did a conservative, successful denomination develop such distinct fundamentalist and progressive wings? Was theology the primary explanation for the differences among Southern Baptists: and even if it was, what explained the differences in theology?

Social scientists have long looked for the ways in which religious beliefs are connected to the everyday worlds in which they are sustained and passed on to new generations. Differences in style from one region to another and differences in beliefs from one culture to another suggest that people whose lives are different make sense of those lives differently. They appropriate the symbols, stories, and traditions that are available and plausible to them. And those same stories, in turn, shape their thoughts and actions. It is as if the sacred world is in conversation with the everyday world, each affecting the other. The universal experiences of birth and death are given meaning by the symbols and rituals with which they are surrounded. But the mundane world of working and eating, in all its varigated diversity, may be sacralized, as well.[2] Across time and around the world, peoples in varying circumstances have made religious sense of their lives with practices as different as the times and places in which they were located.

More than fifty years ago, H. Richard Niebuhr argued that the divisions among American Protestants were primarily the result of just such social differences as class, race, region, and ethnicity.[3] He argued that the denomination to which a person belonged was more a matter of birth than of belief, and that groups of similar belief might divide over matters patently nontheological. The most obvious example in American history was the division of Methodist, Baptist, and Presbyterian denominations over the issues of slavery and sectionalism. But equally glaring were the ethnic churches in the Lutheran and Catholic traditions and the divisions between sedate east and frontier west.

In addition, Niebuhr argued, the cycle of birth, growth, and maturity in religious organizations is intimately linked to changes in social class. He saw new religious groups (sects) often evolving over time into a more institutionalized form (denominations) suitable to their rising status as a group. That, in turn, left denominations vulnerable to rebellion and schism from their own less fortunate members. Another new religious group was then formed from the bottom, to represent the interests of those who are disenfranchised by the middle-class propriety of the denomination's mainstream.[4] A number of studies have since demonstrated the degree to which the religious practices of the comfortable do indeed differ from those of the less privileged. It has not always been clear, however, whether class differences are the only social sources of religious divisions or even whether class differences necessarily produce schism.[5]

Since World War II, the regional and ethnic differences Niebuhr observed have diminished in American life, blurring the social differences between American denominations. Sociologists W. Clark Roof and William McKinney have offered evidence that the old ascriptive bases for religious membership have eroded.[6] People make more individualized religious choices, less influenced by their "ascribed" statuses of region, class, and ethnicity. Although racial divisions are alive and well, other social bases for denominationalism have declined significantly.[7] Similarly, fellow sociologist Robert Wuthnow has argued that there are now broader differences *within* denominational boundaries than *between* them.[8] Niebuhr observed that social forces created distinct denominations; perhaps social forces are now creating distinct and competing parties within those same denominations.

When addressed to the Southern Baptist case, these hypotheses raise insistent questions. To what extent did issues of race or region explain why Baptists were fighting each other? To what extent did differences in social class explain who was discontented and who was satisfied with the establishment? And what role did education play in creating different parties within the denomination? Even if Niebuhr identified the wrong factors, was it still the case that Southern Baptist moderates were as much *socially* different from fundamentalists as they were *theologically* different? While the theological differences were real, it is also necessary for us to explore the ways in which those differences ran parallel to differences in the life experiences of these Baptists.

Differences in Social Status

Niebuhr hypothesized that those he called the "disinherited" were often the source of religious discontent and of new religious movements. He wrote,

> Whenever Christianity has become the religion of the fortunate and cultured and has grown philosophical, abstract, formal, and ethically harmless in the process, the lower strata of society find themselves religiously expatriated by a faith which neither meets their psychological needs nor sets forth an appealing ethical ideal. In such a situation the right leader finds little difficulty in launching a new movement.[9]

To what extent could such status factors account for the differences between the Convention's right and left wings? Did moderates represent the fortunate, cultured, and formal version of Christianity, while fundamentalists represented the more spontaneous, simple, and unconditioned faith in divine revelation that Troeltsch and Niebuhr saw as more characteristic of people living in need?

We asked our respondents about their financial conditions while growing up and found that there was little theological difference between those who grew up rich and those who grew up poor. There were differences, however, between people who grew up in white collar and professional families and those whose parents were farmers or blue collar workers.[10] Those with higher status parents were twice as likely to be on the left side of the Baptist fence. More than a quarter of them (28 percent) were in the theologically moderate camp, compared to 12 percent of those whose parents farmed and 16 percent of those from blue collar homes. Conversely, those from farming and blue collar families were more likely than those from white collar and professional families to be on the fundamentalist side of the fence. The occupational status, but not the income, of the childhood families from which Baptists came seemed to have some relationship, then, to the beliefs they held and the parties they joined in this fight.

This suggests that the status differences that may exist between conservative dissidents and the denomination's establishment may be attributed to differences in culture and style of life more than to differences in raw economic privilege. What makes white collar and professional parents different is much more than the amount of money they make or the prestige they may have in the community.[11] White collar parents are much more likely to value independent thinking, creativity, and expressiveness in their children, while blue collar parents often try to teach obedience, routine, and self-control. Those differing values, after all, reflect the differences between working with supervisors and fixed tasks, compared to making one's own schedule and designing one's own work. These differences in up-bringing may be reflected in the theological party differences we see among Southern Baptists.

Their own place in the occupational structure also played a role in where these Baptists stood (see table 5.1). Again, households in which the husband had a professional job were slightly more likely to be inhabited by moderates than by fundamentalists (27 percent versus 24 percent), and more likely than any other occupational group to contain people left of center. Blue collar and farming households were just the opposite—containing far more fundamentalists than moderates (31 percent versus 7 percent and 34 percent versus 12 percent respectively). Conservative beliefs seemed to have a very strong hold within farming and blue collar households, while those who worked in higher status occupations were somewhat more likely to fall to the left of center and to identify with the moderate party in the denomination. Not only were moderates much more likely to have come from white collar and professional families, they were also more likely to live in such a family as adults. The result was a fairly stark contrast in the occupational composition of the convention's right and left wings. The world of moderates was almost exclusively a white collar and professional world, while fundamentalists were distributed broadly across farming, blue collar, white collar, and professional occupations.

There were also systematic differences in income across these groups (see the middle section of table 5.1). The higher the respondent's family income, the less likely they were to be fundamentalist. The number of self-identified fundamentalists is relatively constant (except in the highest category), but the number whose *beliefs* are to the right of center falls from 37 percent to 17 percent as people in the lowest income range are compared to those in each higher group. Likewise, the number of people to the left of center *rises* from 2 percent to 35 percent across the same range of income. In the lowest income groups, fundamentalists outnumber moderates almost ten to one, while in the highest income groups, moderates outnumber fundamentalists more than two to one. Those most

Table 5.1. Percent in Different Theological Parties by Status Factors

Theological Party	HUSBAND'S OCCUPATIONAL CATEGORY (Laity)				
	Farming	Blue Collar	White Collar	Profes- sional	Average
Self-Identified Moderate	8%	3%	11%	15%	10%
Moderate Conservative	4	4	8	12	8
Conservative	53	62	59	49	56
Fundamentalist Conservative	22	21	15	18	19
Self-Identified Fundamentalist	12	10	6	6	8
Total	99%	100%	99%	100%	101%
(Number of Cases)	(49)	(144)	(130)	(164)	(487)

Theological party	INCOME (Laity)					
	Less than $10,000	$10,000– 19,999	$20,000– 34,999	$35,000– 49,999	$50,000 or more	Average
Self-Identified Moderate	2%	8%	7%	7%	21%	8%
Moderate Conservative	0	3	7	13	14	7
Conservative	61	62	55	54	49	57
Fundamentalist Conservative	23	18	24	15	14	20
Self-Identified Fundamentalist	14	9	8	11	3	9
Total	100%	100%	101%	100%	101%	101%
(Number of Cases)	(64)	(140)	(203)	(100)	(70)	(576)

Theological Party	CHURCH SIZE AND LOCATION (Clergy)				
	Small Rural	Large Rural	Small Urban	Large Urban	Average
Self-Identified Moderate	15%	11%	3%	17%	13%
Moderate Conservative	9	12	15	17	13
Conservative	33	42	41	38	38
Fundamentalist Conservative	30	30	21	21	26
Self-Identified Fundamentalist	13	5	20	7	11
Total	100%	100%	100%	100%	101%
(Number of Cases)	(128)	(74)	(61)	(142)	(405)

NOTE: All differences between categories are statistically significant at $p < .01$. Some percentages do not total 100 due to rounding.

likely to sympathize with the cause of SBC fundamentalists, then, were those with less income. Those who had made it comfortably into the middle class were still a very conservative lot, but were much more likely than their "disinherited" friends to sympathize with the moderate cause.

The result is a left wing that has a much higher average income than those who are more conservative. Well over one third of moderates reported family incomes over \$35,000 in 1984, while fewer than half that many conservatives and fundamentalists were so fortunate. There were enough differences in social standing among Southern Baptists to make it likely that people would be aware of those differences and of the way they corresponded to the theological divisions. Among fundamentalists there was a sense of resentment at the privilege and "snobbery" of the other side. Among moderates there was condescension that varied between snickering and compassion. As Stark and Bainbridge argue, "The conception of who is and who is not 'our kind of people' is endemic in highly stratified groups."[12] In this case, 'our kind of people' had both social class and theological dimensions.

Another indirect measure of status in the Southern Baptist Convention was the size of the church to which one belonged. Bigger churches tended toward the middle- and upper-middle classes, while smaller ones were often thought of as less prestigeous. This was even more true among clergy, of course, where the size of a congregation was a way of measuring one's progress up the status ladder in the denomination. It is especially the case that pastors of very large churches (over 1,000 resident members) leaned significantly to the left and were more likely to identify themselves as moderates than pastors of smaller churches. This was all the more striking because this group contains those very few pastors of "super churches" whose responses were quite the opposite. They were few enough in number to be outweighed on average by the moderate sentiments of pastors in other large (but not huge) churches. Without the conservative super-church pastors, this group of clergy might have looked even more moderate than they did. Secondly, very few pastors of churches more than 300 in membership were willing to wear the fundamentalist label. If church size was a measure of a pastor's status, then status and fundamentalist identity were negatively related. Those who were more "successful" (as measured by church size) were less likely to be fundamentalist in theology and considerably less likely to claim that identity.

The relationship between church size, status, and theological positions can be seen even more clearly if city churches are looked at separately from country and small town churches (see the bottom section of table 5.1). A small church is "normal" in a rural or small town setting. In 1985

three-fourths of all rural and small town SBC churches had total memberships under 300.[13] And indeed, size seemed to make little difference
among rural pastors. The contrast between small and large churches was
much more dramatic among the urban pastors. Barely more than one
third (37 percent) of all SBC city churches had memberships under 300.
Therefore, pastoring a small church in an urban area was less "normal."
In an urban setting, one's neighbors were large, even huge, churches.
Pastoring such a small urban church may have engendered a good deal
more status anxiety than pastoring the same size church in the country.
Similarly, pastoring a large urban church may have carried a good deal
more weight than pastoring a large rural one.

Pastors of different size urban churches occupied very different positions in the denomination, then, and indeed those positions were reflected in theological identifications. Pastors of small urban churches were
almost three times as likely (20 percent versus 7 percent) to identify
themselves as fundamentalist, when compared to pastors of large urban
churches. And at the other extreme, large church pastors were over five
times as likely (17 percent versus 3 percent) to be self identified moderates compared to their small-church neighbors. Indeed, almost no pastors
of small urban churches called themselves moderate. These party identifications reflected real differences in belief. Forty-one percent of small
church pastors fell to the right of center, compared to 28 percent of their
counterparts in large churches. Thirty-four percent of large church pastors fell to the left of center, compared to 18 percent of those in small
churches. Again, it should be remembered that these differences are actually diminished by the presence of fundamentalist super-church pastors
in the large urban category. Without that anomaly, the contrast between
pastors of small and large churches might be even greater.

The churches represented on each side of the SBC's division, then,
were somewhat different. Both sides drew substantially from the small
rural churches that were the backbone of the denomination. Fundamentalists were somewhat more dominated by these small rural churches than
were conservatives and moderates, but in each faction, oldline Southern
Baptist churches were the most numerous. The biggest difference in the
composition of the denomination's two sides was in the distribution of
urban churches. Over one third of moderate pastors were in urban
churches of substantial size. Almost no moderate pastors were in small
city churches. Fundamentalist pastors, on the other hand, were more
likely (if they were in a city) to be in a small church than in a large one.
The tiny fraction of fundamentalist superstar pastors in super churches
formed an ironic contrast to their fellow pastors in churches that were
tiny by comparison.

In a number of ways status in the denomination and in society appears to have been related to the positions people were taking in the SBC controversy. Those who had more comfortable lives—from white collar and professional families, with more income, and a professional at the head of the household—were more likely to be found to the left of center in the denomination and to declare themselves moderate. In addition, pastors of larger urban churches (the denomination's plums) were also likely to prefer the moderate side. Those who came from farming and blue collar backgrounds, who had less money, and whose jobs involved them in a more routine sort of work, were more attracted to fundamentalist ways of thinking. Status cannot explain all the differences between the Southern Baptist Convention's left and right wings, but it does appear to explain a good deal.

The result was clear differences in the objective status resources available on each side. On the left wing, half had come from white collar and professional homes and nearly all the laity worked in middle class occupations as adults. Very few had incomes below $20,000; substantially more had household incomes over $35,000. Over a third of the clergy in the moderate camp were from large urban churches; very few were in the unusual position of pastoring small urban churches. On the right wing, nearly a quarter were pastoring small urban churches. Fundamentalist laity were split about equally between white collar or professional households and blue collar or farming ones. But about three quarters of them had grown up in farming and blue collar homes. Less than a quarter of fundamentalists had family incomes over $35,000, and over one third earned under $20,000. On the fundamentalist side, there was a wide range from well off to underprivileged, from high status occupations and pastorates to low. On the moderate side, the scales tipped clearly in the direction of higher status.

Another result was a difference in personal style and appearance that was regular enough to be noticed by our observers. Rank and file moderates (men and women) were likely to wear nicely tailored suits, and the men often wore oxford-cloth, button-down collar shirts.[14] They were rarely ostentatious; they looked, rather, like they were used to dressing for the office, to fit in with other professional people. The clothing of rank and file fundamentalists varied between outfits that looked new for the occasion and simple dresses or shirts and slacks that had been worn often before. Fundamentalist women were much more likely to wear a fancy dress than a suit, and their husbands occasionally had ties that were a little too wide or shirts that did not match the rest of their clothes. There was, of course, no uniformity to such observations, but the coincidences happened often enough to make us suspect that real differences existed between the two groups.

Those visible differences were also reflected in the subjective preferences and lifestyles our respondents reported on their surveys. In the last chapter, we noted that fundamentalists and moderates took very different positions on the propriety of various "forbidden" practices. The greater acceptance of movies, cards, dancing, and even alcohol among moderates can be linked to their middle class positions in society. Cultural and economic resources have a great deal to do with the recreations one chooses. The consumption of "high culture," for instance, is linked to social class position, and there is even evidence that appreciation for music and art may aid in social mobility.[15] It is not surprising then, that the same pattern of differences among these Baptist groups emerges when they are asked about their cultural preferences. Nearly all the moderates said they enjoyed "cultural events, such as symphony concerts," while less than half the self-identified fundamentalists said they did.

The cleavages in Southern Baptist life, then, coincided at least in part with differences between a left wing that was predominantly middle and upper-middle class, and a right wing that contained many of the denomination's less privileged. The relationship was not perfect, of course. There were many middle- and upper-middle class fundamentalists, and a noticeable minority of less privileged moderates. But Niebuhr was right to point us in the direction of social class as one of the components in the differences between Southern Baptist fundamentalists and their moderate opponents.

Education

People who have different occupations, incomes, and places in the social hierarchy are also very likely to have had different educational experiences. We ought to expect, in fact, that many of the differences we have seen in income and occupation will be related to differences in education. Where one is located in the overall social structure is determined in part by background and by native ability, but people with similar backgrounds who get different kinds and amounts of education often end up in different social locations and have different ideas. Education, in fact, has effects that go far beyond mere placement in occupation and income hierarchies. It has become a major determinant of the lifestyle differences that often make people of similar incomes very different in attitude and habit. A unionized blue collar worker with a $35,000 income and a high school education is likely to hold very different attitudes from a computer programmer with the same income and a Masters degree. What they value for their children and what they expect when they go to church will have been shaped by the education they have received and the kinds of knowledge they need in the work they do everyday.

Wuthnow has argued that education has become a primary source of the differences present in American culture and, as a consequence, in American religion. He cites enormous post-War growth in higher education as clearly linked to the other changes that have transformed American society, especially since 1960. He writes, "The better educated tended to be more liberal on a wide variety of issues; the less educated tended to be more conservative. These differences, moreover, often overshadowed other subcultural differences, such as those rooted in ethnic origins, region of the country, or even income differences."[16] Wuthnow shows that over the past forty years, education has contributed to a kind of homogenizing of America's denominational structure. In part, groups have become more alike because more people are switching from one to another; and it is educated people who are most likely to switch. Denominations are less ethnically and regionally distinct, but differences in education have contributed to new religious divisions that fall along conservative versus liberal lines within the denominations, rather than between them. While denominations increasingly resemble each other, they increasingly are divided within between those whose views are liberal and those who are conservative. That internal division was dramatically apparent in the Southern Baptist case, and there is every reason to suspect that differences in education played a role.

Indeed among both clergy and laity, both amount and type of education were excellent predictors of which side people took in the battle (see table 5.2). Very few pastors who had not been to seminary became moderates. And very few who went to an official SBC seminary were self-identified fundamentalists. Only 4 percent of pastors who had a Bachelors degree or less fell to the left of center, compared to a 36 percent moderate contingent among those who had at least been to seminary. Only a quarter of those who had been to seminary had beliefs that were more conservative than the convention's average, while 59 percent of less educated pastors fell to the right of center. The result is that the more educated the group, the fewer fundamentalists it contained.

A seminary education was both a symbolic and a substantive point of division among Southern Baptist pastors. It symbolized having earned the proper credentials for one's job. In earlier days, only a privileged few went to seminary, with a little bit of college training considered more than enough by most Southern Baptists. But in the education explosion that followed World War II, expectations and opportunities escalated rapidly. Both clergy and laity were going to school in greater numbers and staying in school for more advanced degrees. At the same time, the nature of pastoring changed. New urban churches expected pastors to be fulltime professionals, not people exercising a parttime calling. As the economic

Table 5.2. Percent in Different Theological Parties by Education

	AMOUNT OF EDUCATION (Laity)				
Theological Party	12 Years or Less	Some College	Bachelors Degree	Masters Degree	Doctoral Degree
Self-Identified Moderate	4%	7%	13%	17%	(4)
Moderate Conservative	4	5	17	8	(2)
Conservative	59	60	47	61	(5)
Fundamentalist Conservative	21	23	16	9	(0)
Self-Identified Fundamentalist	11	6	6	4	(0)
Total	99%	101%	99%	99%	—
(Number of Cases)	(313)	(133)	(86)	(60)	(11)**

	AMOUNT OF EDUCATION (Clergy)				
Self-Identified Moderates	0%	1%	4%	16%	26%
Moderate Conservatives	0	4	5	18	17
Conservatives	26	38	45	42	31
Fundamentalist Conservatives	37	33	39	18	19
Self-Identified Fundamentalists	37	24	8	6	6
Total	100%	100%	101%	100%	99%
(Number of Cases)	(70)	(47)	(67)	(174)	(33)

	TYPE OF COLLEGE (Laity)			
	None	Bible College	Secular University	Baptist* College
Self-Identified Moderates	4%	(0)	11%	18%
Moderate Conservatives	3	(0)	8	14
Conservatives	61	(5)	55	52
Fundamentalist Conservatives	21	(4)	18	14
Self-Identified Fundamentalists	11	(2)	8	3
Total	100%	—	100%	101%
(Number of Cases)	(293)	(11)**	(179)	(99)

Table 5.2. (*Continued*)

	TYPE OF SEMINARY (Clergy)			
	None	Non-SBC	Southwestern Golden Gate New Orleans	Southern Southeastern Midwestern
Self-Identified Moderates	1%	2%	4%	34%
Moderate Conservatives	5	4	17	18
Conservatives	37	33	47	31
Fundamentalist Conservatives	34	32	24	16
Self-Identified Fundamentalists	24	29	7	1
Total	101%	100%	99%	100%
(Number of Cases)	(152)	(42)	(108)	(93)

NOTE: All differences between categories are statistically significant at p < .001. Some percentages do not total 100 due to rounding.

*Includes 16 persons who went to other church-related schools.
**too few cases to percentage.

base of Southern Baptist life moved from farming and small town entrepreneurship to urban, large-scale business, the life experiences and expectations of people in the pews changed. They worked in bureaucratic organizations where credentials and efficiency counted. They expected no less of their churches and their pastors. As professionals, pastors needed credentials, and the seminary degree was their "union card."[17]

But education at a Southern Baptist seminary provided more than credentials. It also introduced pastors to denominational ways of doing things and to the people who would be their friends and network of contacts throughout their careers. These were the people who would recommend each other for vacant pulpits and nominate each other for Convention offices. At seminary young pastors met denominational officials and studied the history that would shape their sense of identity. At seminary, people learned to be "real Baptists." The socialization involved in seminary education was considered so important that missionary candidates were required (until 1987) to spend at least one year on a Southern Baptist seminary campus—even if they already had a degree from another school.

The ideas learned at seminary were important, as well. The student learned biblical languages and historical critical methods of interpreting scripture. The long history of the Christian tradition was studied, and Baptist ideas were placed in the context of that history. Students were introduced to the variety of liturgical practices that exist, within the Baptist tradition and beyond. They faced the discipline of thinking systematically about their beliefs and having those beliefs informed by the thinking of theologians from many times and traditions. Students could never leave seminary with a faith that was held in quite the unassuming way it may have been held when they entered. Even if every belief remained intact, graduates became aware of the wide diversity of belief within which they were located. It is not surprising, then, that seminary graduates embraced moderate beliefs and preferred a moderate label over a fundamentalist one. What they learned changed what they believed, and the denominational socialization they received taught them that fundamentalists were troublemakers.

Both sides recognized that education, and especially seminary education, was inimical to fundamentalist beliefs; but not surprisingly the two sides evaluated that fact very differently. On the fundamentalist side, it was greeted with alarm. Charles Stanley spoke of students who had "bailed out of seminary because their faith was destroyed."[18] A messenger to the 1986 convention told us that "education is fine, and I'm for education, but too much religious education can make you dull. . . . I don't think Christ prescribes a whole lot of education for us. We should be knowledgeable of the Word." Pastor Ike Reighard had noted earlier in that convention with great gratitude that his education had not changed his beliefs. "I believed when I was twenty one years old and I had just been saved that this was God's inerrant, infallible Word. Now I want you to know today, after college, after a master's degree and a doctor's degree, I still believe this is God's inerrant, infallible Word."[19] This contrasts to the experience shared by Houston pastor Edwin Young during the previous year's Pastors Conference. He recounted hearing in the classrooms of a Southern Baptist seminary that the miracles of the Old Testament were unimportant and that the resurrection was a spiritual, rather than bodily, event. His professor was a "thorough-going Bultmannian—and Bultmann is to the left of Barth and Brunner and neo-orthodoxy." Of such theories, he declared, to the cheers of his audience, "That dog won't hunt, brethren!" His voice breaking with emotion, Young recalled how he left seminary preaching the ideas he had learned, "scattering in the field those pebbles, those rocks I had been handed—and nothing came up." He started to "wrassle with the Word of God and seek godly men who would share" with him. He read inerrantist scholars who provided him an intellectually-respectable defense of the whole Bible. "And I threw the stones away and I began to scatter the seed of the Word, and miraculous things began to happen."

Such stories of young people corrupted by what they were taught in Southern Baptist schools were common in the sermons of fundamentalist leaders in the Convention. Eighty-four percent of the fundamentalists we surveyed agreed that "There are people teaching in Baptist colleges and seminaries who do not believe what Baptists ought to believe." A 1976 survey of students at Southern Seminary was often quoted as proof that schools were contributing to students losing their faith. Using that survey and other "documented quotations," evangelist E. J. Daniels wrote, "I found indisputable proof that many good Southern Baptists have been asleep while Satan has been destroying the faith of multitudes of future pastors and church leaders of our SBC churches through the teaching of liberal, Bible-denying doctrines."[20] Paul Pressler often told his own story of going to Phillips Exeter Academy and Princeton University seeing there what theological liberalism and neo-orthodoxy was. After he returned to Texas to practice law, he often held Bible studies for young people during the week, and it was students from those groups that eventually got him concerned about what was being taught in Texas' own Baylor University. He did not want such liberalism ruining Southern Baptist youth, especially in an institution he helped to finance.[21] He and other fundamentalists were worried about what happened in Southern Baptist classrooms. They did not want their young people taught ideas that would confuse their faith, and they did not want young preachers taught ideas that "won't preach."

Moderates, on the other hand, were simply not so worried. One pastor said, "I'd like for these boys [fundamentalist leaders] to back off and say, 'Go ahead, the Bible is great enough to withstand some academic scrutiny.'" We saw in the last chapter that moderates simply set wider boundaries and were unlikely to believe that there were people teaching outside acceptable limits. The same pastor claimed, "I've had boys go from [my church] to every Southern Baptist seminary in America. No one has come back a liberal. Southern Baptist education has only enhanced the faith of every one." Moderates had seen no evidence to make them worry—in part because they expected and accepted changes and growth as people moved toward mature adulthood. According to one moderate pastor, "Some folks, at college and seminary and adult stage, need to lay aside some things. Paul said he 'put away childish things.' He didn't mean he put away childlike faith, but he began to use his head. . . . Growth is not alien to the New Testament, and it shouldn't be alien to the Southern Baptist Convention."

The effect of education was no less real for the laity than for the clergy. Among the lay church leaders we surveyed, people with more education were less likely to agree with fundamentalist beliefs or to identify with that movement. For laity, the significant educational milestone was college, rather than seminary. Very few (9 percent) of those who had not been to college were in agreement with moderates, while equally few (6 percent) of those who had been to college were willing to identify themselves as fundamentalist. The completion of college and advanced degrees was associated with much lower levels of agreement with fundamentalist beliefs. Only 13 percent of those with advanced degrees scored to the right of center, compared to 32 percent of those who had not been to college. And a third of those with advanced degrees sympathized with the beliefs of the convention's left wing.

One might wonder, however, whether different kinds of colleges might mitigate these effects. Perhaps those who went to church related schools would be less likely to become liberal than those who went to secular universities. That turned out not to be the case, however. Among the clergy, there were no differences between graduates of secular universities and graduates of church related schools. Whatever differences might have existed were probably overwhelmed by the differences that would emerge out of their later choice of seminary. Among laity, there were differences, but they were not in the seemingly logical direction. Compared to those who went to secular universities, people who attended church related schools were twice as likely to call themselves moderate. Nearly one third of lay leaders educated in Baptist (and other church) colleges were moderate, while less than one fifth of them were fundamentalist in belief. Among the graduates of secular universities, the balance tipped in the other direction, with more fundamentalists than moderates. A quarter of secular graduates scored to the right of center, and less were on the left. Those who went to secular universities roughly mirrored the distribution of belief in the denomination as a whole, while those who went to Baptist (and other church-related) colleges leaned toward the moderate side. What happened for pastors in Baptist seminaries evidently happened for laity in Baptist colleges. They learned ideas and practices that made fundamentalism less attractive to them.

If there were schools where fundamentalist beliefs were being protected, even fostered, they were clearly the Bible colleges and independent seminaries that a small proportion of our respondents attended. Among those who went to a Bible college, not a single person scored to the left of center theologically. Laity who went to these schools were more conservative, in fact, than laity who had not been to college at all. Among clergy who went to non-Southern Baptist seminaries, the story is similar. They were even more conservative than pastors who had not been to seminary at all. Only the three who went to Vanderbilt, Eastern Baptist, and Eastern Mennonite joined the moderate camp. The remainder went to schools such as Luther Rice and Mid-America where they were taught by Southern Baptists who uniformly subscribed to biblical inerrancy and who emphasized traditional doctrines. Well over half (61 percent) of these graduates gave full assent to fundamentalist tenets, and 29 percent claimed that as their theological identity. These graduates of independent schools are almost nonexistent in the ranks of moderates and conservatives, but comprise a substantial minority in fundamentalist ranks.

There were also clear differences among graduates of the six Southern Baptist seminaries. Three of those seminaries were reputedly "liberal," and three were reputedly more "conservative." To see if those reputations had any substance, we compared their graduates. As expected, those who went to Southern, Southeastern, or Midwestern were nearly three times as likely to be moderate in theology as were graduates of the other three schools.[22] Graduates of Southwestern, New Orleans, or Golden Gate were barely distinguishable from the overall theological distribution, with 21 percent falling left of center and 32 percent to the right. These schools evidently represented a kind of status quo within the denomination, with graduates shying away from both party labels and clustering toward the center.

The three liberal seminaries, however, had almost no one willing to identify themselves as a fundamentalist, and only 16 percent agreed with fundamentalist beliefs. Over half (52 percent) of their graduates were to the left of center, and over one third (34 percent) identified themselves as moderates (eight times the proportion found in any other group of clergy). The reputations of these seminaries were obviously well-earned. And their reputations helped to reinforce the reality. Said one faculty member, "As long as I can remember, this was the 'liberal' seminary. It drew me to it, and it still draws students." More open students sought out a seminary experience to match their openness. While these seminaries may not be liberal by any outside criteria, they were clearly the source of leadership for much of the SBC's progressive wing. What was learned there had set their graduates apart from the rest of the denomination, making them less willing to subscribe to fundamentalist dogma and more willing to identify themselves as *not* conservative.

Within Southern Baptist life, education mattered. It mattered how much of it you had and where you got it. The proportion of people left of center was markedly larger in groups of lay people who had been to college, in groups of clergy who had been to seminary, and especially among those who had been to Southern, Southeastern, or Midwestern. The proportion of people sympathetic to the fundamentalist cause was markedly larger among groups of lay people who had not been to college, among clergy who had not been to seminary, and especially among people who had been to a Bible college or independent seminary.

Education was not a perfect predictor. There were many well-educated people who were fundamentalists and many moderates who had little schooling. But the differences between the two wings were tangible and real. Almost no pastors on the moderate side had less than a seminary education, while over two-thirds of the pastors on the fundamentalist side had a college degree or less. Only 17 percent of fundamentalist laity had a college degree, while over half of moderate laity had a Bachelors degree or more. Fundamentalist leaders often had blue ribbon educations and could debate the best-educated moderates on their own terms, but fundamentalist followers were at a considerable educational disadvantage compared to their moderate counterparts. Among the many social sources of Southern Baptist division, then, education must be seen as a leading influence.

Gender, Age, and Race

Although gender often divides people sharply on religious matters, that is not the case here. Lay men and women did not differ from each other in their preferences for one party over another. Neither was more or less theologically conservative than the other. The position of our lay women as presidents of their local missionary society often placed them at odds with the fundamentalist agenda in the Convention. They supported SBC cooperative efforts and had great confidence in the agencies of the denomination as they had existed. But they did not take those positions out of any lack of theological conservatism. There were no more "liberals" among WMU presidents than among the local deacon chairmen we surveyed.

Another cause for differences between people on religious matters is age, but age differences do not explain the variation in belief that was present in the Southern Baptist Convention. On average, older people were no more nor less theologically conservative than younger ones. On other measures of conservatism, age does make a difference, but those differences are not rooted in basic beliefs about the Bible. In other analyses, it was discovered that older lay people were the least likely to support the fundamentalist agenda of reform. Their long years in the denomination had evidently created a loyalty fundamentalists could not easily shake. In addition, it was found that middle aged clergy, those born in the 1930s, were the most likely to identify themselves as fundamentalist, to be antipluralist in attitude, and to support a conservative political agenda.[23] They were no more theologically conservative than other cohorts, but their beliefs led them to a more fundamentalist response to the world—more fundamentalist than either their older or their younger colleagues. After numerous conversations with clergy in this middle aged cohort, I am convinced that the polarizing experiences of the 1950s help to explain this phenomenon. These pastors emerged from seminary at a time of earthshaking change. Some responded with increased conservatism, while others looked forward to leading their denomination into a new era. Many in the latter group, however, eventually became discouraged and left the SBC for other denominations. They include such prominent American leaders as former seminary president Joseph Hough, religious historian Samuel Hill, correspondent Bill Moyers, and *Christianity and Crisis* editor Leon Howell. Without its left wing the remaining cohort became, on average, the most conservative clergy in the SBC. while age has not created discernable patterns in theology, it has created some distinctive ways of responding to the world.

One of the key issues in the 1950s, of course, was race; and race remains an issue today. However, there were not enough nonwhites among our respondents (twelve out of 1,043) to make meaningful comparisons among racial groups. Southern Baptists may be divided *over* race, but not *by* race. These standard demographic variables proved less than useful in untangling the differences among Southern Baptists.

Region

Even the region of one's birth or current residence seemed at first glance to make little difference. Southerners were no more nor less inclined toward the fundamentalist side than midwesterners, northeasterners, or westerners. Divided in this way, neither the region of one's current residence nor the region of one's childhood affected the likelihood of being fundamentalist or moderate. In part, however, differences between regions failed to appear because our respondents were so overwhelmingly southern. The dominance of that category made it unlikely that any deviations in the other categories would be "statistically significant." Consequently, in our follow-up surveys after 1985, we asked not for region of residence, but for state, allowing us to group the southeastern states into sub-regions for those who responded to at least one of our subsequent questionnaires. Table 5.3 shows the resulting patterns of variation.

Some had suggested that the conflict in the Convention was pitting new

Table 5.3. Percent in Different Theological Parties by Region

Theological Party	Establishment South	Old Frontier South	Texas and Neighbors	Expansion States	Average
Self-Identified Moderates	19%	4%	8%	5%	10%
Moderate Conservatives	10	5	7	12	9
Conservatives	45	52	47	53	49
Fundamentalist Conservatives	20	24	28	18	22
Self-Identified Fundamentalists	7	15	10	13	11
Total	101%	100%	100%	101%	101%
(Number of Cases)	(181)	(115)	(115)	(162)*	(573)

NOTE: The Establishment South includes GA, NC, SC, VA, MD, KY; the Old Frontier South includes AL, MS, FL, TN; Texas and Neighbors includes TX, LA, AR, MO, OK; and Expansion States includes everything else. Differences among regions statistically significant at p < .001. Some percentages do not total 100 due to rounding.

*The disproportionate number of cases in this category results from the use of all 1985 cases who reported their region of residence as anything outside the Southeast. Those within the Southeast could only be classified if they had reported state of residence on at least one follow-up questionnaire.

territory ("expansion states" in table 5.3) against old. On average, however, the non-southeastern pastors and lay church leaders who responded to our questionnaire were distributed among the theological camps in about the same way everyone else was. In addition, there were differences within both new and old, that make it impossible to draw the battle lines along the Convention's nineteenth century borders. Within the new territories, the Northeast states, for instance, were strikingly more moderate than the plains and western states into which the Convention had expanded. Those in the Northeast were less conservative, on average, and were far less likely to call themselves fundamentalist. Although we have only 13 cases from which to generalize, it appears that northeastern Southern Baptists had a strong affinity for the other moderates populating the eastern seaboard.[24] Those in the plains and western states were disproportionately likely to fall into the middle category of "conservative"— there were both fewer moderates and fewer fundamentalists among them. But, interestingly, over half of those with fundamentalist *beliefs* in the new midwestern and western areas claimed the label, something only a quarter of fundamentalists in other places did. As Southern Baptists spread out beyond their traditional boundaries, then, those in the west and midwest came to look a good deal like their cousins back home, although slightly less polarized. But those in the Northeast apparently took on a more distinctly moderate character.

Those in the old territories were internally diverse, as well. Southern Baptists in the eastern seaboard subregion of Georgia, North and South Carolina, Virginia, and Maryland (along with Kentucky, the location of the Southern Baptist Seminary) were far more likely to be moderate and to claim that identity than were Baptists in any other part of the country. These states were home to two seminaries, numerous Baptist colleges and universities, the Home and Foreign Mission Boards, and the sites of the founding of the Convention (in Augusta) and of the Womans Missionary Union's first headquarters (in Baltimore). These were the states of the old Southern Baptist establishment. Here there were churches filled with denominational, university, and seminary employees. Here there were pulpits recognized for generations as the "leading" pulpits of the denomination. In the first 100 years of its existence, the Convention had twenty-six presidents; fifteen of them were from these six states.

Just past the seaboard, in Alabama, Mississippi, and Tennessee, along with Florida, things looked very different. These were the first "frontier" states for Baptists, conquered during the camp meetings and revivals of the early nineteenth century. And during that century, Niebuhr observed, there was great tension between those on the frontier and those in the more sedate east. Nearly 200 years later, these church leaders still stand in marked contrast to the "establishment" just east of them. Compared to the seaboard, they were far less likely (9 percent versus 29 percent) to be found on the left side of the denomination's theological center, and more likely (39 percent versus 27 percent) to be on the right. Their sentiments were more clearly with the convention's right wing than with its left.

The rest of the old SBC states (Texas, Arkansas, Oklahoma, Louisiana, Missouri)—all west of the Mississippi—were quite average in their distribution of fundamentalists and moderates. Despite its reputation as the home of Patterson and Pressler, Texas was no more conservative than the rest of the denomination. Neither did it have an extraordinary moderate faction, despite the progressive influences of Baylor. It, and its neighbors, simply reflected the same balance between the left and the right that was present in the denomination as a whole. No significant division appeared, then, along the lines of east versus west, another factor often cited within the denomination as an explanation for their troubles.

Throughout most of the denomination's territory, then, no discernable differences in party loyalty appeared. The exceptions were moderate strongholds in the old establishment states and in the northeast, and fundamentalist strength in Florida, Alabama, Mississippi, and Tennessee. In the northeast, Baptists took on something of the character of their region. In the establishment southeast, Baptist history and institutions shaped church life; and to the west and south of Georgia, the legacy of the nineteenth century frontier spirit remained.

The divisions that occurred in the SBC did not fall neatly, then, along lines of north versus south, east versus west, or new territory versus old. Niebuhr's hypothesis about the role of regions in producing religious conflict is only part of the explanation here. While certain subregions retained a distinctive character that seemed to play a role in the controversy, more important may have been the disruption of Southern Baptists' overall regional identity. We saw in chapter 3 the ways in which both expansion and internal change had begun to alter the self-perception of at least some Southern Baptists. They were no longer tied exclusively to one region, but expansion itself may ironically have heightened regional consciousness. People in Detroit may have found it awkward to name their church Southern Baptist, but they knew they needed some way to signal their distinctive identity. The Convention talked about, but rejected, changing its name. Whatever the meaning of that regional adjective, they were not yet ready to give it up. It may be that the divisions that appeared among Southern Baptists had less to do with their current place of residence than with their differing responses to the possibility of their denomination *not* being southern.

Urbanization

Disruption is also the key word in describing the massive movement of Southern Baptists from farms to towns and cities over the last two generations. Over half of Southern Baptists who were born before World War II grew up on farms or in small villages. Today barely one fourth live in the country. Another one fourth described their current place of residence as a small town, and almost one half of current Southern Baptists said they lived in cities. One third of all our respondents have made the transition from a farm childhood to a town or city adulthood.

Where people grew up and whether they had moved later to a different sort of place did make a difference in which side of the theological fence they chose (see table 5.4). People who grew up in suburbs and small cities were the most likely to adopt a moderate theology, while those who grew up on farms were the least likely to locate left of center. There was, in fact, a direct negative relationship between the size of a person's community of origin and the conservatism of his or her beliefs. People who grew up in cities were simply less conservative than people who grew up in the country.

Table 5.4. Percent in Different Theological Parties by Size of Community

	CHILDHOOD COMMUNITY				
Theological Party	Farming	Small Town	Small City	Suburbs	Big City
Self-Identified Moderates	7%	10%	19%	14%	6%
Moderate Conservatives	5	11	16	16	13
Conservatives	54	46	38	37	47
Fundamentalist Conservatives	23	18	24	28	19
Self-Identified Fundamentalists	11	15	3	6	16
Total	100%	100%	100%	101%	101%
(Number of Cases)	(520)	(189)	(103)	(79)	(66)

	LIFETIME URBAN EXPERIENCE*		
	Stable Rural	Transitional	Stable Urban
Self-Identified Moderates	6%	11%	13%
Moderate Conservatives	5	11	14
Conservatives	55	43	41
Fundamentalist Conservatives	24	19	25
Self-Identified Fundamentalists	9	16	7
Total	99%	100%	100%
(Number of Cases)	(468)	(286)	(106)

NOTE: Differences among categories are statistically significant at p < .001. Some percentages do not total 100 due to rounding.

Stable Rural: childhood and current communities = farm or small town.

Transitional: childhood community = farm; current community = small city, suburbs, or big city OR childhood community = big city; current community = suburbs, small city, small town, or farm.

Stable Urban: childhood community = small town or larger; current community = small city or larger.

The size of the community in which people lived as adults made no difference, however, in where they stood relative to the denomination's battles. People living on farms as adults were no more fundamentalist, on average, than people living in cities. Those whose entire lives had been lived on farms or in small towns ("stable rural" in table 5.4) were different only in that they were slightly less likely to be on *either* side. Over half of them were in the neutral middle. While they tended toward the fundamentalist side in beliefs, they were slightly less likely than others to claim to be fundamentalists. Perhaps the battles that made labels like "fundamentalist" and "moderate" necessary were simply less relevant to people whose world had never included the anonymity of city living.

Beyond this relatively traditional and undisturbed group of rural folk were people who had lived in cities all their lives ("stable urban") and others who had moved between country and city ("transitional"). Different people living in the same urban place—but coming from different backgrounds—took different views of the controversy.[25] Among those people who currently live in cities, for example, 41 percent were from farms, 24 percent were from small towns, and 35 percent had lived in cities all their lives. Those who came to cities from small towns were almost like their neighbors who grew up in the city, except that if they were fundamentalists they were more likely to call themselves that. They are included in table 5.4 as "stable urban." Together with people who grew up in cities and stayed there, they were the least likely to identify with the fundamentalist movement and most likely to identify themselves as moderates. Compared to people who had always lived in the country, they were more than twice as likely to be on the left side of the SBC (27 percent versus 11 percent). Those in at least their second generation of urban living were the most moderate of Southern Baptists.

Those in their first generation of urban living (who grew up on farms and moved to cities) were considerably different. On one hand, they were more likely to be on the moderate side of center than were those who stayed behind (22 percent versus 11 percent). But they were also slightly more likely to be on the fundamentalist side of center (35 percent versus 33 percent) and almost twice as likely to identify themselves with that movement (16 percent versus 9 percent). There seems to be less middle ground in the city, more encouragement to move one way or the other, toward the denomination's progressive wing or toward its fundamentalists. Among this transitional group we can see both the conservative influences of a rural background and the effects of moving from farm to city. They are more likely than any other group to call themselves fundamentalist, identifying with a movement that has historically sought to preserve threatened values. If we can see the effects of cultural disruption, it may be here in these differences between people who have reason to defend threatened traditions (people who have moved from farm to city) and those who do not (those who stayed in rural areas).

The other group most likely to identify with fundamentalism was the group that grew up in a big city but chose as adults to live in the suburbs or in a community of smaller size. This apparently reflected their rejection of urban life. Like their more numerous counterparts who moved in the opposite direction, those who fled the city were disproportionately likely to call themselves fundamentalist. Theirs may have been an attempt to undo the disruption they perceived in the city.

In the effects of urbanization, we have hints that the greatest appeal of SBC fundamentalism was in the times and places of greatest disruption. At a time when the denomination's regional identification had become tenuous, a fundamentalist movement arose. And among the people most disrupted by urbanization—those who moved from farm to city and those who fled big cities for smaller places—fundamentalism had its greatest appeal. If fundamentalism can be defined as a movement in organized opposition to the disruption of a previously accepted orthodoxy, then we would expect to find it thriving in just such places.[26]

Indeed religion's very character is different when it must face a changing environment. In a relatively undisturbed setting, religious practices are tightly interwoven into the fabric of life. One learns prescribed rituals as part of the array of necessary knowledge for membership in the group. Beliefs about the deity or sacred scripture are appropriated alongside beliefs about planting and harvesting, birthing and burying. While the culture is undisturbed by outside intruders, by changes in technology or climate, these everyday ways of being and believing remain central to the group's way of life. But when change occurs, everyday patterns of life are thrown into disarray, and the links between beliefs and practices are disrupted. Things that used to work do not work anymore. Ways of making a living, relating to neighbors, and even relating to God, are made uncertain by the dislocation of the cultural system. What used to come naturally no longer seems plausible. What used to be possible by habit must now be thought about, reevaluated, rationalized, perhaps even given a new sacred meaning. People have to think about why they do what they do, as well as whether they want to do it at all. Both patterns of living and the ideas that legitimate those patterns are "up for grabs" in times of cultural disruption and transition.[27]

What happened in the Southern Baptist Convention may be seen at least in part as differing responses to social change. As the world around them changed, as Baptists themselves were rearranged, relocated, and spread out over the country, some of them embraced the diversity of their new surroundings, seeking new and adapted religious practices that made sense in the new situations in which they found themselves. Others rejected the new, preferring to reassert the orthodoxy that had prevailed in the older rural and small town south.

Responses to Modernity

In traditions throughout the world, existing orthodoxies have found themselves threatened by disruption of the cultural base in which they were lodged. In a creative process of adaptation, they seek out the elements of the old orthodoxy that best explain their new situation and assert these truths as the path to salvation.[28] The disruption against which fundamentalists struggle is often labeled "modernity." Whatever else that label may mean, the "modern" world is one in which change is a fact of life, in which people of multiple cultures live side by side, and in which religious rules have been largely relegated to a private sphere of influence.[29] If this is a fundamentalist movement, then responses to these characteristics of the modern world ought to tell us something about party alignments within the Southern Baptist Convention.

We asked our panel of Southern Baptist local church leaders a variety of questions about modernity. We found all of them, regardless of theological party, remarkably unwilling to say that religion has no effect on their work, their politics, or their family life. If religion has become differentiated into a "private" sphere, these Baptists were unwilling to admit it. But on questions of change and diversity, there was wide variation among them. Most acknowledged these as facts of their lives, but some did so with more enthusiasm than others. Among the statements to which we asked them to respond were

> Public schools are needed to teach children to get along with lots of different kinds of people.
>
> I like living in a community with lots of different kinds of people.
>
> I sometimes learn about God from friends in other faiths.
>
> One of the most important things children can learn is how to deal creatively with change.
>
> Children today need to be exposed to a variety of educational and cultural offerings so they can make informed choices.

These five items together formed a measure of acceptance of the diversity and change that characterize modern life. (For details of scale construction, see appendix B.) The five possible responses to each (from strongly agree to strongly disagree) were scored from one to five and summed. Those who agreed or strongly agreed with all the items (scoring from five through nine) were classified as strongly approving of pluralism. Those who agreed with most but not all (scoring ten thru fourteen) were classified as having moderate approval. And those who disagreed at least as

Table 5.5. Percent in Different Theological Parties by Responses to Pluralism

Theological Party	Strong Approval of Pluralism	Moderate Approval of Pluralism	Disapproval of Pluralism	Total
Self-Identified Moderate	21%	5%	3%	9%
Moderate Conservative	16	8	3	9
Conservative	38	55	43	48
Fundamentalist Conservative	18	24	27	23
Self-Identified Fundamentalist	8	9	23	11
Total	101%	101%	99%	100%
(Number of Cases)	(256)	(500)	(187)	(944)

NOTE: Difference statistically significant at $p < .001$. Some percentages do not total 100 due to rounding.

often as they agreed (scoring fifteen or above) were classified as disapproving. The most "modern" people want their children to learn to get along with lots of different kinds of people, and they acknowledge their own debt to people with different beliefs. They like the diversity of their communities and anticipate that their children will spend a lifetime dealing with change. In saying that they want to raise children who know how to make informed choices, they implicitly acknowledge that tradition cannot be a completely reliable guide, that a more rational base for knowledge is needed.

Indeed positions on pluralism do predict party identification within the Southern Baptist Convention (see table 5.5). And people with an acceptance of these cognitive bases of modernity were more likely than others to find themselves on the progressive side of the denomination. More tellingly, perhaps, those who rejected modern ways of thinking were extremely unlikely to be moderates. Among those who disapprove of pluralism, fundamentalists outnumber moderates nearly ten to one. A modern world view appears to be a necessary, but not sufficient condition for movement into the SBC's left wing.

As a result of these differing responses to modernity, the mood on the two sides of the denomination was quite different. Almost all (91 percent) of self-identified moderates, for instance, agreed or strongly agreed that "public schools are needed to teach children to get along with lots of different kinds of people." Only 43 percent of self-identified fundamentalists agreed. Nearly as many (83 percent) self-identified moderates said that they "like living in a community with lots of different kinds of people," while only 54 percent of self-identified fundamentalists agreed. And an equal number (83 percent) of self-identified moderates said that "children today need to be exposed to a variety of educational and cultural offerings so they can make informed choices," compared to barely half as many (44 percent) self-identified fundamentalists who held that goal for their children. In each case, the remainder of the denomination was spread out about evenly between these two extremes.

The modern world has placed people in situations where inherited wisdom sometimes seems inadequate. Most people exist in a complex society where the relationships among work, family, leisure, and church are not always clear. They must negotiate a viable faith in the midst of that complexity and alongside the pluralism of belief present in such a world. While that may be a difficult task, moderates seemed determined to face it squarely. They would certainly not run from the reality of the modern world in which they lived. In fact, they seemed positively enamored of it. The attitudes of this group were perhaps captured by the editor of the Atlanta *Constitution*'s editorial page, Tom Teepen, in a column reflecting on a trip to Montreal with his wife, Sandy.

> I am struck by how very different the world has become from that of my childhood a half-century past. Sandy and I live in a world whose horizon lines have been pushed far back from the near woods and ridges that surrounded our parents' lives. Yes, that is in part, in big part, because I have a nice income and a job that allows for travel. . . . Still, even the most plain circumstances nowadays have a remarkable window on the world.
>
> My childhood impressions of faraway places were formed from pictures in books—only infrequently in color—and from cherished, enthralling three-dimensional View-Master reels. Now, of course, wars in Afghanistan and the foreign vacations of the rich and fatuous come to me routinely with the flick of the TV's remote control.
>
> To Sandy and me, a spell in a Montreal bistro, the air prettied by the French conversations fluting all around us, is still a wonder and a delight. My children, in common with their generation, have grown up taking the world for granted in a way that until quite recently was unimaginable except for the privileged. Where we could see only the next row of hills, they, bless 'em, see the very curve of the Earth.[30]

For Teepen, and for most of the SBC's progressives, such a widening of horizons is to be welcomed. A young moderate told a similar story.

> I grew up pretty sheltered, in a small town. I'm not belittling my heritage; I'm extremely grateful for it. But it was very narrow, and even provincial, not only culturally but religiously. . . . I have had

a chance to travel to Taiwan, to Korea, and to China. It helped to both confirm who I am and to place who I am more realistically in the world. I have a much broader understanding of what it means to be a Southern Baptist and what it means to be a Christian. . . . I don't feel nearly as obliged to make everybody midwestern as I did when I was growing up. I'm going to share Christ, but how they express their Christian faith—I'm a little more flexible. I have changed culturally.

Diverse cultures, broader horizons, a more flexible faith. For moderates, the challenges presented are far outweighed by the benefits of living in a more inclusive world.

On the other side, self-identified fundamentalists were much less enthusiastic about diversity and change. Addressing a group of Southern Baptists at one of Bailey Smith's RealEvangelism Conferences, Jerry Falwell talked about the problems facing Christians in this time. He talked about how mobility and change have made our world a pressure cooker. Technology and the threats of the nuclear age have made the world a frightening place. He noted that his children knew more at ten than he learned in all his schooling. But despite all the knowledge, he lamented, people were not being taught morality. They needed not just a body of knowledge, but values to guide their living. His audience agreed, as did many of our survey respondents—especially those who identified themselves as fundamentalists. They were quite sure that "informed choice" was not good enough for their children, and over half disagreed about the value of public schools in teaching children to get along with different kinds of people. Almost half claimed that they did not like living in communities with such diversity; and a third disclaimed ever learning about God from people outside their faith. The contrast here was not between two camps each unanimous in opposing views. Rather, the contrast is between a left wing that embraced modern pluralism wholeheartedly and a right wing that was more mixed in its response. While fundamentalists are not unanimous in rejecting the diversity of the modern world, their majority opinion is in that direction.

That fundamentalists would oppose pluralism in the secular world should come as no surprise. We have already seen that theological diversity was one of the chief enemies they oppose within their denomination. Religious faith was not to be found for them in the midst of choices and adaptation, but as a clear and unchanging path toward salvation. They neither celebrate the diversity of their surroundings nor value adaptation, choice, and civility as the principles by which to guide children. Their lives are guided, instead, by principles they see as timeless truths.

Fundamentalists insist that the old orthodoxies are the only way to

God. But because their world has changed, their insistence has to take the form of organized protest. They build congregational cultures in which they can be protected from the cognitive challenges of the world, adding schools, Christian media, and a network of friends to their organizational armor.[31] The old orthodoxies have to be defended if they are to survive in competition with new schemes for making religious sense of life. Baptists in the South were no longer surrounded by other evangelicals who, despite differences in detail, shared most of their basic beliefs. Now they were living alongside Mormons and Lutherans and agnostics, Catholics and Muslims and people whose faith might best be described as private. It required concerted attention to sustain the same beliefs in the Bible that had come naturally in the conservative evangelical world of southern small towns in an earlier era. When everyone else seemed to celebrate the rainbow of urban life, it took a stubborn minority to claim an eternal truth and defend it.

How Southern Baptists felt about pluralism, like where they stood on theology, was in part a product of the different life experiences that are reflected in occupation, education, income, and other categories.[32] Among the laity, those who liked pluralism most were people who had graduated from college (even more so if it was a Baptist college). Those who went to secular universities liked these characteristics of the modern world less than did people who had not been to college at all. Those who liked pluralism least were not, in fact, those with the least education. Rather, it was the group that had some college, but not a degree. Lay people most likely to embrace modernity, not surprisingly, were those who had grown up in cities and chosen to stay there. But those who liked pluralism least were not the people who had lived in the country all their lives. Rather, they were those who were transitional, having moved from farm to city or from a big city to a less urban setting. Smaller differences, but a similar pattern were seen in the effects of occupation and income among the laity. Those who disliked the pluralism of the modern world most were not those at the bottom of the income distribution, but those in the middle ($20,000–$35,000). And farmers were as accepting of modernity as white collar workers. It was blue collar people who were more likely to reject the idea that change, diverse communities, informed choices, and learning from other faiths constitutes a pattern of life to be embraced.

In each case, these middle social categories represent people who are neither the most remote from modernity nor the most entrenched in it. If one were to envision a continuum of categories of people who are more or less "modern," at one end would be farmers, lifetime rural residents, and those who have not been to college. They are relatively remote from the forces of diversity and change. They constitute the status quo from which Southern Baptists are changing. At the other end of the continuum are white collar workers and professionals, lifetime city dwellers, and people with a good education and high income. They are both in the midst of diversity and possessors of the resources and experiences with which to understand and enjoy it. In the middle are people whose exposure to diversity is high, but whose resources are relatively lower. They live in cities, but have not been there all their lives. They have been exposed to the world of higher education, but do not possess the credentials a college degree would afford or the status a white collar or professional job might bring. It was this middle group—well exposed to the modern world, but with relatively less prestige in it—who were most discontented with modernity.[33]

Rejection of modernity was the product of a combination of forces. It was not most prevalent among those most remote from it. While sociologist James Hunter may be right that evangelical beliefs are most common among people with, among other things, less education and less exposure to cities, evangelicalism and fundamentalism are not the same thing.[34] Fundamentalism only exists where there is conscious opposition to the forces of change, and conscious opposition can only exist where there *are* forces of change. Those among Southern Baptists who were the most skeptical of change, choice, and diversity were blue collar workers, those with middle incomes, people who had moved from farm to city, and those who had been to college, but did not have a degree. And combinations were important: people who had moved from farm to city *and* had some college or people with middle income *and* blue collar households, for instance. These were people who knew exactly what the modern world was all about, and they were less enthusiastic about embracing it than were any other Southern Baptists. And the less enthusiasm they had for modern attitudes, the more likely they were to adopt fundamentalist beliefs and identity.

The differences among the Southern Baptist Convention's parties, then, were also reflections of the difference between country and city life, between relatively undisturbed living and life in the midst of change and diversity. Those most likely to side with the Convention's fundamentalists were people who had personally experienced the contrast between city life and more simple settings. Even more basically, people were theologically different not only because of where they lived but because of their response to change and diversity. Moderates responded by applauding the modern world in which they found themselves. Fundamentalists expressed reservations, asserting that an uncritical acceptance of pluralism, rationality, and change was unwise.

Denominational Insiders and Outsiders

The social, cultural, and attitudinal differences that had developed within the Southern Baptist Convention were also apparent in differing patterns of relationship to the denomination itself. Put simply, fundamentalists and moderates had been going to different meetings for quite some time. They did not know how to talk to each other in part because they rarely *had* to talk to each other.

Both moderates and fundamentalists agreed that moderates had been the people most active in Convention affairs for the previous generation. Fundamentalists said that moderates had staked out their territory—in part based on seminary connections—and had excluded fundamentalists from participation. Moderates thought that fundamentalists were merely showing their lack of interest by staying away. Both would probably have agreed that moderates got more respect in denominational circles than did fundamentalists. Whatever the reasons, there were strong perceptions that this fight was also being waged along insider versus outsider lines. While we have no way to measure directly the respect, status, or influence of moderates over fundamentalists, we can compare their patterns of interest, participation, and investment in the denomination. If moderates were the insiders and fundamentalists the outsiders, it ought to show up in how they have related to the official structure of denominational activity.

In some respects the reports of our respondents bear out the contention that moderates were the ones on the inside. Most of the differences in participation between the convention's right and left wings were not very large, but in some ways self-identified fundamentalists *were* significantly less active in denominational affairs. Fundamentalist clergy were more likely than moderates to have stayed away from 1984–1985 state convention meetings, and they were less than half as likely (16 percent versus 44 percent) to have been active enough to attend three or more state meetings in those years. That pattern was even more evident in their attendance at annual SBC conventions. Self-identified fundamentalist clergy were much more likely never to have attended a convention gathering (see table 5.6). They stood out in marked contrast to every other group in this regard. Even those who were equally fundamentalist in belief, but called themselves conservative, had been to annual conventions in larger numbers than had self-identified fundamentalists. There were no differences among the parties in participation at local associational meetings, but in these nonlocal affairs, clergy who had identified with the fundamentalist movement were more likely to be absent.

That was also true in lay participation and in the number of messengers

Table 5.6. Attachment to the Denomination by Theological Parties

	% Self-Identified Moderates	% Moderate Conservatives	% Conservatives	% Fundamentalist Conservatives	% Self-Identified Fundamentalists
Attendance at National Conventions					
Clergy who have never attended	9	22	22	36	50
(Number of Cases)	(39)	(44)	(138)	(105)	(56)
Cooperative Program Giving					
<5 percent	5	5	13	16	21
5–10 percent	38	36	48	51	56
>10 percent	57	59	38	33	23
(Number of Cases)	(86)	(85)	(465)	(211)	(106)
Denominational Identity					
"I can hardly imagine myself as anything but a Southern Baptist."					
Very True	44	61	65	71	55
(Number of Cases)	(85)	(85)	(479)	(215)	(107)

NOTE: All differences between parties statistically significant at $p < .001$.

sent to annual meetings. Moderate laity were much more likely to have attended a state-level meeting than were conservative or fundamentalist laity. The churches of moderate respondents were also more likely to have sent messengers to the 1983 and 1984 conventions. Most churches who sent messengers had routinely sent only the pastor (and possibly his wife). Moderates were more than twice as likely, compared to all others, to deviate from that pattern by sending more than two messengers. Twelve percent of our moderate respondents reported that their church had sent three or more messengers to the convention before the mammoth convention of 1985. On these items, it was moderates who stood out for their high levels of participation. Fundamentalists and conservatives were similar to each other, but less active than moderates. In comparison even to average Baptists, moderates had been more active in convention affairs.

The differences between parties were even more clearly seen in giving to the Cooperative Program. The more fundamentalist the respondent, the more likely they were to report that their church gave less than 5 percent of its budget to the denomination. And the more moderate the respondent, the more likely they were to report that their church gave more than 10 percent. Moderates encouraged a strong tradition of generous denominational support, while fundamentalists were much more tentative in their giving. In a number of concrete ways, then, moderates had stronger investments in the denomination, stronger patterns of activity binding them to it. Fundamentalists had kept their distance, investing less time and money in denominational affairs.

What look at first like patterns that differ along party lines, however, are actually differences produced by social factors, not theology. These differences in participation were only marginally related to beliefs. When people of similar social backgrounds were compared, theology made little difference in how much or little they participated in denominational affairs.[35] The most important factors in determining their level of denominational participation were the size of their church, and where they went to school. No matter what their beliefs, those who were most active were in large urban churches; the least active in small rural ones. The most active clergy had been to a Southern Baptist seminary (It did not matter which one.), and the most active laity had been to a Southern Baptist college; and again, belief mattered very little. Clearly the denominational educational system worked well in introducing people to programs and networks that would frame their church lives.

There is also evidence that resources make a difference in whether one participates in the activities of the denomination. Clergy with more income, and laity from white collar and professional households were more active, on average, than people with less income or different occupations. Because all these social factors are related to theological party identification, it appeared at first that party identification helped to determine how active people were in the denomination. While there were clear differences in participation between fundamentalists and moderates, those differences were products of the social differences that also separated them and not of the theological positions themselves.

In more subtle matters of identity, there were also discernable differences between the denomination's two wings. Most basically, moderates were more likely to have grown up in Southern Baptist churches, while half of self-identified fundamentalists had joined since age seventeen. Moderates were more likely to have had a lifetime of socialization into the denomination's ways, while fundamentalists were more likely to be newcomers. We also attempted to test the subjective attachment of our respondents to the denomination by asking whether they could imagine themselves as something other than a Southern Baptist. Conservatives and fundamentalist conservatives clearly could not. Over two-thirds of all those who chose a "conservative" identity were firmly attached to their denominational home. They said that it was very true that they could hardly imagine themselves as anything else. The two extremes of the denomination stood out in their relative willingness to entertain other denominational identities. This is perhaps not surprising in self-identified fundamentalists, given that their routine attachments had been more tenuous. Self-identified moderates, on the other hand, might not have been expected to entertain alternatives in such large numbers. On every other measure, they were the most loyal, active people in the denomination. But in a proportion larger than in any other faction, self-identified moderates could imagine themselves in other religious groups. Perhaps we see here again their openness to diversity. That openness, however, makes it all the more striking that they were so loyal to Southern Baptists. Their high levels of activity, interest, and giving came not from any lack of alternatives, but from clear commitment to the denomination.

The Results: Battle Lines

In the last chapter, we saw the many ways in which Baptists disagreed with each other over everything from lifestyle to politics, from the role of women to when Jesus will return. All of those issues played a role in defining the differences between the parties. They sketched in the contours of the territories occupied by the convention's progressive wing on the left and its fundamentalist wing on the right. In this chapter, we have seen the extent to which those differences ran parallel to differences in education, social position, even region. But the crucial question for the future of the denomination was not necessarily whether Southern Baptists could agree on the ERA or defense spending, but whether they could agree on their own mission and their own institutional relationships; not whether they were from diverse social locations, but whether those social differences prevented them from working together on the issues that faced them. Would the denomination's agencies go on in the direction set by moderates in the 1960s and 1970s, or would they be redirected by fundamentalists? Would professors be expected to teach solely within the boundaries of majority opinion? Would agencies support the ordination of women? Would local churches continue to ordain women and still be tolerated by other Southern Baptist churches? Would churches remain in a denomination they did not consider to be biblically sound? These internal issues were the essence of the institutional debate.

We have already seen how the various parties differed on most of these issues, but table 5.7 draws that information together for an overview of the conflict. While most self-identified moderates were stubbornly confident that there were no doctrinal problems in the denomination and that differences ought to be tolerated, fundamentalists and many conserva-

Table 5.7. Positions on Denominational Issues by Theological Parties

Issue	% Self-Identified Moderates	% Moderate Conservatives	% Conservatives	% Fundamentalist Conservatives	% Self-Identified Fundamentalists
SBC boards and agencies are doctrinally sound. Not Very or Not at all Confident *(average = 19% N = 1004)*	5	3	16	29	35
SBC boards and agencies are responsive to the desires of ordinary Southern Baptists. Not Very or Not at all Confident *(average = 25% N = 1004)*	7	14	23	34	39
There are people in Baptist schools who do not believe what Baptists ought to believe. Agree or Strongly Agree *(average = 63% N = 365)*	31	58	57	84	84
SBC employees should believe and teach what most Baptists believe. Agree or Strongly Agree *(average = 71% N = 329)*	42	56	75	81	77
Would support a move to disfellowship a church that ordains women. *(average = 28% N = 949)*	0	3	25	44	58
Would support measures against agencies and schools that promote women's ordination. *(average = 45% N = 939)*	2	14	42	66	77
My church should consider leaving the SBC if it is not brought back to biblical soundness. Agree or Strongly Agree *(average = 27% N = 1004)*	2	4	24	39	53

NOTE: Number of cases varies depending on the year in which the question was asked. All differences between parties are statistically significant at $p < .001$.

tives were not nearly so sure. Many did not think the boards and agencies were doctrinally sound, and even fewer thought they were responsive to ordinary Baptists. They felt that convention employees ought to believe like the majority believed and that many of them did not. They were also willing to censure agencies that promoted the ordination of women. Action against the national institutions of the denomination was something they were quite willing to consider. They were somewhat less willing to punish a church in their own local association, but still a majority of self-identified fundamentalists would vote to disfellowship a church that ordained women. Leaving the denomination oneself is the most drastic step, of course. When it happens in large enough numbers, it constitutes an actual schism. The number who would be willing to cut themselves off from the fellowship was roughly equivalent, in each of the parties, to the number who would vote to disfellowship another church with whom they disagreed. Less than a quarter of those in the denomination's conservative mainstream thought things might get bad enough to warrant leaving. But over half of self-identified fundamentalists and more than a third of fundamentalist conservatives were willing to consider that step. It appears clear that the Convention's right wing meant business. If things did not change, they were prepared to leave. These were fighting issues, and Baptists were clearly split along party lines in their responses to them. But were their responses to these issues products simply of their theological positions, or were these issues, too, directly influenced by their differing social locations?

We have seen that the willingness of Southern Baptists to claim fundamentalist beliefs and identity was affected by their educational level and the type of school they attended. Living in the moderate strongholds of the Southeast also had an effect, as did the occupational status of one's parents, one's income, and—among laity—one's own occupation. Clergy in large urban churches were less fundamentalist than those in small urban churches. Even whether one had moved from farm to city made a difference in the tenacity with which certain beliefs were held. These social sources helped to explain why some Baptists were more fundamentalist in belief than others and gave each of the parties a distinctive social flavor.

Did these same social forces, then, explain why Baptists differed on the issues facing the denomination. Were their differences in discontent with the denominational status quo really differences of income or education or region? To test these possibilities, we measured the effects of beliefs and theological identification against the effects of region, education, parent's occupation, income, urban and rural places of residence, and measures of prestige (church size and location for clergy and husband's occupation for laity). Each factor individually was significantly related to beliefs, to theological identity, and to degree of discontent with the denomination; but when all were measured simultaneously, some were simply more important than others.

Which factors accounted for differences in the degree of discontent present among different Southern Baptists?[36] By far the most important factor among both clergy and laity was theology. Controlling for background social differences, people with different beliefs simply took different denominational stands. Baptists with the same income, the same region of residence, the same occupations, but with different beliefs, disagreed on whether there were problems in the denomination and what should be done about them. While those differing beliefs had been formed at least in part out of differing social experiences, it was beliefs that directly shaped their denominational agendas.

Beliefs, however, were not the only significant factor. As we have argued all along, self-identification contributes an effect of its own, over and above beliefs themselves. People with the same beliefs, who did not call themselves fundamentalists, were less unhappy with the denomination and less likely to want to leave (or push others out). The fundamentalist party label indicated identification with a militant movement, and people who chose it were more sure that the denomination needed change than were people who called themselves something else.

Theology and self-identification were the two most important factors in their effects on discontent, but amount and type of education again proved a potent influence in the lives of these Baptists. Laity who had been to Baptist colleges were much more supportive of the denomination than were their neighbors who went to secular universities. And clergy who went to Baptist seminaries were less discontented than either those who did not go at all or, especially, those who went to independent schools. People with the same beliefs and the same backgrounds, then, differed in their feelings about the denomination depending on where they went to school.

The other intervening variable we tested was response to modernity. We wanted to know whether responses to the denomination's diversity were simply a reflection of a larger discontent with the pluralism and change of the modern world. We have already seen that rejection of modernity thrives in the places where exposure to diversity and change is high and resources are relatively low. Controlling for those background variables and for theological beliefs, laity who were less accepting of modern attitudes were also more supportive of the SBC fundamentalist agenda. In part, then, discontent with the Convention's previous progressive direction came from theological conservatism; but in part it came from differences in education and from opposition to the pluralism and change that characterizes the modern world.

While various social forces have created the world in which both fundamentalist religious beliefs and anti-modern attitudes make sense, only one social factor directly affected positions on denominational issues. At each point in the causal process, education is absolutely crucial to understanding what has happened to Southern Baptists. Those who have received more education, and especially those who have sought their education from denominational and/or liberal sources are less likely to hold fundamentalist beliefs; and even if they do, they are less likely to identify themselves as such. They are also more accepting of modernity. Each of those factors, in turn, makes them less supportive of the denomination's fundamentalist agenda. But even beyond those indirect effects, education has its own direct effect on fundamentalist issue support. People with the same theologies, the same self-identity, and the same attitudes toward modernity, but different amounts and kinds of education, were likely to differ on the issues facing the Convention. It is little wonder that the Convention's colleges and seminaries were the primary target of the discontented right wing. Colleges and seminaries had created both the ideology and the social networks, both the sources of meaning and belonging, out of which the old establishment was constructed. They were largely responsible for the changes in belief fundamentalists sought to oppose. Our statistical testing of responses from survey respondents confirmed what fundamentalists already knew—their foremost enemy was the denomination's educational system.

So, the battle lines were drawn. Southern Baptists differed deeply on matters that directly affected their ability to do their work of missions and education. They differed primarily because they had different beliefs, but they had different beliefs, at least in part, because they lived in different social worlds. The insiders were people who had been through the denomination's educational system, while outsiders were more likely to have chosen an independent college or seminary. The social world of insiders was a world of diversity and the resources with which to enjoy that diversity. The social world of outsiders was one in which diversity was an unwelcome intruder. The denomination's progressive wing contained the "new class" of people whose business is knowledge and service. They were the Southern Baptist equivalent of the new evangelicals who embraced the modern world. And the denomination's progressive wing had been in charge for the previous generation. They were the insiders. The outsiders were a fundamentalist movement arising in organized response to the disruption of the orthodoxy that had bound Southern Baptists and southern society into a tightly woven cultural web. They opposed the progressive direction denominational agencies seemed to be taking, and they opposed the modern beliefs their schools were fostering. They were concerned about inerrancy and evolution, women's rights and secular humanism. They were afraid their denomination had drifted too far to the left, and they wanted to correct its course before it was too late.

Social Sources in Perspective

H. Richard Niebuhr's work challenged us to look for the roots of division among Baptists in differences in status, region, and ethnicity. We have discovered that there are indeed remnants of the eastern establishment/western frontier division left in Southern Baptist life. But more important, perhaps, are divisions spawned by the denomination's loss of its exclusively regional identity. We have also discovered that there are differences in status among the parties contending for domination of the SBC's future. There *were* social sources in this denominational battle. The insiders, just as Niebuhr would have predicted, were the more privileged and established, while the outsiders were, on average, people with fewer economic, social, and organizational resources. Niebuhr was right to point us in the direction of social differences and to suggest region and social status as key components of the differences we would find.

But Niebuhr's outlining of the contours of those differences was not entirely adequate. We should never have expected the sources Niebuhr identified in nineteenth and early twentieth-century America to be identical to the forces shaping our own society in our own time. We should expect the social forces that shape and divide today's society to find their way into today's religious divisions. We have discovered that it is education that plays this sorting role today. More than any objective measure of class position (such as income or occupational prestige), education has shaped the ideas and agendas of Southern Baptists. As is the case in the rest of American religion, differences in education have helped to create a broad spectrum of ideological and lifestyle differences within this denomination.[37]

If we were to follow Niebuhr (and subsequent sociological convention), we would, of course, label the better educated, more affluent Southern Baptist moderates "churchly" (or denominational) and their less privileged challengers "sectarian." Those labels, however, are problematic here. Church-like has been defined as more accommodated to the culture, in tune with the surroundings.[38] Groups labeled sectarian are those seen as "in tension" with the larger culture, adopting practices and safeguards that set them apart from the dominant tradition. In American culture, the avoidance of practices such as drinking and dancing, for instance, is sometimes taken as indicative of sectarian tension.[39] As we saw in chapter 4, fundamentalists are indeed more sectarian by those measures, and they are in general more concerned about separating themselves from the world. But because these vices were so widely prohibited in traditional southern culture, at least until recently, being against drinking may indicate church-like integration with the culture, rather than sectarian tension. It was often moderates who experienced tension with their conservative environment because of their less prohibitive practices. Because American society is so varied in its accepted ways of life, almost any practice taken as a sign of tension in one location may be a sign of membership in another. No list of taboos is likely to work as a universal indicator of separateness. In this case, it is simply not clear whether moderates or fundamentalists (or neither) should be considered in tension with Southern and/or American culture. Measuring sectarianism in terms of forbidden practices cannot help us understand Southern Baptists.

This difficulty points us toward the difficulty of conceptualizing or measuring tension in any complex culture. Do we mean refusal to accept certain practices adopted by particular cultural elites? Do we mean refusal to accept certain cognitive assumptions or styles? Do we mean protest against the very foundations on which the culture is built (and if so, which foundations do we mean)? Will we accept the group's definition of *itself* as separate? It may yet be fruitful to retain some focus on the differences between groups that take their task as a universalizing one (churches) and those that see themselves as particularistic (sects), but those terms will only have meaning as we define the nature of the particularism involved and the cultures and cultural forms in which it is located. Not all particularities have the same isolating or exclusivist properties, a point made by Warner about what he calls "elective parochialism."[40] The relevant question may not be whether a group asserts its particularity but in what ways and under what circumstances. Nor is the question whether a group is accommodated, but what aspects of the social structure it accepts.

In part our lack of clarity about tension and accommodation in this case comes from the tension inherent in the culture itself. In the midst of tension between old and new, lines of accommodation are unclear. Which side is in tension with what? The notion of tension versus accommodation, sect versus church, cannot fully describe the dynamics of a situation where different groups within a religious tradition are responding to a changing environment. While the degree of accommodation or tension might illuminate divisive conflicts in relatively static religious cultures, it is less useful in describing the conflict that accompanies change.

But again, we must be specific about which aspects of change are accepted or rejected by various groups. In this case, it has been argued, differences between Southern Baptists hinged on acceptance or rejection of cultural (and religious) pluralism.[41] As we have seen, the term "church" adequately described the relationship between religion and culture in the evangelical heyday of the Bible Belt, when Southern Baptists were just Baptists, not fundamentalists or moderates. But that is no longer the case, and the conflict they experienced in the late twentieth century was not solely the product of one group responding to the privileged and established place of another. Rather, both were responding to a new cultural situation, a situation of pluralism.

Each side was seeking out a viable place in the newly pluralistic world in which they found themselves. To accept the modern rules of religious civility and individual choice was indeed to make a home for oneself in the modern situation, even if other aspects of modernity were questioned. This is the world to which moderates sought to adapt themselves. They were willing to leave their Southern church-like status to become a denomination in the larger American religious mosaic. The dissidents within this denomination, however, were responding differently to change. In a newly pluralistic setting, they were seeking to reestablish homogeneity. They would recreate inside the religious world what was no longer viable in the world outside. For that reason, we have called this a fundamentalist movement, not merely a sectarian one. Again, if the study of religious change and conflict is to take full account of the relationship between movements and their contexts, those contexts must be made analytically specific and placed in the perspective of time. The followers of Niebuhr have pointed us toward accommodation and acceptance of pluralism as distinguishing features of denominations. The Southern Baptists challenge us to look for responses to change, as well.

Who Would Win?

The experience of the Southern Baptist Convention also expands Niebuhr's ideas about the relative power of "privileged" and "disinherited" groups. He assumed that groups having the most of this world's goods would prevail and that the disinherited would be forced into schism. While moderates clearly were the privileged ones by outside standards, that privilege did not translate into victory.

Battles are not fought on ideas alone, nor on the status of the contenders. Winners are not simply determined by the strength of their arguments, nor are they predetermined by the social locations of the combatants. What would happen in this battle would be determined by the organizational resources each side could bring to bear. Put most plainly, the winner would be the side that could get the most people to go to annual convention meetings and vote. The methods and resources of the two sides are the subject to which we now turn.

6. Mobilizing the Troops:
Resources and Liabilities

Thinking in political terms did not come naturally for most Baptists. They have thought of their denomination in many other terms—as family, as sender of missionaries, as the source of high quality programs and training, as a pulpit for great preachers—but the language of politics was not their native tongue. Those who had formulated the Convention's constitutional structure had assumed that natural leaders would rise to the top and be accepted by consensus. There were no constitutional provisions for contending parties.[1] And the people of the Convention had no experience in being asked to support candidates for any reason other than their reputation as preachers or denominational statesmen.

But fundamentalists had concluded that denominational statesmen did not necessarily value doctrinal purity enough to be trusted with leadership. They had decided that only men committed to correcting the leftward drift of the denomination should be elected to the SBC presidency. That might, of course, have happened by chance under the existing system. W. A. Criswell, after all, had been elected for two terms in the earlier part of the decade. But fundamentalists did not want to leave things to chance any longer; and so they organized to elect presidents who would carry out their program of reform. And organizing meant getting sufficient messengers to the convention to vote for the right candidate.

The presidency in itself was not actually very important; almost anyone could preside at the meeting. But the president was the key to the entire appointment and nomination process by which trustees were placed at the helm of the denomination's agencies (see fig. 6.1). If the Southern Baptist Convention were going to be changed, it had to start with the presidency. Such a top-down strategy is ironic in a denomination that presumes to be "congregational" in polity. The official rhetoric of the denomination has it that congregations tell the denomination what to do, not the other way around. While fundamentalists wanted the congregations to tell Nashville to be more conservative, they wanted Nashville to change because they recognized the power of the agencies to shape church life.

Even as fundamentalists organized to fight for the change they wanted, they sought to resist the label "political." Many of the rank and file seemed to believe quite sincerely that encouraging people to attend a convention and vote for a president who would protect the integrity of the Bible was a normal activity, not out of the ordinary, and certainly not political. One group of messengers at the Dallas convention recalled that they had attended a meeting in their state where Paul Pressler had spoken about his concerns. There they had been "encouraged to attend" the Dallas convention; but, one of them said, "there was certainly no organized effort to get out the vote." Even one of the leaders of the fundamentalist movement told us that he "hadn't really been active" that year. He had only made four or five trips in the month before the convention—as he had promised he would. Whether consciously or unconsciously, fundamentalists seemed not to perceive their activities as any departure from the usual ways of doing things.

Moderates, on the other hand, looked around themselves and noticed immediately how different things were from the way they remembered the conventions of the past. An elderly messenger to the 1985 convention lamented that she "used to come and have a good time. It would be real spiritual, and I'd go home and feel like I'd been in heaven. But not these days. I wish it would go back to the way it was." Perhaps more tellingly, a moderate leader remembered the days when he and his friends were in charge. "These were my people. We'd gather, and it was like a homecoming." In the days they remembered, sermons and mission reports were the highlights of the convention meeting. Foreign missions night was something to remember, and the agency reports were duly noted and reported to the folks back home. But on Tuesday night in Dallas, missionaries who had lined up in the back of the hall for their part on the program watched in anger as thousands of messengers streamed out of the convention center after a weary day of issues and elections. They had finished the business they came to do, and many were leaving town. Messengers were demonstrating by their behavior that the annual meeting had become more political than inspirational.[2]

The annual meetings had always been political occasions, of course. The business done there had to do with the policies that would govern the common life of this group of Baptists, as well as with which rewards would be available to which people. For the first 100 years of its existence, the Southern Baptist Convention had made those decisions largely by consensus. For the period between 1931 and 1979, most of the work of the denomination went on in its institutions and agencies, relatively undisturbed by the annual gathering to which they reported.[3] Churches accepted that authority and allowed the programs and materials of the denomination to shape what they did. Policies were set and rewards allocated largely inside the network of pastors, trustees, and bureaucrats who were in charge. Power was at issue when people met for their annual meeting; they just never noticed it because they accepted the legitimacy of the leaders who governed and the staff who executed policy. Without

Figure 6.1.   Elections and Authority in the Southern Baptist Convention

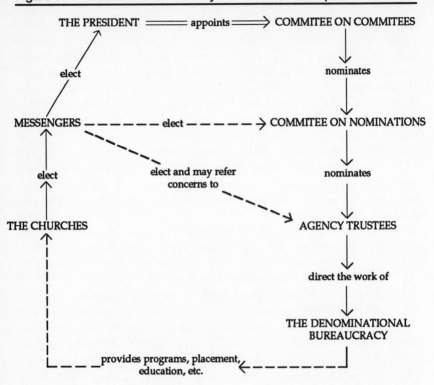

any challenge to the existing structure of power and rewards, the meetings were placid and unpolitical.

When fundamentalists decided to challenge the old powers, they had to organize their own system of rewards and bring to bear a new set of resources. It was not that the Convention had become political for the first time. Rather, there were for the first time contending political parties, each with its own platform, leadership structure, resources, and rewards. In challenging the old structure, the fundamentalists faced a formidable opponent. Their victory attests to their even more formidable marshalling of the resources necessary for the campaign.

In analyzing the political processes by which the fundamentalists came to power in the Southern Baptist Convention, we will use the perspective known in sociology as the "resource mobilization" approach to social movements. This perspective, especially as developed by Zald,[4] will turn our attention to the "infrastructure" of "means of communication, work schedules, and discretionary resources . . . preexisting networks, associations, and organizations of involved groups."[5] Achieving change in an organization requires changes in the beliefs people hold about that organization's goals and procedures, as well as changes in their behavior relative to the decision-making process. They have to come to believe that change is necessary and that they can and should act to try to effect that change. Southern Baptist fundamentalists wanted to change the denomination, and to do so they had to establish themselves in legitimate positions of power. But to do that, they had to have effective movement leadership, a clear agenda, efficient and convincing means of communication, ways of minimizing social and material costs, and means for facilitating the participation of messengers who would vote to support their candidates. To stop them, moderates would have to mobilize resources of at least equal strength. Moderates may have started with the advantages of established institutional positions, but fundamentalists soon found ways to overcome their apparent disadvantage.

Leadership and Coordination

During the 1950s and 1960s, fundamentalist pastors had largely been excluded from the normal channels of leadership in the denomination. They had rarely been nominated for any office at any level and rarely received invitations to preach in places of honor or to join agency staffs or seminary faculties. They were not recommended to the best pulpits by their state and associational leaders. That system of leadership training, career advancement, and recognition was largely monopolized by moderates (although they did not yet call each other by that name). Fundamentalists simply did not represent the direction in which the Convention was headed. They disagreed with the goals of the organization, and they were kept at the margins of the existing status system.

That did not mean, however, that they had no opportunities to become leaders, to gain recognition and influence. As we noted in chapter 3, the growth of alternative fundamentalist institutions in the 1970s offered an arena in which leadership could be developed. The new schools, Criswell, Mid-America, and Luther Rice, could train young men for fundamentalist ministries and offer more seasoned men opportunities to teach and to be honored by speaking invitations and honorary degrees. The new channels of communication—at first the *Journal* and later the *Advocate*—not only provided news but also offered recognition for the accomplishments of fundamentalist pastors.

In addition, fundamentalist leaders were making a mark for themselves in one arena long honored among Baptists—evangelism. They were dynamic preachers who knew how to recruit large numbers of people into their churches and how to move many to "walk the aisle." Their churches exploded along with the population explosion in many southern cities. They established their congregations as the most exciting, dynamic, growing churches in exciting, dynamic, and growing cities. Most were young and attractive, with an easy style that charmed those who watched them, in person or on television. As the people moved in from the countryside and immigrants arrived from outside the south, churches pastored by fundamentalists were the place to be. They built multi-million-dollar "family life centers" and equally impressive sanctuaries. They broadcast their services and produced Sunday morning events to which people were eager to return. Their congregations sometimes exceeded 10,000 members, and multiple services were held on Sunday to accommodate them. They baptized hundreds and adopted hundreds more "by letter" from other Baptist churches. Their remarkable success and growth, along with their television exposure, made them highly visible in their local communities, whether or not other Baptists liked them.

Their success also brought speaking invitations, especially to revivals, evangelistic crusades, and conferences on evangelism. For many years, each Baptist state convention had hosted a January "evangelism conference" that had become a kind of mid-year retreat for preachers. It was their chance to get away from the local parish, renew old acquaintances, hear good preaching (from someone else), and go back rejuvenated for the months ahead. Because fundamentalists were recognized as dynamic, evangelistic preachers, they were often invited to speak to these events. They were also invited to speak at the annual SBC Pastors Conference. And there were dozens of other rallies and conferences, sponsored by local churches and by independent evangelistic organizations, to which a corps of leading pulpiteers regularly made its way. In those conferences and revivals, conservative pastors firmly established themselves as leading preachers, able to draw a crowd of listeners who would go away moved and impressed.

On that circuit of revivals and conferences, links were being forged among these leaders. They stayed in each other's homes, went out for doughnuts and coffee together, and talked about their common concerns for the direction in which their world and their denomination were headed. Some of them had known each other since childhood—their fathers having pastored adjacent churches, perhaps, or having grown up in the same congregation. Some of them met through spouses or siblings. Some met in seminary, when a common alarm at what they were being taught bound them together. A network of fundamentalist leaders did not have to be constructed from scratch. It already existed in the ordinary connections that bound together people in similar circumstances.

But the network did have to be mobilized *as* a network. During the 1960s, various concerned pastors had from time to time tried to rally enough people to fight particular local issues. Small groups met, wrote letters, and tried to figure out what to do. Eventually people in one area noticed what those elsewhere were doing, and a broader group began circulating information among themselves, slowly adding names to their mailing list. Finally, in 1973, at First Baptist in Atlanta, the Baptist Faith and Message Fellowship (BFMF) was born. In this, the network had its first publicly-organized national form.

At about the same time, Paige Patterson was completing a Th.D. at New Orleans Baptist Seminary and was sought out by Judge Paul Pressler from Houston. Pressler had been told that Patterson was somebody "who thinks as you do."[6] They began to talk about what could be done to turn the Southern Baptist Convention back to its biblical roots, and in the coming months and years they joined the circuit of speakers at evangelism and pastors' conferences. By 1978, they were convinced that a new form of organization was needed. The BFMF was fine for fellowship, communication about issues, and moral support; but it had not helped them change the direction of the Convention. Patterson and Pressler helped to organize another key Atlanta meeting. Conservative author Hefley reports that at least one conservative pastor from each SBC state attended.[7] They decided that electing presidents and overseeing appointments were the keys to the process; and they set their sights on 1979, the next time there would not be an incumbent in the SBC presidency.

The names of those who attended can only be surmised. These early meetings were kept quite secret by pastors who feared they would be ostracized and ruined for such organizing. The only public figures who emerged to speak for the movement were Patterson and Pressler. Since Pressler was a lay person, and Patterson was in an independent institution, the usual sanctions could not be applied to them. The pastors simply went home and quietly organized their states, while Patterson and Pressler became the visible "bad guys."

Bound together by their common purpose and by the very secrecy of their coalition, this core group of leaders formed a highly cohesive team.[8] Apparently no one defected in the first ten years of the struggle. Whatever strategy they agreed on prevailed. The candidates they chose to run were unopposed by other conservatives. Although there must surely have been disagreements from time to time about who would serve in which position, those disagreements never became public. None of the men publicly complained that he had not been rewarded properly for his sacrifices. As the movement began to succeed, they took their places on boards of trustees; others chaired key committees and planned Pastors

Conference programs; still others became SBC presidents or heads of agencies. Some merely preached and organized, without holding office. Some moved or became less active, but none rejected the cause or repudiated its methods.

The job they took on in that first meeting was to build outward from their inner core a viable coalition that could mobilize enough messengers to assure victory. To do so, they recruited fellow pastors who shared their concerns; and they, in turn, called others who would probably want to cooperate. The net eventually reached from the super-churches to the county seats and suburbs and finally to the mass of rural pulpits that still dominated the convention. The inner core itself grew slowly as other leading pastors and rising young stars joined the cause. When they met in Atlanta in 1989, their number had grown to about 100, and they were much more public about their participation.[9]

In the early days, Fundamentalists rightly discerned that existing denominational authorities opposed the changes they wanted to make. And they knew that such a concentration of legitimate power in the hands of their opponents could spell their doom. Moderates, however, were never able to turn that official authority into a cohesive coalition that could mobilize voters in opposition to the fundamentalists.

The first difficulty for moderates was that no one believed the problem was real. In the first months after Adrian Rogers' victory in Houston, the old guard dismissed it as a fluke, as a momentary storm stirred up by a few from the radical fringe. They remembered J. Frank Norris and reassured themselves that fundamentalism had never received much of a welcome in Southern Baptist life. Those in leading pulpits, in seminary classrooms, and in the denominational agencies simply could not believe that such a movement could succeed. They thought that after a few expressions of outrage, a few attempts to label Pressler or Patterson as a new Norris, people would return to the status quo, ignoring the troublemakers. There was no need for a leadership coalition, because there was no problem against which to organize.[10]

However, in early 1980, Pressler was widely quoted explaining the movement's plans as "going for the jugular" of the Convention by electing presidents and thereby controlling appointments. A few denominational leaders began to suspect that something more was afoot than a recurrence of Norris's tirades. After the next convention, a group of a dozen or so leaders gathered in Gatlinburg, Tennessee, to assess the situation. They were mostly pastors recognized as leaders of the denomination's progressive wing, and they became known as the "Gatlinburg Gang." They decided to go on the offensive to try to ensure that the fundamentalist movement would be stopped.

In the coming years they attempted to build the kind of coalition among alarmed nonfundamentalists that the fundamentalists had already created for their own cause. They traveled to the churches of their friends, spoke at forums, and otherwise spread the word that the situation was serious. They fairly readily gathered an extended group of urban, well-educated, larger-church pastors—people like themselves. But they did not readily enlist either a broad-based coalition that extended into the countryside or a cadre of rising young stars. They may have failed to rouse the countryside because they lacked contacts and affinities outside urban areas. They failed to enlist younger progressive pastors who had recently emerged from the seminaries at least in part because many in this younger cohort recognized the extent to which their views were at odds with mainstream Southern Baptists. They did not believe they themselves could command a wide following, nor did they wish to spend their career energies in this battle. Leadership was left, then, to somewhat older, urban pastors who were more willing and more able to fight for the denomination in which they had already invested half a career.

A moderate leadership coalition was in place in the early 1980s, but varied in the degree to which it was public. In the middle of the decade, various ad hoc state organizations—in North Carolina and Virginia, Friends of Missions, in Kentucky, Friends of SBC Cooperative Missions, and in Georgia, Concerned Southern Baptists—formed openly, officially incorporated, and had publicly-designated leaders. In other states, the equivalent groups chose to keep their existence more secret. During the first half of the decade, this coalition sought to work by consensus, shunning the idea of any one leader setting policy. As a result, they were only occasionally a united group, sometimes letting institutional loyalties and rivalries stand in their way. By the time of the Atlanta convention in 1986, moderates claimed that fifteen or sixteen states were organized well enough to be able to report approximately how many moderate messengers would be coming. In that year, they had also sought, for the first time, a unified national strategy, with coordination from someone they recognized as their leader/advisor. That person was never publicly named, but he supplied a level of cohesion that had been sorely lacking in earlier years.

In the early years of the struggle, moderates not only had no single coordinator, they also had no single presidential standard-bearer. Even after Pressler made it clear that the election of presidents was the key to the fundamentalist strategy, moderates failed to counter with a single opposition candidate each year. Moderate leaders were used to thinking of nomination to the presidency as a high honor. Election meant only a little more honor than nomination. Multiple nominees had always been the order of the day, sometimes requiring multiple run-offs. By refusing to drop that custom, moderates lost the chance for a clear candidate behind whom to rally, a national spokesperson for their cause. In 1979, there were five candidates opposing Rogers; in 1980, five opposed Bailey Smith; in 1982, two opposed Jimmy Draper; in 1983, Draper was reelected without opposition; and in 1984, two moderates opposed Charles Stanley. Only in 1981, in Los Angeles, did moderates present a united front behind Baylor president Abner McCall. In 1985, after six years of fundamentalist victories over their divided opposition, moderates finally seemed to understand that presidential elections were no longer the popularity contests they had always been. When that happened elections became clearly partisan for both sides, and even moderate messengers became accustomed to looking for the party labels on their candidates. By 1988, the politicization was evidently complete. Two surprise, nonpartisan candidates were nominated against party candidates Jerry Vines and Richard Jackson. Of the 31,274 votes cast, the two independent candidates received 358 between them.

The most logical standard-bearers for the moderate cause were the high-level office holders in the denomination's agencies, people who were well known and respected across a wide cross-section of the Convention. They were the people who had naturally risen to the top in a moderate-dominated career system. They were the preachers and scholars whose message the Convention was accustomed to hearing and heeding. It was they who held the positions in which, traditionally, moral authority resided. They were leaders of the missions and Sunday School Boards, presidents and professors in colleges and seminaries. If they suggested that the Convention faced a crisis, action usually followed. If they had a bold new vision, a program was developed. If they had new doctrinal or biblical insight, it usually found an official denominational channel for publication. They should have been the most persuasive leaders in the fight to stop the fundamentalists.

But leaders in voluntary organizations have very few resources at their disposal, especially compared to leaders in hierarchical and business organizations. They cannot offer rewards or threaten sanctions, at least not beyond the immediate scope of their own organizational staff. When relating to the local units or the voluntary members who make up the bulk of the organization, they must rely on persuasion, symbolic rewards, and the intangibles of friendship. They must maintain their authority based on the very normative grounds on which the organization is founded.[11] Based on extensive study of the conditions under which church leaders can implement policies consonant with church goals—but at odds with members' wishes—James Wood has concluded that in a number of ways legitimacy is the key.[12] First, there must be a formal structure that grants leaders the legitimate power to act—something clearly missing from Southern Baptist polity. Second, both the members and the leaders must believe that it is legitimate for leaders to take controversial positions, and members must be convinced that they should tolerate actions with which they disagree. But most importantly, both the belief in legitimacy and the willingness to tolerate disagreeable actions are dependent on the leaders' ability to link their actions to shared values. It is ultimately the leaders' ability to reinterpret and evoke the core values of the organization that establishes their legitimacy. If they are no longer seen as symbols or guardians of the ideals of the group, they lose their ability to take unpopular stands or to shape the organization's concrete goals.

And these core values were the very grounds on which the fundamentalists chose to attack. By 1985, only 24 percent of our survey respondents would say that they were very confident that the SBC's schools and agencies were "doctrinally sound." The next year, 63 percent of them reported that they believed there were people teaching in Baptist colleges and seminaries who did not "believe what Baptists ought to believe." The seeds of distrust had clearly been sown. A substantial number of the voluntary members of the Southern Baptist Convention did not believe that their employed leaders represented the values of the group. And even those with modest confidence in the institutions as a whole were willing to believe that there might be a few "bad apples" in them.

Denominational leaders were caught in a fatal dilemma. As Harrison demonstrated in his study of American Baptists, denominations whose official polity is congregational have no basis for acknowledging the very real power wielded by their bureaucrats.[13] They refuse to grant legitimacy to a group that, under normal circumstances, has enormous influence over the local churches. They continue to assert that it is the local congregation that is the only legitimate source of authority, while allowing a de facto oligarchy to prevail.[14] But these were not normal circumstances, and influence never legitimated can be denied. Since the denomination had never ceded legitimate leadership status to these agency heads, they had never had any authority beyond their "moral" and symbolic power to influence. And in the early days, when they were still not convinced that their help was needed, their moral authority was already being destroyed. Once the fundamentalists had taken that, efforts to defend their institutions appeared motivated only by self-preservation, not by high and holy principles. Because their symbolic legitimacy had already been undermined, they could never regain a platform from which to address the majority of Baptists.[15] Whether or not the impressions were true mattered little. The most powerful leaders moderates could have mustered were effectively delegitimated by the early unanswered attacks of fundamentalists. By the time agency leaders joined the fray, in 1984–1985, the only authority that remained was the authority of office, and that had never been recognized by Baptists as a legitimate form of influence. For many Southern Baptists, these leaders had become merely symbols of an unfeeling bureaucracy and perhaps guardians of heretics.

The authority of office proved a liability not only because of the distrust and anti-establishment mood that had been created, but also because denominational employees felt that they could not use their offices to their advantage. In 1984–1985, when several denominational leaders were active, they were severely criticized for taking unfair advantage of their offices to campaign against a president elected by the people who "paid their salaries." As a result, they had to accept stringent limitations on their ability to lead the moderate cause. Because fundamentalists were outsiders, they ironically had more freedom to organize and speak out than did those who occupied the denomination's highest executive positions.

In the early 1980s, then, fundamentalists had a clear leadership advantage. They had taken an informal network of super-church pastors and evangelists and molded it into a cohesive coalition with a passionately-held agenda. These leaders were preachers of remarkable ability, able to stir crowds with their words, able to evoke response in their hearers. They had developed a following after years on the revival and Pastors Conference circuit and were broadly admired as the leading pulpiteers of the day, even by people who later joined the moderate cause against them. Moderate leadership, on the other hand, had developed through the normal denominational channels of training and career, with the best among them moving into institutional roles. There, ironically, their very success under the old system proved a liability in their attempt to persuade Southern Baptists that the fundamentalists should be turned back. The pastors who took up the moderate fight were very good preachers, often with polished literary and rhetorical flair. But a Cecil Sherman was unlikely to move a crowd as an Adrian Rogers could. And Roy Honeycutt's doctrinal expositions could not match the popular appeal of Jimmy Draper's. Many moderates were relatively remote from the majority of Baptists, having left behind the simple smalltown life. Both their positions as official denominational leaders and their remoteness from their roots diminished their ability to lead.

Symbols and Agenda

We have already seen that the primary symbols in this denominational fight were the Bible, on one side, and freedom, on the other. But from the beginning, fundamentalists had seized the initiative in defining the conflict in their terms. While most Baptists might agree with the moderates about the importance of interpreting scripture for oneself and tolerating others who disagree, they were not willing to go so far as to allow interpretations that seemed to violate a basic trust in the veracity of the Bible. They could say "yes" to the moderate call for cooperation, but could also say "yes" to the fundamentalist call for the ouster of professors and writers who "do not believe the Bible." The moderate rhetoric of freedom and cooperation was simply not powerful enough to overcome the fundamentalist rhetoric based on unquestioning belief in the Bible.

By claiming the Bible as their chief symbol, fundamentalists also gained the initiative in defining the rest of the agenda for the conflict. They wanted employees who believed the Bible and agencies that would run by biblical rules. They wanted an end to onerous practices like the ordination of women, and they wanted the adoption of a social agenda more in keeping with their conservative instincts.

The actual moderate agenda, in place among the leaders of the denomination over the previous two decades, was not one often touted openly. It involved opening the denomination to a broad range of influences beyond its traditional southern core and thereby questioning many of the cultural elements that had defined being southern and Baptist. Convention leaders had fostered the introduction of historical critical methods of biblical interpretation, had supported the ordination of women, had taken a progressive view on race relations and other social issues, and had not sought to stop the erosion of traditional southern taboos on dancing, card playing, and the like. During the 1960s, these issues had occasionally been addressed directly in SBC programs and periodicals, but almost inevitably a conservative backlash followed.[16] As a result, moderate leaders were reluctant to hit the trail in open support of the agenda that had in fact guided their actions. They were simply convinced that they could not rally majority support for that agenda (and they were probably right). As a result, moderates were reduced to general calls for "freedom" and to responding to the agenda defined by the fundamentalists.[17]

This lack of a clearly-defined moderate agenda showed up in analysis of the data gathered through our surveys. The questionnaires contained a number of items about which moderates had specifically been concerned, yet it proved nearly impossible to construct a scale out of those items. Scales are groups of items that go together because people answer them similarly. Our scale of items related to the fundamentalist agenda had an alpha score of .76 (a measure of internal coherence with a high score of 1.00)—an indication of just how closely the various parts of that scale fit together. People who lacked confidence in the boards were also likely to want churches and agencies censured for ordaining women, and they were likely to consider leaving the convention if it did not return to "biblical soundness." But no such cluster of issues ever emerged for moderates. Wanting freedom of interpretation was only marginally related to an emphasis on the importance of cooperation, which in turn was only marginally related to support for the separation of church and state or congregational limits on the pastor's authority. The only empirical way to define the moderate agenda was to define it as opposition to the fundamentalist platform. In other words, the denomination's rhetorical battles were not fought between pro-moderates and pro-fundamentalists, but between pro-fundamentalists and anti-fundamentalists.

As we examine the different resources available to the two sides in this conflict, then, we will concentrate on agreement or disagreement on the fundamentalist platform. That platform of issues will be defined as

- lack of confidence in the "doctrinal soundness" of convention agencies;

- lack of confidence in the responsiveness of convention agencies to ordinary Baptists;

- willingness to censure agencies that promote women's ordination;

- willingness to disfellowship churches that ordain women; and

- willingness to leave the convention if it is not "brought back to biblical soundness."

Up until now we have been concerned with how the convention was divided over ideological and lifestyle issues, but political organizing took place around political issues, and it is to those we will turn. Theology and positions on these issues are certainly related (see table 6.1). Indeed, as we saw in the last chapter, theology and theological self-identification (along with education) were the key determinants of where people stood on denominational issues. Those we will term "profundamentalist" are the people whose beliefs and educational experience had led them to the conclusion that a number of things needed changing in the Southern Baptist Convention. They were in high agreement with the fundamentalist platform. Those we will call antifundamentalist are the people whose beliefs and education had led them to the conclusion that the denomination was working just fine and fundamentalist changes would be unwelcome. Those termed undecided here are people who agreed with the fundamentalists on some things, but not all. By those definitions 36 percent are profundamentalist, 29 percent undecided, and 35 percent antifundamen-

Table 6.1. Support for the Fundamentalist Agenda by Theological Parties

SBC Political Position	Self-Identified Moderates	Moderate Conservatives	Conservatives	Fundamentalist Conservatives	Self-Identified Fundamentalists	Total
Anti-fundamentalist	86%	71%	32%	20%	5%	35%
Undecided	12	23	38	22	23	29
Pro-fundamentalist	2	7	30	58	72	36
Total	100%	101%	100%	100%	100%	100%
(Number of Cases)	(88)	(79)	(454)	(201)	(103)	(925)

NOTE: Difference between parties is statistically significant at p < .001. Some percentages do not total 100 due to rounding.

talist. Neither side had a clear majority. To win, either would have to convince people in the middle to go along with them.

Communicating the Message

A social movement requires more than leaders and an agenda, of course. It must also have followers, and recruiting people who will take up the cause requires that they hear the movement's message. There must be people for whom the agenda of the movement makes sense. There must be people for whom this movement provides sensible explanations for life's quandaries and practical ways to survive in the world they inhabit. We have already explored the extent to which the changes and dislocations of recent southern history created a cohort for whom the message of a fundamentalist movement made sense. Those same changes also created a climate in which a moderate Southern Baptist message made sense to others. Both sides faced the task of communicating their message beyond a leadership core, making the symbols and arguments of their movement available to a waiting constituency.

The most natural form of communication among Southern Baptists is, of course, the pulpit. And in that medium, as we have noted, fundamentalists excelled. Their preaching styles and their message of clear answers and certain directions lent themselves to mass mobilization. Moderate style, on the other hand, was more likely to be subdued, somewhat scholarly, and open to the ambiguities of life. Fundamentalists asserted, "This is the way!" Moderates outlined a list of alternatives.

Fundamentalist leaders also had greater access to pulpits where large numbers of people might be gathered. Their own churches were often huge, and the revivals and evangelism conferences to which they preached made them widely recognizable. Moderates, on the other hand, were less likely to host revivals and evangelistic crusades and had no comparable social form at which a pulpiteer might gain a following. Moderate pastors did not have the extensive staffs enjoyed by the super-church pastors and were thus not so free to travel as were the independent evangelists and pastors with multiple associates.

While it was relatively rare for a moderate pastor to preach in widespread pulpits, (moderate) denominational officials were everywhere. They traveled extensively and enjoyed a wide hearing at state conventions, workshops, and in local churches. Again, had denominational officials, rather than pastors, led the moderate cause, their access to large audiences would have been a distinct advantage. Each year, we asked our respondents whether they had been to a meeting at which any of a long list of activists had spoken. The only moderates who ever came close to the listenership of fundamentalists like Draper and Rogers were seminary presidents Honeycutt and Dilday in the campaign year of 1985. Over time, then, fundamentalist speakers had built up a very broad base of recognition in the denomination. When pastor Winfred Moore faced Adrian Rogers for election to the denomination's presidency in 1986, nearly twice as many people had heard Rogers preach, both in person and through various mass media.

The other striking advantage fundamentalist speakers had developed was the opportunity to preach in situations not specifically defined as political, where their messages would be heard by a wide variety of Baptists. Over a quarter (27 percent) of the clergy in the undecided camp had heard a fundamentalist speaker in 1985, while only 20 percent of them had heard a moderate speaker (see table 6.2). Of all the people who had heard fundamentalist speakers in 1985, over half (56 percent) were non-fundamentalists. Of those who had heard a moderate speaker that year, only 43 percent were not moderates. Anti-fundamentalist clergy were almost as likely, in each year, to hear a fundamentalist speaker as to hear a moderate one, while profundamentalists were generally about twice as likely to hear one of their own as to hear someone from the opposition. It appears that moderate speakers were preaching more often to people already committed to the cause, while fundamentalist speakers were broadly known and heard by a cross-section of the denomination. In 1985, the two parties' total audiences among our respondents were roughly even: 30 percent of clergy and 8 percent of laity had heard a fundamentalist speaker; 28 percent of clergy and 6 percent of laity had heard a moderate speaker. But the distribution of people in those audiences may

Table 6.2. Political Communications Received by SBC Political
Parties, 1985

Communication Source	% Anti-fundamentalist Clergy	% Undecided Clergy	% Pro-fundamentalist Clergy	Total All Clergy
Fundamentalist speaker	29	27	33	30
Moderate speaker	49	20	15	28
The *Advocate*	59	69	79	69
SBC Today	62	62	47	55
(Number of Cases)	(122)	(65)	(140)	(328)

reflect a significant advantage for fundamentalists in getting their message to people who were not already convinced.

That pattern was also apparent in what messengers did with their pre-convention time. The Pastors Conference was, of course, the traditional event to attend. The Forum was the upstart, and was overtly political. Far fewer attended the Forum (by a factor of at least four or five to one), and those who went were likely to be already-convinced moderates. In 1986, only one third of our respondents who attended the Forum were from the undecided or profundamentalist camps. In 1987, none were. Moderates, on the other hand, were quite likely to attend the fundamentalist-dominated Pastors Conference, where they would hear messages designed to convince them that change was needed. Since before 1979 fundamentalist preachers had used this preconvention platform as an opportunity to assail heresy in the seminaries and wickedness in the world, and their message always had a large audience that spanned the Convention's political spectrum. In 1986, as many moderates went there as to the Forum. Again, moderates were much more likely to be exposed to the fundamentalist version of events than were fundamentalists to hear what their opposition had to say.

Fundamentalists were also more likely to utilize mass media for disseminating their message. Charles Stanley actually had a nationally syndicated TV program, and nearly one fourth (23 percent) of our 1985 respondents said that they "regularly" watched his "In Touch" ministry. Even if Stanley never directly addressed problems facing the denomination on his broadcasts, this regular, national exposure greatly extended his potential influence. Moderates had no comparable broadcast exposure. In 1986, moderates in Georgia hoped to get Winfred Moore's message to likely messengers by televising the church service at which he spoke on the Sunday before the convention.[18] The service, however, was aired late that Sunday night, and the sermon Moore delivered could hardly have helped the cause very much. He offered neither dramatic solutions for life's problems nor any direct commentary on what should be done in the SBC. In 1987, moderate candidate Richard Jackson did have a regular viewing audience, but he voluntarily gave it up in the weeks before the convention. He had been the regular preacher on "The Baptist Hour," a program carried by the denomination's ACTS cable network. However, he feared charges of unfair advantage if he continued to preach while he was an active presidential candidate.[19] In both instances moderates were unable to use television effectively, either to keep their candidate before the voters or to address directly the issues in the Convention.

Some of the media exposure for each side came from sources outside the denomination, however. Both Jerry Falwell and Pat Robertson, preachers watched regularly by 12 percent and 13 percent, respectively, of our respondents, have mentioned or featured the SBC on their programs.[20] In 1985, CBN offered a forum for the fundamentalist perspective. Former Convention presidents Rogers, Smith, and Draper appeared with Pat Robertson on the 700 Club, citing examples of doctrinal irregularities and emphasizing the importance of Charles Stanley being re-elected that year.[21] The moderate cause got its chance in 1988, on PBS. In a program aired just before the convention meeting, former Southern Baptist Bill Moyers examined the denomination's "Battle for the Bible." He gave ample air time to denominational moderates and progressives and painted the fundamentalists as departing from the democratic ideals of historic Baptist practice. While he did not speak directly about the presidential election, there could have been little doubt who he favored.

Perhaps the most dramatic endorsement fundamentalists got was from the most famous "TV preacher" of all, Billy Graham. On the eve of the 1985 convention, he sent a telegram that he later claimed was meant to be a private message of encouragement. It was publicly released, however, and was communicated to the gathering crowds in Dallas.[22] As the favorite son of Southern Baptists, Graham stood in a uniquely influential position, and his endorsement added considerably to the legitimacy of the fundamentalist cause. The next year, they got another "celebrity endorsement" in the form of a letter of commendation from President Ronald Reagan. This time the letter was saved until after the election, but it was the first order of business after the results had been announced. While not specifically endorsing Adrian Rogers, Reagan did make clear his support for the conservative agenda in the denomination. Moderates simply had no such nationally-recognized figures who could help them draw attention to the message they wished to communicate.

   Both sides in this conflict adopted one of the fundraising and mobilization techniques perfected by TV preachers, namely the mass mailing. In 1985, W. A. Criswell sent a letter and brochure to every Southern Baptist pastor (all 36,000 of them) urging the reelection of Charles Stanley. Calling Stanley "God's prophet" and referring to First Baptist Atlanta as "one of the great strategic churches in our Southern Baptist zion," Criswell argued that Baptists should work with Stanley to win the world for Christ. In 1988, moderates followed suit. Winfred Moore, the moderates' previous candidate for president, sent out a letter, brochure, and tape. While the letter urged pastors to pray for the upcoming San Antonio convention (and asked that they return an enclosed reply card saying they would), the brochure took a different tack. It included a section linking Patterson, Pressler, and other fundamentalist leaders to Reconstructionism (which the brochure called a "scary cult"). The attempt backfired, and this mailing probably lost more votes than it gained. Meanwhile, that same year, First Baptist of Jacksonville, Florida, had paid to send copies of their pastor's 1987 Convention Sermon to every SBC pastor. Their pastor was Jerry Vines, and he would be the nominee of the fundamentalist party at that year's convention. In 1989, moderates tried again, this time with a taped sermon from candidate Daniel Vestal. Both sides hoped these mass mailings, usually in the weeks before the convention meeting, would communicate their message as broadly as possible.

   The messages of each side were carried largely by preachers, although those preachers often extended their reach by using television, radio, mass mail, and cassette tapes to communicate with the masses of Southern Baptists. Communication from the two parties in this Baptist battle was not limited to the pulpit, however. While oral means were the most natural among a people accustomed to "hearing the Word," written words became important, as well. Fundamentalists entered the field first, with the Baptist Faith and Message Fellowship's *Southern Baptist Journal*. Started in late 1973, with William A. Powell as editor, the *Journal* was seen as an alternative to the denomination's Baptist Press service and the state Baptist papers. Because Baptist Press was organizationally located within the Executive Committee, fundamentalists saw it as merely the mouthpiece of the bureaucrats who were leading the Convention in directions fundamentalists did not want to go.[23] The *Journal* was published sporadically (generally four or five times a year) during the 1970s, but it was instrumental in beginning to build the coalitions fundamentalists would need.

   It always had, however, something of the look and tone of a scandal sheet. Powell was tireless in seeking out evidence of liberalism and often published the book and article excerpts that conservatives used for ammunition against people in schools and agencies. By 1980, a number of the leaders of the movement had become convinced that the *Journal* had become too strident to serve their needs. At first they tried to replace Powell as editor, but when that failed, a whole new publication was launched. The *Southern Baptist Advocate* would be headquartered in Dallas and edited by Paige Patterson's brother-in-law Russell Kaemmerling. The *Journal* would continue to be published from time to time, and up to 25 percent of our respondents claimed to read it, but the torch had clearly passed to the new publication.

The *Advocate* was published in magazine format, rather than as a newspaper. It was attractively laid out, often with two-color printing and always with a variety of articles. Friends at *Christianity Today* provided Kaemmerling with support and guidance. He read widely from the newsletters of numerous conservative organizations. Despite his lack of journalistic experience, he put together a monthly paper of wide-ranging coverage and appeal. It still covered the events and trends it considered evidence of liberalism in the denomination—a feminist litany used in chapel at Southeastern or a invitation to a gay man by a student group at Southern.[24] It still celebrated the successes of conservative churches and advertised products offered by conservative pastors (tapes, cruises, Holy Land tours, and the like). It added a number of features focusing on political and social issues (communism and abortion, for instance), but it also added attention to denominational programs that deserved support by conservatives. And it provided very explicit instruction on attending annual conventions and background on the issues that would face those gatherings.[25] Its stories were usually short and to the point, without extensive detail or analysis. It was easy to remember what the *Advocate* had to say. Periodically it was mailed to all Southern Baptist pastors, and in 1985 two-thirds (69 percent) of our clergy respondents claimed that they got news about the Convention from its pages (see table 6.2).

During the early period, moderates depended for their news on the official denominational sources. Nearly 90 percent of our respondents claimed that they got news about the convention from their state Baptist papers. Many churches bought bulk subscriptions for twenty or more members, who then received a paper each week at their home. What they read in these news-magazines was everything from Bible studies to lists of the churches that gave most to the Cooperative Program. They featured the successes of missionaries far and near, and they promoted the programs being developed in Nashville.

Although each paper had some local staff for reporting its own state issues, much of what they printed came from the denomination's news bureau, Baptist Press. Staffed in Nashville by seasoned journalists, and fed by reporters in several other "bureaus" (mostly staff people in agencies such as the Baptist Joint Committee or the Home Mission Board), Baptist Press had become among the most respected denominational news operations in the country. They issued releases to subscribers five days a week, all year long. Most stories were the kind of denominational insider news that one would expect.[26] But they also covered the stories that would be of interest to readers beyond the denominational inner circle. Fundamentalists did not trust them, but moderates and the secular press found "BP" indispensable for solid stories backed by good reporting.

When a group of fundamentalists announced their intention to change the direction of the Convention, it was a story Baptist Press could not ignore. It was the kind of "real news" reporters like BP's news director Dan Martin thrive on. In the early 1980s, BP followed the fundamentalists wherever they went. In the months before the 1985 convention, for instance, when both sides were working furiously to get out the vote, BP covered fundamentalist rallies in Birmingham, Wichita, Knoxville, Oklahoma City, Little Rock, and Lexington, South Carolina. They also covered moderate rallies in Myrtle Beach, Louisville, and Knoxville. They reported the charges and countercharges, even those aimed at their own news operation. To an outsider, their accounts seemed even-handed, but their stories were often printed alongside editorials written by state paper editors who, almost to a person, opposed what the fundamentalists were doing. As a result, the entire denominational media establishment was soon branded as blatantly proliberal. But through such reporting the messages of both sides were being extended into the homes of virtually every Southern Baptist who cared to keep up with such things.

In 1983, BP and the state papers had been joined on the scene by an explicitly moderate publication, *SBC Today*. Walker Knight, longtime editor of *Home Missions* magazine had left the Home Mission Board to edit this "national, autonomous publication of news and opinion for Southern Baptists." Its twenty-eight-page tabloid format made it much longer than the *Journal, Advocate*, or any state paper. It clearly assumed a well-read audience.[27] It covered a wide range of topics, including much of the standard denominational news, but with a political savvy and candor never allowed someone inside the establishment. It covered foreign missions, but focused on such things as debates about the influences of liberation theology and whether missionaries should stay nonpolitical. It reported on opposition to women in ministry and on the accomplishments of women ministers. It consistently took the "New Christian Right" to task, often wondering in print when Jerry Falwell would become a Southern Baptist. It published sermons and book and movie reviews, along with updates on various church-state issues. And, of course, it highlighted the controversy in the denomination from a moderate point of view and alerted readers to issues facing upcoming Convention meetings. It was never as single-mindedly political as moderate political activists wished, but Knight's experience and training in journalism were clearly evident, as was his excellent access to denominational insiders. It would be several years before the magazine had anything like a comfortable budget, but they never missed publishing an issue. They, like the *Advocate*, periodically mailed their magazine to every SBC pastor, and by 1985, nearly as many pastors read *SBC Today* as read the *Advocate* (see table 6.2).

Other moderate groups added the *Baptist Laity Journal* and *The Call* to the list of independent publications circulating among Baptists. The *Laity Journal*, as the name implied, was aimed at mobilizing laity, and *The Call* was published only in the months immediately before the 1985 convention. Both were almost exclusively political journals, containing little about missions or other denominational matters. They contained shorter, more hard-hitting articles than *SBC Today*, making the moderate case in its most direct and simple form. In 1988, *Laity Journal* joined forces with the new moderate coalition, "Baptists Committed" and published only an occasional newsletter thereafter.

The result of all this publishing and mailing was that by 1985, 75 percent of our clergy respondents said that they got news about the Convention from one or more of the political journals. Nearly half (45 percent) said they read both. The readers of *SBC Today* were more likely to say they also read the *Advocate* than were the *Advocate*'s readers to read *SBC Today*. This parallels the patterns of the two groups in hearing political speakers. Moderates were more likely to have heard and read messages from the other side than fundamentalists were to have heard or read the moderate view. At least partly because people from all sides were reading it in substantial numbers, the *Advocate*'s audience among clergy was larger than *SBC Today*'s clergy audience. Just over half (55 percent) of the pastors said they read the moderate journal, while two-thirds (69 percent) said they read the paper published by the fundamentalist side. Among laity, readership of the two was nearly identical at about 9 percent for each. What the fundamentalists had achieved, then, was a substantial majority of pastors (and a small number of laity) who were well-versed in the rhetoric and issues of the conservative cause. On the other side, somewhat fewer people were reading *SBC Today*, and fewer still relied on it as their sole source of information on the conflict.

In 1986, personal difficulties forced Kaemmerling to resign as the *Advocate*'s editor. He was succeeded by Robert Tenery, a North Carolina stalwart of the movement. Tenery had been publishing a newsletter for

North Carolina conservatives, but he had no other journalistic experience or formal training, a deficit that was apparent in the paper's subsequent unpolished literary style. In addition, as a busy pastor, Tenery could not devote full time to the operation, and often failed to produce any paper at all. Only twelve issues appeared between February 1986 and June 1989. This sporadic publishing record seemed not to have hurt the cause, however. Readership among our survey respondents had dropped off slightly by 1987, but so had the readership of *SBC Today*. The drop-off appeared to reflect decreasing interest in the controversy rather than any specific disaffection with the *Advocate*.

Perhaps that general lack of interest explains the failure of a third fundamentalist journal that entered the arena in 1988. *The Cause* was to be published in Jacksonville and was to be a full-color magazine featuring missions and evangelism at least as prominently as politics. Their first issue appeared just before the 1988 convention (coinciding with Jacksonville pastor Jerry Vines' successful presidential bid), and a second followed soon after the convention. But no further issues were forthcoming until a farewell newsletter in June of the next year. The editor had told me in 1988 that they had "more paid subscriptions than *SBC Today*," promising that they anticipated a long-term demand for their magazine. But a year later an editorial acknowledged that they had been counting on regular financial support from "several leading conservative SBC pastors," support that had not materialized.[28]

Nevertheless, the cause of fundamentalism had found ample channels of communication over the previous decade and a half. Its preachers were widely heard and its journals widely read. While moderates could claim the loyalty of denominational officials and sources of information, those officials and reporters could not overtly "campaign." When moderates finally began to organize explicitly moderate channels of communication, they had to catch up. And because their speakers and journals were organized in the heat of an explicitly political battle, they remained more ghettoized than the fundamentalist speakers and journals. They more often delivered the message only to people who were already convinced.

The Costs and Benefits of Participation

All the communication in the world was of little use to either side if those who received the message were not willing or able to get involved. Since going to an annual convention costs both time and money, and since taking a stand has social and political costs, both sides sought to minimize costs while maximizing the rewards to potential messengers and campaign workers.

The monetary costs of convention attendance were initially less burdensome for moderates. They came from larger churches and sometimes had larger personal incomes. However, the churches of our moderate respondents were no more likely to provide financial support for convention attendance than were the churches of our fundamentalist respondents. Fundamentalists soon overcame whatever monetary disadvantage they had with an innovation of their own. They chartered buses for the trip, thus holding transportation costs to a minimum. And they asked people only to attend for one day—the crucial presidential election day on Tuesday. Anyone who lived within about 200 miles of the convention site could catch an early bus on Tuesday morning and be home before bedtime. People who lived slightly farther away might have to pay for one night's lodging and miss two days of work, but the costs were still minimal compared to the meals and hotel bills (not to mention air fare) being borne by those who went and stayed for three, or even four or five days.

The costs in time, of course, partially explain the predominance of clergy among the messengers. Retired people, school teachers, housewives, and people with ample vacation policies could attend; but most laity found that missing more than one day of work was not feasible. By finding a way to lower the time-and-money costs of participation and by carefully recruiting within the radius of a half-day's drive, fundamentalists mobilized a whole new cohort of messengers, often from small churches that had never before been involved.

Not everyone could come by bus, of course. Some would have to come by plane and would have to stay in hotels. And both sides soon became involved in the travel business. They had to make sure that those who wanted to go had transportation and that hotel rooms were available for those who wanted to stay. Each side advertised in its respective journal the services of travel agents who would offer special discount air fares and special hotel rates. Moderates once circulated a horror story about losing a block of hotel rooms to some mysterious person who paid for them in cash. In most convention cities, rooms were at a premium, especially when crowds were so huge. Planning ahead was essential. When the Emory contingent arrived in Dallas on Friday night before the convention to discover that our reservations had not been received, panic set in; there was literally no room in any inn. Although we did get space, our experience was typical of what would have faced any Baptist foolish enough to make a last-minute decision to attend, especially if he or she did so without the aid of a broker. Going to conventions was no longer an individual enterprise; it was an activity controlled in large part by the parties who held the keys to transportation and lodging.

The story of the hotel rooms paid for in cash raises the perennial question that has haunted this controversy: Where has the money come from? It is a question each side has asked about the other, and it is a question on which no full accounting can be given. In some cases (the 1988 mailing of Vines' sermon, for instance) a local church has carried the expense for a specific project. In other cases (the mailing of a tape of 1989 moderate candidate Dan Vestal's sermon), a single anonymous donor footed the bill. Pressler admitted in the Firestorm Chat tape that he had some financial help for his travel, but that the rest came from his own pocket. When the agency heads campaigned in 1985, they were careful to avoid using institutional funds for their trips. Instead, either their host group or anonymous donors made their travel possible. Both the Pastors Conference and the Forum are financed each year by a free will offering taken during the sessions. *SBC Today* had support from its host church and from a number of other churches, but was financed primarily through subscriptions and small donations. After 1986 the *Advocate* survived on donations alone. Each side probably had well-to-do laity who were willing to write substantial checks from time to time. And each side suspected the other of having secret sources of vast sums of cash. What seems more likely is that each side repeatedly "passed the hat" among the faithful, gaining most of their support from masses of ten and twenty-dollar bills.

There were other costs, as well, beyond the monetary and logistical costs of attending a convention or supporting the cause. Especially for clergy, there were costs to be incurred in taking sides. For a few of the pastors from the smallest and most conservative churches, supporting SBC fundamentalists meant getting involved in a denomination that had always been held at arm's length. Landmark traditions were still strong enough to keep some Baptists away from full Convention participation. One pastor from a country church in Tennessee told me at the Dallas convention that he had to ask his church's permission to come. They had never before sent a messenger, and they were frankly a little suspicious.

But most churches with fundamentalist pastors were probably not so reluctant. As we have seen, fundamentalist pastors are likely to claim a good deal of authority and have a good deal of influence in their churches. They were likely to be able to add resources to the cause by marshaling their members' support. Members, individually and collectively, became donors, and some went along to vote. We have the testimony of some fundamentalist leaders, in fact, that they expected the messengers they took to vote as a fundamentalist bloc. An active Florida organizer advised other organizers in 1985, to make sure their church's messengers were "led by the Spirit of God." He noted, "I don't want anyone going from my church that I have questions about." Fellow fundamentalist Homer Lindsay agreed, "I'm not telling you how to vote, but if you do what God wants you to do, then we'll vote the same way. [God's] not going to lead you to do one thing and me another."[29] Once the fundamentalist pastor had gained the respect of his flock, he could be fairly certain that he would not incur undue costs for his activities in the Convention. He could also be fairly sure that where resources would allow, his laity would attend and vote for a cause they too saw as holy.

The social costs fundamentalist pastors were likely to incur were, in the early days at least, costs connected to collegiality and career. In the early days, anyone caught organizing opposition to the established system could expect to be labeled a troublemaker and shunned. They had broken the unwritten codes of Southern Baptist conduct that prescribed niceness and cooperativeness as prime virtues. It was for that reason that Patterson and Pressler were the primary visible organizers and spokesmen. The social risks conservatives faced were real, and their involvement testifies to their sheer passion for the cause.

By the late 1980s, however, Pressler and Patterson were less often needed as public scapegoats. The network of profundamentalist pastors was well in place and was able to offer its own rewards in the form of recognition, participation, and appointments to denominational offices. For many pastors in churches long outside the denominational reward system, participation in this conservative resurgence involved far more rewards than costs. Smaller urban and rural churches had long been ignored by "headquarters." Enthusiastic (fundamentalist) evangelists had been passed over in favor of innovative (moderate) program developers. The fundamentalist movement reversed all that.[30]

For moderate pastors, there were costs and benefits, as well. Just as participation itself brought rewards for fundamentalists, moderate pastors might also gain by speaking out for the moderate cause. Like their opponents, they often felt the thrill of involvement in a worthy crusade, the satisfaction of doing something they saw as important for themselves and others. Within the ranks of their compatriots, involvement brought the rewards of appreciation and admiration.

But social rewards were often outweighed by the costs borne by moderate pastors who took up this cause. Because so few people believed that a problem existed, early moderate activists were as likely as fundamentalists to be seen as troublemakers. That gradually became less the case, but the majority of Baptists wanted desperately to believe that there was nothing really wrong. In the interest of preserving their vision of peace, they were often willing to shun the messenger—moderate or fundamentalist—who proclaimed that there was no peace. Although moderates were more securely established in the SBC career system, becoming involved in this struggle threatened to destroy the advantages they had accumulated.

In addition, moderate pastors often faced real risks inside their own congregations. Many pastored "Old First Churches." These downtown churches in small and medium cities often contained the elite of the community and a broad cross section of theological views. While many in the congregation might be well-educated and progressive, others might be just as well-educated and both culturally and theologically conservative. Conservatives might, in fact, be among the most powerful people in the church, perhaps holding both key positions and giving large sums of money. They wanted an eloquent and cultured pastor from the most prestigious seminary, but they did not want to abandon either their traditional beliefs about the Bible or their traditional southern ways of living. Moderate pastors who chose to oppose fundamentalism sometimes risked the wrath of such members. A few even found themselves without jobs.[31]

More commonly, moderate pastors had at least some room to make unpopular statements. But they could rarely count on active and unanimous support from the congregation. Even if they took ten messengers to a convention, three or four of them might vote for the fundamentalist candidates and agenda. The moderate pastor's own commitment to tolerate diversity would not allow him or her to prevent fundamentalist messengers from attending and voting their consciences.

Moderate lay messengers often faced costs they never anticipated when they agreed to go to a Southern Baptist Convention. Most went expecting the exhilaration of participating in a massive exercise in democracy, and many were bitterly disappointed at the lack of debate and their loss of every vote. They came away feeling as if it had done no good at all to be there. In some cases, it had been quite unpleasant. Naively sitting in the midst of people who were voting the other way, they had to listen to the vigorous applause and gloating comments around them. When they bravely raised their cards in opposition, they might be reminded that people like them needed the prayers of people who knew the correct way to vote.[32] And when the winner of the presidential election was announced, fundamentalist supporters cheered as if a war had been won. They sometimes mounted their chairs, waving Bibles in the air, and shouted their feelings of vindication. Many moderates vowed they would never subject themselves to such an experience again.

Moderate leaders sometimes endured more direct verbal assaults on the floor of the convention. They could not be attacked during official reports or debate; the rules of decorum prohibited angry or accusatory public comments. People attempting such comments from microphones soon found themselves cut off or their remarks stricken from the record. However, the rules of decorum did not apply to what was said outside official debate. On at least a half dozen occasions, I witnessed what seemed the verbal equivalent of schoolyard fights. Although moderates sometimes initiated arguments with fundamentalists, most of the ones I witnessed started with a fundamentalist seeking out a moderate with whom he was particularly upset—sometimes over something that had just happened, sometimes over events in general.[33] Approaching that person, the attacker would begin a deluge of accusations and angry comments. Soon the two would be surrounded by twenty or thirty spectators, pressing in on the pair, sometimes shouting encouragement to one or the other. In one such encounter, the fundamentalist accused the moderate of really being an Episcopalian at heart; and someone shouted from the back, "Why don't you admit you don't believe the Bible?" The moderate protested that he *did* believe the Bible *and* that his church had given more to the Cooperative Program than any other in his state—including the much larger church of the man who had just been elected SBC president. As the two men talked, they moved closer together. Eventually each placed a hand on the other's shoulder, and used the other hand to jab an angry finger at the other's lapel. None of these encounters ever came to real blows. Some victims, in fact, were able to maintain an almost super-human graciousness in the face of the anger they were receiving. Usually, the encounter ended as abruptly as it began, sometimes at the behest of some outside agent. It was simply another of the costs of involvement, especially for visible moderate leaders. Not only did they lose every vote, but they also had to face angry opponents in unpleasant arguments.

Defeat was a cost that eventually took a toll on the moderate cause. People were unwilling to return year after year only to lose every vote. One outgoing moderate trustee explained to me in 1987 that he was not going to the convention that year because "I'm tired of butting my head against a wall." Going only to cast losing ballots seemed to him a waste of time and money. Some moderates suspected after Dallas that the fight was over, and their suspicions were confirmed by the defeat in Atlanta. If massive organizing, a friendly location, and the absence of an incumbent were not enough to ensure victory, they saw no reason to believe that victory would follow in subsequent years. Ironically, however, even those who said on their surveys that they were "grieving" and that moderates should seek other alternatives remained at least as politically active as those who left each annual meeting vowing "next year we'll win." Perhaps these survey respondents were like the moderate activist I interviewed in 1986. He vowed that he was through organizing, that he thought moderates ought to boycott the St. Louis convention, that going on with the fight was a waste of money. But he remained active, went to St. Louis, and somehow could not give up the cause—he loved the denomination too much to walk away. By 1988, however, 20 percent of our moderate survey respondents said that they thought their churches would be participating less in future conventions.

Moderates often described themselves as not being "fighters." They pointed out that they rarely painted the world in passionate black and white. Most said they would rather just go back to pastoring their churches. Nevertheless, a few of the moderate leaders seemed to thrive on the conflict and on the ever-elusive possibility of victory. They watched their margin of defeat get narrower, and they derived hope and energy for the coming year. Like the fundamentalists, they had a cause about which they were passionate—returning the SBC to its heritage of freedom and cooperation. Whatever costs they experienced seemed outweighed by the benefits of leading a worthy cause.

Political Action and Convention Attendance

To find out just how mobilized the two sides were, to assess which side had best been able to induce involvement, we asked our respondents a series of questions about activities in which they might have engaged as a specific response to the conflict in the convention. These were explicitly political activities, ranging from merely attending a meeting to recruiting messengers to actually going to the convention (see table 6.3). In 1985, nearly three quarters of the clergy (73 percent) and almost half (44 percent) of the lay church leaders who returned our survey said that they had been involved in at least one political activity that year. Those numbers changed little in 1986, but dropped off considerably (at least among moderates and the undecided) in 1987. They were up again in 1988, but did not regain their 1985–1986 levels. (This pattern of political activity parallels, of course, the sizes of the conventions in those years.)

These numbers would seem to indicate a rather high level of political activity and the presence of an on-going political infrastructure. They also suggest that the pleas of the Peace Committee for a campaign moratorium went largely unheeded. On the moderate side, activities became less visible after 1985. When we talked to more than a dozen leading moderate organizers in the weeks before the 1986 Atlanta convention, it was apparent that they had attempted to honor the Peace Committee's requests by refraining from public attention to the cause. The agency heads who had actively campaigned the year before were silent, as well. Although many moderates were clearly still working behind the scenes, they had given Baptist Press little, if anything, to cover.

Fundamentalists, on the other hand, were somewhat more public about their efforts during the Peace Committee's 1985–1987 tenure. In December 1985, Homer Lindsay, Jr., copastor with Jerry Vines of First

Table 6.3. Activism by SBC Political Parties, 1985

Activity	% Antifundamentalist		% Undecided		% Profundamentalist		Total	
	Clergy	Laity	Clergy	Laity	Clergy	Laity	Clergy	Laity
Went to meeting of concerned Baptists	36	22	26	14	29	16	31	17
Tried to influence someone on the issues	35	19	22	21	26	25	28	22
Tried to recruit messengers	39	20	31	13	41	23	38	19
Went to Dallas	54	11	53	3	42	8	49	7
Number of messengers Church sent to Dallas	1.87		1.40		1.15		1.47	
(Number of Cases)	(125)	(177)	(66)	(186)	(141)	(164)	(332)	(527)

Baptist in Jacksonville, announced that Adrian Rogers would be the conservative candidate and that organizing was underway. In January, he sponsored a Conservative Pastors Rally during the Florida state Evangelism Conference. Those meetings, along with an April rally in Nashville, included accusations against the liberals in the denomination and encouragement for conservatives to attend the convention in June.[34] In Nashville, Georgia layman Lee Roberts, then the chair of the Committee on Boards, claimed that professors were feeding their students spiritual "slop" (a remark for which he later apologized). Although they were experiencing some pressure to cease organizing, fundamentalists were still publicly pursuing their goals.

Not everyone in the denomination was involved in all this organizing, however. Those who were less clear about the issues were also less involved. Consistently the "undecideds" were less politically active than those in the pro- and antifundamentalist camps. Having a clear agenda and being actively involved went together, each undoubtedly facilitating the other.

The partisans on each side were about evenly matched on most activities (see table 6.3). If anything, anti-fundamentalists had a slight edge in the proportion of their clergy who were actively working for the cause. Moderates were somewhat more likely to go to meetings than were fundamentalists, and moderate clergy were more likely to proselytize for their cause. That advantage, however, was partially offset by the enthusiasm of fundamentalist laity. They were considerably more likely than were moderate laity to try to persuade someone to see the Convention their way and go along to the annual meeting.

The goal of the rallies and persuasion, of course, was getting messengers to the annual meeting, and on this score, moderates actually did better than fundamentalists—despite what the election outcomes might lead us to believe. Antifundamentalist clergy were more likely to attend than either the profundamentalists or those who were undecided. And antifundamentalist laity were about equal in their convention attendance to laity who supported the other side. Combined clergy and laity on the antifundamentalist side reported that their churches, on average, sent more messengers each year than did either the undecided or the profundamentalist respondents (see table 6.3).

The net result of all of this was that moderates were actually showing up at conventions in numbers slightly ahead of their proportions in the denomination, while fundamentalists were represented proportionately. While 35 percent of our respondents disagreed with the fundamentalists, 44 percent of those who went to Dallas did. The most under-represented group in Dallas was the undecided. They comprise 29 percent of our sample, but only 20 percent of those who went to Dallas. They were destined to be even fewer in number in following years as the convention became even more polarized. What seemed to evolve over the four years we surveyed was a dual process of more people making up their minds which side to be on and fewer of those who remained uncommitted wanting to attend the convention.

The moderate advantage in sending messengers was more than just political organizing or even resources. It was also a matter of tradition and habit. Moderates, as we saw in the previous chapter, had been going to conventions longer and were generally more active in denominational affairs. Some were in official capacities where they were expected to attend annual conventions, but the proportion of denominational officials among messengers never exceeded 6.1 percent between 1981 (the first year for which information is available) and 1988. In most years only one messenger in twenty-five was a state convention, agency, or other denominational employee whose way had been paid by the denomination. More typically, moderates were simply in the larger, urban churches where participation in all of the denomination's activities was part of the normal routine. They had a longer and deeper history of involvement.

Upon closer examination, we discovered that attendance at the Dallas convention was a product both of continuing denominational activity and of political mobilization. The process seemed to work differently for each side, however.[35] For moderates, high activity in routine denominational affairs and high approval of the state of the denomination naturally went hand in hand. They were involved and thought things were in pretty good shape. Because they were already active in attending denominational meetings, they were more likely also to get involved in the political organizing that began to take place. In part this was again demographics. People from larger churches were more likely to be moderates, and people from larger churches were also more likely to go to conventions. The proportion of messengers from churches of more than one thousand members far exceeded the proportion of churches in the SBC of that size.[36] In fact, it was not ideas that led moderates into political activity, but their already-established routine of going to meetings.[37]

Some moderates, then, went to Dallas because they had been going to conventions all their lives. They routinely went to associational and state meetings, supported the Cooperative Program, read the SBC periodicals, and sent messengers to conventions. They went out of habit and out of commitment to the denomination's mission. Other moderates went *both* because they were committed to the SBC and because they had been to political meetings, heard political speakers, read the moderate press, and knew that important issues were at stake. Those who opposed the fundamentalist agenda came to the convention through two distinct, but connected, paths—one traditional denominationalism, the other political activism. One group had had its consciousness raised; the other had not.

The pattern for fundamentalists was somewhat different. Their discontent with the denomination had kept them away from routine denominational meetings. They were less likely to have gone to state meetings, to read the missions magazines, to support the Cooperative Program, or to have gone to previous conventions themselves (or to have had anyone from their church there). They were not involved and did not like the way things were going. When they went to a political meeting, it was not simply out of the habit of attending Baptist meetings. For fundamentalists, ideas, not routine activity, had gotten them involved. And fundamentalist political activity brought many people to Dallas who had never been involved in the denomination before. The net advantage moderates enjoyed in levels of recruitment, meeting attendance, and persuasion was not a matter of better political organizing, but of a more well-established network and routine of going to meetings.

Because fundamentalists did not come to their political organizing by way of denominational participation, they also did not go to Dallas by way of habit. They went because they had been recruited and persuaded. They went because they had heard and read the message. And they went because they had an agenda. Eighty-six percent of the pro-fundamentalist clergy said that their primary reason for going to Dallas was to support Charles Stanley. A few chose various other reasons: hearing the reports and sermons, seeing old friends, or just because they always go. Not a single fundamentalist said that support for Winfred Moore was his or her motivation. The vast majority knew exactly why they were there and were relatively uninterested in anything else. Many would arrive in time for the vote on Tuesday and leave after they heard the results.

By contrast, over one third of anti-fundamentalist clergy said that they went for some reason other than support for Winfred Moore, a pattern that did not change appreciably in the years we surveyed. Nearly one-fifth said that the reports and sermons were their primary concern, and others admitted they really wanted to see old friends. A few (7 percent) even said that they had come to support Stanley, not Moore. Antifundamentalists were anything but a united voting bloc. A sizable number of those who agreed with the moderate cause nevertheless were uncommitted to the moderate candidate. And in the middle, over half of the undecided went to Dallas committed to doing the denomination's business, but uncommitted to a candidate. However, those who did come with a favorite candidate leaned in the direction of Stanley by three to two.

Most of the undecided, then, and a sizable group of those who opposed fundamentalism, could not be counted on to vote in support of moderates. In fact, 10 to 15 percent of those who were moderates by every measure we had—their own self-designation, their beliefs, and their positions on the issues—nevertheless seemed to support the rhetoric and candidates of the fundamentalist party. They somehow agreed that a "course correction" in favor of more strict belief in the Bible would benefit the Convention. Such a split between ideology and political behavior was simply not present on the other side. Virtually all those who agreed with fundamentalists about the ills of the Convention regularly supported the candidates and platform of that party.

Moderates were also hindered in their political activities by the intense desire among them to believe that peace was at hand. Over half of the anti-fundamentalists and the undecided left Dallas convinced that there were "many signs of reconciliation between fundamentalists and moderates who have been fighting each other." That number dropped off somewhat in 1986 and 1987, and was reduced to barely more than a quarter by 1988, as hopes for peace evaporated among moderates. What is most significant here, however, is that people who believed that peace was at hand were much less likely to organize than were other anti-fundamentalists. The desire to believe that the fight was over prevented nearly half the moderate constituency from organizing to do the things that would help the moderate cause.

Those who opposed fundamentalism were not all equally opposed or equally willing to work for the cause. While on paper the opponents of fundamentalism may have outnumbered supporters, they could not form that opposition into a cohesive voting bloc. Some among them believed the rhetoric of the other side about the need for orthodoxy and for some minor corrections in the way things were being done. Others were simply too entrenched in their traditional convention-going habits to act like political participants. Moderates may ironically have been hurt by the very patterns of attendance that helped them to turn out messengers so easily in the first place. Many of those messengers were likely to act in a nonpolitical fashion, to treat the business of the convention as if these were the traditional nonpartisan conventions they had always attended before.

The moderate failure to understand that liability is perhaps best evidenced by their failure to take account of the strength of the tradition of presidential incumbency. The SBC constitution specifies that a president is elected for a one-year term and may be reelected for a second consecutive term. (The constitution is silent on the total number of times a president may be elected.) Since the office has always been considered an honorific, the thought of unseating a president who wanted to serve a second term never entered anyone's mind. It would have been an unbe-

lievable insult under the old system. And for most middle-of-the-road
Baptists, the old system would not be given up easily. While they may
have recognized that the presidency was no longer simply an honor, they
refused to give up the idea that a sitting president who wanted to continue
his service should be reelected. Even those who opposed the fundamentalists were not always willing to recruit messengers, go to the convention, and vote for an opponent to a sitting president. Our survey data
suggest that anti-fundamentalists were more active in 1986 than in 1985
and in 1988 than in 1987, putting their energies into elections where
there was no incumbent.

But under a system in which the power of the presidential office had
been recognized and invoked, moderate activists—unlike the rank and
file—thought incumbency was no longer sacred. If a president had been
elected as a political candidate with a political agenda, then reelection
was no longer simply a matter of honor or insult. The first major moderate
effort to get out the vote for a single, identifiable, moderate candidate was
in 1981, when Bailey Smith was up for reelection. They lost on a sixty to
forty vote. In 1983, they did not oppose the reelection of Jimmy Draper,
but their next major effort to get out the vote was not 1984 (when two
moderate candidates split the anti-Stanley votes), but 1985, when Stanley
was seeking his second term. Although they came closer that year (55 to
45) and achieved a similar proportion of the votes in 1987 and 1989, their
cause was hurt by the reluctance of the people who were their natural
constituents to give up their traditional voting habits.

Those traditional habits of convention goers worked against moderates
in a number of ways. More moderates were willing to go to conventions,
but not because they were committed to a political cause. They remembered the days when conventions were high spiritual experiences and the
convention's business was a routine affirmation of the directions set by
trusted officials. They wanted the convention to be like it used to be.
They wanted to believe that they could act as if it were the way it used to
be, a consensual body where they could trust those in charge.

Legitimate Authority and the Forms of Debate

Trusting those in charge meant, of course, trusting the very fundamentalists with whom they disagreed. Those with the legitimate authority to
shape what happened at convention meetings were the duly elected
presidents and other officials appointed and elected to work with them.
That authority extended in both obvious and subtle ways into every aspect of what messengers experienced during their three days of convention business. Until fundamentalists made it an issue, no one had ever

quite realized the extent to which the office of the presidency stood at the center of everything the Convention did. The president not only set in motion the selection of trustees, he also shaped the meeting's agenda and the sort of resolutions that would be debated.

The SBC president has the legitimate authority to appoint a Committee on Committees each year, a group that begins the nomination process for all other committees and boards (see fig. 6.1). In its conception, this committee was to be a kind of extension of the president's eyes and ears into all the states, seeking out representatives from all the territories who would best know fellow Baptists who could serve the denomination well. Its job was to nominate any special committees that the convention might decide it needed; but in practice, its mission was almost solely to nominate members for the Committee on Nominations. This sixty-five member committee would then seek out the 250 or so people who would be needed each year to fill vacancies on the standing committees and boards of trustees that shaped the details of denominational life.

Both the Committee on Nominations and the trustees they eventually nominated were subject to election by the messengers, of course. This election was presumably not automatic, but in reality the positions might as well have been appointive.[38] In 1979, under the old moderate regime, the sixty or so members of the Committee on Boards (the old name for the Committee on Nominations) were elected in a five-minute slot on the agenda, with no opposition and apparently (from the recorded Proceedings) no discussion. Immediately following that, the 200 or more nominees to convention boards and committees were elected in another five-minute slot, again without opposition.[39] It was clear that messengers trusted the process of electing a president who would seek out fellow nominators who would in turn find the best people to serve. To speak of these offices as in any real sense of the word elective is, however, stretching that word. Once the people had spoken in electing a president, they essentially gave up their role in the process.

After the election of Adrian Rogers in 1979, however, the trust that had made the system work for almost fifty years was gone. Since those being nominated did, technically, have to be elected by the messengers, moderates sought to abort (or at least slow) the domination of trustee boards by fundamentalists by offering substitutes for the nominations brought to the convention. By 1981, when the first slate of fundamentalist trustees was presented, the time for their election still occupied only a five-minute time slot. But moderates were prepared with an amendment that struck three fundamentalist nominees and replaced them with moderates. The motion was made by Ken Chafin, outspoken member of the Gatlinburg gang, and just two years earlier himself chair of the Committee on

Boards. The house was closely divided, and a ballot vote was necessary, but moderates won.[40] In 1982, Chafin again returned with two substitutions, and again his amendment passed. This time a second moderate amendment challenged a third nominee. That also passed. Apparently fearing a rout, fundamentalists moved to refer the entire report back to committee. That effort failed, but there were no further changes forthcoming. For the first time, the five-minute time slot proved insufficient, and a motion to extend the time was necessary.[41] In nearly every year after that, motions to extend the time became routine. Not all messengers were content with their old role of rubber stamping the work of the nominating committee, but only an extension to several hours would have made this election process anything but perfunctory.

In 1982, President Bailey Smith established a new policy about challenges to committee nominees. As if to preserve an aura of southern consensual gentility (and pretending that this was not a political process), he requested that those offering substitutions say nothing negative about the person they wished to replace, offering only positive comments about the person they wished to elect. This policy, accepted by the messengers, strained the meaning of debate on these issues. Moderates were reduced to speaking in code words understandable only to those already initiated into the cause. They argued, for instance, that their substitutions offered greater geographic balance, when what they really meant was that their nominee offered greater theological balance. When they tried to make links between nominees and the fundamentalist organization or agenda, they were invariably ruled out of order.

Nevertheless, moderates had won on those first two efforts to alter—admittedly in very small measure—the list of nominees offered by fundamentalists. Their ability to win, however, depended on the timing of the votes. Because fundamentalists had often recruited messengers for presidential election day only, many of their voters were no longer available on Wednesday and Thursday. At least in 1981 and 1982 (and apparently in most years after that) moderates could sometimes muster majority votes on the last two convention days. After losses in these first two years, fundamentalists took no more chances. Because they dominated the Committee on Order of Business fundamentalists were able to move these elections to a more advantageous time on the program; in 1983, the reports of the Committee on Committees and Committee on Boards were moved from Wednesday morning to Tuesday afternoon. In every year after that, moderate attempts to substitute nominees failed.

In 1985, of course, moderates tried their most daring challenge yet. They attempted to offer an entire slate of substitute nominees—not for the board and committee positions, but for the Committee on Nominations itself. It was this attempt, and President Stanley's rulings relative to it, that precipitated much of the chaos in Dallas. Convinced that the President's ruling had exceeded his legitimate powers, a group of moderate messengers led by Robert and Julia Crowder of Birmingham, decided to bypass existing channels of authority, now dominated by fundamentalists, and take their dismay to an outside authority. They filed suit in federal district court.[42] They wanted someone to declare that Presidents must abide by the will of the majority of messengers. The courts, however, refused to involve themselves in this internal church matter. The attempt to marshall outside resources, in fact, backfired, leaving the Crowders and the moderate cause discredited for having so blatantly violated the presumed consensus of the denomination. The only internal result was a change in the by-laws that further limited the ability of messengers to participate in the election process. Substitutions could be offered, but no more than one at a time. Given a limit of fifteen or twenty minutes for more than 200 nominations to be considered, even successful challenges could never change more than a few members on any Committee or Board. What appeared on paper as a democratic process of election was in reality an oligarchical appointment process.

In any large organization, power is always delegated to smaller groups to work out the will of the majority. In this case, the churches delegate to their messengers the right to vote. The messengers delegate to their president the right to select nominators and to the nominators the right to propose those who will serve. Messengers reserved the right to ratify the work of those bodies, but only gross negligence would ordinarily cause them to overrule that delegated responsibility. With no legitimate mechanism for broadening the base of the selection process, choices about all the denomination's leadership had come to rest in the hands of a very few.

Not only did Southern Baptists have no official mechanism for dispersing power, they also had strong traditions that made them reluctant to admit that power was indeed concentrated at the top. They had lived for nearly 150 years with a myth of democracy. It was sustained primarily by a culturally-based consensus that prevented any real need for debate or organized opposition. The Southern Baptist model of democracy was not that of competing interests. Rather it was a democracy based on what Farnsley has called the "rough spiritual equality" that comes from both a common scriptural authority and a common cultural heritage.[43] They assumed that consensus would emerge from their common efforts to discern the will of God. Once having entrusted a task to people they believed to be "men of God," they believed that God would guide those people to correct decisions. To call those decisions into question was to cast doubt on all the presuppositions by which they had governed themselves all this time. On a number of levels, moderates were fighting a losing battle in seeking to offer substitute nominees. Both the legitimate authority of the committee and the traditions of consensus and trust were being questioned by their actions.

We asked our 1986 respondents, for instance, whether they generally voted for or against substitute nominees and why. Ninety-two percent of the pro-fundamentalist messengers always voted against substitutions. They clearly knew that a slate of committed fundamentalists was important. They were joined in those votes by nearly three-quarters of the undecided messengers and almost a quarter of the anti-fundamentalist ones, as well. Those who said they voted against substitutions overwhelmingly said that they did so because they trusted the committee to prayerfully do its work. The force of tradition and perceived legitimacy weighed heavily against building a successful moderate coalition and in favor of the fundamentalists in charge.

Fundamentalist influence on the Order of Business Committee also ensured that all the prayers, testimonies, sermons, choral anthems, and "theme interpretations" for the annual meeting were placed in the hands of loyal fundamentalists. The choir and orchestra from one of the super-churches might have the pre-session music, a nearby pastor the opening prayer, and a suitably orthodox seminary professor might be entrusted with interpreting the convention theme (which had also been set by the Order of Business committee). Various freelance musicians might be showcased in the periods before the sessions. The tone throughout was revivalist and triumphant, and the content was always conservative. And of course, the official Convention Sermon and the presidential address would be expositions of the values and issues fundamentalists wished to promote in the denomination.[44] Whether in moments of inspiration or in the scheduling of debate, the Committee on Order of Business shaped what happened from beginning to end.

The other key committee appointed by the president was the Resolutions Committee. Each year, the convention took the opportunity of its meeting to adopt a number of statements on issues facing individual Christians, churches, the denomination, or the nation. They ranged from the innocuous resolution of appreciation to the host city to controversial statements on abortion or race relations or SALT II. In the 1970s, the committee had generally been filled with ethicists, academics, and progressive pastors. As late as 1979, they presented a slate of resolutions that covered domestic violence, family farms, the need to support public education, hunger, energy, abortion (condemning excess, but affirming choice), peacemaking, inflation, and appreciation of the seminaries.

Almost every item submitted to the committee that year was either incorporated into a resolution or sent directly to an agency for action. All the resolutions took moderately progressive stands, and with minor changes, they all passed. If an SBC agency was called on the carpet for its progressive stand on some issue, it could turn to these resolutions as a defense of its position (as the Christian Life Commission sometimes did on abortion).

By the end of the 1980s, the situation had changed radically. Those appointed to the Resolutions Committee and active in writing resolutions were often also active in state and national conservative politics. The resolutions passed in 1987 and 1988 included affirmations of Christian homes and homemakers, opposition to school-based clinics and other "value-neutral" efforts at sex education, opposition to any legislation that would allow the federal government to apply civil rights standards to church institutions, condemnation of homosexuality as a deviant behavior that is the primary cause of AIDS, and so on. AIDS, sex education, abortion, the family, and the Civil Rights Restoration Act were all the subject of resolutions in *both* those years (despite the presumed policy of not presenting resolutions on subjects recently addressed). While the Committee did report out a resolution on hunger in 1987, it differed markedly from the four strongly-worded offerings on hunger and economic justice that had been submitted. They had contained extensive lists of economic reasons for hunger and poverty and specific recommendations for government and church actions. The rewritten resolution contained a single line acknowledging that hunger is a problem, and it counseled only Christian concern and the use of existing denominational resources.[45] (On the other side of the political fence, the 1987 committee also passed over a thinly-veiled anti-Mason resolution and another that advocated home schooling as the only Christian way.) In general, conservative concerns found their way into the finished products proposed by the committee, while more liberal concerns were left behind. In 1988, for instance, resolutions submitted but ignored by the committee included statements opposing capital punishment and apartheid, and on stopping aid to the Contras. An affirmation of the current convention officers made its way into a resolution, but commendations of Randall Lolley and of the Baptist Joint Committee died before reaching the floor. Resolutions Committees were receiving far more suggested resolutions from messengers than before, and some were relatively far from the political mainstream (on both sides). However, those recommended for approval (and those written from scratch by the committee) had moved from the left side of the stream distinctly toward the right. When SBC agencies sought justification for their policies, they could turn to a host of conservative resolutions for backing.

The fundamentalist control of what happened at conventions went far beyond even scheduling and resolutions, however. They also influenced who was seen and heard (and in what context) during debates over convention business. Doing business with 40,000 potential debaters is, of course, an absurd proposition. The bulk of the crowd was spread out over an enormous hall in which multiple floor mikes had been placed. The rest were in auxiliary halls, linked only by video feed and their own one or two mikes. No one could possibly control the flow of debate from any one vantage point. Some limits, some method of control was essential. In Dallas, the limits were sometimes exercised arbitrarily from the platform. The chaos was so blatant there, however, that the Executive Committee mandated a new system for subsequent years. Called a Microphone Ordering Box (MOB), the system provided electronic control. Anyone wishing to speak registered that desire at the remote microphone, and the system recorded whether they wished to speak "for" or "against" or whether they had a point of order. It then placed them in an electronic "line" accordingly, and one of the parliamentarians could tell the chair which speaker was next in line.

The system worked quite well for allowing an equitable distribution of speaking opportunities among those who wished to offer motions, points of order, or arguments in debate. The actors in these debates, however, were still not evenly matched. Everyone could be heard, but not everyone could be seen. It will be remembered that convention planners had responded to the vastness of the halls by using giant video screens to project platform images into the hall. In years past, the stage had been relatively open to people who wished to speak. Even in 1985, many moderate motions came from the platform (although almost no moderate debate came from that location).[46] But with the installation of the MOB boxes, platform mikes were reserved exclusively for "official" use. Speakers there were easily covered by the video cameras and could clearly be seen against a standard blue backdrop.

Floor mikes were another matter entirely. Those speaking from remote halls were almost always disembodied voices. Some locations in the main hall could be covered, but only if the camera operator could locate the relevant speaker and refocus quickly. Even if the speaker showed up on the screen, the image was one of a jumble of people crowded around a microphone, some listening, some not. It was not always visually clear even who was speaking. People speaking from the floor never created an authoritative visual image, if they had any image at all.

This visual disadvantage was augmented by various rules and customs that also gave official speakers a decided edge. In the debate over substitute nominees, for instance, any challenge was immediately countered with a prepared speech, from an official microphone, by an official member of the committee. Since the challenger could not specifically counter anything claimed by the committee, "debate" was reduced to the word of an anonymous voice from the floor against the powerful image of the committee.

In still other ways, the dynamics of debate in such a convention setting strongly favored officials. Both the mass of people and the mass of information to be assimilated worked against the possibility of extensive debate on substantive issues. Among the most central decisions each year were the ten to twenty recommendations brought by the Executive Committee. These were the actions that most directly affected what would happen during the other 362 days of the year. But almost never was there any debate about any of these recommendations. In a careful analysis of the proceedings of the 1979, 1985, and 1986 conventions, we found only three questions, comments, or amendments to the total of forty-two recommendations brought in those three years—one each year. None substantially altered what the Committee had proposed. We have already seen that, until 1981, the Committee on Boards and trustee nominees were routinely approved without discussion. And through 1979, reports from all of the agencies were also routinely presented without questions or comments. Few messengers had read the 200-page "Book of Reports" they were handed when they registered. Unless they had already come with specific grievances, meaningful questions about agency reports were unlikely.

The two points at which messengers could most easily affect the outcome of the convention were in resolutions and motions. Still, in 1979, about two-thirds of the resolutions went through without comment. In 1985 and 1986, about half were actively discussed and/or amended. As we have seen, more suggested resolutions went to the committee for consideration in those years, and most died there. Only eleven and twelve, respectively, were reported out, compared to twenty-one in 1979. Both under the previous moderate regime and under fundamentalist leadership, then, messengers averaged active discussion of six or eight resolutions each year (a number that is probably a function of the time available); fundamentalist committees simply gave them fewer to choose from.

Messengers were also taking the initiative to make more motions. One of the biggest differences between the convention of 1979, the last year in which a moderate presided, and the tumultuous conventions of 1985 and 1986 was the dramatic increase in the number of motions being offered from the floor. There were motions about everything from the display of flags at meetings to when the presidential address should be scheduled. In 1979, only eleven motions and one suggested by-law change were offered. As was the custom, the by-law change and the two motions having to do with the internal affairs of an agency were referred directly to that agency for response. Of the other nine, four were officially scheduled for later debate, and five were acted upon immediately when presented. In 1985, thirty-six motions and seven by-law changes were brought; and in 1986, thirty-six motions and thirteen by-law changes came from the floor. Had they been scheduled for debate in the proportion that 1979's motions were taken up, messengers might have had to stay an extra week.

Most motions were referred from the floor directly into the agency and committee system (a process one cynical moderate described as letting the fox guard the chickens—something fundamentalists had discovered long ago).[47] Almost all of the by-law changes were offered by moderates and went to an Executive Committee increasingly dominated by fundamentalists. They came back in 1986 and 1987 as four by-law revisions bearing only minor resemblance to the original moderate motions.[48]

The other motions brought to the 1985 and 1986 conventions were about evenly divided among moderate causes, fundamentalist causes, and concerns not readily identifiable with either party. Motions clearly identifiable with *either* side were much less likely than neutral motions to get an immediate vote or an official place on the schedule. Of the seventy-two motions on which we have complete information, only twenty-one were actually voted on in those two years. Five passed, one was approved by a ruling of the chair, fourteen failed, and one was referred to committee by a vote of the messengers. Two of the five that passed were motions to collect a special offering for world hunger. Without such a clearly worthy (and apparently neutral) cause, the chances of emerging from a convention with an adopted motion were slim indeed. In two years, less than one in ten motions had succeeded.

Most of the remainder of messengers' motions went, like the by-law changes, into the agency and committee system. Each body would review the motions referred to it, but none was under any obligation to do more than say they had thought about it. If the motion was congruent with the direction that agency's trustees wanted to go, the motion would likely come back in the form of a recommendation. (Such was the case with a motion on a Sanctity of Life Sunday referred to the Calendar Committee in 1985.)[49] But if the motion was contrary to the wishes of the trustees, they could simply include in their written report at the next convention that they had considered the motion and found it unwise.[50] As fundamentalists had learned a decade before, the direction of agency business cannot easily be changed from the floor.

When motions, resolutions, and recommendations came to the floor, they were, of course, subject to debate. Messengers could offer their arguments about whether they supported the measure and why. We have already noted some of the constraints placed on such speeches. Nothing negative can be said about an opponent, and time is generally limited to two or three minutes. What we have not directly noted, however, is just how rare the give-and-take of debate became during the years of controversy. In each year, messengers were adopting ten to twenty recommendations, ten to twenty resolutions, and a dozen or so other amendments and motions. On only a handful of these was there any debate at all—perhaps eight or ten measures each year—and that debate typically consisted of one or two brief comments on each side. The nineteenth century days of day-long debates and thirty-minute eloquent speeches were clearly gone.

In 1979, nearly half of all the speeches by ordinary messengers was debate on some measure that was before the body. By 1986, that proportion was barely more than 10 percent. Messengers were speaking much more, but debating less. They were instead using their microphone time to make motions and propose by-law changes (most of which, as we have seen, were referred and probably died in the system), to point out technical problems (microphones and lights not working properly, for example), and to call for points of order. In 1985, with more than twice the number of messengers to the 1979 convention, the number of points of order was quadruple (23 in 1985 compared to 8 in 1979). Even that does not do justice to the situation, for in that year countless attempts to register points of order were simply never recognized by the chair. At one point President Stanley replied to a questioner that if the chair had not recognized a point of order, there had not been one. In 1986, the assistance of a professional parliamentarian and the use of the electronic microphone ordering system meant, among other things, that all the desired points of order got registered—all forty-nine of them. Not surprisingly, the vast majority of these were brought by moderates protesting perceived slights by the chair. And equally unsurprising was the fact that in the two years combined, only four such moderate challenges were ruled "well taken." In 1985, moderates may have had room to protest unfair presiding, but in 1986, the convention was so closely controlled by the parliamentarian that deviations from the rules were unlikely.[51] Yet moderates used fully half of their floor time calling the chair to task.

The annual meetings themselves, then, were not well suited to communication or debate. Most issues went by without comment. The real issues had been debated long before the convention gathered, within the committees and trustee boards the messengers delegated to do their business. The communication advantage at the convention did not lie with the messengers, but with those who had set the agenda, those who would present reports and statements as "officials," those who could speak with the legitimate authority of office. In the 1980s, the authority of elected office was with the fundamentalists, and they used it to shape what would happen in the annual meetings.

But the authority of staff offices still rested with moderates, and they, too, got a chance to influence what happened at annual meetings. Each agency got an annual opportunity to try to convince the messengers that what they were doing deserved support. The Home and Foreign Mission Boards and the Sunday School Board got featured evening program time, with opportunities for testimonies, audio-visual presentations, and sermons. The seminaries and other agencies generally got ten to fifteen minutes for a report or feature. All were welcomed to the platform (after 1985, to the side microphone). They had the legitimate opportunity to communicate their message to all those who cared to listen.[52] Most sympathized with the goals of the SBC's progressive wing. They knew that they were sometimes at odds with the majority of their constituents, but most had worked for years under the assumption that gradual change was possible. They thought that the commitments to missions, to education, to ministry, and to evangelism that they shared with the vast majority of Southern Baptists would far outweigh any other disagreements. It was these common goals they emphasized in their reports.

Still, their words about common goals could never overcome the enormous advantages accumulated by the fundamentalists. Out on the denomination's right wing, fundamentalists had forged a cohesive and powerful leadership coalition, identified symbols and rhetorical styles that would move the masses, devised strategies for minimizing the costs of involvement, effectively communicated their message, and consistently brought enough people to the annual meeting to elect a president. They had gained the legitimate authority to govern a body that still liked to think of itself as a consensual democracy. They had slowly amassed the broader legitimate authority that resides in committees and boards of trustees. From that base, they first changed the shape of the annual meeting, altering its tone and content. But by 1986, they were ready to begin to change the agencies that are the on-going structure of the denomination, as well. Their aim was a day when both elected officers and agency heads would fully support a fundamentalist agenda, and they had earned the legitimate authority to pursue that goal. What they would do with their authority to govern the Southern Baptist bureaucracy was the question on everyone's mind.

7. The Tasks of Governing: Fundamentalists and the Southern Baptist Bureaucracy

Having succeeded in sustaining a decade of electoral victories, Southern Baptist fundamentalists were no longer outsiders. They controlled what happened at annual convention meetings, and they dominated the elected boards of trustees that were charged with governing the agencies and institutions of the denomination. By 1986, the first boards came under fundamentalist majorities, and in the years that followed, the remainder of the boards were added to the list. Fundamentalists had gained the power by which to hire and fire and to set the policies that would shape the curricula in seminaries and Sunday Schools and direct mission efforts at home and abroad. What they would do with that power would depend both on dynamics within their own movement and on the organizational dynamics of the lion they now had by the tail.

As we saw in chapter 3, the Southern Baptist Convention had grown into an enormous, bureaucratically organized, highly professional aggregation of agencies and institutions. To say that they were bureaucratically organized is not necessarily to imply the negative connotations associated with that word. In this case bureaucracy implies merely a way of organizing, a particular understanding of authority. As Max Weber pointed out in the earlier part of this century, modern forms of organization contrast sharply with the way other people have thought about government, economy, or religion. Rather than organizing around family and land, guild and apprenticeship, or even around a powerful charismatic figure, modern organization is based on consciously chosen goals and intentionally developed structures for reaching those goals. Among the characteristics of such "rational" organizations are:

- rules that limit what is to be done and how it is to be done;

- a hierarchy of authority;

- permanent records kept on paper (now electronically) in files;

- expert training for one's job and hiring based on training and credentials;

- jobs that are fulltime, lifetime "careers" and carry a set salary; and

- respect and influence in the organization based on one's position and expertise, rather than on outside factors.[1]

While no human organization is ever as rational as it may first seem, these ideas about how organizations ought to work are well ingrained in the modern psyche. We want to know who is in charge, that they are well trained, that they will follow the rules, and that they will make and file a record of our business with them.

In every sense of the word, then, the Southern Baptist Convention was a bureaucracy. After messengers had done the work of electing trustees and approving budgets, the tasks of the denomination were handed over to two mission boards, a huge publishing house, an annuity board, six seminaries, and nine "commissions" (see again table 1.1). Each "entity" (as they were collectively called in the denomination's lingo) had a program statement that outlined its functions within the denomination. It planned and budgeted for years in advance, and it recognized clear lines of authority within its structure. Employees were required to have educational credentials and relevant experience, in addition to their affirmation of the Baptist Faith and Message. The organizational system the fundamentalists wished to tame was a peculiar mixture of sacred callings and secular credentials, of ecclesiastical mission and business-like procedures. As one staffer told me, "This is where God wants me to be and where my preparation has led me to be"—the divine and the rational working together!

The people who had found their way into the denomination's agencies often spoke passionately about their sense of calling to their work. Whether they edited Sunday School lessons or developed programs for campus ministry or Christian citizenship, whether they supported people starting new churches or screened foreign mission candidates, whether they managed the work of several departments or planned and researched for future needs or taught in a seminary, these were people who had a keen sense of their role in the church. They wanted to help local church leaders do their jobs better and provide learning resources for individual Christians. By definition, status quo was not good enough; change and development were to be sought. These were people who had been to college and usually to seminary. They had trained for the work they did and felt confident in their ability to do it well. They were also loyal Baptists and active church goers. Many had served on church staffs before joining a national organization. They had a very high regard for the life of the local churches and a firm conviction that churches willing to remain open to new possibilities could provide ever stronger ministries to their own members and to their communities. They were people who had placed their credentials and skills in the service of the Southern Baptist Convention's mission of reaching people with the gospel.

These Baptist bureaucrats had all agreed to work within the doctrinal boundaries set by the Baptist Faith and Message, but their education and professional training meant that they usually read that statement through a moderate lens. They were likely to be open to a variety of interpretations of scripture and know about the variety of church practices that have existed across time and space. They were likely to live in a world where travel and reading and professional associations had brought them into contact with a wide variety of others whose language and habits they had learned to respect, if not adopt. Their own Baptist doctrines were held dear, but held in a context of wide experience and tolerance. More importantly, doctrine was simply not the most central element in what they did. What they did was defined more by specialization and professional standards than by a fine tuned reading of any tightly-drawn theological statement. It was not that they did not believe; it was just that doctrine had been more assumed than explicit. If they were accomplishing their tasks of supporting church programs and extending the denomination's mission outreach, it was assumed that they must believe the right things.

A number of studies of religious organizations have demonstrated that factors such as size, complexity, and professionalization have at least as much to do with the way they do business as does theology. The bigger the denomination, the more people it will have working at the national level; and more workers, inevitably means more departments and more levels to the hierarchy.[2] And as organizations get more complex, the people occupying their very specialized niches are likely to find a good deal in common with others who occupy similar positions in other organizations. In other words, they are likely to think in terms of their professional identities, associations, and credentials, as well as in terms of their place in the hierarchy of their own organizations. In fact, cooperation with transdenominational organizations of all sorts (from the Consultation on Church Union to the National Campus Ministry Association) is as much a function of the complexity and professionalization of a denomination as of that group's theological position on ecumenism.[3] The Southern Baptist Convention, in fact, while ideologically opposed to joining the National Council of Churches, nevertheless participated actively in committees of that body.[4] At the Sunday School Board, representatives regularly worked with the NCC group that outlined scriptures for use in the International Lesson series. At both Mission Boards, there were regular contacts and joint efforts with other evangelical organizations. Denominational workers recognized the common task in which they and other ecclesiastical professionals were engaged, and they cooperated with non-Baptist colleagues in a variety of ways.

The implication of all this professional activity was not so much that Southern Baptist institutional staff members were theologically liberal as that they were influenced by the organizational and professional world in which they lived. Large organizations have a logic of their own. As they grow and develop, they expect increasing skill and specialization in their personnel; and that skill and specialization pushes the organization and its personnel toward a rationalized view of the world and a specialized set of relationships with that world. Theology may affect the content of the denomination's program, but it is unlikely to alter the structure of the organizations through which that program is administered. Fundamentalists entering the Southern Baptist system were likely to find themselves tugged and shaped by these same modern assumptions.

Fundamentalists were also likely to find themselves tugged and shaped by the very size and legitimacy of a system they were entering from the outside. Without an overnight revolution, they were faced with a gradual process of organizational change and the dangers (as they saw them) of being absorbed into the existing organizational culture. Being a minority voice can be very lonely, and being a constant critic can bring immense pressures to conform. So long as one dominant coalition is clearly in charge, that coalition stands a good chance of converting dissidents. This is a variation on the process described by Selznick as "cooptation."[5] He notes that when there is conflict between the organization's goals and need for stability on the one hand and the goals and needs of its constituency on the other, the organization is likely to seek to create bridges between itself and the constituency by bringing new elements and leaders into the organization. In so doing, the organization is changed, but the process of change is managed so as to be minimally disruptive. The new leader may adopt the values of the organization wholeheartedly or at least may be able to translate them into terms acceptable to his or her constituency.

In this case, new leaders were generally not being brought in voluntarily—they were coming at the behest of a movement hostile to the organization. Nevertheless, once they entered the organization, they were subject to its existing norms and goals and were sometimes coopted by them. Faced with a successful dissident movement, SBC organizations would have to respond. But faced with the enormity and complexity of those organizations, fundamentalists would inevitably be drawn toward existing structures and goals, away from radical change.

The Fundamentalist Strategy for Change

What fundamentalists sought to alter in the Southern Baptist Convention was not so much the structure, but the policies and personnel located within that structure. Although they came in on an antiestablishment platform, it was the establishment's programs and policies they sought to change, not the establishment itself. They wanted programs that would more clearly reflect a single-minded attention to evangelism, and they wanted personnel who would agree with them on how the Baptist Faith and Message (and the Bible) should be interpreted.

The first step in that process had been assembling boards of trustees who would actively pursue an agenda of change.[6] That meant consistent nominations of people who were proven inerrantists (and conservative on other important issues). Some flavor of their concern is heard in what one Committee on Nominations member told us: "I knew my men [nominees] believed in the Bible, that they were anti-abortion, that they believed in the miracles. I knew they could pass the test."[7] His testimony and other reports from the Committee on Nominations made clear that conservatism of all sorts was taken as a prime qualification for board membership.[8]

Finding committed conservative trustees was complicated by the fact that many conservatives had been relatively isolated from the denomination. In the early years, people who had only recently joined Southern Baptist churches and who had never been to an annual convention were sometimes elected to the governing boards of denominational agencies.[9] Some were from churches that had shunned the programs of the Convention as too liberal and gave more mission money to independent causes than to the Cooperative Program. Moderates and agency staffs began to complain loudly that it was absurd to bring in trustees who had no experience in or commitment to the denomination they were being asked to govern. Since Cooperative Program giving was the most easily measurable indicator of denominational support, moderates sometimes used that as a basis for challenging nominees. Slowly, fundamentalists responded by checking more carefully the denominational credentials of those they nominated. A 1986 Committee member lamented that "it wasn't so much what they believed, but CP. . . . I'm strong for CP. I've been a Southern Baptist all my life. But if we're making CP a standard by which we measure the calibre of men. . . . My first nominee would have been outstanding, and I had to withdraw him because his church doesn't give more."

He also regretted giving up that nominee because the man was a strong leader, "an executive, not just some little factory worker—very dynamic, verbal. He would stand up." Fundamentalists not only needed people who believed the right things about the Bible (and abortion and women's ordination and other issues); they also needed people who would not easily be persuaded that things in the agencies were really satisfactory after all. As another Committee on Nominations member told us, "It's not just how many, but who—whether they're aggressive and strong or intimidated and passive." Not every nominee who entered the boards after 1981 became a loyal fundamentalist voter. Almost every agency person I talked with had at least one story to tell of a fundamentalist who joined the board determined to make waves but soon decided that there were too many good things happening and too few things that deserved change. New trustees sometimes testified after their first round of meetings, "I couldn't find one thing to complain about!" Indeed, the agencies were doing many things that most Baptists would find admirable. They were, in general, managed very efficiently and they carried on an impressive array of missions and educational work. It was easy for a new trustee to get lost in it all and forget that a thorough housecleaning was needed. He or she got to meet the staff and found them to be pious, believing, dedicated professionals, as well as likeable human beings. New trustees might even get a personal visit from the president of the agency, along with lots of attractive information on the program and structure of the entity they were now helping to govern. In many instances, the agencies' careful attention to orientation and inclusion paid generous dividends in the conversion of dissidents into supporters. The cooptation process sometimes worked.

New trustees soon discovered that there was indeed a great deal of information to be digested. For instance, at each meeting of the Home Mission Board directors (that agency's trustees), an inch-thick stack of reports awaits them. Color-coded by subject, it contains biographical information on new staff members to be elected, financial statements on all the programs, loan requests from churches, and so on. To the uninitiated, much of it might as well be Greek. At the Foreign Mission Board, one older trustee remarked, "New board members can't know everything happening . . . it's too vast." In the past, trustees largely assumed that the staff had done its homework in dealing with such routine matters. Few trustees worried about whether every detail was in order. Under the old establishment, the rapport between staff and trustees was such that trustees never thought they had to ask detailed questions. A staff member described the process this way.

> Usually the people on the board lean heavily on the staff people to help them make decisions. We always try not to make decisions for them, but we try to be ready with information for them and ready with recommendations at certain points. We feel like we have the chance to study something for a month, and they are looking at it for the first time. . . . We try to be prepared to analyze it for them so that they can make good decisions.

Even the new fundamentalist trustees were often frankly intimidated by the enormity of the task they faced. They knew they could not come in and learn everything they needed to know in two or three days twice a year.

But going along with the system was not the point for the new fundamentalist trustees. To make sure that trustees would be active and aggressive, the Nominations Committee often looked to those who had experience in politics. Organizers for Eagle Forum and right-to-life groups, candidates for local and state offices, lawyers, and other political activists began showing up in numbers probably disproportionate to their numbers in Southern Baptist life. These were people experienced at understanding organizational systems and able to organize successful opposition.

New trustees, then, might raise questions about anything. They wanted to make sure that nothing was left to the discretion of staff people who might continue to pursue a progressive agenda. At the Baptist Joint Committee, they even wanted copies of staff correspondence and expense accounts.[10] At the Sunday School Board, they got the right to ask for copies of any internal communication among editors (a move which considerably decreased the amount of light-hearted banter that had occupied the electronic margins of material being edited). Trustees wanted to do their jobs well. They wanted to be fully responsible for the agencies they governed, and to do so meant a considerable increase in their access to information about the inner workings of the organization.

Ironically, however, the new composition of these boards may have decreased some of the informal ways in which trustees used to influence staff. Boards during the "moderate" era usually contained a healthy sprinkling of top-level professionals and business people. These were people agency staffs saw as similar to themselves and therefore easy to talk to about problems they faced. In addition, board members often had specific experience or skill on which agency staffs might call. The level of trust that had existed between boards and staffs not only meant that trustees accepted the judgement of the staff, but also that staff regularly sought the advice of trustees in making those judgements. The different backgrounds and orientations of the new trustees established a barrier between them and the staff that made such informal influence much less likely.

The barrier between trustees and staff could, of course, be eliminated by changing the composition of the staff. To that end, trustees began to seek a much more active role in the hiring process. They wanted more information about the people being recommended for vacancies. In the past, positions had often been filled between board meetings by using a mailed resumé and ballot, but now trustees wanted to talk with candidates about their beliefs and assure themselves that liberals were not sneaking in under their noses. In this review of the changes in each agency, personnel will be a recurring theme (summarized in table 7.1). The fundamentalists who had been elected as institutional trustees were determined that personal piety, proper belief, and sound biblical practices would characterize anyone hired under their trusteeship.

The vigilance of these new trustees created a new atmosphere in the board room. During the years in which the balance on the boards was nearly equal, issue after issue would be challenged and debated. Emotions often ran high.[11] Sometimes issues defeated one year would be passed the next year when the balance changed. As a growing group of fundamentalists took their places on these governing bodies, they began to work together privately to map strategy and set agendas. Huddles would be observed in the hallway. In an occasional slip of the tongue, a fundamentalist member would allude to something "we" decided. At the fall 1987 Southeastern Seminary board meeting, an alternative slate of board officers and committees was offered from an unnamed ad hoc group. Moderates objected vehemently to such caucusing. Moderates expected the boards, like the convention itself, to be run by consensus, with the group deliberating as one body. Fundamentalists, on the other hand, perceived that they were in an adversarial situation and that organized party efforts were necessary. They wanted to be prepared for the issues they would face and to know that no one would have to speak as an isolated dissident. They seemed intuitively aware of the pressures toward conformity that could be brought to bear if they did not act in concert.[12]

New fundamentalist trustees gradually became, of course, not isolated dissidents, but leaders of the majority. Their numbers and their electoral victories had given them the power to effect the course correction they desired. They could point to various resolutions to legitimate their agenda; and after 1987, they could point to the report of the Peace Committee as the mandate under which they were to act. It officially reported that the convention's troubles were the result of theological differences, and it called on institutions to be responsive to the dominant conservatism of the people in Southern Baptist pews. Fundamentalists had long been saying that they did not want to pay the salaries of people who would teach things at odds with Baptist beliefs. In the Peace Committee report, they had an official document, passed by the convention, that gave their goal legitimacy.

I am convinced that none of the people who worked so hard in 1984–1985 to put together a Peace Committee envisioned it as the vehicle by which the fundamentalist agenda would be legitimated. Fundamentalist leaders tended to see it as a useless exercise that if for no other reason, they would do for the sake of appearances. Hard-line moderates were also skeptical about the possibilities. But many traditional Southern Baptists were convinced (or wanted desperately to believe) that men of good will, children of the same God who read the same Bible, could work out their

Table 7.1. Controversy-Related Personnel Actions, 1985–1989

Case	Complaint	Disposition
1985		
Debra Griffis-Woodberry, HMB-supported mission church pastor	woman in a pastoral role	not "defunded" but last woman approved for CPA
Janet Fuller, HMB-supported campus minister	woman in a pastoral role	hired on a close vote, but last ordained woman missionary
Edward Taylor, Foreign Missionary	unwillingness to evangelize all Catholics	resigned
1986		
Richard Harmon, Director, HMB Interfaith Witness Department	vocal dissent from Board's new direction	forced resignation
Temp Sparkman, MWBTS professor	unorthodox beliefs, especially "universalism"	passed second doctrinal review
1987		
Al Shackleford, VP for Public Relations & Director, Baptist Press	engaged in biased journalism (against fundamentalists)	hired on a tie vote
James Carter, nominee to SWBTS faculty	church ordains women, low baptism record, liturgical worship style	nomination withdrawn
Elizabeth Barnes, SEBTS professor	doctrinal questions	hired on 14-13 vote
Larry Baker, Director of CLC	opposition to capital punishment, support for women in ministry, would allow some abortions	kept job on tie vote

differences. If people could just spend time getting to know each other, they would discover they were not so different after all. Perhaps they would agree to compromise on a few things, each genuinely giving in for the sake of the other. At worst, maybe they would work out an amicable divorce settlement, splitting the denomination's property between the parties. That kind of personal conflict resolution had worked in the past, and Charles Fuller, chair of the committee, believed it could work again.

But this was not the past. While these committee members could pray together and exchange jokes over dinner, they could not agree on the issues facing the Convention. Chairman Fuller reported after each meeting that he was still hoping for a breakthrough, hoping that good will and personal diplomacy would prevail.[13] But the divisions represented in the committee were too deep. Those divisions were linked to well-

Table 7.1. (*Continued*)

Case	Complaint	Disposition
Randall Lolley, President, and 3 SEBTS administrators, followed over the next two years by eight more faculty and seven administrators	dissent from new trustee direction	resigned
1988		
Molly Marshall-Green, SBTS professor	universalism and lack of support for missions	tenure challenged, but approved
George Sheridan, HMB Interfaith Witness staff	unwillingness to evangelize Jews	forced resignation
Michael Willett, Foreign Missionary	"doctrinal ambiguity"	dismissed
Larry Baker and four other CLC staff members	dissent from new trustee direction	resigned
1989		
Benny Clark, nominee to HMB Atlanta staff	SBA membership, low CP giving, no Sunday night services, low baptisms, women deacons	nomination withdrawn
Greg & Katrina Pennington, foreign mission candidates	would be divisive because of her ordination	appointment denied
Lloyd Elder, President BSSB	political activity	censured and asked to stay neutral
Russell Dilday, President SWBTS	political activity	he and trustees mutually agree to stay neutral
David Benham, HMB staff	dissent from "resurgent racism" of new agency direction	resigned

organized—and very different—institutional networks and systems of belief. At the heart of it, fundamentalists insisted that inerrancy was essential, and moderates insisted that it could not be. The use of that word was simply never settled. After countless hours of debate between the best minds each side had to offer, each recognized that, as one put it, "We're not wired the same."

While agreement could not be reached on a common language or common beliefs, the committee nevertheless wrote a final report that would be taken as the norm by which Southern Baptists and their institutions were to be governed. They refused to recommend any specific constitutional changes or enforcement mechanisms, however, leaving their directives up to the discretion of those affected. As a result, those directives had power only where they served the interests of people who wished to follow them. Their recommendations on political activity, for instance, were in the interests of neither side. So long as presidents stood at the helm of an appointment process that could shape the convention, neither side was likely to give up efforts to elect a president.

The committee's one apparent effort to change the realities of the Convention's power structure was an exhortation in the final report that there should be "fairness in the appointive process," with nominees "drawn in balanced fashion . . . representative of the diversity of our denomination."[14] Interpreted literally, that recommendation appeared to call for something like quotas in committee nominations. Fundamentalists, however, did not choose a literal interpretation. Asked if his appointments that year met this criterion, Adrian Rogers asserted that they certainly did. The Peace Committee report would do nothing concrete to alter either the political process or the winner-take-all structure of the denomination. The party in power would have to do nothing to give up any of that power. If this was the concession moderates won, it was an empty one.

What the committee wrote about theology illustrates the success of fundamentalists in getting the conflict defined in their terms. The committee had begun its work by declaring that theology was at the heart of the controversy, and it went on to report that there was indeed theological diversity within the denomination. In its first statement, several examples were cited, among them: "Some accept and affirm the direct creation and historicity of Adam and Eve, while others view them instead as representative of the human race in its creation and fall." The report continued by saying that they were "working earnestly to find ways to build bridges between those holding divergent views so that we may all legitimately coexist and work together in harmony to accomplish our common mission."[15] In that first statement neither of these diverse views was apparently being touted as preferable to the other. Responding to this initial statement and to the concerns of the committee, the six seminary presidents issued a statement of their own in the fall of 1986. Called the Glorieta Statement (for the location in New Mexico where it was issued), it affirmed that they believed the Bible to be "not errant in any area of reality" and pledged vigilance in keeping the boundaries set by the Baptist Faith and Message. They also pledged that they would actively work to involve conservative scholars on their campuses, hold conferences on conservative beliefs, and so on. They admitted that inerrancy might not have been treated fairly in the past, and they pledged to be "balanced" in the future. Some moderates thought they had given up far too much—Cecil Sherman, for instance, resigned his place on the Peace

Committee—but this was their effort at the kind of compromise from which bridges could be built.[16]

When the final report was adopted the next year, however, there were no theological bridges in it. Both the moderates and the middle-of-the-road members we interviewed agreed that the fundamentalists had never given an inch on beliefs, forcing those on the other side to make concessions. In the case of each example of diverse views cited in the first report, the most conservative belief was now declared to be what the great majority of Southern Baptists believe and therefore what employees ought to accept and teach. Southern Baptist institutions were called on "to build their professional staffs and faculties from those who clearly reflect such dominant convictions and beliefs held by Southern Baptists at large." The committee recognized that its own members differed on these beliefs, but had learned "to live together . . . in mutual charity and commitment." But uniformity of belief, rather than mutual charity and commitment would be the guiding principle in institutional life. Within weeks, the Peace Committee report would be cited by the Home Mission Board's new conservative chief as the reason for his concern with the doctrinal integrity of his staff.[17]

The Peace Committee report was, then, something of a treaty written by the victors. Fundamentalists throughout the denomination had become convinced that their schools and agencies were not being run by biblical principles. By patient organizing they had elected trustees who would pursue their concern. The Peace Committee report finally provided the legitimate mandate for that task. While some new trustees found less to complain about than they had anticipated, others were able to maintain their critical posture in the midst of efforts to convince them that the agency's work was both orthodox and worthwhile. By banding together, setting a clear agenda for themselves, and insisting on an active, fully-informed role, these trustees began to change the course of the institutions they governed.

The Home Mission Board

The first skirmishes in the effort to change institutional policy took place at the Home Mission Board in Atlanta. For years the ordination of women had been a festering issue, and it was over this issue that they first fought. At the 1984 Kansas City convention, conservatives proposed and passed a resolution that endorsed "the service of women in all aspects of church life and work *other than* pastoral functions and leadership roles entailing ordination." (italics my emphasis) Women were excluded from pastoral roles, the resolution noted "to preserve a submission God requires because the man was first in creation and the woman was first in the Edenic fall (I Tim. 2:13ff)." The Board, however, had not excluded women (ordained or otherwise) from support of various kinds, including Church Pastoral Aid (CPA) for struggling mission churches with either male or female pastors. At least one woman pastor, Debra Griffis-Woodberry of Maryland, had been approved for CPA, and fundamentalists were outraged. Armed with the Kansas City resolution, fundamentalist trustees attempted to change the board's policy. Moderates argued back that the Board had no business telling a local church who could be hired as pastor. But fundamentalists said they wanted to make decisions on "biblical grounds, in line with the historic Baptist position." The Convention had spoken, they said, and it was the trustees' job to abide by the will of the constituents.

Their first 1985 attempt failed on a vote of thirty-nine to thirty-two, but the issue was not dead. When a contingent of new fundamentalist trustees had been added to the board that summer, a study committee was appointed; and when they made their report in 1986, CPA was ruled unavailable to churches with women pastors. The tenuous balance of power on that 1985–1986 board was demonstrated, however, in another decision focused on women ministers. The personnel committee recommended that the Reverend Janet Fuller (because she was ordained) be denied appointment as a "student work missionary" for Yale University and four other New Haven schools. The daughter of Southern Baptist missionaries to Lebanon, Fuller had already been serving at Yale for two years. After a passionate plea in her behalf by a dissenting member of the personnel committee, the full board reversed the committee's recommendation, appointing her by a slim thirty-seven to thirty-four vote. She would, however, be the last ordained woman appointed. Moderates vowed not to let the issue die, but their efforts to reverse the board's new direction were in vain.

Fundamentalist ideology would, in the coming years, continue to change the character of the agency's personnel. Trustees were concerned about more than just ordained women on their missionary force. They were also looking for evidences of deviation of other sorts. In 1987, personnel policies were changed in two other areas, each helping to draw more clearly the boundary defining the new Southern Baptist identity. On one side, the trustees moved to distinguish themselves from their evangelical neighbors in the "modern charismatic movement." Those "actively participating in or promoting glossolalia" would not be "appointed [missionaries], approved [for Church Pastoral Aid and other programs] or endorsed [as chaplains in hospitals, industry, or armed services]." Fundamentalists who had been influenced by a "dispensational" view of scripture saw glossolalia as unique to the first century and invalid for the present church. If a fundamentalist understanding of scripture was to be the guiding principle, then glossolalia could not be allowed.[18]

Distinguishing Southern Baptists from their neighbors on the left, trustees chose divorce as their issue. Only sexual infidelity or desertion (by the other party) were legitimate grounds, and even the innocent party could not remarry. Anyone in a "pastoral role" should, they said, exemplify the highest Christian standards for family life. In a world where "family" was defined with decreasing certainty, fundamentalists turned to the Bible for a clear and certain standard. Merely saying that one believed the Bible was not enough. Southern Baptist missionaries would have to demonstrate that they also lived by the rules fundamentalists deduced from the biblical text. Ideology was shaping a personnel policy that would clearly affect who would work for this organization.

The question of who would *lead* the Home Mission Board also had to be decided. In early 1986, William Tanner, the organization's president left for another post. Fundamentalists who had worked for ten years to change the direction of their denomination saw this as their first opportunity to select a chief executive officer. When Tanner left, however, the trustees were still a closely divided body, with moderates occupying key officer and committee positions. Official procedure called for the officers of the trustees, in consultation with the staff, to name a search committee. The people they named were described by one staff member as "respected by the staff persons who have seen them operate in committees. There's some good experience on there. I think the committee has the best interests of the Home Mission Board at heart. I don't see any of them as set on one side or the other." But fundamentalists saw it quite differently. Not one member of the committee was firmly aligned with the new trustees. The moderate trustee chair spoke of the group as a "team," with "experience," that could work together in "harmony." But fundamentalists saw it as a deliberate attempt to exclude them from the process.

Before the committee chair could make his first progress report to the Board at the August 1986, meeting, trustee Ann Frazier moved that the Board go into an executive session in which they requested the resignation of the original search committee. All but one of the original members complied, and the committee was reconstituted with three old members and four new ones. All the records of the first committee were destroyed, and resumés and recommendations had to be resubmitted. They would start with a clean slate in their search.

By that time there was finally a clear and dependable majority of fundamentalists on this board. They elected a new slate of officers for themselves, and there was little doubt that the search committee would bring a conservative recommendation that would be approved. Speculation was rife about who would be rewarded with this first major fundamentalist staff position. The person they selected, Larry Lewis, was not one of the movement stars, but he had impeccable credentials—both for experience in Home Mission work and for his loyal participation in the movement. The committee was unanimous in recommending him, and only fifteen trustees (out of sixty-seven) voted against his election. Describing himself as a "church planter" at heart, he had pastored growing and active urban churches both in Missouri and in New Jersey. And he had helped to pass "doctrinal integrity" and anti-abortion resolutions in Missouri and at the SBC, chairing the 1985 SBC Resolutions Committee. He had not often been visible, but he had worked hard to see that Southern Baptists moved in a more conservative direction. Now he would get the chance to put that commitment into action.

Some doubted that Lewis had the ability or experience to run such a large organization. Others feared that he would immediately begin a staff purge. Neither fear proved accurate. Lewis quickly began the process of getting to know the work of his organization. One staffer reported with amazement that Lewis knew more in six weeks about the inner workings of the Board than the previous President had known after ten years. Fears of a doctrinal purge peaked in the early weeks of Lewis' tenure. Speaking to the staff in a chapel service, Lewis said that he intended to "give careful attention to the doctrinal integrity" of the agency and that those "who will not be responsive will be replaced."[19] A storm of protest ensued, and Lewis soon realized that he had no legitimate authority to change the terms of employment of those already serving. The rationally established rules of the bureaucracy limited his power. He eventually circulated a memo requesting that anyone who had doubts about the Baptist Faith and Message talk to him about their disagreements, a request most considered impossible to enforce. When Lewis announced that he wanted to reorganize the Board, rumors of a purge were again rampant. *SBC Today* reported that the "corridor talk" at the Board included fears that the "reorganization might call for elected employees to change their titles, thus setting in place the opportunity for such employees to be 're-questioned' and threatened with termination."[20] No such tactics emerged.

While fears of a wholesale purge were subsiding, hiring and firing were still a recurrent concern. Even before Lewis had arrived, the conservative pressures were being felt. In the summer of 1986, Richard Harmon, head of the Interfaith Witness Department, had delivered a staff chapel sermon that was highly critical of fundamentalism and of the developing new majority among trustees. When word of his sermon reached fundamentalists, they pushed for his ouster. Considering the options available and the direction in which the organization was headed, resignation seemed the only reasonable alternative. His department was, in fact, another of the top items on the agenda of the new trustees. They had long complained that Interfaith Witness had become merely "interfaith dialogue." They were unimpressed with the ecumenical work being done there. The department's location in the Missions Ministries Division (rather than under Evangelism) seemed to symbolize the absence of an evangelistic focus to their work. The department had often been challenged in the past by disgruntled pastors or church people, but they had always had the support of the administration and the trustees. By 1986, that situation had changed. Within eighteen months a second staffer, George Sheridan, would resign after being demoted for unwillingness to evangelize Jews. And in the 1988 reorganization of the Board, Interfaith Witness was finally moved into the Evangelism section. Its primary purpose, Lewis said at the time, was "training and equipping Baptist people to witness to people of other faiths."[21]

The upheaval in Interfaith Witness was perhaps the most traumatic change effected in the early days under a fundamentalist board of trustees. Even when Lewis' reorganization plan was announced in the fall of 1988, few wholesale philosophical changes could be discerned. Rather, the plan reflected Lewis' focus on evangelism and church starting and the imperatives of a rationally-organized bureaucratic structure. Four sections were expanded into five. Departments were slightly reshuffled, and some personnel were reassigned. Fundamentalist stalwarts Charles Chaney and Darrell Robinson were given the vice presidencies for the key Evangelism and Extension sections; but no one was fired, and no ultimatum accompanied the reassignments. Even when budget cuts precipitated extensive staff cutbacks in 1989, those decisions seemed more dictated by a desire for a leaner organization than by any doctrinal motives.

In his reorganization, Lewis had acted like an efficient corporate manager. He had set out his objectives—evangelism and new churches—and with the help of a task force of "experts" he reorganized the institution's departments and personnel so as to reach those objectives. Since his objectives were not significantly different from what the Board was already doing, no wholesale reconstruction was necessary. Even those who were doing the work he apparently valued least—social ministry—actually benefitted (at least temporarily) by having their own new section. The focus of that section's work was changed by the addition of an office on alternatives to abortion, but no existing work was discontinued. Throughout the institution, then, each staff person felt the mandate to focus his or her work on fostering new converts and new churches, but no one was prevented from continuing to do the work he or she had always done. So long as staff members could live with an over-arching emphasis on evangelism and with the agency's conservative climate, their jobs seemed safe. The job of reshaping the Home Mission Board would be accomplished neither by purging it of current personnel nor by ceasing to be a bureaucracy. Instead, Lewis was going about the task of setting organizational policies shaped by his fundamentalist faith. Ideological commitments would be bent to the demands of the rationally organized structure within which he and the others worked.

While there was to be no wholesale purge of existing staff, new staff were being subjected to intense doctrinal scrutiny. The prefundamentalist search process had already included church recommendations, statements of faith, and agreement to abide by all sorts of behavioral norms. But with a fundamentalist board of trustees and Lewis as President, additional criteria and assurances were added to the process. Elected staff (the professionals who work mostly in Atlanta) were now personally interviewed by Lewis and quizzed on their understanding of and assent to the Baptist Faith and Message. In their appearances before trustee committees, candidates again had to prove their doctrinal integrity. Even in the final stage of full board approval, candidates might be called in for questioning. The new trustees and the new boss were taking a very activist role in assuring themselves and their constituents that this SBC agency would no longer be dominated by people whose beliefs differed from majority Baptist positions.

And it soon became clear that this screening process would include more than just beliefs. In early 1989, the Reverend Benny Clark was entering the last stages of the process, having successfully passed through his interviews with Lewis and with the personnel committee. He had even announced his resignation to his church. At that point one member of the personnel committee and several other members of the board stepped in, raising several concerns about Clark's possible employment. The three central concerns were that Clark was a member of the Southern Baptist Alliance (the organization formed in 1987 by members of the denomination's progressive wing), that his church ordained women deacons, and that they did not have Sunday evening services.[22] Elimination of Sunday night services was often seen by conservatives as a sign of liberalism, as of course was the ordination of women to the diaconate. And membership in the Alliance was a clear signal of one's position on the left wing of the denomination. While trustees couched their concerns in rhetoric about denominational support and avoiding divisive issues, the message was clear: Clark was a member of the very group against which fundamentalists had rebelled. If they hired him, their campaign would have been for naught. Once the concerns were raised, the pressure was on Lewis and, in turn, on Clark. The position was offered, but Clark chose to decline it.

Clark's case nicely illustrates the conflicting pressures felt by an ideologically committed executive. The approval of Clark, after full screening by Lewis and relevant committees, indicated the extent to which the rational structures that outlined job qualifications and career tracks could still channel ideologically unacceptable candidates into the pool. There were well worn paths into this bureaucracy, paths that led through training, pastoral experience, mission involvement, and network connections. People who had been on those paths for the past generation were likely to be inclined toward a progressive agenda. They had accummulated the credentials necessary for working in the denomination's institutions. And many could even pass the new doctrinal tests. But they were not fundamentalists, and they were not the kind of people that SBC fundamentalists wanted working for them. On the one hand, they clearly failed the ideological tests of the committed conservative activists who wanted "purity" in their institutions. But on the other hand, they had the credentials and experience those same institutions demanded in professional staff. Lewis had recognized Clark's credentials and even accepted Clark's doctrinal compatability; but his activist trustees had recognized the incompatibility between Clark and their long-range goals. Lewis was then caught between the mandates of the rationally organized institution he had been hired to run and the mandates of the ideologically committed trustees who were ultimately his bosses. In this case, ideology won. Whether ideology could continue to supercede the structural imperatives of the bureaucratic process remained to be seen. This would certainly not be the last time Lewis faced such a conflict.

The pressures of the existing structures and policies again came to bear when the existing staff asked Lewis whether the criteria by which Clark had been judged would also be used on them. Those whose churches had women deacons (or ministers), no Sunday night services, or Alliance membership feared that they too would be suspect. Lewis assured them, however, that those standards would not be used against them. So long as they were living within the guidelines set by the organization for their work, their church affiliation (so long as it was Southern Baptist) would not be relevant. The modern, rational imperative that sets limits on the powers of work organizations supported the employees' contention that non-work-related affiliations should not be used in work-related judgments. For in-coming staff and missionaries all sorts of behavior and affiliations would be used as a measure of true doctrinal loyalty. But for existing staff, at least for now, job performance would outweigh ideological purity.

The Home Mission Board, then, was the first institution to come under the new regime, and it affords us a look at the countervailing pressures inherent in attempting to bring a new ideology to bear in a bureaucratic organization. By redefining its goals and reshaping personnel policies, the fundamentalist board of trustees and the fundamentalist executive began the process of concrete institutional change that the SBC's dissidents had desired for nearly a generation. No attempt was made to change the presuppositions of the way work was organized. Rather, the new bosses sought to refocus the substance of what was being done and gradually change the personnel who would be carrying out their goals. Lewis believed strongly in the power of ideas to shape behavior. He believed that if the people working for the organization held true doctrines about the Bible, the organization itself would be transformed.

The Foreign Mission Board

Similar concerns for mission goals and orthodox personnel were present at the Foreign Mission Board in Richmond, and they too saw a strong shift toward direct evangelism and church planting. But there was no new chief executive to be hired in these early years, and no major reorganization of structures. The shifts were more subtle in Richmond than in Atlanta.

The first major change in personnel policy was a change that for the first time allowed graduates of independent seminaries to be appointed without any study at an official SBC institution. Long before there was a Mid-America, the Board had determined that at least one year of study at one of the denomination's seminaries was essential to developing what one staff member described as "the sense of family" and understanding of "the unique SBC milieu" that would enable an overseas mission group to work together as a team. He noted that "when you are put in the situation of being a minority, oftentimes under stress, you don't want to introduce other factors that enhance the dissonance." But by 1988, the board of trustees reversed that position, allowing graduates of any accredited seminary to be appointed.

At about the same time, the trustees reaffirmed their doctrinal guidelines by dismissing an errant missionary. Michael Willett, still in language study in Costa Rica, came under the suspicion of a fellow missionary (one of the first Mid-America graduates to be appointed). Willett had just published an article supporting women's ordination in *SBC Today*, but his

coworker was also worried about Willett's adherence to orthodox interpretations of Jesus' life, death, and miracles. He detailed his suspicions
to friends in Tennessee, and his letter apparently "received some circu-
lation" before any complaint was every voiced directly to Richmond. After
a series of conferences and confrontations, Willett was eventually fired for
"doctrinal ambiguity."[23] Three years earlier, another Latin American missionary had also gotten into doctrinal difficulties. Edward Taylor resigned
after he came to the conclusion that not all Catholics needed evangeliza-
tion.[24] In that case as well, accusations about unorthodox beliefs circulated through conservative channels on their way to the Board.

Many fundamentalists had become convinced that very few Southern
Baptist appointees were in fact orthodox. Since the SBC seminaries were
"liberal" and all missionaries had to attend them, all missionaries were
suspect. Board President Keith Parks reported receiving requests for lists
of "genuine, Bible-believing evangelistic missionaries." He obviously declined to designate only some of his missionaries as orthodox.[25] The Foreign Mission Board had always had strict theological requirements, and
Parks was quite conservative himself. His basic conservatism and passionate commitment to missions had already helped him weather the protests
over his public opposition to Charles Stanley's 1985 reelection. It is not
clear, in fact, that either Taylor or Willett would have survived a doctrinal
inquiry even before the fundamentalists dominated the board of trustees.
Their departures were not so much part of an organized effort at purity as
incidental casualties in a time when doctrinal and denominational identity
were being renegotiated.

It was clear, however, that Greg and Katrina Pennington would have
been appointed without hesitation, were there not a fundamentalist board
of trustees. In the summer of 1989, this Oklahoma couple had passed
through all the preliminary tests, had all the necessary credentials, and
were within days of official appointment. But Katrina was ordained, and
her ordination had caused some stir in Oklahoma when it happened.
A trustee from her home state was determined that this "divisive" young
woman should not be a foreign missionary. Asked what would convince
him that she was not divisive, he replied that she should renounce her
ordination. Other fundamentalist trustees looked at the Penningtons' experience on the staff of a progressive church in San Francisco as a warning
of unfit beliefs. With a last minute effort, fundamentalists succeeded in
blocking their appointment, infuriating many on the staff who had found
the Penningtons well-qualified.[26] The board of trustees, just like their
counterparts in Atlanta, had begun the process of changing the substantive criteria for appointment.

At about the time they had fired Willett, the board had established a committee to review the entire appointment process. Since World War II, the Board had developed an elaborate screening process designed to maximize the skills and commitment of its mission force and minimize the factors that lead to predictable problems for missionaries. Candidates were screened by doctors and psychiatrists; and because they recognized the problems of uprooting teens into a strange context, families with older children were seldom appointed. Candidates were often refused or told to wait. The process was so strict that one fundamentalist leader declared that even the Apostle Paul would never have made it. He and others were unconvinced that every missionary needed a college and seminary education or that all the other requirements were really necessary. They wanted to make appointments more on the basis of evangelistic zeal than on credentials and psychiatric evaluations. Again, the demands of ideology were in conflict with the procedures established by a rationally organized bureaucratic system. The result would likely be new policies on missionary qualifications.

The Foreign Mission Board's new trustees, like those at the Home Mission Board, wanted new hiring criteria and more active involvement in the appointment process. They wanted face-to-face interviews with the candidates in addition to the written profiles they usually received. They also wanted to be more involved in the supervision of those missionaries once they were on the field. The trustees were unhappy with a system that made missionaries responsible first to their local mission group, then to an area supervisor, and only then to the administration in Richmond and the board of trustees. They wanted to eliminate the middle levels of that hierarchy, establishing direct accountability between missionaries and the Richmond office (which of course, is directly responsible to the trustees). At least until they could be sure of the commitments of all those on the field, trustees did not want doctrinal and other concerns to get buried in "the system." Nor did they want new, more conservative missionaries to be subject to the authority of older, establishment colleagues. The hierarchy into which the SBC's more than 3,000 missionaries had been organized would, they hoped, be dismantled. They were seeking to change personnel policy both by greater attention to the conservative theology required of missionaries and by changes in the structure through which missionaries did their work.

The new trustees at the Foreign Mission Board were also interested in changing the goals of the work being done. In 1988, a new "70–30" plan was announced. Within ten years, the board would have 70 percent of its missionaries devoting at least half time to direct evangelism. Somewhat fewer missionaries would then be doing the medical, educational, agricultural, and other social work that had often been seen as the missionary's main entree into nonwestern cultures. Echoing the Home Mission Board emphasis on new converts and new churches, the measure of productivity was to shift toward baptisms and church starts.

The changes in Foreign Mission strategy and personnel were more gradual than those implemented in Atlanta, but they were no less decisive. Fundamentalist trustees aimed to use ideological standards more than bureaucratic ones to determine who would do the work, in what structures, and with what goals.

The Sunday School Board

At the publishing house in Nashville, the tension between ideology and structure had long been a fact of life. While on the one hand the Sunday School Board was the largest and most rationalized of the denomination's entities, it was also the most subject to ideological and cultural constraints. It had always answered not only to its board of trustees, but also to the market. Whenever its products strayed beyond the boundaries of Southern Baptist sensibilities, customers were likely to protest, and adjustments would be made.

Some of the pressure on the Sunday School Board in the late 1980s, in fact, came directly from changes in the market. One senior administrator called it "declining brand loyalty." He lamented that churches were no longer routinely committed to buying their denomination's products. They are willing to shop in the marketplace of independent publishers, buying what best suited their tastes, concerns, and budget.[27] The Board had already lost some customers to the Baptist Literature Board, begun by members of the Baptist Faith and Message Fellowship in the 1970s. But more significantly, they were losing customers to Scripture Press, David C. Cook, and other evangelical houses. By 1988, they were suffering a fairly serious tightening of the budget that only added to the sense of siege that prevailed in Nashville.

Unlike other SBC institutions, the publishing house receives no Cooperative Program funds. Its work is subsidized by the products it sells— including in 1985, some 78 million pieces of literature. There might be declining brand loyalty, but nearly every Southern Baptist church used *something* that came from Nashville. Ninety-six percent of our respondents claimed that their churches used at least some of the quarterly Sunday School lessons published there. Available for every age from the cradle to the grave, with three separate series for adults, these quarterlies were the primary source of biblical instruction for most Baptists. Every Sunday 2 to 3 million adults spent an hour reading and discussing what the Bible and their quarterly had to say.[28] The products of this publishing house, then, had great influence and got regular, careful scrutiny. There was little chance that doctrinal deviations could be buried inside the organization.

When a professor at Southeastern Seminary wrote a 1985 lesson on Job suggesting that the Satan portrayed there was not the same personification of evil described in later Jewish writings (including the New Testament), his idea did not go by unnoticed. Nearly 150 letters were sent to Nashville protesting his lack of orthodoxy. The organization's response was to blame the process—the lesson missed a step in the editorial sequence and thus slipped through. The solution was to tighten procedures. An experienced editor explained to us,

> There always has been a concern to minister to all Southern Baptists, regardless of their theological position, and a concern to write carefully, so as not to be stepping on landmines unnecessarily. It may be that the difference that the theological controversy has made is that we have had to develop mechanisms and procedures that will ensure that we do that. We have become more conscious.

Even before fundamentalists had a majority on the board of trustees, they could mobilize direct pressure on the editorial process. The writer of the Job lesson was removed from the list of approved writers, just as the editor of the *Baptist Student* magazine would be relieved of his editorial duties for publishing controversial articles on women in ministry (and on the New Christian Right). The organization responded to pressure by changes in staffing and by implementing new procedures, new safeguards against offending their customers.

Recognizing that they were writing for a diverse audience one editor noted that they looked for writers with enough experience "to understand the nuances of what makes Southern Baptists tick . . . [to be] aware of some of the pitfalls, landmines, red flag words and ideas. We say we don't want people to write to be understood, but so they will not be misunderstood. That's a tall order." Another talked about the differences between pastoring and writing.

> As a pastor I could be a little more confrontational with folks in my sermons, because they heard the inflection in my voice, they knew the beat of my heart. We had this personal relationship. Well, you can't do that in cold print. All you have are the cold hard words in black and white. . . . The people put their own inflections in, and a lot of times it is a lot different from what the writer intended or what I intended. So we cannot be confrontational, we must be educational, move them along an inch, or a quarter of an inch, at a time.

Like most of the staff, he wanted desperately to help Southern Baptists better understand the Bible, to help them to grow and change, even if only a quarter of an inch at a time.

Some of the pressures had always been there as part of the nature of being a market oriented organization. But other pressures were increasing with the changes in the denomination and, specifically, in their board of trustees. "I continue to sense more limitations to what I am called to do," this staff member said. "We are in a very conservative atmosphere in the convention right now. The conservatives are in control of it, of our board of trustees, and they are putting more and more restrictions on us as to what we can and cannot do." The presence of a fundamentalist board of trustees channeled the already present forces of the market, amplifying the already present conservative voices of customers. As in the other denominational institutions, trustees sought more information, more voice in hiring, and doctrinal oversight of staff and programs.

The most visible change in the substance of the Board's work was the addition of a new commentary series. Having chafed at the Broadman commentaries published in the 1970s, fundamentalists gained the opportunity to publish a multi-volume series that would "demonstrate that biblical inerrancy represents a viable, scholarly approach."[29] Of the five consulting editors who would guide the project, two were from Criswell College and one from Mid-America. This marked the trustees' willingness to bypass existing professional staff to make sure that a conservative constituency was pleased.[30] The staff of the Board had argued that their market research did not support the need for such a commentary. Whether they or the trustees were right would ultimately be tested by the strength of the commentary's sales. If it failed, the market pressure against exclusively inerrantist products might prove a formidable argument against the ideological pressures of activists committed to that point of view. If it succeeded, future inerrantist materials were assured. Their longterm success in reshaping published products would depend on their success in developing appropriate markets.

In the short term, the most difficult struggle faced by the fundamentalist trustees at the Sunday School Board was the question of political rewards and punishments. Would they use their power to punish those who had opposed them in their struggle to gain their positions? As fundamentalists saw it, Sunday School Board President Lloyd Elder had been visibly on the wrong side of a number of battles. They not only blamed him for all the doctrinally controversial products they had already attacked (the lesson on Job, for instance), but they also resented the way he seemed able to use the power of his office to favor moderate causes.[31] In the summer of 1989, one trustee circulated a forty-page list of criticisms that amounted to a call for Elder's dismissal. When the trustees gathered, cooler heads prevailed, and Elder was merely censured.[32] For the time being at least, political causes alone would not be enough to justify personnel changes.

At least in the initial period of transition to a fundamentalist governing body at the Sunday School Board, no structures changed and no one was fired. Already conservative writing guidelines were tightened further, and the range of products was expanded in a conservative direction. Trustees gained greater access to the internal affairs of the agency and took a more active role in hiring. But in many ways they merely focused and intensified the conservative pressures that already existed. Although this organization had always been committed to educating Southern Baptists and "moving them along a quarter of an inch at a time," it had always known that any quarter of an inch might precipitate a market reaction requiring them to move at least an inch back to the right.

The Christian Life Commission

If the changes at the Sunday School Board were like a giant glacier moving slightly to the right, the changes in its tiny Nashville neighbor, the Christian Life Commission, were like a continuing series of explosions that eventually left few existing structures intact. The Commission had been a thorn in the side of conservatives since its inception in the 1930s. Its persistent push for integration had never been popular. In the 1980s, however, the problem was abortion. The agency had taken a modified pro-choice position, arguing that abortion was in a few instances the lesser of evils. Their position infuriated the right-to-life activists who brought repeated resolutions and motions calling for a clear and active pro-life stand. So long as they did not control the board of trustees, however, those motions were repeatedly reported back to the convention with polite refusals to change.[33] As late as the 1985–1986 convention year, the CLC's board still had a moderate majority.

And it was in that year that the agency's long-time executive director, Foy Valentine, notified his trustees that he would soon be retiring. An all-moderate search committee was named. Fundamentalists were as furious about this as they had been about the similar tactics of the Home Mission Board. They did not, however, have enough votes yet to reject either the committee or its eventual recommendation of Larry Baker to fill Valentine's post. By the time the committee brought Baker before the board, additional fundamentalist trustees had taken office. They questioned him about capital punishment (which he opposed), the role of women in ministry (which he supported), and especially abortion. He stated that there are rare exceptions "when, while abortion may not be justified, it may be excused. Because we live in a broken and sinful world, . . . there may be occasions when the exception needs at least to be an option."[34] The fundamentalists on the board were less than pleased, but they fell two votes short of the fifteen they would have needed to defeat his election; in March of 1987, Baker took office.

Not surprisingly, one of Baker's first decisions was to give more attention to abortion. He reassigned staff member Robert Parham from full-time work on hunger to work divided equally between abortion and hunger. They planned a major consultation on abortion, and Parham spoke enthusiastically about the possibility of working toward "knitting a seamless garment of pro-life issues."[35] He had in mind, the kind of "consistent pro-life ethic" talked about by Catholic Cardinal Bernardin, the evangelical lobby JustLife, and others. It would include opposition to abortion and to capital punishment, along with support for child welfare and economic justice measures. But that was not the approach fundamentalists wanted to take. They wanted abortion outlawed, and they wanted the CLC to lead Southern Baptists in the fight.

Even if Baker had done everything fundamentalists wanted him to do, he might still have been doomed by their anger over the process that brought him to the Commission. Even as he took office, there were threats to his job. At the annual SBC meeting in June, a group of dissident trustees brought a minority report, condemning the procedure by which Baker was hired and complaining that he was out of line with key Baptist positions. When the 1987–1988 board took office, a fundamentalist majority was in place, and at their September board meeting a motion for Baker's dismissal was brought. But even some of the new trustees were unwilling to fire him after only six months on the job. With a tie fifteen to fifteen vote, he kept his job.

This decision to seek Baker's dismissal actually went against the strategy fundamentalist leaders wanted to maintain. Their effort had been to avoid dismissals wherever possible. They wanted to discredit accusations that a "bloodbath" was in store for agencies under their control, and they wanted to avoid creating martyrs. The general strategy was to change hiring practices for new personnel along with changing agency policy, hoping that current staff unwilling to live within new guidelines would leave voluntarily. Those who had guided this movement from its beginnings recognized that precipitous actions could create the kind of schismatic situation that had faced the Lutheran Church Missouri Synod when conservatives took over there. Southern Baptist conservatives wanted to effect their course correction without losing any significant portion of the denomination. (The exception was their eagerness for the exit of the 5 to 10 percent of the denomination they saw as truly liberal.) While they assumed that some dismissals would be necessary, they wanted those to be very carefully chosen and very cautiously accomplished. The decision to seek Baker's dismissal may have reflected the strong activist character of this board of trustees more than a careful decision reached by fundamentalist leaders from throughout the movement. Once committed vocal trustees were in place, not even the leaders of the movement could keep them in line.

While trustees had failed in their attempt to fire Baker, their message had not been lost on him. Within the next year he and four other staff members would be gone, leaving only two professional staff members and an administrative assistant from the previous era. Said one of the five, "I am leaving because of the low comfort level and the low security level." The staff had been warned to look for other opportunities, and he took that suggestion seriously. He waited until after the 1988–1989 board had met, but said, "My low comfort level was not helped in any way by the things I heard [at the meeting]. There was not any sign of direct affirmation or support for any of the current staff." Expressing his regret at leaving, he said, "For thirty-six years, Southern Baptists through the Cooperative Program have made it possible for me to follow God's calling in my Christian ministry. . . . The past seven years have been good ones as I have been able to help Southern Baptists through the Christian Life Commission to . . . become more aware of the ethical imperatives of the Christian faith."[36] The strong sense of vocation that had brought him and others into this ministry had become irreconcilable with the equally strong sense of vocation shared by fundamentalists with a very different vision of the "ethical imperatives of the Christian faith."

After Baker left, a new search committee set out to find a man who was "an avowed inerrantist" and also opposed to abortion, capital punishment, and women's ordination, who was academically qualified and had a strong record of social activism. It took them less than three months to recommend Richard Land for the job. With degrees from Princeton and Oxford, he carried more academic weight that any other visible fundamentalist. He was a former administrator at Criswell College and a former administrative assistant to Texas governor Bill Clements. And his biblical and social views were impeccably conservative.[37] In late 1988, Land took over the agency, and the new era began.

One of the major problems faced by Land was the recreation of the CLC's identity. For more than a generation, conservatives had seen the CLC as an adversary, while progressives had called it home. During the Valentine era the CLC's annual seminars were the regular gathering place for the denomination's progressive wing, often drawing several hundred registrants. Seminars were held at a hotel in a major city and resembled in format the professional conferences many of these folk were accustomed to attending. Speakers from the American religious mainstream and from the political left were often surprised to find such a receptive Southern Baptist audience. Even as late as 1988, the program had included Union Seminary ethicist Roger Shinn, Congressman William Gray, and an ordained woman talking about social justice for the poor.[38] Although Land did not get to plan all of the 1989 seminar program, the presence of speakers from Dallas Theological Seminary, Criswell College, and *Christianity Today* gave it a decidedly more conservative cast.[39] And not surprisingly, few of the old progressive constituents were in attendance. As with the agency itself, the old audience was gone, and a new one would have to be created.

Land's goal was to create an agency that would bridge the gap between conservative and liberal constituencies. He described his task as "convincing conservatives to see the CLC as a resource and not an adversary, while convincing moderates that the agency is committed to more than just a narrow conservative agenda." In his first year, the agency sponsored both a race relations conference and a sanctity of life conference. The race relations conference, in particular, was an attempt to bring the denomination's two wings together by featuring Foy Valentine as well as prominent conservatives on the program. But the task of rebuilding the CLC's identity would not be easy. Both conservatives and progressives would remain skeptical.

In addition, the organizational environment faced by a new CLC was formidable. The old CLC had offered a very particular blend of commitment to progressive social action with loyalty to doing that action within the Southern Baptist Convention. The new CLC had a conservative constituency that was already well connected with a variety of established conservative organizations outside the SBC, through which they were pursuing their conservative moral agenda. Conservative activists might not need one more Christian lobby. Having almost completely changed the staff of the agency, and having put in place a new agenda of conservative concerns, the task of creating a niche for the agency in the larger organizational and political environment remained. In the crowded organizational environment of New Christian Right politics, the new CLC's only unique mission appeared to be the conversion of uncommitted Southern Baptists to conservative political action. It might only survive if it could take over as the chief Southern Baptist lobby in Washington, but to do that would require displacing the Baptist Joint Committee on Public Affairs.

The Baptist Joint Committee on Public Affairs

The Baptist Joint Committee had since its inception been treated as if it were a full-fledged SBC agency, but that was not, in fact, the case. Its unique structural relationship to the denomination created unique dynamics as fundamentalists moved into positions of power in the denomination. Even if they occupied every Southern Baptist seat on the Baptist Joint Committee, they could still not control its decisions about staff or policy. This was an agency jointly supported and governed by nine Baptist bodies, black and white. Although the Director, James Dunn, was a Southern Baptist, and both staff and budget were dominated by Southern Baptist contributions, Southern Baptists did not hold a majority of seats on the board of directors. The positions taken by the Baptist Joint Committee on issues of church and state represented not just the wishes of Southern Baptists, but the collective wisdom of nine Baptist groups.

The Baptist Joint Committee had rarely in the past disagreed with official Southern Baptist positions. They were in line with official SBC policy in opposing an ambassador to the Vatican, helping ministers with tax problems, supporting "equal access" for after-school religious activities, and advocating balanced textbook treatment of the role of religion in American history. But they emphatically would not support a school prayer amendment, and they refused to argue that the Civil Rights Restoration Act was a grave threat to the freedom of religion (the grounds on which the Moral Majority and other conservative groups attacked the bill). On those two issues, Southern Baptist fundamentalists repeatedly condemned the BJC as liberal. They passed SBC resolutions in support of school prayer and in opposition to the Civil Rights Restoration Act, but those resolutions had no binding power on the BJC.

Fundamentalists reserved their choicest words for James Dunn himself. Because of his structural independence, Dunn had been more outspoken in his opposition to fundamentalists than any other leader from the SBC's progressive wing. He had even joined Norman Lear's People for the American Way and accused Ronald Reagan of "despicable demagoguery." There was no other staff member in the entire SBC bureaucracy fundamentalists would rather fire. One fundamentalist leader said it flatly, "His whole approach and attitude is not ours, and anything I can do to see him replaced or get our money diverted from him, I'll do."

The fact that they could neither fire Dunn nor change BJC policy on conservative issues set up a series of structural innovations aimed at moving the Southern Baptist Convention out of the Baptist Joint Committee. For several years, annual motions had been brought from the convention floor requesting that the BJC be "defunded" and/or that ties with them be severed. Each time, these efforts (usually considered on Wednesday or Thursday—moderates' strong days at the convention) were defeated. But a 1986 motion was referred to the Executive Committee, and the first of three special study committees was formed. They struck a compromise that had the support of Executive Committee member Paul Pressler and therefore looked like it would put the matter to rest. The board of the Baptist Joint Committee was to be reorganized, giving Southern Baptists eighteen, rather than fifteen, seats. In addition, the number of SBC agency executives sitting on the committee would be reduced, and the number of at-large (elected and therefore fundamentalist) members increased. The BJC board agreed, and the plan easily passed at the 1987 SBC annual meeting.

Still Southern Baptists were only one-third of the Joint Committee's trustees. If control of the Baptist Joint Committee had been the aim, Pressler and others supporting the reorganization had clearly failed. However, what they apparently wanted most was not so much the increased representation, but another feature virtually ignored both in the Executive Committee and on the convention floor. The new bylaw also allowed the eighteen SBC members (called the Public Affairs Committee [PAC]) to "function as a separate committee serving the Southern Baptist Convention." From their first meeting it was clear that they intended to do just that. They wanted their own separate budget and they wanted SBC money going to the BJC to go through them. If the BJC even wanted exhibit space at the annual convention, the PAC would have to approve the request. They set out to establish themselves as an independent body and as the structural link between the Baptist Joint Committee and the SBC.

Some indication of the way the PAC intended to represent Southern Baptists in Washington came in their first few months of operation. They sent a letter to members of the U.S. Senate formally endorsing the nomination of Judge Robert Bork to the Supreme Court (an action unprecedented in Southern Baptist history).[40] They also opposed the Dodd-Kildee child care bill (for its imposition of regulations on church day care centers and its "discrimination against mothers who stay home").[41] When they again clashed with the staff of the Baptist Joint Committee that fall, they voted simply to sever ties.

The Executive Committee of the SBC told them that they could not walk out and that BJC money would still go directly to Dunn's Washington office. But the Executive Committee also said that it would set up another study committee to talk about the question of finances. The solution offered this time left no question about who would represent Southern Baptists in Washington. A Religious Liberty Commission was proposed. It would have its own budget, some portion of which could be sent to the Baptist Joint Committee, if it chose. But both money and representation to the BJC would be solely determined by the new Commission.

A new agency cannot simply be created by the Executive Committee, however. It must gain a majority vote of messengers in two consecutive annual conventions. And after the proposal left the Executive Committee, the Religious Liberty Commission met with some unexpected ideological and structural obstacles.[42] To be established, it would have to gain the ideological support of messengers. They might have to think hard about condemning an organization for arguing that the state should stay out of the business of sponsoring religious rituals in the classroom. While some Baptists might want prayer back in their southern schools, others—even conservative ones—might wonder whether historic Baptists like John Leland or Roger Williams would agree. And some of those who disagreed with the BJC on school prayer were still not convinced that the Committee should be discarded. The ideological battle over the need for a Religious Liberty Commission was at best too close to call.

The structural questions, on the other hand, weighed heavily against the new Commission. Creating a new organization under the Southern Baptist institutional umbrella implied adjustments in existing organizations. A new niche would have to be created in the institutional environment—represented most concretely by a slice of the budget. In 1989, when the Commission was proposed, the Executive Committee was also proposing the first no-growth budget in recent SBC history. Both mission boards were accepting a small decrease in their funding, and neither looked kindly on the possibility of giving up additional money to fund a new agency. Keith Parks spoke against the idea in the Executive Committee debate, and even fundamentalist Larry Lewis voiced his opposition after it was officially proposed. As the 1989 annual meeting approached, SBC President Jerry Vines announced that he was requesting a postponement of the first vote on the proposal. The Executive Committee agreed and left the new Commission pending. By the time they met in the fall, the proposal had been buried. But in its place, the CLC inherited more money for its Washington office and an expanded mission that would include church-state issues.[43] Fundamentalists had not been able to create any new structures or directly demolish any of the old ones, but they had finally crafted a compromise that would accomplish their purposes.

While fundamentalists were working out a way to sever ties with the Baptist Joint Committee, their attack on that body created the first tangible break in the unquestioning loyalty of moderates to the Southern Baptist Convention and its Cooperative Program. For years moderates had condemned fundamentalists for designating money to pet projects and giving minimally to the cooperative budget of the denomination. Now it was their turn. When the Convention reduced the BJC's funding in 1988, three state conventions and numerous churches designated additional gifts directly to Washington. The Committee actually had its best budget year ever. The Baptist Joint Committee gave moderates their first opportunity to explore the options available to them as outsiders—a process we will explore more fully in the next chapter.

The Seminaries

From the beginning the seminaries had been the most visible target for fundamentalists who wanted change in their denomination. They had correctly discerned, as we saw in chapter 5, that the staff and graduates of the three "liberal" seminaries formed the backbone of their opposition, and writers from those seminaries were the most common targets of fundamentalist speakers who wanted to demonstrate the presence of liberalism in the denomination. Since seminary professors are likely to write books on the Bible, on the church, and on theology, their ideas made them the most vulnerable to attack.

In addition, seminaries were the institutions in the Southern Baptist social structure that seemed most directly linked to the churches. Churches wanted to be sure that when they sent their most dedicated youth to seminary, those youth would return with faith intact. They also wanted to know that when they went looking for a pastor, they could trust people with degrees from Southern Baptist schools. Fundamentalists wanted to assure Southern Baptists that what was being taught in their seminaries was true to traditional beliefs. So it was in those institutions that the battle for control of the hearts and minds of Southern Baptists was most dramatically fought.

In the heat of the controversy some had suggested that perhaps the six institutions should just be divided between the two contenders. But the fundamentalists had no intention of giving up the "bricks and books" of even one campus. If seminaries were "bricks, books, and brains," it was only the brains they wished to replace—losing the infrastructure was not in the plan. As one leader put it, "That's not what I have given the last eight years of my life for." Nothing would have made him happier than to see all the liberal students and professors at one or more of the seminaries walk out to form a "Seminary in exile" (as the Concordia [Lutheran] Seminary students had done in St. Louis after the conservative takeover of their school). Such a wholesale exodus would have greatly facilitated the importation of the inerrantist scholars who would create the kinds of seminaries fundamentalists wanted. At none of the seminaries was "Seminex" duplicated, however. In part that was because faculty members knew that change could not really come unless they left, and they vowed to stay as long as possible, even against their own self-interests.[44] Each teacher and institution responded to growing fundamentalist majorities on their boards of trustees with the resources available in their particular context.

New Orleans and Golden Gate suffered little disruption. They were already considered acceptably orthodox. In late 1986, Golden Gate got a new president, and there had been wide speculation about which fundamentalist would be rewarded with a prestigious seminary presidency. In the end, the position was filled on ideological, but not political, grounds. William Crews was clearly in sympathy with the inerrantists in the Convention, but he had not been active in the fundamentalist movement. He could be trusted to continue the seminary's conservative direction. Likewise at New Orleans, conservative policies continued without disruption. These two schools experienced none of the conflict present at other seminaries.

The basic conservatism of giant Southwestern Seminary and its president Russell Dilday were never really in doubt, either. Dilday, however, had been very active in seeking to defeat Charles Stanley, and he continued in the years ahead to speak out against the fundamentalists. He wanted the kind of seminary that would be open to scholarly inquiry and respected in the larger arena of theological education, and he did not want a small group of fundamentalists interfering in the way the school was run. But interfere they did. Like the new trustees in other institutions, they wanted the information necessary to change the shape of the institution's policy and personnel. One moderate trustee described the ensuing tug of war as the work of a group of troublemakers who hung around together, caucused before every meeting, and were "constant pin pricks" making Russell Dilday's life difficult. In 1985, they succeeded (at first) in preventing him from firing a faculty member with a long record of problems. By 1987, they were able to block the nomination of Fort Worth pastor James Carter to the faculty. Carter presumably passed all the tests of "character, commitment, credentials, and confession of faith," but he failed because his church's practices seemed to hint at liberalism: they had not baptized large numbers of people; they ordained women to both diaconate and ministry; and they practiced a more liturgical form of worship than is common among most Baptists.[45] What policy and program changes trustees had in mind for the seminary had still not become apparent, but their concern for the orthodoxy of the school's staff had begun to make a difference.

Southwestern's trustees also had to decide what to do about Dilday himself. They failed in 1985 to censure him for his political involvement, but the issue came up again in 1989. This time the threat to his freedom, even his job, was real. After a five-hour closed door meeting, Dilday agreed to watch what he said and asked trustees to do the same. With no clear doctrinal grounds on which to attack him (and with over 100 supporters singing hymns outside and a battery of lawyers poised to file suit), trustees chose not to move against Dilday.[46] As in the case of Sunday School Board president Lloyd Elder, political grievances alone would not precipitate dismissal.

Fundamentalists could find no one to fire at Golden Gate, New Orleans, or Southwestern, but that was not the case at the other schools. At Midwestern, Southern, and Southeastern, concerns about personnel were long-standing and vigorous. The Peace Committee had refused to give them a clean bill of health after the first year, coming in with lists of questionable faculty and piles of suspicious writings.[47] One fundamentalist leader asserted that there were no more than three or four real conservatives on the entire faculty at either Southern or Southeastern. "Hit lists" of faculty that should be fired circulated in fundamentalist conversations.[48] And near the top of everyone's list was Midwestern Seminary's Temp Sparkman. As early as 1977, Sparkman's writings were the subject of controversy. Fundamentalists did not like the way he incorporated developmental psychology into his understanding of salvation, and they accused him of being a "universalist" (a belief that all will eventually be saved). During 1977–1978, Sparkman was investigated by the Midwestern trustees, and he convinced them that his views were within the bounds of the Baptist Faith and Message. But the furor did not die. By 1984, an unsigned document listing Sparkman's heresies began circulating in fundamentalist circles. By the fall of 1986, another major investigation was underway. Again Sparkman passed the test, this time on a 21 to 11 vote. Fundamentalist trustees were not happy, but most said that they would let the matter drop. Privately some worried that any future action for dismissal would precipitate a lawsuit. Individual and organized efforts to demonstrate Sparkman's heresy continued. Students disrupted his classes, and pastors called him at home with accusations. But the official case was closed.

In the months that followed, seminary president Milton Ferguson worked hard to establish the relationships and lines of communication among his trustees that would overcome their hostility to each other and to the seminary—and it apparently worked. When the Instructional Committee of the trustees met in the spring of 1988, they "shared their spiritual testimonies," creating an atmosphere that was "almost like a revival."[49] One trustee said, "I listened to these people talk about where they were in their relationship with the Lord, and I began to see them in a whole new light . . . [After that] I saw a willingness on their part to hear what I was saying and to try to understand, even if they didn't agree." Another committee member said, "We wish we could take the whole Southern Baptist Convention and put them in a small room just to talk to each other."

What could not be done in the whole convention, could be done in a small group of trustees, dealing with the governance of the smallest of the seminaries. A common ground based on religious experience was established that enabled them to deal with their conflicts and work toward consensus. While both the cultural and structural supports for Southern Baptist consensus were gone, such small group efforts could still sometimes succeed. The future policies and personnel of Midwestern would, at least for a time, be worked out by fundamentalists and moderates who were willing to construct mutually agreeable solutions.

The situation at the denomination's oldest and most prestigious seminary was different in many ways from the situation at Midwestern. The institutional resources of The Southern Baptist Seminary in Louisville seemed to offer a wider array of options to a potentially embattled administration. Southern was the only seminary that had significant connections and resources beyond the Convention itself. Many of its faculty enjoyed recognized, secure places in the larger scholarly community. Some of its students came from denominations beyond the SBC. And with the largest board of trustees, it would simply take longer for fundamentalists to be a majority, allowing more time for the institution to convert them to its way of working.[50] But most importantly, Southern had a sizable endowment. Only about half of the seminary's annual operating budget came from Cooperative Program funds. The seminary world might be dominated by the Southern Baptist Convention, but the SBC did not define the boundaries. All of this combined to create the perception that Southern could chart a more independent course, perhaps defying attempts by fundamentalists to change her policies or personnel.

The course chosen by seminary president Honeycutt, however, was not independence, but compromise. In his 1987 address to alumni, gathered for their annual convention luncheon, he assured them that he was committed to maintaining the seminary's high reputation and scholarly standards. But, he said, Southern has the institutional maturity and scholarly stability to be able to tolerate diversity. Competent conservative and inerrantist scholars would be added to the faculty, invited to lecture and preach, and welcomed into the seminary community of scholars. He would trust that the bright light of scholarship and the norms of the academic community would eventually work to his advantage. He could only hope that he was not welcoming the Trojan horse inside the gates. He had evidently become convinced that there was no other viable way for the institution to survive.[51] He likened the only apparent alternative to the bull that chose to pick a fight with the locomotive that passed through his territory each day. "We might admire his courage, but not his judgment."

Honeycutt's most visible implementation of his strategy came in April of 1988. He had instructed his faculty search committee to fill an opening in New Testament with someone who was an inerrantist. They came back with a recommendation that David Dockery, of Criswell College, be hired. But at the same time, Dr. Molly Marshall-Green was up for tenure, and Honeycutt argued that these two decisions represented his willingness to reach out "in both directions." Dockery's election, of course, posed no problem for the board, but Marshall-Green had been under fire since she joined the faculty as the first woman to teach theology in a Southern Baptist Seminary. She was ordained and had served in pastoral roles. Her dissertation was taken by conservatives to support the same dreaded universalism of which Sparkman had been accused. Conservatives were especially concerned that Marshall-Green's universalist theology would erode students' commitment to missions. And, as in Sparkman's case, they had circulated excerpts and summary statements about her work. She had been retained for her second term under protest, and conservative trustees wanted to make sure she did not get tenure. Before the meeting, they estimated that they had two more than the seventeen votes they needed to keep her from remaining on the seminary's faculty.

Marshall-Green and Honeycutt proved formidable opponents, however. After "the most extensive and thorough interview ever held with a faculty member," the academic personnel committee brought a unanimous recommendation for tenure. They had become convinced that she really did believe the Bible and that she believed that faith in Jesus was necessary for salvation. When some trustees still objected, Honeycutt argued that they should not leave him "amputated in this process of reconciliation, leaving me to say, 'As it turned out, I failed. I could reach out only toward Dr. Dockery; I could not reach out toward Dr. Marshall-Green.'"[52] One fundamentalist, struggling with how to vote, said, "I am in a dilemma . . . [Dr. Honeycutt] has given outstanding leadership toward trying to listen and respond and be fair . . . and he's paid a great price for this. It's weighing on me that maybe some of us need to pay a price." In the end he abstained, but a dozen other fundamentalist trustees who had come prepared to take a stand against heresy voted for tenure instead. Only seven determined fundamentalists finally opposed Marshall-Green. At least in this initial skirmish, the effort to "reach out to both sides" had succeeded. By agreeing to add a conservative scholar, a less conservative one had been retained.

At all of the seminaries, fundamentalists faced formidable challenges in seeking to dismiss existing faculty. Theological language is notoriously slippery, and clear cases of heresy are difficult to prove if the accused does not wish to be a heretic. Southern Baptist seminary professors who were genuinely committed to their vocation of service to the denomination had already had long years of practice in translating their less traditional interpretations into terms traditional folk could understand. A few professors would simply give up under the pressure and go elsewhere, choosing not to expend their energies in this fight. But those who chose to stay could usually make their case for orthodoxy. As a result, the changes fundamentalists could bring to the seminary campuses were somewhat limited. They could bring in new professors of their own kind, but for the most part they would have to wait patiently for openings created by retirement and voluntary moves.

Although there were few changes in faculty forthcoming, changes in policy and teaching were already underway. The six seminary presidents had already promised to promote "fairness and balance" in teaching, exposing their students to conservative points of view and emphasizing the primacy of evangelism and spiritual growth. In the years of the controversy, faculty at all the seminaries had already learned to teach in a more guarded, defensive way. As one teacher put it, "I think the subtle changes of caution may be hard for us to see . . . looking over our shoulders was three or four years ago. Now . . . you know what is there." They had learned that what they said in the classroom might be used against them. On each campus, a few students emerged as the "troublemakers" who would take classes primarily to get incriminating evidence on the professor, constantly asking questions designed to paint professors into a corner. As a result, classroom topics that were too controversial might simply never be discussed. And all topics were discussed in ways that minimized the possibility of conservative objection. One professor acknowledged that even the language in the classroom shifted from terms and categories used in the larger ecumenical community to "language that will address our own constituency."[53]

The positive side some teachers saw in this process was that they had learned how to communicate more effectively with their conservative students. A number of teachers admitted that in the 1960s and 1970s a kind of arrogance prevailed on campus. Students confronted their teachers about being "relevant," and teachers confronted their students about untenable forms of belief. Some even admitted that they routinely delivered lectures designed to be "fundamentalist busters." Now they had to take conservative positions and objections more seriously. More than one seminary person described the result as better teaching. And more than one student described the result as a bland and cautious version of theological education. Seminary had always been an opportunity to test and refine the faith of childhood. A messenger to the 1987 convention remarked wistfully that he owed a great deal to Southern Seminary for "freeing [him] from a very provincial upbringing." One teacher worried about that continuing. "The seminary still draws students who feel a certain tension between themselves and the church they grew up in. They feel this seminary might be an open door or open window for them. I think we dare not lose that." It was clear that the door would not be open as wide in the 1980s and 1990s.

Fundamentalists wanted professors to support traditional faith, not challenge it; and classroom practices were subtly changing in that direction. At five of the six seminaries, new fundamentalist policies were slowly being implemented amidst nagging fear and occasional skirmishes. Faculty who were unwilling to live with the compromises could—as fundamentalists hoped—seek employment elsewhere. The changes in policy would gradually produce changes in personnel, as well as changes in teaching.

At the sixth seminary, however, the process of change was very different. At Southeastern changes in personnel and policy were abrupt and considerable, set in motion in a fiery 1987 confrontation between the school and its fundamentalist trustees. The bull who finally chose to fight the locomotive was not Roy Honeycutt, but Southeastern's president Randall Lolley.

People at the seminary anticipated trouble. They had watched their board of trustees approach a fundamentalist majority and had little hope that these trustees would be convinced to go along or compromise. In the spring, Elizabeth Barnes had been added to the theology faculty on a fourteen to thirteen vote. With new trustees coming on in the fall, fundamentalists could be expected to begin enacting whatever changes in policy and personnel they had in mind. In his fall convocation address, Lolley described the Southeastern tradition as a "free conscience, free church, free country way of doing theological education." He declared that if Baptists wanted a seminary "different and destructive of the idea which this school has sought through its history to incarnate, then this president will give not one moment of the time or one millibar of the energy he has left to producing that kind of school."[54] A line had been drawn, a challenge issued.

Alumni and students were behind Lolley. They organized a large rally for the evening before the fall trustee meeting was to begin. Trustees arrived to a campus full of banners, arm bands, and yellow ribbons; but they were undeterred. After two days of parliamentary maneuvers, tense and angry exchanges, closed door sessions and public meetings bulging with students and reporters, fundamentalist trustees had clearly established that they would direct the future policies and personnel of the school.

After electing their substitute 'slate of board officers and committee members, the new trustees proposed and passed the first of the structural changes fundamentalists wanted to see in all the seminaries. They wanted to remove current faculty from the faculty selection process, making hiring the prerogative of the president, who would be directly responsible to the trustees. Such a structural change represented an imposition of ideology over the rational structures of seminary organization. No longer would faculty be sought through the recognized processes of academic screening and selection by peers. Rather, the doctrinal concerns of the trustees would take precedence.

Within ten days, Lolley announced that he would resign. "I cannot fan into a flame a vision which I believe to be contradictory to the dream which formed Southeastern," he said. At the same time, Academic Dean Morris Ashcraft announced he would no longer serve as dean, but would return to the classroom. Two other administrators joined Lolley and Ashcraft in announcing their intention to leave, and four others followed in the next few months. Within less than six months, a new president had been hired, with a new dean following the next year. And by the end of the 1988–1989 academic year, one-third of the faculty and over half the administration that had staffed the school in 1986–1987 would be gone. At Southeastern, fundamentalists came closest to their dream of forcing wholesale turnover by the implementation of new policies. They would inherit the bricks and books of the seminary and have the opportunity to staff the institution with "brains" of their own choosing.

The victory at Southeastern was not without a price, however. Enrollment for the 1988–1989 school year was down by 20 percent and declined again the next year to less than half its original level. Alumni contributions disappeared almost entirely, and there were hints that the seminary's accreditation might be in jeopardy. The Southern Association of Colleges and Schools (SACS) and the Association of Theological Schools both sent visiting committees to the campus to determine whether the school could still operate within guidelines of "academic freedom and institutional integrity." SACS was concerned that the new faculty selection process did not conform to accreditation guidelines, but the agency gave the seminary a year to draft a formal response. The trustees' immediate reaction was to blame Lolley's "failed leadership" for their problems.[55] They may also have been thinking about alternatives to official accreditation. The March 1989, issue of the *Advocate* contained an editorial arguing that Southern Baptist seminaries should not be subject to the review of outside agencies, and in the fall the Executive Committee of the SBC urged the seminary not to be intimidated by outside accrediting agencies.[56]

Fundamentalist trustees wanted schools that would be solely responsible to the wishes of Southern Baptists, but the wishes of Southern Baptists were not the only factor in the institutional environment of a seminary. Institutions are built not only on ideas, but they also rely on people who are willing to invest money and careers in them, on reputation in the marketplace in which they compete, and on other factors in the larger organizational environment. Fundamentalists had effected new policies and new personnel and had changed the structures in which theological education would take place. They had set out to make Southeastern a fundamentalist school, placing it essentially in the same educational market with Mid-America. Yet with over half the faculty from the old era remaining, it was not yet clearly attractive to fundamentalist students. In its first years as a fundamentalist school, it would be caught between identities and thus between markets. As the new trustees created a new institutional identity for the school, they would also have to create a new institutional support system. Its old pool of staff, students, donors, and accreditors was likely to disappear. Southeastern would remain a viable reality only if the Convention chose to provide financial props in the interim.

The fundamentalist victory at Southeastern had also created the first moderate martyr. Randall Lolley was anything but silent in the months following his resignation. On the heels of the Southeastern battles, moderates were energized. They beat back a fundamentalist challenge to Georgia's Mercer University, elected moderate presidents in several states, and passed numerous state resolutions condemning the Public Affairs Committee's recent endorsement of Robert Bork. In the late fall of 1987, moderates thought the tide just might have turned in their favor. They had long hoped that the fundamentalists would engineer their own demise, and at last it seemed to be happening. They had gone too far. Surely forcing a seminary president out and violating church-state traditions would finally convince Baptists in the middle that fundamentalist changes were not so benign.

But the moderate momentum could not be sustained long enough to elect a moderate SBC president. Although fundamentalist candidate

Jerry Vines got only 700 more votes than his moderate challenger, 1988 would mark the tenth fundamentalist presidential victory (with Vines re-elected in 1989). It had seemed like such an ideal opportunity. The convention was in the relatively friendly territory of San Antonio; there was no incumbent to challenge; moderates' own candidate Richard Jackson was an inerrantist himself; and there was outrage fueling the campaign. But still moderates could not win. Fundamentalist electoral victories would continue, and fundamentalists would continue the process of redirecting the policies and personnel of the denomination's institutional life. While "modernity" might be the longterm victor in the culture, this institutional segment of the culture had been reclaimed by a fundamentalist movement. The course correction was underway, and Southern Baptists would have to decide how they would adjust to the new direction their denomination was taking.

8. Southern Baptists and the Future: Accommodation, Reconstruction, and Innovation

When an organization has experienced a hostile takeover, loyalties can no longer be taken for granted. Those who supported the old order may or may not accept the new goals of the organization. Equally, those who were dissidents against the old order will have to be convinced that a new administration really will make a difference. Their loyalty will not come automatically to the new regime. Once fundamentalists had firmly established their direction of the Southern Baptist Convention's bureaucracy, they would have to gain the loyalty of both their employees and the voluntary members of the denomination's 37,000 churches. They would need at least neutrality, at best sympathy, and continuing monetary and participatory support.

Meanwhile, those who had clearly lost this battle would have to decide what to do about their loss. The options that had faced dissident fundamentalists in the 1960s and 1970s now faced dissident moderates and progressives for the 1990s. Hirschmann has described the choices available to dissatisfied members as "exit, voice, or loyalty."[1] When members become dissatisfied with the way their organization is being run, they can exercise any combination of loyal accommodation, vocal opposition, and threats of exit. In a complex organization like the Southern Baptist Convention, those options could be exercised at three or more levels. Individual church members could alter their participation or leave their local church. Congregations could change their relationship to the denomination or withdraw. And employees within the bureaucracy could accommodate, voice dissent, or resign. We will look first at employees.

Working in a Fundamentalist Bureaucracy

The conditions of work had clearly changed for Baptist employees. The list of activities, associations, and beliefs that constituted deviation from approved Southern Baptist standards was slowly being lengthened. Decisions about new staff were clearly being made on new grounds, and existing staff could not avoid wondering when the same tests would be applied to them. Many knew that they would not pass the new ideological tests. For many there was real dissonance between personal beliefs and dreams and the new goals of the agencies. They could deal with that dissonance by redefining or ignoring it, by learning to get along in the new system, by suffering silently; or they could leave. The choices they made depended both on their loyalty to the organization (especially their commitment to their work) and on the resources or constraints that defined their potential career paths.

Not every employee, of course, disagreed with the new directions of the agencies. Some had been in wholehearted agreement with the fundamentalists all along. Others found the distance between their positions and those of the new management easily bridged. Having not done a comprehensive survey of agency staff, I cannot say with certainty what proportions experienced dissonance and what proportions welcomed the changes. Of the fifteen randomly-selected staff members we interviewed, however, only one embraced the anticipated new programs of his agency with open arms. Another anticipated major changes, but thought he could live with most of them. Four thought their jobs would be relatively unaffected, and so anticipated little direct, personal conflict. But nine of the fifteen had serious reservations about the directions and rules being established by their boards of trustees. All nine had given serious consideration to whether they should stay. In addition to these formal interviews, I have had dozens of other conversations with agency people about the degree of disquiet present in the corridors. Although I was most likely sought out by those who were more discontented, the degree of soul-searching also present among those I randomly chose leads me to believe that the "gloom, despair, and agony" I heard about was fairly widespread.[2]

Some agency employees knew that they would stay, whether they agreed with the new management or not. The reasons were very pragmatic: They were only a few years from retirement and did not want to lose benefits; they had kids in college and could not afford a period of unemployment; or they simply did not know where they could go. One of the career dilemmas faced by Southern Baptist employees in search of new jobs was the relative insularity of the Southern Baptist career system. Most who were over about forty-five had gone to Southern Baptist schools, gotten degrees tailored to their Southern Baptist work, and built up networks of fellow Southern Baptist professionals (who were all now in the same predicament). Their credentials were perfectly designed for a career serving Southern Baptists, but the organizational structure in which that career could be pursued was now closed to them. Among other things, the new management meant that they could not easily move even within the Southern Baptist system. [The same was true of a group of pastors who had risen to the pulpits of leading moderate churches and had dreamed of moving from there into seminaries or agency jobs. The only career moves available in the new system would be lateral moves to other moderate pulpits.] Having invested their lives along one career path, they suddenly had very few options for exit. Many agency people had only minimal parish experience or were decades distant from their work in a congregation. Even pastoring was not a readily available (or attractive) alternative. Those who felt stuck expressed a deadening sense of resignation about their jobs. They would stick it out because they had to, but the excitement and fulfillment were gone. Instead, they would follow orders and try not to step out of line. When asked about a new job assignment, one person replied, "That's what I'm doing if I want to have a job."

Others chose to stay because of loyalty to the vocational goals that had drawn them to the agency in the first place. They loved their work and wanted to continue doing it just as long as they could. Some had invested heavily in developing programs or in supportive relationships. Their very identity was shaped by the circle of friends and activities located within these Southern Baptist organizational structures. While they recognized that conscience might someday demand that they leave it all behind, that would not be an easy sacrifice. They remained convinced that more good than bad was being done by their organization, and they would stay until that assessment changed.

Their problem, of course, was discerning when the balance had shifted, when the little grey compromises of their ideals had accumulated into a vocation they no longer could own. Could you continue to work for new bosses whose heroes were repugnant to you? Could you continue to work among people who ridiculed people and causes you supported? Could you continue to work for an agency that would not hire someone from your church to a new position? Could you continue to give up parts of the job that had been the most meaningful? One group of Nashville employees started meeting for weekly "reality check" lunches to help each other see more clearly where the compromises were happening and whether they represented important or trivial concerns.

Most employees, however, had thought about the problem more abstractly. They tried to envision (and prepare themselves to resist) some demand, some new program, or some working condition that would represent a breach of conscience they could not bear. One person spoke metaphorically about the dilemma they faced, "If the organization says you will wear blue shirts on Tuesday, and you can't wear a blue shirt on Tuesday, your option is leave and go to another place. It's that simple." For many of those I talked to, the "blue shirt" order they feared was the one in which they would be forced to sign a more restrictive doctrinal creed. That was the line they could not cross. Partly they were unwilling to commit themselves to beliefs more conservative than those found in the Baptist Faith and Message; partly they were independent-minded Baptists who balked at signing any creed. One young campus minister vowed she would not even sign a statement saying she liked hot dogs for lunch. But something as decisive as signing a creed did not appear to be what fundamentalists had in mind. They expected the kind of assent that comes in actions rather than assent pledged in ink. Moderate staff members would not have the luxury of a showdown test of conscience. Rather, they would have to wonder each day if the job they were doing was still the job they had once felt called of God to do.

Some, of course, did not stay. Some, like those we discussed in chapter 7, were forced out. But others quietly decided that they could no longer give their life energy to the work they were being asked to do. They sent out resumés and left as soon as the opportunity arose. Younger people were much more fortunate in this regard. They simply had more time to rebuild a career. Their age made moving more feasible, and their credentials were sometimes less exclusively Southern Baptist than those of their older colleagues. Many had gone to recognized universities, worked for non-profit organizations, and kept up their ecumenical and professional ties. Those at the older end of a career also found leaving relatively easy. Some who would otherwise have worked until they were sixty-five or even seventy chose to retire at sixty-two. Exit was most likely, then, among those whose options were most plentiful—those old enough to count the days until an early retirement, and those young enough to begin again.

Those who stayed, young or old, had already endured the long and painful political struggle. They had already learned to look over their shoulders for hostile fire. They had learned to live with the anxious uncertainty of years in which the future direction of their work was being renegotiated by outsiders they did not know and with whom they had an adversarial relationship. Most had learned to go on with their work in spite of it all, but any upsetting news (or rumors) quickly made the rounds in Nashville or Atlanta, reviving the sense of siege that pervaded many corners of the denomination's agencies. Some had acquired a kind of gallows humor about the whole situation. The best they could do was laugh and hope.

I asked each staff person I interviewed to talk about what they envisioned doing in five or ten years. Almost invariably they responded first with a nervous laugh and a remark prefaced by "*if* I still have a job." Those who had been thinking about their goals often shook their heads in doubt that their dreams would become reality. More often, though, they were taken aback by the question. "Gosh," said one, "I guess when you are living with a kind of survivalist mentality it is hard to dream of where you would like to be ten years from now." These were people whose training and life experience had pushed them constantly toward growth, new challenges, being on the cutting edge. To the extent that they perceived that they no longer controlled their own destiny, they had also ceased to dream about the future.

If employees stayed, they were unlikely to envision voicing their discontent. While they might negotiate some minor concessions on specific assignments, they doubted that it would be tolerated if they spoke out. The most visible evidence that their assessment was right was the fate of Richard Harmon: his open dissent resulted in his dismissal. So long as one was an employee, one would wear the blue shirt on Tuesday. Dissent could be voiced only after leaving. Otherwise, employees learned to build their vocational wardrobes around the new dress codes. They rebuilt self-images, vocational identities, and career goals around the new realities represented by boards of trustees and management they never would have chosen for themselves.

Dilemmas of Individual Membership

Most Southern Baptists, however, were not tied to the organization by employment. They were bound instead by ties of congregational membership. They could theoretically voice their dissent without fear of reprisals, and they could exercise their option of exit simply by joining the church down the street. To put it in such voluntaristic terms, though, is to miss the powerful ways in which congregation and denominational identity were crucial landmarks in Southern culture. People who had been members of a church for fifty years, whose parents were perhaps buried in the cemetery outside, could not merely walk away to join the church down the street any more than they could walk away from their family to join another one. In traditional Southern towns being Baptist (or Methodist or Pentecostal or Lutheran) was a very public part of one's identity. Almost two-thirds of our respondents (64 percent) said that it was very true that they could hardly imagine themselves as anything but a Southern Baptist. The relationships, activities, and cultural norms that surrounded and constituted their church membership were far too strong to be dislodged by the winds of this controversy.

That is not to say that no individual Baptists left their churches. This is a question on which I have no systematic data, but there is every reason to believe that among less tradition-bound Baptists of the newer South a good deal of denomination-switching took place. As upwardly-mobile, well-educated Baptists looked at the programs and image of a feuding, increasingly conservative denomination, some undoubtedly did what upwardly-mobile Baptists have always done—they joined Methodist, Presbyterian, and Episcopal churches.[3] Some cosmopolitan Baptists may have switched with ease to a congregation whose image and practices more nearly suited their tastes, but many left with real regret. One lifelong Baptist wrote to his old congregation, "I hope that you can accept that my Christian identity is no longer nurtured in Baptist life. . . . Accepting these changes has been difficult for me, but I am confident of the Spirit's movement in my life." Just as employees were struggling with questions of vocation, some Baptists were struggling with questions of their own sense of religious identity and mission. The option of individual exit would not come easily for many.

Clergy, of course, were more like employees than like voluntary members. They had invested training, career, and network in this denomination. Worst, the denomination controlled their retirement benefits. The running joke in this controversy was that if a split came, clergy would go with whichever side took the Annuity Board. Fears of actually losing money were probably overstated. No money already contributed to a Southern Baptist annuity by a pastor would be lost if he or she left the denomination. But if a pastor ceased being employed by a Southern Baptist institution, no additional funds could be invested.[4]

For those most marginal to the career system, who had invested the least, exit was easier. Some Baptist clergywomen, for instance, joined the relatively more secure Methodist system, and a few of their male colleagues did, as well. A few very visible progressive pastors became Episcopal priests. And American Baptists reported that the number of clergy requesting transfer information increased dramatically. The number who actually did transfer was probably fairly low, however. Since the ABC is a far smaller denomination, there are fewer jobs available. Once SBC pastors realized the placement hurdles that might face them in the ABC, most turned to other alternatives. Most, in fact, remained securely tied to the Southern Baptist Convention—bound by loyalty, habit, and investments of all sorts that made exit a very costly option.

The Potential for Schism

If individual employees left, the Southern Baptist Convention would merely replace them. If individual members or pastors left, their congregations would mourn their leaving. But if churches or groups of churches left, a schism would be underway. That was the possibility that had haunted Southern Baptists throughout the struggle. Many people went to Dallas honestly fearful that the denomination would not survive the

Table 8.1. Effects of Controversy on Local Churches as Perceived by Different Theological Parties

Issue	% Self-Identified Moderates	% Moderate Conservatives	% Conservatives	% Fundamentalist Conservatives	% Self-Identified Fundamentalists
The controversy has had no local effect *(average = 42% N = 340)*	36	22	45	40	53
SBC fundamentalist control will *not* affect the local church *(average = 77% N = 361)*	57	71	81	83	77
No recent SBC event or issue raises concern *(average = 64% N = 260)*	34	52	66	73	83

week intact. It did survive, however, and is likely to do so for the foreseeable future.

In part the denomination survived because so many people honestly believed that all the fuss really did not matter. Over three fourths (77 percent) of our respondents could name no concrete effects they expected in their local churches from the newly fundamentalist agencies (see table 8.1). One Georgia man declared as he left San Antonio in 1988 that he would go back to doing exactly what he had done before. "Southern Baptist headquarters is not in Nashville; it's in every local church. They can do whatever they like, and it won't make one bit of difference to me!" Almost two-thirds (64 percent) named no event or trend in the denomination that concerned them, and nearly half (42 percent) said that their church had not even informally discussed the issues. They perceived their congregation to be "locally autonomous" and anticipated that they would simply proceed with business as usual. Former President Jimmy Carter often laughs about the delight his church takes in gathering on the Sunday after the convention to repudiate everything SBC messengers have passed.

It may be that the independent-minded Maranatha Baptist Church of Plains—which formed when its parent congregation refused to integrate—has created programs and identity for itself that are in fact autonomous. But even President Carter teaches Sunday School from quarterlies published in Nashville. What Southern Baptists read every Sunday, the person they hear in the pulpit, the very programs that give shape to their church life, are the products of the denomination, not of any local church.

No one can ever make President Carter believe or teach ideas with which he disagrees, but he may find himself disagreeing more often in the years ahead. And the next time Maranatha needs a pastor, they may find that the sort of seminary graduates they have to choose from has changed. Should they choose to begin a ministry to unwed mothers, they will find ample denominational support. But should they choose to attack some problem of hunger or poverty or arms control, they will find little in Nashville that will help them do their ministry. When they get ready to give their Lottie Moon Christmas Offering for foreign missions, they will know that they are supporting vigorous programs of evangelism and church planting overseas, but less of their money will support education or agricultural training or other services. And of course, none of their money will be used to support churches with women pastors, and little will go to support the Baptist Joint Committee's efforts to defend the separation of church and state. The shifts in the denomination have been gradual enough to make them hard to discern, but the shifts are there, and they do have effects on how local churches do their own work and extend their influence throughout the world.

Sociologists Cantrell, Krile, and Donahue have developed a scale with which to measure the degree of parish autonomy that exists in a denomination.[5] But even their questions illustrate the difficulty in making clear distinctions between local and nonlocal control. Of the fourteen questions on their scale, Southern Baptists clearly submit to nonlocal control on only one, the requirement of yearly demographic reports. On five items, power is in local hands (ordination, accounting procedures, the legal officers of the corporation, and the like). But on eight items decisions sometimes (or always) are made in consultation with nonlocal entities. Even the disposal of property, for instance, may not be a purely local matter if the church has a loan underwritten by the Home Mission Board. If the church receives Church Pastoral Assistance, it is not in full control of its pastor's salary (or even choice of pastor). And churches always depend on local and state denominational officials for pastor search help. Beyond the everyday ways in which the denomination shapes local church life, even in these legal and personnel decisions, Southern Baptist congregations are not always autonomous entities.

If Maranatha, or any other congregation, remains aware of the many ways in which it is connected to the denomination—as well as the ways in which it is independent—its options for dissent or change in participation remain open. To the extent that churches *believe* themselves to be autonomous and unaffected by policy at the national level, their options for change are limited. Churches are not likely either to protest or to exit an organization they perceive to be irrelevant. They will continue to use

Table 8.2. Changing Loyalties in the SBC

Position	% Self-Identified Moderates	% Moderate Conservatives	% Conservatives	% Fundamentalist Conservatives	% Self-Identified Fundamentalists	Total
Would *not* support a move to leave the SBC						
1985	83	97	81	76	67	80%
1986	80	93	89	79	74	85%
1987	72	95	84	82	89	84%
FUTURE CHURCH RELATIONSHIP TO THE SBC (Average Scores)*						
Support for CP giving	.91	1.06	1.20	1.24	1.33	1.17
Using denominational programs	.77	.94	.98	1.06	1.04	.97
Using SBC Sunday School literature	.86	.93	1.06	1.13	1.05	1.03
Attendance at routine meetings	1.01	1.08	1.21	1.10	1.25	1.15
Attendance at SBC annual conventions	.96	.91	1.03	1.21	1.34	1.08
Support for foreign missions	1.00	1.21	1.28	1.37	1.52	1.28
Support for home missions	.94	1.09	1.26	1.33	1.44	1.25
Sending youth to Baptist colleges	1.01	.99	1.06	1.04	1.26	1.07
Sending youth to SBC seminaries	.96	.90	1.03	.98	1.17	1.02

*Averages are calculated by assigning scores of +1 for a report of "more" involvement, −1 for "less" involvement, and 0 for "same." 1.00 is then taken as the base. Scores above 1.00 indicate increasing involvement; scores below 1.00 indicate decreasing involvement.

the denomination's programs and send the denomination their money, all the while protesting that they are free to do anything they please. On every measure of denominational involvement, between one half and two thirds of our respondents said they anticipated no change at their church. And where change was seen as most likely, people anticipated that their church's support would increase, not decrease (see table 8.2). Churches have always tried to give more each year to the Cooperative Program and the mission offerings. Most, apparently, would continue to do so. Routine involvement and efforts toward regular growth would continue to be facts of life for the conservative mainstream, would likely grow among fundamentalists, and would wane only among the denomination's most progressive segment. The dominant belief in the symbol of "local church autonomy" therefore made exit less likely and helped to prevent schism.

The avoidance of schism in the Convention was not merely a matter of inertia, however. In some ways, schism was actually less likely in 1989 than in 1979. The total amount of loyalty to the denomination may have increased, on balance.[6] Even if some self-identified moderates were putting distance between themselves and the SBC, fundamentalists were at the same time moving solidly into the denomination's embrace. In 1979, fundamentalist churches were only marginally committed. If they had failed to correct the Convention's course, they would have left with little regret. As late as 1985, only 17 percent of self-identified fundamentalists and 32 percent of fundamentalist conservatives said that their church should stay in the Convention even if it were not "brought back to biblical soundness." In both 1985 and 1986, over half of the self-identified fundamentalists who responded to our survey said that they agreed or strongly agreed that leaving was the best course of action. As we saw in chapter 5, fundamentalists had been only marginally involved in the routine life of the denomination, gave less of their money to the Cooperative Program, and were more likely than were moderates to have grown up in some other tradition. They had been outsiders and were willing to leave entirely if the SBC's drift toward liberalism was not halted.

In the years following 1985, however, fundamentalists became convinced that leaving would not be necessary. Steadily increasing numbers (from 67 percent to 89 percent) said that they would *not* support a move in their church to leave the SBC (see table 8.2). When in 1988 we asked them to anticipate the involvement of their churches in the SBC over the coming decade, self-identified fundamentalists anticipated growing involvement on every front, with greatest growth in giving, going to meetings, and sending their youth to denominational schools. Fundamentalist conservatives were leaning in the same directions, although not quite as heavily. It appeared that the Convention's right wing was becoming convinced that doctrinal soundness was returning to the SBC and that full commitment to the denomination's institutions was in order.

It makes perfect sense, of course, that fundamentalists should increase their loyalty to the denomination. This was, after all, their victory. When we asked our respondents each year about their view of the future of the SBC (see table 8.3), increasing numbers of fundamentalists (from 29 percent to 56 percent) said that they were "excited that Bible believers are continuing the process of regaining our rightful place at the helm of this great denomination." The future health of the Southern Baptist Convention, however, would depend on sustaining the loyalty of the rest of the denomination, including those who disagreed with them.

Table 8.3. Changing Views of the SBC's Future

Opinion	% Self-Identified Moderates	% Moderate Conservatives	% Conservatives	% Fundamentalist Conservatives	% Self-Identified Fundamentalists	Average
Excited that "Bible believers" have regained control						
1985	1	4	16	20	29	15%
1986	4	6	18	32	46	20%
1987	0	21	29	28	47	25%
1988	2	12	21	47	56	25%
Like the conservative direction, regret the division						
1985	9	10	25	40	51	27%
1986	8	21	24	26	29	22%
1987	8	15	13	25	23	16%
1988	5	23	15	12	26	15%
Hopeful, see signs of reconciliation						
1985	33	56	51	37	20	43%
1986	22	52	40	38	20	36%
1987	21	38	47	43	23	39%
1988	14	23	35	28	18	27%
Hopeful that moderates can win next year						
1985	51	28	9	3	0	13%
1986	36	12	16	3	6	15%
1987	42	18	11	3	3	14%
1988	30	23	23	9	0	20%
Grieving that SBC has been lost						
1985	6	2	0	0	0	1%
1986	30	9	3	1	0	7%
1987	29	9	1	0	0	6%
1988	47	15	5	2	0	12%

Fundamentalists especially needed the acquiescence of the broad conservative mainstream, and they apparently had no difficulty in getting it. Between 1985 and 1987, the willingness of conservatives to oppose moves to take their own church out of the denomination had fluctuated slightly (see table 8.2). But in 1987, only 3 percent agreed that they would support leaving, while 13 percent were unsure. As they looked toward their church's future involvement in the denomination, the number who foresaw more giving and mission support greatly outweighed those who foresaw less. Their tradition of regularly increasing financial support, then, remained intact. Conservatives were even, on balance, looking forward to attending denominational meetings more regularly. Their anticipation of increasing support was not as strong as the increases envisioned by fundamentalists—but fundamentalists were starting from lower levels of participation and had more room to increase.

On balance, the mainstream of the convention seemed willing to proceed with fundamentalists in a more conservative direction. Conservatives were not, for the most part, excited about the convention's new direction (see table 8.3). Each year, the dominant response of conservatives to our question about the future of the Convention was that they were hopeful that the fighting was almost over. The primary concerns they listed were the disruption and "bad press" caused by the conflict, not any particular issue, fundamentalist or moderate. In 1985 and 1986, even those who sympathized with the fundamentalist cause were worried about the division they saw. But by 1987 and 1988, conservatives seemed to be less worried. Among those who clearly favored the Convention's new direction, the number who were excited had come to exceed the number who were worried about division. They may have disagreed with the tactics by which the new trustees had come into office (over half thought exclusive fundamentalist appointments were unfair), but they were apparently not disturbed by what they were seeing. Most, in fact, remained convinced that there would be no significant changes affecting their local church (see table 8.1).

Conservatives had, during this time, become less convinced that peace was at hand, and many of those who changed their views during these years actually moved into the moderate camp. Their hope for a moderate victory had, by 1988, reached about the same low level as the hope left on the moderate side. Some conservatives seemed slowly to have become convinced that there was a takeover underway and that it should be stopped. As we have seen throughout, the denomination's conservative middle was an ambivalent mix of people who agreed with the fundamentalists about the Bible, but agreed with the moderates about authority, polity, and freedom of conscience. By the late 1980s, they appeared to be deciding that polity issues were really most important. At the same time that they were joining the moderate cause, however, some on the progressive side were dropping out. The result was a shift to the right in the moderate political effort. Even the Forum took on a more conservative flavor, with speakers like Robert Schuller on the 1989 program.

The organization that emerged as the voice of this conservative/moderate political coalition was "Baptists Committed to the SBC." Led by men like Winfred Moore, they vowed to remain the kind of vocal "loyal opposition" that fundamentalists would not be able to ignore.[7] They would continue to attend conventions, sponsor presidential candidates, and hoped to build the kind of broad-based anti-fundamentalist movement that could eventually succeed. As Moore told one gathering, "It isn't over until the fat lady sings, and at least where I'm from, the fat lady hasn't sung yet." These were people who refused to concede defeat and who thought they could outlast the fundamentalists. In one of those verbal schoolyard fights on the convention floor, a fundamentalist made the mistake of asking a moderate (in a somewhat taunting tone) whether he would be back the next year. "I'll be back for the next thousand years," he replied. "We were here before you came, and we'll be here when you are gone. So you'd better come back every year with busloads of your people, because we're going to be here!" After generations of investment in the denomination, some Southern Baptists were simply unwilling to walk away and leave the inheritance to people they saw as intruders. Baptists Committed was an effort to rally moderates and conservatives for a long-term investment in political struggle. They might be the party out of power, but they still identified themselves most centrally as a party within the Southern Baptist Convention.

Some of those who wanted to stay and fight started thinking about how they might be able to "hurt the fundamentalists in the pocketbook." Since they knew they typically gave more to the denomination than fundamentalist churches did, they thought they might be able to demonstrate their power at the bank, even if they were losing at the ballot box. Some suggested escrowing money until fundamentalists agreed to play fair. Others suggested reducing their percentage gifts to the level given at First Baptist Jacksonville (Jerry Vines' church) or First Baptist Atlanta (Charles Stanley's church): 2 to 4 percent. They were searching for whatever levers of power might return them to leadership in the SBC. They did not want to quit giving their money to missions, but they also did not want fundamentalists deciding how their money was spent. Having built a denomination with a unified budget and central decision making, however, they could never quite figure out how to organize a monetary protest without hurting the agency employees and the missionaries who were still their friends.

The organizing base for Baptists Committed was a combination of conservatives who had finally decided that fundamentalist leadership was not a good idea and those slightly to their left in the "moderate conservative" camp. Moderate conservatives were people whose theology was less traditional, but whose identity was still with the conservatism of the Convention. Their responses were a complex and peculiar mixture. Despite their own personal theological positions, a significant minority (about one third) actually favored the fundamentalist direction of the convention. They were either excited about "Bible believers" being in charge or gave the fundamentalists worried affirmation (see table 8.3). About a quarter yearly kept up the hope of a moderate political victory. An increasing, but small, minority shifted from hope for peace to grief. They were slower than others to give up their hope that peace was at hand. These were people who had been very involved, both in the Convention and in the controversy. They were less likely than any other group to say that the controversy had had no effect on their local church (see table 8.1). Almost half named an event (such as the "priesthood of the believer" resolution or the political tactics of the fundamentalists) that made them concerned about the Convention's future. But until 1988, the vast majority rejected the view that the Convention was lost. Even then, 46 percent retained their optimism; they believed things would get better. Either the moderates would win, or people would quit fighting.

By 1988, however, a few more were having doubts. The number of moderate conservatives who said they were "grieving" over the Convention's future had increased, and when looking toward the future, some of them saw less involvement in the SBC (see table 8.2). On some items the yea-sayers outnumbered the nay-sayers, and on others it was the reverse. Only increases in foreign mission support got a strong vote of confidence from moderate conservatives. Annual convention attendance, seminary support, and use of Sunday School materials promised to decrease among them. At least some of them were beginning to agree with the self-identified moderates that the convention had changed drastically for the worse.

They were not, however, ready to leave. The people most likely to reject any move to take their church out of the denomination were moderate conservatives (see table 8.2). We saw in chapter 5 that moderate conservatives had been very much the denominational insiders, very involved in Convention life. They were also those most likely to say that they could not imagine themselves as anything but a Southern Baptist. Their activities, friendships, and very identity were built around this denomination. Even when they turned to grieving, it was a fiercely loyal kind of grief. Said one man, "I was raised in Southern Baptist orphanages; I went to Southern Baptist schools; and I have served Southern Baptist institutions all my adult life. This convention is like my mother. And just because my mother has been raped and beaten by a band of hoodlums, I can't walk out on my mother!"

Such grief was widespread among those who had staked their theological identities along the Convention's left border. They had abundant metaphors, although a mother's death was the most common. Being vanquished in a war was another. Being hijacked or robbed was another. One slightly more optimistic person mused that maybe they had merely been locked out of the house for a while. Some used the biblical metaphors of being in exile or wandering in the wilderness on exodus. These were people who were becoming disengaged from something they loved. Self-identified moderates had been no less involved in the denomination than those slightly to their right who called themselves conservatives. They had been born in it, heard tales of its glories in their childhood, came of age in its institutions, and gave it their best energies as adults. Unlike moderate conservatives, however, they had built their identities less completely on being Southern Baptist and could more often imagine themselves as something else. Between 1985 and 1989, their commitments to maintaining their Southern Baptist ties were visibly weakening. Almost no one had given up the fight in 1985, but in 1986, when they lost the presidency (even without an incumbent), the number who said they were "grieving [that the] convention has been taken over" increased to nearly one third (see table 8.3). The 1987 defeat appeared not to discourage many more; but when they failed again in 1988 (again with no incumbent), the number of self-identified moderates who said they were grieving reached nearly half (47 percent). Over that period, there were actually small increases in the number who were willing to entertain notions of leaving the denomination. By 1987, 12 percent of them said they would support a suggestion that their church leave the Convention (up from 5 percent in 1985), while another 16 percent said they were unsure (up from 12 percent in 1985).

It is worth noting that between 1985 and 1988, responses to our question about the future became increasingly polarized in the denomination as a whole. In 1985, 70 percent of all our respondents said either that they were hopeful of peace or that their agreement with the fundamentalists was tempered by regret for the division that existed. By 1988, the numbers in those two equivocal categories had dwindled to 42 percent. Self-identified fundamentalists, along with fundamentalist conservatives were excited, and no longer regretful—they had either decided that the division had really disappeared or that it no longer mattered. Meanwhile, people on the left had increasingly given up hope. Moderates who had been fighting for ten years were becoming increasingly discouraged. The contrast between their grief and the newly aroused political consciousness of some conservatives was apparent at the Southern Baptist Alliance "listening session" in the fall of 1988. Some of those in attendance talked about how they had just gone to the convention for the first time that year or the year before. They were appalled at what they saw and were convinced that if moderates would just work hard at organizing they could win. Finally a weary member of the Gatlinburg gang stood to respond, "Some of us have *been* organizing for ten years. Where were you when we needed you?"

In 1988, a significant minority of self-identified moderates (about a quarter) reported that they envisioned their churches moving away from active involvement in the denomination (see table 8.2). Almost none anticipated increased use of denominational programs or Sunday School literature, while one in four anticipated less. Less than one-fourth anticipated increased giving to the Cooperative Program and to missions, while larger numbers anticipated cutbacks. The number expecting routine increases in foreign mission support was exactly balanced by the number expecting decreases. They expected to keep on going to regular denominational meetings as usual (80 percent expected no change), but they thought that on balance there would be fewer moderates at future annual conventions. Even those who saw no change in their church's support may have been reflecting a new apathy. These were the churches that had given the denomination steadfast support, continually challenging themselves to do more. Discontinuing that upward spiral was the way some churches expressed their displeasure.

Becoming more marginal to denominational life did not mean, however, that moderate Baptists had clear alternatives in mind. Nearly half (42 percent) of those who anticipated less involvement with the SBC checked none of the organizational alternatives we offered (and did not write in any alternative of their own in the space provided). Although they were dissatisfied, they did not yet know what they might do about it.

On the surface, the most logical destination for disgruntled Southern Baptists was the American Baptist Churches. Indeed, churches did not even have to sever ties with Southern Baptists to join, but could declare their cooperation with both bodies. "Dually-aligned" churches gave money to both denominations, got their resources from either or both, and could vote in both systems. In the border states, this arrangement was fairly common. Some churches, like First Baptist in Washington, D.C., had simply refused to choose one side or the other in the original split between North and South.

Yet dual alignment was the least popular organizational alternative among Southern Baptists (see table 8.4). The total number of all our respondents who favored this option varied between 4 percent and 7 percent over the years we surveyed, and self-identified moderates (until 1987) were no more likely to favor dual alignment than were any other groups. In the minds of most Southern Baptists, the distances between them and the American Baptists were great. Most Southern Baptist

Table 8.4. Institutional Alternatives Favored by Moderates and Others

Option	% Self-Identified Moderates	% Moderate Conservatives	% All Others
Would like to see church align with both SBC and American Baptists			
1985	10	7	7
1987	16	9	4
Personally favor cut in CP giving (1986)	24	6	9
Anticipate less church support for CP in the future (1988)	27	13	8
Anticipate designated CP giving in the future (1988)	28	16	13
Personally favor church support for alternative institutions			
1986	26	9	8
1987	36	7	9
Anticipate church support for alternative institutions (1988)	27	4	8
Anticipate church support for the Southern Baptist Alliance (1988)	27	15	4

churches had had little if any contact with American Baptists. Even after Southern Baptists had declared the nation their mission field, American Baptists had hesitated to move into the South. Only about 250 (mostly black) ABC churches existed in the entire region. A miniscule SBC schism would overwhelm them, and they were not eager to see that happen. On the Southern side, isolation was magnified by the regional and denominational pride that remained. Even if their own denomination was in a mess, they still assumed that it was superior to a much smaller—and declining—denomination from the North. One otherwise-progressive Southern Baptist church, for instance, studied the matter and concluded that since the two groups had found it necessary to divide in the first place (and had been separate for 140 years), perhaps one should leave well enough alone. Whether out of ignorance, prejudice, or practicality, our respondents did not seem to be rushing into the American Baptist Churches. Nor did that Northern denomination seem to be extending especially open arms toward the South. While a few Southern Baptist churches would probably move eventually into the ABC, even a partial denominational reunion of this last remaining civil war split did not seem likely.

About the only alternative most moderates seemed able to think about by 1988 was designated giving to the Cooperative Program, and only about a quarter were even contemplating that (see table 8.4). However, that number seemed likely to grow in the ensuing years. Now that fundamentalists were in charge, moderates would give their money selectively, supporting the good things and eliminating the bad. The trauma at the Baptist Joint Committee had already given some moderate churches a chance to try out this technique. After the BJC's allotment was cut by the Convention, some churches simply sent them a separate check, in some cases decreasing their check to the Cooperative Program accordingly. Moderates had always bragged about their generous, cooperative support for the denomination's programs. They had condemned fundamentalists for wanting to support only pet projects. Now they were ready to say they had been wrong, that perhaps selective giving was not so bad after all.

Some moderates were also thinking about supporting "alternative" institutions. When asked about their personal support for that idea, over one-third of self-identified moderates had agreed in 1987, up from one-fourth the year before. If increasing numbers of moderate individuals continued to pursue this idea, the number of supporting churches would likely grow, as well. These churches and individuals were perhaps looking forward to a new school or publishing house or mission group that would embody moderate goals. Without leaving the denomination, they would nevertheless be able to enjoy the benefits of institutional support from agencies that shared their dreams. Just as fundamentalists had started Mid-America and had worked through independent mission boards, these progressive Southern Baptists hoped to be able to do the same thing.

What seemed likely to emerge, then, was a reconstructed denominational coalition that would no longer be held together by a Cooperative Program monopoly. Neither fundamentalists on the right nor moderates on the left would see Nashville as the only place to send money and find program assistance. Even though fundamentalists were in charge of the Nashville bureaucracy, their decades of institution building and a tradition of local church independence conspired against any exclusive loyalty to the denomination. Meanwhile, those on the left seemed poised to seek other ways to support missions, other sources of educational material, other voices in Washington. At the very least, by designating their Cooperative Program moneys, they would refuse to support new fundamentalist programs within the SBC.

For at least fifty years, Southern Baptists had been among the most tightly-knit, hierarchically functioning denominations in America. The Cooperative Program meant that all funds went through one channel, and SBC program loyalty meant that almost all churches shaped their identities and activities in a denominationally-prescribed manner. Tradition, ethnicity, region, and culture created this monolith, and a full embrace of modern bureaucratic methods sustained it. But culture, region, tradition, and even ethnicity were no longer uniform. Southern Baptists now lived in a culture where choice was an increasing reality. Individual congregations could increasingly choose to relate to any combination of a vast array of religious organizations, denominational and otherwise. Throughout American religion, congregations were exercising a good deal of freedom to adopt programs more shaped by the lifestyle demands of their members than by denominational traditions.[8]

Local church autonomy was not just a symbol. For those churches that chose to exercise it, autonomy allowed a great deal of room for organizational innovation. Most of those who were choosing to innovate were merely repeating the strategies practiced earlier by fundamentalists— reduced and/or designated giving and support for alternative institutions that would meet their special needs. In part the denomination's resilience can be credited to its congregational polity. While some researchers have hypothesized that the lack of tight control in such denominations renders them vulnerable to schism, just the opposite seemed to be the case among Southern Baptists.[9] Lack of tight hierarchical control meant that churches could remain nominally within the bounds of denominational life, while maintaining a good deal of distance from official programs and agencies. The fundamentalists had done this for years; and by the late 1980s, moderates were experimenting with a similar distanced, nominal participation. No official divorce was necessary; separate bedrooms and bank accounts would do.

The Southern Baptist Alliance

The "separate bedroom" to which some Southern Baptist progressives retreated was the Southern Baptist Alliance. When moderate political activists gathered after their 1986 defeat in Atlanta there was a good deal of anguish among them. Some were beginning to realize that they might never win and that the Southern Baptist Convention as they had known it might be gone forever. Some analyzed the anger and denial they had been feeling as stages in the process of grieving. To continue to fight to revive the SBC began to seem (as one person later put it) like a child clinging to the dead body of her parent. While some were ready to go on organizing, others vowed that it was time to create something new.

During the fall of 1986, a small group, mostly from North Carolina and Georgia, began meeting to formulate plans. If they were not going to spend their energy on political organizing—and they were not going to leave the denomination—just how could they survive? They were gradually working out the outlines of a new coalition when the news of their plan broke. They hastily scheduled simultaneous newsconferences in Raleigh, Charlotte, and Atlanta; and on February 12, 1987, the Southern Baptist Alliance was officially, if a bit prematurely, born. They arranged for a makeshift office and waited to see what would happen.

At its birth, the Alliance announced that members would commit themselves to a "covenant" of seven principles. These were ideas and practices they perceived as essential to Baptist life, but increasingly endangered by the fundamentalist direction of the SBC. They would support

- the freedom of the individual, led by God's Spirit within the family of faith, to read and interpret the Scriptures, relying on the historical understanding of the church and on the best methods of modern biblical study;

- the freedom of the local church under the authority of Jesus Christ to shape its own life and mission, call its own leadership, and ordain whom it perceives as gifted for ministry, male or female;

- the larger body of Jesus Christ, expressed in various Christian traditions;

- the servant role of leadership within the church;

- theological education in congregations, colleges, and seminaries characterized by reverence for biblical authority and respect for open inquiry and responsible scholarship;

- the proclamation of the Good News of Jesus Christ and the calling of God to all peoples to repentance and faith, reconciliation and hope, social and economic justice;

- the principle of a free church in a free state.

While these principles were largely drawn from historic Baptist positions, they also reflected the progressive character of those who wrote them. Their emphasis was not just on the traditional principles of freedom and cooperation, but on their specific expression in "modern biblical study," the calling of men *and women* to ministry, ecumenical cooperation, "open inquiry," and a gospel that includes "social and economic justice." This was a covenant that would place the Alliance to the left of most Southern Baptists.

In those early days, the Alliance was not quite sure what it would do. The originators talked about their role in terms taken from the Hebrew prophets: they would point out the ways in which the covenant was being violated by the current SBC and call trustees and others to task for failing to be true to the Baptist heritage. They did not expect to change anyone's mind, only to be a voice of conscience for those who could not simply go along in silence. They also said, however, that they would serve as a channel for funds to agencies and causes that might be defunded by the SBC.[10] If they could not change the SBC, they could at least protect good causes within it from extinction.

The organization was to be directed by a thirty-member Board that would represent both the churches and the individual members that joined. Individuals could contribute annual dues of $25, and churches would be assessed $1 per resident member per year. By September, fourteen churches and over 1,300 individuals had cooperated by sending money. By their first birthday, there were thirty-eight churches and 2,100 individual members. A year later, the number of churches had nearly doubled (to seventy-three), and the number of individuals had almost reached 3,000.[11] Individual members came from thirty-nine states, the District of Columbia, and overseas; but they were concentrated in the states of the old nineteenth-century SBC establishment—along the eastern seaboard from Florida to Virginia, and Kentucky. Two-thirds of SBA members came from this one area that contained only one-third of Southern Baptists. And none of the churches that had joined were located outside the Convention's original territory. Once the eastern seaboard members are counted, however, the remaining SBA population was distributed fairly evenly throughout remaining Convention territory.

The Alliance's first activity was a convocation called for May 1987. About 400 people gathered at a Baptist women's college in Raleigh, where they worshipped in the creative liturgical styles to which many had become accustomed. They held workshops on the SBA convenant and talked about the future of the organization. They approved a constitution and bylaws, elected their first officers, and started the process of establishing state and regional groups that would be linked to the national body.[12] The ad hoc group that had dreamed the Alliance into being was now an official, legal, organization. They would regather each spring for an annual convocation and organize to act on their concerns during the rest of the year. Charlotte pastor Henry Crouch was elected president and executive director, but by the end of the first year, that job was divided between a new president and a parttime, nonsalaried administrator. Before the second year was up, Stan Hastey, formerly with the Baptist Joint Committee, was hired as a fulltime, salaried administrator, with new SBA offices in Washington. Just two years after it was formed, the annual budget reached $400,000. With money, staff, and growing membership, the Alliance assumed an increasing presence in Southern Baptist life.

In talking about the members' needs, the first convocation's participants agreed to establish four task forces: on educational materials, on women in ministry, on religious liberty, and on placement. In making that move, they turned the corner from an organization that pointed out where Southern Baptists were going wrong toward an organization that would establish structures and programs independent of the Convention. In these early years of its life, the Alliance would gradually move toward institutionalizing its vision, offering concrete alternatives to SBC programs, schools, and causes that its members no longer found satisfactory.

But the other major function served by the Southern Baptist Alliance in those early years was its very existence as a place of refuge. It provided a sense of identity for people who were no longer sure they could wholeheartedly call themselves Southern Baptists. It offered a place of fellowship, where common concerns and griefs could be shared. And it offered a place to laugh—at themselves, at fundamentalists, at Southern Baptist traditions, at the world. It was a place where the best progressive preachers (including women) could be heard and voices could blend in both the hymns of the church and the protest songs of liberal activists. An early brochure invited potential members to "step out of the crowd . . . and discover you're not standing alone." Progressive Southern Baptists, who had felt like a tiny minority for a very long time, were finally creating a home for themselves.

In their early days together, the participants in the Alliance often used the term "like-minded" to describe the comfortable way they felt in each other's presence. It also described the near unanimity that existed on certain key issues. Among the respondents to our 1988 questionnaire, twenty-two said they thought their church would support the SBA. Of those twenty-two, everyone agreed that individual Baptists should be free to interpret the Bible and should be tolerant of people who differ, that separation of church and state was an important Baptist distinctive, and (with one dissenter) that the pastor should not be the final authority in the local church. They were not, however, so unanimous in their theology. Ten said that the Bible is inerrant, and five agreed that God put everything in the Bible He wants us to know. On those issues the SBA average is certainly to the left of the rest of the Convention, but not uniformly "liberal" in theology. Nor are they uniformly over-educated or financially well-off (although every one of them said they enjoyed attending "cultural" events).

These twenty-two SBA supporters are, however, less conservative on political issues than average Southern Baptists. They uniformly embrace the civil rights movement, and nine of them think civil rights ought to be extended to homosexuals. There is even a slight majority (fourteen) on the side of the ERA. In addition, sixteen of the twenty-two favor the ordination of women, and seventeen reported that their church ordains women as deacons, sixteen as ministers. The freedom about which the SBA talked meant a consensus among their supporters about equal rights for women and minorities, in the church and elsewhere. In many ways, SBA members were people who had been taking minority stands themselves for quite some time. They were often the political activists who had frequented the annual Christian Life Commission seminars. The Alliance offered a re-creation of the kind of place were progressive politics and progressive theology did not make one an outsider.

Fellowship and function formed the two poles of SBA existence, sometimes complementary and sometimes in tension. On one side (perhaps represented by its individual members) were efforts simply to sustain people who felt isolated and wounded. The SBA was a place to plant a flag of principle and rally around it. On the other side (perhaps represented by the churches who joined), the SBA was the organizational channel that would substitute for denominational functions no longer acceptably performed by the Southern Baptist Convention. On its fellowship side, the Alliance gathered for banquets, receptions, and worship. On its function side, it organized into committees and task forces. Some who came to the annual convocations enjoyed the fellowship most; others wanted to "get down to business and *do* something." The structure of the organization was still so amorphous that both fellowship and function, spontaneous dreaming and systematic planning were present.[13] At the SBA's after-session gathering at the San Antonio convention, for instance, fellowship yielded to dreaming, which in turn became organization. Set up as a time of fellowship, the first part of the evening was dominated by the expression of anger and grief felt by the defeated messengers. But the grief could not last forever. Nancy Hastings Sehested, pastor of Prescott Memorial Baptist in Memphis, took the microphone and began to call the participants away from "crucifixion" and toward "resurrection." They began to envision together the new world of ministry they might create. And they began to organize. Someone suggested that a major "listening session" was needed, a time for systematic reflection on the future. Someone else volunteered a location. Before they went home for the night, the initial plan had been formed.

They held their listening session in Nashville in September 1988. Over 700 people registered, nearly half of them laity. The range of personal agendas represented among them was vast. At one pole were people who had just discovered there was a problem and thought political organizing might be the answer. They were not at all ready to declare the SBC dead. Not far from them were those who wanted to organize financial channels that would enable the Alliance to be the means by which the fundamen-

talists would be hurt in the pocketbook. Several people came with elaborate plans for establishing escrow accounts or foundations or "shadow"
Executive Committees. These two groups saw the Alliance as an instrument of power for the restoration of the SBC to its former glory.

But there were others there whose vision stretched beyond a return to
former glory. They were not so sure that the "good old days" were nearly
good enough. They had begun to see the old SBC as a bureaucracy interested in its own survival and willing to accommodate to conservative demands on everything from race relations to biblical interpretation to the
role of women. Women, especially, had no desire to return to the SBC of
1978. If this group talked of returning to anything it was a return to the
seventeenth century, to days of Baptist struggle against established religion, days in which the principles of democracy, religious liberty, and a
mutually-responsible regenerate membership were being forged as Baptist distinctives. It became increasingly clear that the Alliance was not the
proper home for those whose primary loyalties were to 1960s and 1970s
Southern Baptist Convention structures. Those who would stay with the
Alliance were people willing to disengage from the old, to grieve, and to
call each other toward new things. Among the twenty-two SBA supporters from our 1988 survey, fourteen said that they were grieving because
the convention had been lost.

Those who wished to continue trying to regain power in the Convention soon formed Baptists Committed. Although there was a good deal of
overlapping membership between the two new organizations, their aims
were very different. As the Alliance moved away from old ways of thinking about being Southern Baptist, moderates still committed to their traditional Southern Baptist identities could not go with them. Further
political defeats would probably convince some of them that the Alliance
was a viable alternative. Each year, the number who had given up the
political fight increased. But even defeat would not create progressives
out of the conservatives in and near the SBC mainstream.

Of those among our respondents who said they envisioned supporting
the SBA, twelve said their churches would be using fewer denominational
programs and less Sunday School literature from the SBC. Eleven said
that their churches would probably support the Cooperative Program
less, with thirteen saying that designated giving was likely. An equal number said that they would support alternative institutions. Although they
were certainly not uniformly convinced, there appeared to be significant
sentiment among these SBA supporters in favor of finding new educational materials, institutions, and ways to spend their mission money.
Those were also the concrete concerns heard among participants in the
Alliance's various programs.

The organization moved most quickly on the need for new Sunday

School materials. Reporting on the work of the educational materials task force, Everett Gill wrote to SBA president Henry Crouch, "The meeting confirmed what we have been hearing all along: that there is serious and long standing disaffection with the Bible study materials coming out of Nashville, and many people fear that it will only grow worse." Working with *SBC Today*, the Alliance moved toward publishing lessons keyed to the same biblical texts being used in the official SBC adult "Life and Work" curriculum. The first edition appeared in January 1989. It was a modest beginning, a compromise. Some had wanted a whole new SBA curriculum, while others merely wanted advice on adopting an existing non-SBC program. Still others were timid about cutting themselves off from any traditional activity. Under this plan, churches could continue to buy quarterlies from Nashville, but supplement (or replace) the commentary contained in them with the materials printed in their monthly *SBC Today*.

The Alliance also began, as soon as extra funds were available, to provide a channel for mission support. By 1989, they were budgeting over $95,000 for various projects. The Baptist Joint Committee on Public Affairs would get $10,000 toward making up the $40,000 they had lost from the SBC. Southern Baptist Women in Ministry would get a substantial grant for support of their organization. The Southeastern Seminary chapter of the American Association of University Professors (formed for the protection of faculty against their new administration) would also get a grant. In addition, housing projects for the poor would be supported through Habitat for Humanity, and peace efforts through the North American Baptist Peace Fellowship. Beyond such direct SBA funding, the organization also began to serve as a channel, linking individual projects with supporting individuals and churches. Donors could designate gifts to SBA-approved projects that would then be supported beyond the regular SBA mission budget.

As the budget grew, so did the ability to fund mission projects that might not receive SBC support. No one was being asked to cut what they gave to the Cooperative Program, although a fair number of member churches did. Rather, they were being offered a second unified "Global Ministries Budget" to support. The SBA had not set up a shadow Cooperative Program, but a supplementary program that for some churches substituted for all or most of their SBC missions giving. But those decisions were made on a local basis, not by any unified prescription handed down from the SBA office. To retain their membership, local churches only had to give their $1 per member per year fee. Beyond that, how much they gave, and to whom they gave it was up to them. The Alliance retained the SBC's emphasis on local autonomy.

These efforts in publishing and mission support were typical of the kind of organizational identity the SBA was trying to create, an identity *within* the SBC. Its biggest problem was its image as a schismatic group, and in the beginning Alliance organizers tried to dispel that notion. Some talked about it as an "auxiliary" to the Convention, noting that after women were officially denied access to the floor of annual meetings in the 1880s, they formed the Woman's Missionary Union as an auxiliary to be run by women, for women, but as an aid to the overall work of the Convention. They stressed that they had no plans to leave the denomination, that they were only serving as a prophetic voice within it and supplementing its work where necessary. They argued that by providing a place for self-expression and service they might actually keep some people from leaving. This would be a last-chance effort to keep the denomination's progressive wing attached.

But every time the Alliance made concrete efforts to meet the institutional needs of its constituents, it was faced again with the accusation that it was a new denomination in the making. At no time were such accusations more prevalent than when the Alliance decided to start a seminary. By the time the Alliance held its second annual convocation in March 1988, Randall Lolley was about to be replaced by Louis Drummond at Southeastern, and a vision of fundamentalist theological education there was taking shape. Alan Neely, an exiting professor at Southeastern, had become the Alliance's parttime executive, and his presence made the crisis at that seminary all the more real. It was in fact probably more pressing in the minds of the leadership than among other supporters of the Alliance. Of the twenty-two SBA supporters among our respondents, only eight said that they anticipated less support for SBC seminaries. But people connected with Southeastern were ready to pour a great deal of energy into developing alternatives. By the time the listening session met in September 1988, a task force for theological education had been formed and was encouraged to explore various possibilities. They entered conversations with Duke University about starting a House of Baptist Studies connected to that Divinity School.[14] Wake Forest University established its own task force to determine whether they might start a Divinity School on that Baptist (but independent) campus.[15] Finally, in January 1989, the Alliance board announced that plans were underway for a joint venture with theological institutions in the Richmond area.[16] It would be a freestanding, accredited school that would share resources with Presbyterian and black Baptist seminaries and would have representatives from American Baptist seminaries on its planning body. It was envisioned both as an alternative to Southeastern and as a symbol of the Alliance's willingness to overcome the black-white and North-South divisions that had created the SBC.

The debate at the March 1989, convocation was a lively one. It took over two hours, and the program had to be rearranged to accommodate it. The several hundred people who had gathered turned the sanctuary of First Baptist Greenville, South Carolina, into a town hall, enjoying the kind of free debate many of them had missed as Southern Baptist Conventions got bigger and more tightly controlled. A succession of speakers, young and old, men and women, pastors and lay people, made their way to the microphones to speak their minds. Although many had grave doubts about the wisdom of starting a seminary, the final vote was overwhelmingly favorable. People had listened to each other and had formed something close to a consensus. Although the SBA was certainly a coalition built on many common cultural bases, it also contained people with conflicting institutional loyalties. Some of those who still disagreed after the vote spent time with their opponents, struggling to find ways to continue to cooperate. The SBA's ideology affirmed the right of dissent and the value of conflict. This seminary vote was, among other things, an experiment in how dissent would be accommodated.

In these early days, the Alliance was still acting more like a social movement than like an institution. Its structure was fluid, and the rules were being made up as they went along. Its "fellowship" and "function" poles roughly paralleled the potential tension between this charismatic phase and the routinization that might follow. Some leaders were already anticipating that official lines of representation and authority needed to be delineated. They did not want to evolve into the kind of oligarchy masquerading as democracy the SBC had, as they saw it, become. They proposed to the Greenville convocation a structure that would designate about 150 elected delegates to do business, while everyone else came together for reports and inspiration. After the heady experience of open debate, however, it is little wonder that the members turned down that proposal. They were not yet ready to give up their sense of direct participation. They wanted to stay a movement a little longer.

The concern with "healing" that was expressed in the proposed structure of the new seminary was a concern more and more frequently heard in SBA circles. Perhaps first voiced publicly by organizer Jim Strickland at the 1988 convocation, growing numbers of members talked about the heritage of culturally-based division to which they did not wish to return. They were ready to confess the sins of Southern Baptists' origin. They began to speak of breaking the religious barriers of region and race that had been erected in defense of slavery. By the end of the 1989 convocation, a motion to study dropping the "Southern" from their name received a very warm reception.

Members wanted to reach out to American and National Baptists, but hardly knew how.[17] A prominent black pastor preached at the 1989 convocation, but when they had met in Nashville the previous fall, no one thought to invite the locally based black Baptist officials. Even though SBA members tended to be passionate supporters of the civil rights movement, they still traveled largely in southern white circles. Establishing real links across those long-standing divisions would take sustained and concerted effort.

While including blacks and American Baptists might take special efforts, women were already in their midst. A few strong female leaders had been part of the original group that had birthed the Alliance, and from the beginning it was clear that female leaders would be accorded legitimacy in this organization. It was not clear, however, just what their legitimate roles would be. During the 1987 convocation, Nancy Sehested led one worship service, and in 1988, one of three interpreters of the "SBA vision" was board member and former missionary Ann Neil. Susan Lockwood Wright, pastor of Cornell Baptist in Chicago, had been a founding vice president. But only one-fourth to one-third of the Directors were women, and they still had to help many of their brethren understand the fine points of inclusiveness. Women members did not want to be addressed as "Mrs. George So-and-So," and they did not want to hear about the needs of "mankind." They wanted concrete help with placement and maybe even a quota of female positions on the Board. Men who had lived in the male world of the traditional SBC would have to learn how to work with women to create a new kind of institution.

SBA women still struggled with old presumptions and stereotypes, but their place in the SBA at least allowed them a visible and legitimate space in which to work on those problems. The covenant itself affirmed the right of churches to ordain and call women ministers. The Alliance also agreed to a voluntary covenant on the use of inclusive language in its worship and business. But more concretely, the SBA began to provide funding to the Southern Baptist Women in Ministry organization and to the mission churches with women pastors that the Home Mission Board would no longer support. A placement service was also set up, seeking to help women (and men) find jobs. There would still be more women seeking pastorates than there were Southern Baptist churches willing to hire them, but the Alliance would try to facilitate the process where possible.

The placement service was a recognition that the Southern Baptist career market had gotten treacherous. Individual churches had always elected their own members to a "pulpit" committee, but the committee often relied on the advice of local and state Baptist officials. They might also get a number of recommendations simply from other interested parties. Both churches and pastors could sometimes get unpleasant surprises when they discovered too late that the match they had made was not a good one. SBA pastors could tell stories of moderates fired by churches that insisted on a fundamentalist leader. And they could tell stories of conservative and moderate churches who unknowingly hired fundamentalists. Every pulpit committee had routinely been receiving resumés from local fundamentalists recommending other fundamentalists to the church.[18] The lay people on those pulpit committees might simply not have the political insight to ask the right questions. Only after the pastor arrived might they find out that he had very different ideas about his role and authority (and about what the Bible does and does not allow). Fundamentalists hoped that such pastors would be able to teach churches the biblical way and that the number of solid Bible-believing churches would thus be increased. The SBA recognized that they would have to be equally intentional about pastor placement if they wished to halt such fundamentalist transformations of local churches (and start a few of their own).

The placement service provided a specialized kind of communication among members in a time when communication among "like-minded" people was not always easy. For other kinds of communication, the SBA linked up with *SBC Today*. New members got a year's subscription to the newspaper with their membership. They would get, in fact, a special edition of the newspaper with a section devoted exclusively to Alliance news. Member churches were encouraged to buy bulk subscriptions in the same way that they had formerly bought multiple subscriptions to their state Baptist papers, and by the middle of 1989, over 4,500 new subscriptions had been added through this connection with the Alliance. Through *SBC Today*, members could stay informed about what was happening in the denomination as a whole and about the plans and activities of the Alliance. The newspaper helped to bind together a widely-scattered, but growing constituency.

During its first two years, the Alliance's membership and budget actually exceeded expectations. Still it was tiny compared to the denomination in which it created a haven. From our data, its potential pool of sympathizers can be guessed to be perhaps 10 percent of the church leaders. About that many say they would support alternative institutions and/or changes in their gifts to the Cooperative Program. But most importantly, about that many report that they are grieving and have declared the Convention lost. Such emotional closure on the old era seems to be necessary before attraction to the SBA is possible. Those who are not ready or willing to make such a break with the past will not find the SBA a congenial home.

Gaining support from 10 percent of church leaders does not, however, mean that the SBA might look forward to signing up 10 percent of the SBC's 37,000 churches. In fact, the notion of "membership" proved an obstacle for many churches. The Alliance urged individual churches to take their time, hear all sides, and make the decision carefully, but nevertheless to join. Many traditional Southern Baptists could not be convinced that they could "join" the SBA without in effect leaving the SBC. Randall Lolley pled with the group at the listening session to create some other way to support the Alliance's work. As a pastor of a traditional moderate church, even he could not easily guarantee that his congregation could be persuaded to join. As we have noted before, moderate churches are very likely to contain a mixture of conservative and progressive members. Moderates were more likely, for instance, than either conservatives or fundamentalists to report that there had been division in their church over the SBC controversy. They also reported that differences of opinion among the members was one of the reasons their church would not change its denominational involvement. Individual pastors and members might join the SBA, then, without disturbing their more conservative fellow members. But they shied away from the conflict that might come if their churches pursued a vote on membership.

Such conflict sometimes produced new SBA member churches, however. In some cases, groups from old traditional First Churches, often with moderate pastors, simply endured the tension as long as they could and finally left. After years of deferring progressive programs and trying to avoid offense, some groups of moderates struck out on their own. Often tiny fledgling congregations—having left the budget, buildings and prestige of the old church behind—had an opportunity to embody their new vision of church life. By 1989, perhaps half a dozen such splits had occurred, with the Alliance as a primary source of identification and moral support.

The Future?

These local church schisms raise again the question of permanent, formal division in the larger body.[19] As we have seen, the vast majority of Southern Baptists appear today to be settling in under their new administrators. Most think that the changes will not really affect them, that their locally autonomous churches can go on as before. So long as they think there has been no change, they can certainly not be expected to exit. Therefore, fundamentalists can expect to keep the denomination's mainstream intact.

Within the institutions, there will continue to be a significant degree of exit among the staff from the old era. Some agencies and schools have already lost large portions of their old staff, and we might expect that by the middle of the next decade few of the employees from the early 1980s will remain. Many will still be Southern Baptists, but they will no longer be working for the denomination. Within local churches, some individual members and some pastors will seek a new denominational home. But will any sizable and organized group of churches leave?

Hirschmann notes that under normal circumstances "voice" and the threat of "exit" are instruments for effecting change in an organization.[20] People protest because they want things to be better. Because they are loyal to the organization, they do not simply leave at the first sign of trouble. They may be quite patient—so long as they perceive that their patience may be rewarded. For that to happen, they must first gain support from a significant number of others with similar concerns and, second, perceive that there is some chance that their complaints will be effective. Normally there is a good chance that some change may occur. Organizations do not usually want to lose their members and therefore have some incentive for making the changes about which members are complaining.

However, in the case of the Southern Baptist Convention, none of these factors that might discourage the exit of the denomination's left wing seem to be present. The voice being exercised by moderates is unlikely to be effective against fundamentalists who are not only convinced that their own goals are divinely sanctioned (and therefore should not be changed), but would, in fact, like to see the Convention's left wing leave. Fundamentalist leaders often said that they admired people who chose to leave for conscience's sake and that they expected the 5 to 10 percent liberal fringe to exit. The threat of exit by these members, then, could have no effect in inducing change.

Nor was their voice likely to be heard. The effectiveness of a progressive voice in the Southern Baptist Convention would be hampered—as it had always been—by its tiny size and now also by the hostility of the denomination's official leadership. The progressive voice had always been overwhelmed by the voices of more conservative members, even when moderates had been in charge. The potential effectiveness of progressives remaining in the Southern Baptist Convention appeared small indeed. Neither their voice nor their threat of exit could be expected to make any difference; only their intense loyalty, against all odds, might still overcome the forces pushing them out.

If the Southern Baptist Alliance survives and continues to grow, it may be expected to play a key role in the coming years. It will probably never attract more than a few hundred churches and a few thousand additional individuals. It was formed as a vehicle for the expression of protest, but it could also be the vehicle for exit (something its leaders always acknowledged as a possibility). By 1989, the Alliance was gradually accepting responsibility for both the services that support church programming and the organization through which joint mission efforts are done. Only a few churches had switched loyalties entirely from the SBC to the SBA. For some the SBA was a minor supplement, an auxiliary, a place to go for one or another program or function. For a few, the SBA would become one among many sources they might use in putting together local programs. From the plethora of independent religious organizations on the left and right, they might choose various combinations of publishers and mission efforts, political action committees and youth camps. SBA itself might in fact choose to become primarily a networking organization; a broker, providing churches with information about existing programs from other publishers, agencies, and denominations.

But the SBA might also continue to build institutions and programs of its own, distinct from the Southern Baptist Convention. If joint venture activity with other Baptist bodies continues, a formal merger might eventually take place with another group or groups. As members talk of healing, they might seek out some formal realignment of their Southern churches with Northern and/or black Baptists. The proposed seminary in Richmond certainly seemed to lay the foundation for such a move.

SBA members might also remain simply a marginal and disaffected group within the SBC. They might come together primarily for comfort and fellowship, while they maintain institutional alignments that are essentially unchanged. That, however, seemed the least likely alternative.

Once an institutional infrastructure is in place outside SBC boundaries, the possibility of remaining within the denomination becomes increasingly tenuous. Some wish to stay to ensure that a progressive voice is heard. But if that voice is perceived to be ineffective, the reason for staying is less clear. To keep these grieving progressives in the SBC, at least some of the Alliance's complaints will have to be heard and heeded, some people or policies influenced by their message—and that appears quite unlikely. In the long term, the Alliance would appear to have few reasons to stay, and increasing possibilities for exit. A continuing sense of estrangement, coupled with separate organizational networks, is *possible* within Southern Baptist polity, but it is not likely. People can go to different meetings, give to different causes, honor different heroes for only so long. When a group discovers that it no longer needs what the organization has to offer and cannot contribute to the goals of that organization, exit becomes more likely.

Perhaps the element that makes exit most likely for Alliance members, however, is their gradual recreation of their past and future identities.

They have begun to leave behind their dreams of regaining power in the old system; the future for them no longer lies in a re-creation of the recent past. They are rewriting their longterm history, as well. One hears more about the seventeenth century than about the nineteenth century in these circles. In an odd way seventeenth-century Baptist cries for freedom seem better suited to the late twentieth-century world than do nineteenth-century Baptist visions of a Christian civilization. It took a fundamentalist revolution to force progressives toward rejection of the cultural accommodation that had characterized Southern Baptists from the beginning. They were ready to leave their "churchly" status in the established religion of the old South and were talking about returning in "sectarian" fashion to the purity of their roots.

In other ways, it was the sectarian, anti-pluralist ways of the fundamentalists that were pushing them toward schism. They appeared to be forming what Stark and Bainbridge have called a "church movement," a group separating from its parent body because the parent body has become too concerned with purity, a group wishing to embrace a larger range of the culture than is permitted by those in denominational power.[21] But those labels of church and sect fail to take account of the dynamic process in which both fundamentalists and moderates had engaged. They were constructing a new future out of various elements of their past. Each was shaping bits of old and new into ideas and structures that would carry them into the twenty-first century.

At least a few Southern Baptists were refusing to accept the terms of peace offered by the victors in this battle. The synthesis of old and new offered by Southern Baptist fundamentalists could not make sense of their lives. They knew that the world in which their denomination was the guardian of traditional southern culture was gone, and they did not wish to see it return. They had accepted the pluralism of the new South, recognizing that neither their old culture nor their unquestioning denominational loyalty could or should be restored. While a small group on the denomination's right wing had engineered an attempt to re-create a doctrinal and cultural consensus, and the vast majority in the middle had chosen to go along, this small group on the left had seized this as a creative moment. They began to speak of it as exodus rather than exile. It is not yet clear what the form of their new identity will be—nor even if it will survive. But their struggle to bring something new out of the depths of their despair could well be the birth pangs announcing a new kind of Baptist.

Appendix A.
Methods of Study

D ata reported in this book have been gathered by a number of means. Statistics reported include official data gleaned from various denominational sources as noted in the text. In addition, original data come from the survey of Southern Baptist clergy and lay church leaders conducted by the Emory University Center for Religious Research in 1985, with follow-up questionnaires in 1986, 1987, and 1988.

The Sample and the Survey

In selecting a population for study, we decided against attempting a sampling of all Southern Baptists. Logistically, such an undertaking would have been immense and complicated.[1] More importantly, we were most interested in hearing from the people who would be recognized leaders in their congregations, people who could be expected to have influence on how the church related to the denomination. Pastors, of course, are the natural persons to select as local leaders. But we wanted to include the opinions of lay people, as well. In most congregations, the most respected men (and in some congregations women) are chosen as deacons. The person elected as chair would likely be one of the leading men in the congregation. Women may fill various offices, but the one that brings them most clearly into contact with the denomination and most visibly into leadership in the church is serving as president of Baptist Women, the local component of Woman's Missionary Union.

In 1985, the Center contracted with the Baptist Sunday School Board for a sample of these three groups drawn from their records on Southern Baptist churches. Each year over 90 percent of the denomination's 37,000 churches return their Uniform Church Letter. Completing this document is rather like doing one's taxes; it asks for everything from current membership figures to how many members are enrolled in preschool choir to the market value of the church property. These finally make their way to Nashville, where some of the information is stored on computer and some remains on paper. Churches which do not report one year are likely to have reported the previous year; so almost no records are more than two years old, and the file on pastors is updated daily.

We received a listing of randomly-selected names and addresses. Twelve hundred pastors had been selected from the list of slightly less than 33,000 churches with pastors. Nine hundred WMU presidents were selected from the list of churches reporting such a person. And nine hundred chairs of local diaconates were selected from the list of churches reporting a deacon chair. As we expected, all the pastors and deacon chairs in our sample were male, and the WMU presidents were all female. These latter two lists were compiled by randomly selecting churches that had reported the item and then assembling the names by hand from the paper files.

The sample sizes were determined by taking into account both the final number of respondents desired in various subgroups (messengers at the Dallas convention, for instance) and the anticipated response rate. Researchers at the Sunday School Board and at the Research Division of the Home Mission Board had warned that pastors rarely exceed a 25 percent response rate and that they expected laity to respond in even fewer numbers, especially to a long and potentially controversial survey. James Guth, political scientist at Furman University, however, had obtained response rates as high as 50 percent of SBC pastors, using first class mail and multiple reminders. The Center would not have a budget for first class mail or for more than two reminders, so we anticipated a response rate between those two extremes. The 1985 rate was 36 percent on the clergy sample and on the WMU sample, 31 percent on the deacon sample.

After the first year, the original lists were used again for follow-up questionnaires. Because in 1985 we did not anticipate subsequent surveys, original questionnaires were not coded so as to easily identify respondents. Through a complicated matching procedure a list of almost 800 respondents was assembled. We supplemented that with every fourth name drawn from the list of nonrespondents. Surveys in 1986 and 1987 were then mailed to previous respondents, plus the reduced nonrespondent list. Response rates for previous respondents averaged 49 percent, but people who had already refused to return a questionnaire once proved quite intransigent, with very few additional respondents being added from that pool in 1986 and 1987, and a response rate that never exceeding 12 percent. In 1988, budget constraints dictated mailing only to previous respondents. In 1985, 1986, and 1988, initial mailings were at bulk rate. In 1987, surveys were sent first class, resulting in numerous corrections to our mailing list. In 1985–1987, the initial mailing was followed by a reminder and a second questionnaire. In 1988, the second questionnaire was the only follow-up.

Samples of this size could reasonably be expected to contain a full representation of churches in the Convention. However, there is some bias in the populations from which our samples were selected. Only about 70 percent of churches—less than 60 percent of rural churches—reported an on-going WMU, for instance. That constraint is less true of deacon chairs, an office that is likely to be present in almost any church of any size. Rural and smaller churches may, however, be less likely to submit complete reports that would list that person's name. It is likely then that smaller, rural churches were underrepresented in the population from which our samples were drawn. As we see in table A.1, small and rural churches are indeed underrepresented among our respondents, while large and city churches are overrepresented. Since we have reason to suspect that this distortion is inherent in the population from which the sample was drawn, weighting factors for church size and location were used to bring the responses more nearly into line with population characteristics.

To further check the representativeness of the respondents, we compared the educational levels of our clergy with those reported in a study done two years earlier by the Home Mission Board. With data on over half of all clergy, they reported significantly more clergy with a high school education, and fewer with a seminary degree or more. As table A.1 shows, our clergy respondents are significantly better educated than is the norm in the SBC. Since education is a key

Table A.1. A Comparison of Survey Respondents to Known
Characteristics of the SBC—Unweighted and Weighted Results

	% Respondents Unweighted	% SBC Total	% Respondents Weighted
Church Size *			
1–99	18.2	31.7	29.0
100–299	37.2	39.3	37.0
300–499	22.1	16.7	18.0
500–999	15.2	8.8	11.1
1000+	7.4	3.6	4.9
Church Location **			
Open Country	33.1	48.4	42.8
Small Town	23.6	21.2	24.6
Small City	14.7	15.1	16.0
Large City	28.7	15.3	16.7
Region			
South	80.8	80.9	79.1
Midwest	12.2	11.4	13.5
Northeast	1.4	.9	1.5
West	5.6	6.7	5.6
Educational Level (Clergy)			
Less than 12 years	2.8	1.3	2.7
High School Diploma	3.5	14.9	15.4
Attended Bible College	3.2	3.2	3.2
Completed Bible College	2.7	6.2	2.7
Attended Other College	12.2	8.3	8.9
Completed Other College	16.2	13.5	14.6
Some Seminary or more	59.3	50.8	52.9

SOURCES: For clergy education levels, C. Price, "A Study of the Educational Attainment of Southern Baptist Pastors, 1983." (Atlanta: Home Mission Board, 1984). For SBC church size and location, ed. L. S. Barr, *The Quarterly Review* 46(4) (July, August, September 1986): 24.

*Since we asked for *resident* members, and the SBC reports *total* members, we have adjusted their categories to account for an average 28% nonresident members as follows: 1–149 = "1–99"; 150–399 = "100–299"; 400–749 = "300–499"; 750–1499 = "500–999"; 1500+ = "1000+."

**Our community size categories are compared to SBC reported categories as follows: open country or village = "open country"; town and small city (population 500–9,999) = "small town"; medium city (population 10,000–49,999) = "small city"; and large city (population 50,000 or more) = "large city."

factor, especially among clergy, we used the Home Mission Board data to construct weights for our clergy respondents.

We also compared our lay respondents to the U.S. population, as reported in the 1980 Census and found that they were better educated than the general population. Because they are leaders in their congregations, however, there may be reason to expect that they may be better educated than ordinary church members (and than the general population). But our respondents' higher levels of education may also result from the same response bias that caused better educated clergy to overrespond. It is not surprising that people who are more educated would be more likely to respond to a questionnaire. The least educated would have difficulty even completing the task, and the most educated would be most accustomed to such written reports. We have not however, weighted the lay responses, since we have no reliable comparison data with which to construct weights.

Taking into account the underrepresentations that were built into our population, these respondents appear to be a good cross section from which to generalize about the positions of local church leaders in the denomination. They do not represent all Southern Baptists, but they are leaders in churches of all sizes, locations, and regions.

Whether they represent the range of political positions in the denomination is harder to guage. In 1985, we compared our early and late responders as an approximation of the possible differences that may exist between those who responded and those who did not. Almost all of the differences we found were related to levels of activism, both denominational and political, but not to which side the person was on. Late responders were less likely to have been to political meetings or to have made special efforts to attend the convention. They were less likely to read SBC periodicals, went to fewer denominational meetings, and talked to fewer people about convention affairs. There is reason to believe, then, that the people who did not respond to our questionnaire were simply less involved in SBC affairs and cared less about what was at stake.

The survey instruments we used are contained in Appendix C, and the scales constructed are discussed in Appendix B. Items in the 1985 questionnaire were pretested in two Atlanta congregations—one strongly fundamentalist and one strongly moderate. Items added in subsequent years sought to elaborate and extend information gained in the first year. Items repeated from year to year were intended to form a picture of changing levels of activism and opinion. The section on Dilemmas in Daily Living was added by Arthur E. Farnsley to gather data relevant to his dissertation.

The Interviews

Much of the information reported here came from informal conversations with relatively anonymous people. As we observed at annual convention meetings and at other gatherings, we sought out ordinary participants who helped us to see what was happening from their point of view. We usually tried to learn a little about their backgrounds (where they were from, where they went to school, what they did for a living) and a little about their relationship to the denomination (how active they were, how much they cared, and where they stood on various issues). Over the course of four years, several dozen of these conversations made their way into the project files.

Other informal conversations resulted both from my preexisting network of acquaintances in the denomination and from my position as an increasingly public person. People who knew me sought me out to talk about the controversy. And I was often invited to speak to groups in the denomination. In these circumstances I was a participating observer. I responded as a friend or as an "expert," but their questions and responses were of interest to me as a researcher, as well. In some instances, dialogue and discussion sessions at such meetings were taped and transcribed, and in additional instances I made detailed notes. While some fundamentalists were included among those with whom I had routine casual hallway conversations, this population of informal and invited conversations is admittedly skewed toward the moderate side. I simply had access to a richer and broader range of moderate informants who filled in details and insights. I tried to make up for that disparity by spending disproportionate amounts of time during conventions in places where I knew I could talk to more conservative people about what was going on.

Because such informal conversations can never be representative, in 1985 we began a more deliberate process of interviewing. In the weeks immediately prior to the 1985 and 1986 convention meetings, we talked by telephone with a total of twenty-five pastors who were reputed to be politically active. In 1985, these were all in the Atlanta area; in 1986, they spanned the country. In addition, a total of seventy-nine formal interviews were completed, covering three other populations: moderate and fundamentalist activists; elected members of key boards of trustees; and staff from several key agencies. Lists of activists were assembled by reputational means. We failed to complete interviews with only three of those we originally contacted. From our original pool of activists, then, we completed interviews with ten fundamentalist leaders and fourteen moderate leaders. Lists of staff and board members were assembled from the 1985 SBC *Annual* and samples were selected by using a table of random numbers. Eighteen staff members were selected, including people from the Foreign Mission Board, the Home Mission Board, the Sunday School Board, and the agencies housed at the Executive Committee building in Nashville. Fifteen of these interviews were eventually completed. Ten other staff people were identified as "key informants" and were also interviewed. By a similar random procedure, twenty-eight names were selected from the boards of trustees of the Foreign and Home Mission boards, the seminaries, the Christian Life Commission, and the Public Affairs Committee, as well as from the Executive Committee, the Calendar Committee, and the Committee on Boards. Three of those we originally contacted refused, and four could not be reached. Those names were replaced, and twenty-four of these board members were interviewed. In addition, six members of the Peace Committee were interviewed, making a grand total of 104 formal interviews.

These interviews covered the religious and social backgrounds of the persons involved, their career histories, and, for activists, the stories of how they became involved in Convention affairs and what they had done to win support for their cause. We asked them what they valued most about being a Baptist and what they were willing to fight for. We asked staff people and board members how the controversy had affected their work and what they envisioned for the future. Staff people especially were asked what they thought would change and if there was anything over which they would leave. We asked everyone about their connections with organizations and causes outside the denomination, as well.

Most of the interviews were conducted in person, with a tape recorder. Subjects from Atlanta or Nashville were usually interviewed in their office. Most of the rest were done at odd moments and in odd places during the annual conventions; I interviewed one fundamentalist leader on a loading dock outside the Dallas convention hall. We met several people in hotel lobbies and restaurants and a few in hallways or empty conference rooms. A few who never came to the convention and were beyond our travel budget were contacted by phone. I was assisted in the interviewing process by Deborah Finn, Art Farnsley, and Marilyn Metcalf.

Observations

Annual convention meetings in 1985–1988 formed the major focus of our observational task. During those gatherings, we concentrated on talking to people about how they felt, why they were there, and what they thought. Our observers concentrated on the way the interactions of those vast crowds were structured. We talked to the people who went to the floor microphones to speak, and we watched the rituals of reunion. We noted how the sides organized themselves and the mood of the moment. At the Dallas convention, I worked with Scott Thumma and Deborah Finn, two Emory graduate students. In Atlanta, I worked with a large group of students who chose this as an opportunity to hone their research skills. Included were Scott and Deborah, Art Farnsley, Gary Hauk, James Thobaben, Fred Glennon, Les Weber, Melissa Sexton, and Laurel Kearns. I was accompanied to St. Louis by Marilyn Metcalf, who was beginning research on Southern Baptist clergy women at the University of North Carolina at Chapel Hill. In 1988, I went to San Antonio by myself, and Art Farnsley attended the 1989 Las Vegas meeting (portions of which I watched via satelite in Atlanta).

In addition to direct observations, we had access to audio tapes and manuscripts of all major addresses and to videotapes of the denomination's official gavel-to-gavel coverage for its BTN satellite network. Detailed notes on the official proceedings of the meetings were accumulated through examination of those videotapes, which are housed at the Historical Commission library in Nashville. Tapes from all four years were reviewed in full. In addition to noting the content of various reports and speeches, all debate was analyzed in detail. I recorded who spoke, about what, from what auditorium location, and with what response.

We also observed as many of the preconvention activities as time and bodies would allow. In 1986, our coverage of the whole array of specialty meetings was quite thorough. In other years, observations were generally limited to the Pastors Conference, the Forum, the Women in Ministry conference, and limited portions of the Womans Missionary Union meeting. Audio tapes from the Pastors Conference and the Forum were purchased from the Radio and Television Commission, and transcripts added to the project files.

Other meetings observed included local church services and reporting sessions before and after the 1985 and 1986 conventions. We were also able to observe a few of the meetings of Concerned Southern Baptists, the moderate group in Georgia, and attend a RealEvangelism conference, at which many of the fundamentalist leaders spoke. Eight meetings of the Home Mission Board Directors were covered by one or more observers, as were three key meetings of the SBC Executive Committee. Finally, three national and two local meetings of the Southern Baptist Alliance were included among the events we recorded for our files.

Written Sources

Three publications were covered with some regularity, noting especially the issues they were covering and their efforts to mobilize messengers. This was not, however, a formal content analysis. The publications surveyed were *SBC Today*, the Southern Baptist *Advocate*, and the Southern Baptist *Journal*. In addition, I accumulated a large collection of miscellaneous state Baptist papers, alumni newsletters from the seminaries, and various Baptist magazines.

Preceding the 1986 convention, we asked a random sample of churches to send us their church newsletters. About thirty did, and they were read and analyzed for the ways in which they reported on convention events.

Our most carefully analyzed written sources were the daily releases from *Baptist Press*. All releases from September 1984, through May 1987, were coded as to their primary subject matter. Those bearing on the controversy were then added to our files. Releases dated from January through June in 1988 and 1989 were also coded and filed.

Data Analysis

Written sources, notes from observations, along with interview and sermon transcripts (all in multiple copies) were analyzed for subject content, marked for source, and filed. Art Farnsley handled most of this preliminary qualitative analysis. I then analyzed the material from each subject folder for common themes and key events.

Survey data from a merged file containing all four surveys were analyzed using SPSS-X. Details on the various procedures are contained in text and notes.

Appendix B.
Scale Construction and Equations

Various items from the questionnaires were combined to yield composite scales measuring underlying common predispositions or attitudes. For most items there were five alternative responses, varying from "strongly agree" to "strongly disagree," with "unsure" in the middle. In all instances, scale items were scattered throughout the instrument to avoid a response set. Each set of items was tested using RELIABILITY analysis, and a standardized item alpha was derived.

Table B.1. Scale Items, Distribution, and Reliability

FUNDAMENTALIST BELIEFS

Items	Scoring
The scriptures are the inerrant Word of God, accurate in every detail.	Strongly agree = 5
God recorded in the Bible everything He wants us to know.	Strongly agree = 5
The Genesis creation stories are there more to tell us about God's involvement than to give us a precise "how and when."	Strongly disagree = 5
The Bible clearly teaches a premillennial view of history and the future.	Strongly agree = 5
It is important that Christians avoid worldly practices such as drinking and dancing.	Strongly agree = 5

Distribution

Range	Percent
5–10	5
11–15	14
16–20	47
21–25	34

Alpha = .71

Table B.1. (*Continued*)

OPPOSITION TO MODERNITY

Items	Scoring
I like living in a community with lots of different kinds of people.	Very untrue = 5
Public schools are needed to teach children to get along with lots of different kinds of people.	Strongly disagree = 5
I sometimes learn about God from friends in other faiths.	Very untrue = 5
One of the most important things children can learn is how to deal creatively with change.	Strongly disagree = 5
Children today need to be exposed to a variety of educational and cultural offerings so they can make informed choices.	Strongly disagree = 5

Distribution

Range	Percent
5–9	29
10–14	52
15–19	17
20–25	2

Alpha = .53

SUPPORT FOR THE FUNDAMENTALIST AGENDA

Items	Scoring
How confident are you that the staffs of SBC boards and agencies are doctrinally sound?	Not at all confident = 4
How confident are you that the staffs of SBC boards and agencies are responsive to ordinary Baptists?	Not at all confident = 4
Would you support measures being taken against convention agencies and schools that support the ordination of women?	No = 0 Yes = 2
Would you support a move in your association to disfellowship churches that ordain women?	No = 0 Yes = 2
If the SBC cannot be brought back to biblical soundness, our church should consider leaving.	Strongly agree = 5

Distribution

Range	Percent
3–5	29
6–8	33
9–11	19
12–17	19

Alpha = .76

Table B.1. (*Continued*)

DENOMINATIONAL ACTIVISM		
Items	Clergy Scoring	Laity Scoring
Number of state-level meetings attended.	none = 0 1–2 = 1 3+ = 2	none = 0 1 = 1 2+ = 2
How often have you personally attended the Southern Baptist Convention?	never = 0 1–5 times = 1 6+ times = 2	same
How many messengers did your church send to Pittsburg? to Kansas City? (sum the two scores)	none = 0 1–2 = 1 3+ = 2	same
What percentage of its undesignated funds does your church give to the Cooperative Program?	none = 0 <5% = 1 5–10% = 2 >10% = 3	same
Do you (or your church) receive Missions USA? The Commission?	yes = 1 yes = 1	same

Distribution

Range	% Clergy	% Laity
0–2	3	21
3–5	21	48
6–8	41	23
9–13	35	8

Alpha = .70

Equations

The predictors of support for the fundamentalist agenda discussed in chapter 5 were tested using an Analysis of Variance model (ANOVA) deriving betas from Multiple Classification Analysis. Several variables that had significant bivariate relationships with the dependent variables were tested in preliminary equations but eliminated from the final model because they did not have significant direct effects in any of the multivariate equations. Those eliminated included denominational activism, parent's occupational category, husband's occupational category, and in the clergy equation, income and church size and location. Because region does have effects in some equations, it was tested in each of the equations shown in table B.2. However, it too is eliminated in equations where an initial test showed no evidence of effects. Categories used in the equations were the categories shown in the bivariate tables in chapter 5.

Table B.2. Predictors of Denominational Discontent among Clergy and Laity

Predictor	Fundamen-talist Beliefs	Opposition to Modernity	Fundamen-talist Identity	Denomina-tional Discontent
Region	.18	.21	xxx	xxx
Education (Type)	.48	.31	.27	.16
Urban Experience	.19	.14	.15	n.s.
Fundamentalist Beliefs	xxx	xxx	.19	.57
Opposition to Modernity	xxx	xxx	.19	n.s.
Fundamentalist Identity	xxx	xxx	xxx	.14
R^2	.37	.20	.23	.61
		AMONG LAITY		
Region	xxx	.20	xxx	xxx
Education	.21	.27	n.s.	n.s.
Income	.14	.11	n.s.	.15
Urban Experience	n.s.	.15	n.s.	n.s.
Fundamentalist Beliefs	xxx	xxx	.20	.30
Opposition to Modernity	xxx	xxx	n.s.	.15
Fundamentalist Identity	xxx	xxx	xxx	.22
R^2	.10	.14	.07	.26

NOTE: Effects shown are betas derived from Multiple Classification Analysis. xxx = variables not in the equation. n.s. = effect of less than .10.

Appendix C. The Questionnaires

A STUDY OF THE SOUTHERN BAPTIST CONVENTION
1985

Center for Religious Research
Candler School of Theology
Emory University

Part 1: Convention Activities and Issues

Did you watch any part of the Dallas convention on BTN?

_____ yes   _____ no

How often have you personally attended the Southern Baptist Convention?

(0) _____ never   (2) _____ 6-10 times
(1) _____ 1-5 times   (3) _____ more than 10 times

In what year did you first attend an SBC annual meeting? _____

How many messengers has your church sent to recent Southern Baptist Conventions?

_____ Pittsburgh (1983)   _____ Kansas City (1984)   _____ Dallas (1985)?

About how many people do you talk to fairly regularly about convention affairs?

(0) _____ no one
(1) _____ 1-5
(2) _____ 6-20
(3) _____ more than 20

In the last twelve months, how many meetings have you attended

_____ (#) in your association?
_____ (#) in your state convention?
_____ (#) that were convention-wide?

Did you attend any meetings in the last year where any of these people spoke? (check all that apply)

_____ Paul Pressler   _____ Roy Honeycutt   _____ Jimmy Draper
_____ Paige Patterson   _____ Russell Dilday   _____ Adrian Rogers
_____ Cecil Sherman   _____ Randall Lolley   _____ Bailey Smith
_____ other conservatives _____
_____ other moderates _____

I get news about the Southern Baptist Convention from (check all that apply)

_____ my state Baptist paper
_____ SBC Today
_____ The Southern Baptist Advocate
_____ The Southern Baptist Journal
_____ word of mouth
_____ none of the above

The single most important criterion for choosing SBC leaders today is (check one)

(1) _____ their concern for the biblical soundness of our schools and agencies.
(2) _____ their loyalty to and support of the Cooperative Program.
(3) _____ their neutrality in the present conflict.

How confident are you that the staffs of SBC boards and agencies are doctrinally sound and responsive to the desires of ordinary Southern Baptists?

Doctrinally Sound	Responsive	
(1) ___	___	very confident
(2) ___	___	somewhat confident
(3) ___	___	not very confident
(4) ___	___	not at all confident

People have responded to the conflict in the convention in a number of ways. For each of these activities, indicate whether you have been involved for more than a year, for a year or less, or never.

	Yes, for over a year (2)	Yes, in the last year (1)	No, Never (0)
Made special efforts to attend the annual convention meeting	___	___	___
Encouraged people who agree with me to attend the annual convention	___	___	___
Tried to convince someone to change his/her mind about an issue	___	___	___
Attended a meeting of people concerned about the convention	___	___	___
Donated money to a group concerned with convention issues	___	___	___
Served as an officer in a group concerned with convention issues	___	___	___
Prayed for the convention and its leaders	___	___	___

If you have participated in a group that is concerned about the Southern Baptist Convention's future, please tell us the name of that group. _____

Next, we would like to know where you stand on some of the controversial resolutions that have come before the SBC in recent years.**

Do you believe abortion should be prohibited
(1) _____ in all cases?
(2) _____ except to save the life of the mother?
(3) _____ except in cases of rape, incest, or to save the life of the mother?
(4) _____ rarely, if at all? It is a matter of individual moral choice.

Do you support a constitutional amendment to outlaw abortion?
_____ yes   _____ no

Do you think Southern Baptist churches should be active in opposing abortion?
_____ yes   _____ no

Do you believe that women
(1) _____ should never be ordained?
(2) _____ may be ordained as deacons, but not as pastors?
(3) _____ may be ordained as pastors or deacons?

Would you support a move in your association to "dis-fellowship" churches that do ordain women?
_____ yes   _____ no

Would you support measures being taken against convention agencies and schools that promote women's ordination?
_____ yes   _____ no

In the final part of this section, we have some questions about you and your church.

Which best describes the location of your present church?

(1) _____ village or open country
(2) _____ small town (not in an urban area)
(3) _____ small city (not in an urban area)
(4) _____ new suburban area
(5) _____ old suburban area
(6) _____ central city

What is the resident membership of your church?

(1) _____ 1-99
(2) _____ 100-299
(3) _____ 300-499
(4) _____ 500-999
(5) _____ 1000+

What percentage of its undesignated funds does your church give to the Cooperative Program?

(0) _____ none
(1) _____ less than 5%
(2) _____ 5-10%
(3) _____ 11-25%
(4) _____ more than 25%

How would you describe the missions education and Church Training programs in your church?

Missions Education	Church Training	
(1) ___	___	very weak
(2) ___	___	weak
(3) ___	___	strong
(4) ___	___	very strong

Admittedly, categories do not tell everything, but most of us think of ourselves more in some terms than in others. When you think about your theological position, which word best describes where you stand?

(1) ___ Fundamentalist   (2) ___ Conservative   (3) ___ Moderate   (4) ___ Liberal

What translation of the Bible do you like best? (check one)

(1) ___ King James	(4) ___ New American Standard
(2) ___ New English	(5) ___ New International
(3) ___ Revised Standard	(6) ___ other ___

Which of these publications do you (or your church) receive? (check all that apply)
___ Sunday School quarterlies published by the Baptist Sunday School Board
___ Royal Service
___ Missions USA
___ The Commission
___ The Baptist Program

Which of these TV programs do you watch regularly (at least 2-3 times per month)? (check all that apply)
___ The 700 Club   ___ The PTL Club
___ James Kennedy   ___ Charles Stanley
___ Jerry Falwell   ___ Jimmy Swaggert

Part 2: Your Ideas and Everyday Life

To better understand who Southern Baptists are, we have some questions about your everyday life. In this section, decide whether or not each statement describes you and your situation. Is it true for you? Check whether each is very true, somewhat true, somewhat untrue, or very untrue. If you are not sure or undecided, check the "unsure" column.

	Very True (1)	Somewhat True (2)	Unsure (3)	Somewhat Untrue (4)	Very Untrue (5)
Things are changing so fast that what worked yesterday is likely to be obsolete tomorrow.	—	—	—	—	—
I often have to deal with people that I do not know very well.	—	—	—	—	—
I try to share the plan of salvation with others whenever I get a chance.	—	—	—	—	—
I support passage of the ERA to guarantee equal rights for women.	—	—	—	—	—
I would like to see my church consider aligning with both the SBC and the American Baptists.	—	—	—	—	—
I don't like to think about some of the frightening uses of recent technology.	—	—	—	—	—
[C] I enjoy working with people from other denominations.	—	—	—	—	—
[L] When I am at work, I rarely think about religious beliefs.	—	—	—	—	—
I like the idea of having a Christian Yellow Pages.	—	—	—	—	—

I rarely talk to my family about my work.

I like living in a community with lots of different kinds of people.

If my members [our pastor] suggested that our church leave the SBC, I would support them [him].

[L] I rarely talk to people at church about my work.

God hears and specifically answers all my prayers.

I can hardly imagine myself as anything but a Southern Baptist.

I sometimes learn about God from friends in other faiths.

My church puts a lot of emphasis on members being loyal patriotic citizens.

My church puts a lot of emphasis on evangelism and soul-winning.

My church puts a lot of emphasis on providing care for the needy.

My church puts a lot of emphasis on organizing to promote social change.

Part 3: Your Opinions

In this section there are statements of opinion on a variety of issues. There are no "preferred" answers. We just want to know what you think. For each one, please indicate whether you Strongly Agree, Agree, Disagree, or Strongly Disagree. If you really don't know how to respond, check the "unsure" column. If you don't care, check "neutral."

FIRST, we want to know some of your opinions on education, politics, and everyday life.

	Strongly Agree (1)	Agree (2)	Unsure (3)	Disagree (4)	Strongly Disagree (5)	Neutral (0)
National and international news is rarely as interesting as what happens in the local community.						
Husbands have the God-given responsibility to lead their households.						
Some of the problems in today's world are just too complex to think about.						
It is important that Christians avoid worldly practices such as drinking and dancing.						
Public schools are needed to teach children to get along with lots of different kinds of people.						
It is important to return this country to the Christian principles on which it was founded.						

One of the most important things children can learn is how to deal creatively with change.

When it comes to sexual morality, some things are simply right or wrong, not matters of individual "preference."

Children today need to be exposed to a variety of educational and cultural offerings so they can make informed choices.

It is good that groups like the Moral Majority are taking a stand for Christian principles.

It seems like there's an expert for everything these days.

In a complex society, public schools cannot be expected to teach values.

The bloated defense budget is one of the biggest problems facing this country.

Even if homosexuality were wrong, the civil rights of gays should still be protected.

America must protect weak nations from communism so we can continue to spread the gospel.

NEXT, we want to know your opinions on some religious beliefs and issues.

	Strongly Agree (1)	Agree (2)	Unsure (3)	Disagree (4)	Strongly Disagree (5)	Neutral (0)
God hears the prayers of all people.	___	___	___	___	___	___
God recorded in the Bible everything He wants us to know.	___	___	___	___	___	___
The Bible clearly teaches a "pre-millennial" view of history and the future.	___	___	___	___	___	___
Pastors should have the final authority in the local church.	___	___	___	___	___	___
If the SBC cannot be brought back to biblical soundness, our church should consider leaving the convention.	___	___	___	___	___	___
The Southern Baptist Convention is like a family--people shouldn't even think about leaving.	___	___	___	___	___	___
The Genesis creation stories are there more to tell us about God's involvement than to give us a precise "how and when."	___	___	___	___	___	___
The scriptures are the inerrant Word of God, accurate in every detail.	___	___	___	___	___	___

It is not fair for fundamentalists in the SBC
to appoint only other fundamentalists to agency
and seminary boards.   ___   ___   ___   ___   ___

Homosexuality can be a viable Christian alternative.   ___   ___   ___   ___   ___

No matter what the dilemma, God can reveal the
right answer.   ___   ___   ___   ___   ___

Belief in the separation of church and state is an
important Baptist distinctive.   ___   ___   ___   ___   ___

Part 4: Basic Background Information

Age: _____   Sex: Male (1) _____   Female (2) _____

Which of the following best describes the community in which you spent most of your childhood? Which best describes
where you live now?

Childhood   Now

(1)   _____   _____   farm or rural area
(2)   _____   _____   small town (not within an urban area)
(3)   _____   _____   small city (not within an urban area)
(4)   _____   _____   suburbs of a big city
(5)   _____   _____   big city

What is your ethnic background?

(1) ___ black
(2) ___ white
(3) ___ oriental
(4) ___ other _____

Did you now, or did you when you were growing up, speak a language other than English in your home?

___ yes   ___ no

Where did you spend most of your childhood? Where do you now reside?

Childhood   Now

(1) ___   ___   Northeast (ME, NH, VT, MA, CT, RI, NY, PA, NJ)
(2) ___   ___   South (MD, DE, WV, VA, NC, SC, GA, FL, KY, TN, MS, AL, TX, OK, AR, LA)
(3) ___   ___   Midwest (OH, MI, IN, IL, WI, MO, IA, MN, ND, SD, NB, KS)
(4) ___   ___   West (MT, ID, WY, CO, UT, NE, NM, AZ, CA, OR, WA, AK, HA)
(5) ___   ___   Outside the US (specify) _____

Between your childhood and now, have you lived in any additional regions?

___ no   ___ yes (specify) _____

About how much was your total household income last year?

(1) ___ less than $10,000
(2) ___ $10,000 - $19,999
(3) ___ $20,000 - $34,999
(4) ___ $35,000 - $49,999
(5) ___ $50,000 or more

How many wage-earners were there in your household last year?

_____ # full-time

_____ # part-time

How would you describe your family's situation during <u>most</u> of your childhood?

(1) _____ genuinely poor

(2) _____ got by on a shoestring

(3) _____ comfortable, but few luxuries

(4) _____ well off

(5) _____ genuinely rich

Which best describes the school your children attend?

(1) _____ no children in school

(2) _____ public school

(3) _____ private Christian Academy

(4) _____ parochial (Lutheran, Catholic, etc.)

(5) _____ private, non-church-related

Generally, how do you describe your political leanings? How might your parents have answered while you were growing up?

You   Parents

(1) _____ _____ Conservative Republican

(2) _____ _____ Moderate or Liberal Republican

(3) _____ _____ Independent, closer to Republican

(4) _____ _____ Independent, closer to neither

(5) _____ _____ Independent, closer to Democrat

(6) _____ _____ Conservative Democrat

(7) _____ _____ Moderate or Liberal Democrat

(8) _____ _____ Other _____

Now some questions about the kind of work you and your family do. First during most of the time when you were growing up, what kind of job did the principal wage-earner in your home have? Second, what kind of job do you nw have? And third, if you are married, what kind of job does your spouse have? NOTE: If you are retired, check the kind of job you last held.

	Parent's Occupation	My Occupation	Spouse's Occupation
			clergy
			homemaking
			farming
			clerical (secretary, bank teller, keypunch operator, etc.)
			technical (medical technician, electronics specialist, programmer)
			managerial (manager, executive, owner)
			professional (doctor, lawyer, professor, consultant, etc.)
			service professions (social work, nursing, teaching, etc.)
			sales (retail clerk, travelling salesperson, etc.)
			other service work (police officer, cook, waiter, janitor, orderly, etc.)
			skilled trades (mechanic, repairer, construction worker, welder, etc.)
			factory work (assembler, inspector, etc.)
			general labor (freight handler, miner, service station attendant, etc.)
			transportation (truck driver, heavy equipment operator, etc.)
			other _____

(01)
(02)
(03)
(04)
(05)
(06)
(07)
(08)
(09)
(10)
(11)
(12)
(13)
(14)
(15)

What is the highest level of education you have completed?

(1) _____ less than 12 years
(2) _____ high school diploma
(3) _____ 1-3 years of college
(4) _____ Bachelors degree
(5) _____ Masters degree
(6) _____ Doctoral degree

If you have attended college, where did you go?

(1) _____ an independent Bible college
(2) _____ a Southern Baptist liberal arts college or university
(3) _____ a non-Southern Baptist, but church-affiliated college or university
(4) _____ a secular college or university

[C] If you attended seminary, which one did you attend?

(1) _____ Southern   (4) _____ Southeastern
(2) _____ New Orleans   (5) _____ Midwestern
(3) _____ Southwestern   (6) _____ Golden Gate
(7) _____ Other (specify) _____

[C] Have you completed training in Clinical Pastoral Education?

(1) _____ no
(2) _____ yes, one unit (quarter)
(3) _____ yes, more than one unit

FINALLY, how do you feel about the future of the convention?

(1) _____ Excited. Bible believers are continuing the process of regaining our rightful place at the helm of this great denomination.

(2) _____ Hopeful. There are many signs of reconciliation between fundamentalists and moderates who have been fighting each other.

(3) _____ Hopeful, but sad. Dr. Stanley is leading us in the right direction, but we are deeply divided.

(4) _____ Sad, but hopeful. Perhaps next year in Atlanta the moderates can stop the fundamentalist takeover.

(5) _____ Grieving. The convention has been taken over, and moderates must now consider other options.

The Dallas Convention

This section is for those who attended the Southern Baptist Convention meeting in Dallas this summer. If you did not attend the convention, skip directly to the next section.

What was your most important purpose in attending?
(1) _____ to support Charles Stanley and the conservatives
(2) _____ to support Winfred Moore and the moderates
(3) _____ to hear the mission reports and sermons
(4) _____ to see old friends
(5) _____ other_____

Who or what most influenced you in deciding to attend?
(1) _____ my congregation
(2) _____ a friend
(3) _____ a speaker
(4) _____ reading about the issues
(5) _____ other_____

Did you vote for the presidential candidate for whom you originally planned to vote?
_____ yes _____ no

If not, what made you change your mind?_____

On Wednesday, the parliamentarians ruled that nominations for agency and seminary boards of trustees cannot be submitted from the floor. Others claimed that the By-laws allow all committee reports to be amended from the floor, but the parliamentarians did not agree. How do you feel about their ruling?

(1) _____ They are the experts and should be respected.
(2) _____ They probably made a mistake, but that is understandable.
(3) _____ They were used by Dr. Stanley and his friends to prevent legitimate debate.

In the Committee on Boards debate and at several other times, Dr. Stanley refused to recognize "points of order" and other requests from the floor. How do you feel about his presiding during business sessions?

(1) _____ Such a large group demands a strong president. He only did what he had to do.
(2) _____ He shouldn't have to listen to unruly protestors. Ignoring them is only right.
(3) _____ He sometimes lacked skill. When he mishandled debate, it was out of ignorance.
(4) _____ He and his friends do not want to open debate and did everything possible to prevent it.

Some of the issues that come before the convention are hard to understand. If you found yourself unsure of how to vote, was there someone to whom you could turn for advice?

(1) _____ no, no one.
(2) _____ yes, others from my church
(3) _____ yes, people on the floor that I recognized as supporters of Dr. Stanley
(4) _____ yes, people on the floor that I recognized as moderates
(5) _____ other _____

A STUDY OF THE SOUTHERN BAPTIST CONVENTION

1986

Center for Religious Research
Candler School of Theology
Emory University

Part 1: Convention Activities and Issues

From what sources do you get news about the Southern Baptist Convention? (check all that apply)

_____ your state Baptist paper
_____ SBC Today
_____ The Southern Baptist Advocate
_____ The Southern Baptist Journal
_____ word of mouth
_____ none of the above

About how many people do you talk to fairly regularly about convention affairs?

(0) _____ no one
(1) _____ 1-5
(2) _____ 6-20
(3) _____ more than 20

In the last twelve months, how many meetings have you attended

_____ (#) in your association?
_____ (#) in your state convention?
_____ (#) that were convention-wide?

Did you attend any meetings in the last year where any of these people spoke? (check all that apply)

_____ Paul Pressler   _____ Roy Honeycutt   _____ Jimmy Draper   _____ Lee Roberts
_____ Paige Patterson   _____ Russell Dilday   _____ Adrian Rogers   _____ Jerry Vines
_____ Russell Kaemmerling _____ Randall Lolley   _____ Bailey Smith   _____ Winfred Moore
_____ other conservatives_____
_____ other moderates_____

What do you think is at the heart of the controversy in the SBC?

(1) _____ differences in theology
(2) _____ a struggle for control
(3) _____ both
(4) _____ other (please specify)_____
(5) _____ don't know

People have responded to the conflict in the convention in a number of ways. For each of these activities, indicate whether you have been involved for more than a year, for a year or less, or never.

	Yes, for over a year (2)	Yes, in the last year (1)	No, Never (0)
Made special efforts to attend the annual convention meeting	‖	‖	‖
Encouraged people who agree with me to attend the annual convention	‖	‖	‖
Tried to convince someone to change his/her mind about an issue	‖	‖	‖
Attended a meeting of people concerned about the convention	‖	‖	‖
Actively participated in a group concerned about the convention	‖	‖	‖
Donated money to a group concerned with convention issues	‖	‖	‖
Served as an officer in a group concerned with convention issues	‖	‖	‖

Has the controversy in the SBC affected your local church in any way? ___ yes ___ no
If so, please explain. _____

If a qualified ordained woman were recommended for a staff position in your church, would you support calling her?
___ yes ___ no

Do you favor continuing SBC support of the Baptist Joint Committee on Public Affairs?
___ yes ___ no ___ don't know

Part 2: A Few Background Questions

YOUR AGE: _____ Sex: Male (1) _____ Female (2) _____ In what state do you now reside? _____

What is the highest level of education you have completed?
(1) _____ less than 12 years
(2) _____ high school diploma
(3) _____ 1-3 years of college
(4) _____ Bachelors degree
(5) _____ Masters degree
(6) _____ Doctoral degree

About how much was your total household income in 1985? in 1984?
1984 1985
(1) _____ less than $10,000
(2) _____ $10,000 - $19,999
(3) _____ $20,000 - $34,999
(4) _____ $35,000 - $49,999
(5) _____ $50,000 or more

Which best describes the location of your church?

(1) _____ village or open country
(2) _____ small town
(3) _____ small city
(4) _____ older suburban area
(5) _____ new suburban area
(6) _____ downtown in a large city

In what year did you first attend a meeting of the Southern Baptist Convention? _____

If you attended seminary, which one did you attend?

(0) _____ did not attend
(1) _____ Southern   (4) _____ Southeastern
(2) _____ New Orleans   (5) _____ Midwestern
(3) _____ Southwestern   (6) _____ Golden Gate
(7) _____ Other (please specify) _____

If you graduated from seminary, in what year did you receive your degree? _____

At what age did you accept Jesus as your savior? _____
At what age did you join a Southern Baptist Church? _____

Have you moved to a new residence since you completed our 1985 questionnaire?   _____ yes   _____ no

Part 3: Your Opinions

In this section there are statements of opinion on a variety of issues. There are no "preferred" answers. We just want to know what you think. For each one, please indicate whether you Strongly Agree, Agree, Disagree, or Strongly Disagree. If you really don't know how to respond, check the "unsure" column.

	Strongly Agree (1)	Agree (2)	Unsure (3)	Disagree (4)	Strongly Disagree (5)
Baptists should have the individual freedom to interpret the Bible for themselves and be tolerant of differing interpretations.	—	—	—	—	—
My church should consider aligning with both the SBC and the American Baptists.	—	—	—	—	—
If someone suggested that our church leave the SBC, I would support them.	—	—	—	—	—
Pastors should have the final authority in the local church.	—	—	—	—	—
If the SBC cannot be brought back to biblical soundness, our church should consider leaving the convention.	—	—	—	—	—
The scriptures are the inerrant Word of God, accurate in every detail.	—	—	—	—	—
It is important that Christians avoid worldly practices such as drinking and dancing.	—	—	—	—	—

God recorded in the Bible everything He wants us to know.

| | | | | | | | | |

The Bible clearly teaches a "pre-millennial" view of history and the future.

| | | | | | | | | |

This dispensation will end with the "Rapture", when Jesus will take believers out of this world to heaven.

| | | | | | | | | |

The Genesis creation stories are there more to tell us about God's involvement than to give us a precise "how and when".

| | | | | | | | | |

It is not fair for fundamentalists in the SBC to appoint only other fundamentalists to agency and seminary boards.

| | | | | | | | | |

If we can agree on what we want to <u>do</u> together, we do not need to worry about agreeing on what we believe.

| | | | | | | | | |

If fundamentalists take over SBC agencies, our church should consider cutting its Cooperative Program giving.

| | | | | | | | | |

If fundamentalists take over SBC agencies, my church should consider supporting alternative agencies.

| | | | | | | | | |

There are people teaching in Baptist colleges and seminaries who do not believe what Baptists ought to believe.

| | | | | | | | | |

FINALLY, how do you feel about the future of the convention?

(1) _____ Excited. Bible believers are continuing the process of regaining our rightful place at the helm of this great denomination.

(2) _____ Hopeful. There are many signs of reconciliation between fundamentalists and moderates who have been fighting each other.

(3) _____ Hopeful, but sad. Dr. Stanley has lead us in the right direction, but we are deeply divided.

(4) _____ Sad, but hopeful. Perhaps next year in St. Louis the moderates can stop the fundamentalist takeover.

(5) _____ Grieving. The convention has been taken over, and moderates must now consider other options.

Part 4: The Atlanta Convention

From what sources have you heard news of the Atlanta convention? (check all that apply)

_____ None.
_____ A report at church.
_____ Watching the sessions on BTN.
_____ I attended the convention myself.
_____ From other sources (please specify) _____

_____ A sermon from your pastor.
_____ Your state Baptist paper.
_____ Your daily newspaper.
_____

How many messengers did your church send to Atlanta? _____

Did your church provide financial support for its messengers?

(0) _____ No, none.
(1) _____ Yes, partial support, staff only
(2) _____ Yes, full support, staff only
(3) _____ Yes, partial support for lay messengers, too
(4) _____ Yes, full support for all messengers

People decide who they favor for president of the SBC on a variety of grounds. Which of this year's candidates would you rate highest on these grounds:--

Theological soundness
(1) ____ Moore higher
(2) ____ Rogers higher
(3) ____ both the same
(4) ____ don't know

Ability to lead the SBC in the right direction
(1) ____ Moore higher
(2) ____ Rogers higher
(3) ____ both the same
(4) ____ don't know

Christian character
____ Moore higher
____ Rogers higher
____ both the same
____ don't know

Persuasiveness of the nominating speech
____ Richard Jackson's speech for Moore higher
____ Nelson Price's speech for Rogers higher
____ both the same
____ don't know

What (or who) was most important in influencing your decision about who you favored? _____

Have you every heard Dr. Moore or Dr. Rogers speak? (check all that apply)
____ yes, Moore in person
____ yes, Rogers in person
____ yes, Moore on TV, radio, or tape
____ yes, Rogers on TV, radio, or tape
____ no, never heard either

ANSWER THE QUESTIONS ON THIS PAGE ONLY
IF YOU WENT TO THE ATLANTA CONVENTION

What was your <u>most</u> important purpose in attending the convention?

(1) ____ to support Adrian Rogers and the conservatives.

(2) ____ to support Winfred Moore and the moderates.

(3) ____ to hear the mission reports and sermons.

(4) ____ to see old friends.

(5) ____ It's my obligation to go whenever I can.

(6) ____ other _____

Did you combine vacation time with your trip to Atlanta?

____ yes ____ no

Some of the issues that come before the convention are hard to understand. If you found yourself unsure of how to vote, was there someone to whom you looked for advice?

(0) ____ no, no one

(1) ____ yes, others from my church

(2) ____ yes, people I recognized as supporters of Dr. Stanley

(3) ____ yes, people I recognized as supporters of the moderates

(4) ____ other _____

How would you rate Dr. Stanley's presiding over this year's convention?

(1) ____ He did an excellent job of handling such a large group.

(2) ____ He sometimes lacked skill in parliamentary procedure.

(3) ____ He again did everything possible to prevent open debate.

Do you think the parliamentarian and the new microphone system
(0)____ made no difference?
(1)____ helped a little?
(2)____ helped a lot?

When substitute nominations (such as for agency trustees) were made from the floor, how did you usually vote?
(1)____ for the substitute   (0)____ against the substitute

What was your main reason for voting that way? _____

What was the best thing that happened at this year's convention? _____

What was the worst thing that happened at this year's convention? _____

Which activities did you attend in Atlanta? (check all that apply)

____ Pastors Conference   ____ Tuesday morning   ____ Thursday morning
____ WMU convention   ____ Tuesday afternoon   ____ Thursday afternoon
____ Women in Ministry   ____ Tuesday evening   ____ seminary luncheon
____ SBC Forum   ____ Wednesday morning   ____ Evangelists conference
____ other pre-convention meeting ____ Wednesday evening   ____ other related meetings

A STUDY OF THE SOUTHERN BAPTIST CONVENTION
1987
Center for Religious Research
Candler School of Theology
Emory University

Part 1: Convention Activities and Issues

1. From what sources do you get news about the Southern Baptist Convention? (check all that apply)

   ___ BTN news program
   ___ your state Baptist paper
   ___ SBC Today
   ___ The Southern Baptist Advocate
   ___ The Southern Baptist Journal
   ___ word of mouth
   ___ daily newspapers

2. In the last twelve months, how many regular denominational meetings have you attended

   ___ (#) in your association?
   ___ (#) in your state convention?
   ___ (#) that were convention-wide?

3. Did you attend any meetings in the last year (besides the SBC) where any of these people spoke?
   (check all that apply)

___ Paul Pressler	___ Roy Honeycutt	___ Jimmy Draper	___ Norman Cavender
___ Paige Patterson	___ James Slatton	___ Adrian Rogers	___ Jerry Vines
___ Charles Stanley	___ Joel Gregory	___ Bailey Smith	___ Winfred Moore
___ other conservatives (please specify) _____			
___ other moderates (please specify) _____			

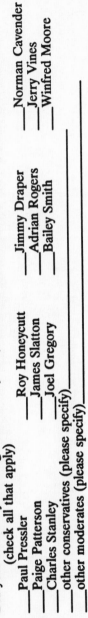

4. People have responded to the conflict in the convention in a number of ways. For each of these activities, indicate whether you have been involved <u>during the last year.</u>

	Yes, this year (1)	No, not this year (0)
Made special efforts to attend the annual convention meeting	___	___
Encouraged people who agree with me to attend the annual convention	___	___
Tried to convince someone to change his/her mind about an issue	___	___
Attended a meeting of people concerned about the convention	___	___
Actively participated in a group concerned about the convention	___	___
Donated money to a group concerned with convention issues	___	___
Served as an officer in a group concerned with convention issues	___	___

5. The controversy in the SBC has affected some local churches in a variety of ways. In which of the following ways has your church been affected? (check all that apply)

___ not affected at all
___ informal discussion of the issues
___ special meetings to discuss the issues
___ more interest in the convention among members
___ more messengers have been sent to conventions
___ division among members over the issues
___ division between members and pastor over the issues
___ less willingness to support the Cooperative Program and mission offerings
___ more willingness to support the Cooperative Program and mission offerings
___ loss of members who disagree on SBC issues

6. Now that conservatives have gained control of most SBC agency boards, what effects do you anticipate in your local church? _____

7. When you think about what makes a Christian's life different from a non-believer's, which of these practices do you think should <u>not</u> be a part of the Christian's life? (check all that apply)

___ drinking alcoholic beverages   ___ social dancing
___ card playing   ___ going to movies (not G-rated)
___ swearing   ___ smoking

Are there any of these practices for which you think a person should be expelled from church membership? If so, which one(s)? _____

8. Does your church support the ordination of women as deacons? ___ yes ___ no
Are women currently serving in your church as deacons? ___ yes ___ no

9. Does your church support the ordination of women as ministers? ___ yes ___ no
Has your church ever ordained a woman to the ministry? ___ yes ___ no

10. Do you think women's ordination is a major issue in the SBC? ___ yes ___ no

Part 2: A Few Background Questions

YOUR AGE: _____ YOUR SEX: Male (1) _____ Female (2) _____ In what state do you now reside? _____

1. What is the highest level of education you have completed? _____

   (1) _____ less than 12 years   (4) _____ Bachelors degree

   (2) _____ high school diploma   (5) _____ Masters degree

   (3) _____ 1-3 years of college   (6) _____ Doctoral degree

2. Which best describes the location of your church?

   (1) _____ village or open country

   (2) _____ small town

   (3) _____ small city

   (4) _____ older suburban area

   (5) _____ new suburban area

   (6) _____ downtown in a large city

3. About how many baptisms will your church report for this church year? _____
   Of those baptized, about how many fell into each of these categories?

   _____ (#) children of members   _____ (#) adults from outside the church

   _____ (#) children of non-members   _____ (#) adults who had been members, but only recently truly accepted Jesus

4. In what year did you first attend a meeting of the Southern Baptist Convention? _____

5. If you attended seminary, which one did you attend?

   (0) _____ did not attend

   (1) _____ Southern   (4) _____ Southeastern

   (2) _____ New Orleans   (5) _____ Midwestern

   (3) _____ Southwestern   (6) _____ Golden Gate

   (7) _____ Luther Rice   (8) _____ Mid America

   (9) _____ Other (please specify) _____

Part 3: Your Opinions

In this section there are statements of opinion on a variety of issues. There are no "preferred" answers. We just want to know what you think. For each one, please indicate whether you Strongly Agree, Agree, Disagree, or Strongly Disagree. If you really don't know how to respond, check the "unsure" column.

	Strongly Agree (1)	Agree (2)	Unsure (3)	Disagree (4)	Strongly Disagree (5)
I enjoy attending "cultural" events, such as symphony concerts.	—	—	—	—	—
The civil rights movement helped to move this country in the right direction.	—	—	—	—	—
If fundamentalists take over SBC agencies, my church should consider supporting alternative agencies.	—	—	—	—	—
It is usually better to do things the way they have always been done.	—	—	—	—	—
If someone suggested that our church leave the SBC, I would support them.	—	—	—	—	—
Most people who are on welfare could easily work for a living, if they wanted to.	—	—	—	—	—

My church should consider aligning with both the
SBC and the American Baptists.

⎯   ⎯   ⎯

It is not fair for fundamentalists in the SBC to appoint
only other fundamentalists to agency and seminary boards.

⎯   ⎯   ⎯

If we can agree on what we want to do together, we do not
need to worry about agreeing on how to interpret the Bible.

⎯   ⎯   ⎯

If fundamentalists take over SBC agencies, our church
should consider cutting its Cooperative Program giving.

⎯   ⎯   ⎯

People on the convention payroll ought to believe
and teach what the majority of Baptists believe.

⎯   ⎯   ⎯

The best answers come from a careful search of all
available information.

⎯   ⎯   ⎯

FINALLY, how do you feel about the future of the convention?

(1) ____ Excited. Bible believers are continuing the process of regaining our rightful place at the helm of this great
denomination.
(2) ____ Hopeful. There are many signs of reconciliation between fundamentalists and moderates who have been
fighting each other.
(3) ____ Hopeful, but sad. Dr. Rogers has lead us in the right direction, but we are deeply divided.
(4) ____ Sad, but hopeful. Perhaps next year in San Antonio the moderates can stop the fundamentalist takeover.
(5) ____ Grieving. The convention has been taken over, and moderates must now consider other options.

Part 4: Dilemmas in daily living

On this page are 5 situations in which ordinary people might find themselves. For each one, imagine that you are the person involved, and think about what you might do. If none of the suggested alternatives fits, write in your own solution on the "other" line. For the first three, you may check more than one response, and in each case, we would like to know why you chose as you did.

1. You notice that someone who works in the department you head has been avoiding you and that his work has been slipping. You hear from others that he has developed a drinking problem. When you ask him about it, he claims that it is "nothing" and is all over anyway. Do you--

_____ fire him?
_____ report him to your superior?
_____ refer him to a counselor?
_____ hope it really is over and do nothing?
_____ pray for him?
_____ other _____
Why?

2. Your fifteen-year-old son has been identified as the father by a sixteen-year-old pregnant girl. He admits that it is possible that he is, but he can't be sure. Do you advise his to--

_____ marry the girl?
_____ accept financial responsibility?
_____ accept no responsibility until forced to do so?
_____ other _____
Why?

3. Because you are a deacon and a friend, the church secretary tells you that six months ago the pastor made a "loan" with church funds to a local Christian businessman, which has been repaid. Do you--

_____ do nothing--it's better to "let sleeping dogs lie"?
_____ do nothing--the pastor knew what he was doing and had the authority to do it?
_____ go to the other deacons with the information?
_____ go to the church publicly with the information?
_____ confront the pastor privately?
_____ other _____
Why?

4. You live in a family in which the wife/mother does not work. It becomes clear that the husband/father's income cannot meet all of the family's expenses. Which is the best alternative? (check only one)

_____ Cut expenses further, even if it means doing without
_____ The father should take a second job.
_____ The mother should work part-time.
_____ The mother should work full-time.
_____ other _____
Why?

5. During the "new business" portion of a church business meeting, a good friend of yours moves that the deacons question the associate pastor about an affair she believes him to be having. The pastor rules your friend out of order, insists that she sit down, and accuses her of causing trouble. How do you respond? (check only one response)

_____ The pastor did the right thing.
_____ The pastor was wrong to rule my friend out of order, but she should not have made such a motion.
_____ The pastor was wrong. My friend was not out of order, and the matter should have been discussed.
_____ other _____
Why?

Part 5: The St. Louis Convention

1. From what sources have you heard news of the St. Louis convention? (check all that apply)

   ___ None
   ___ A report at church   ___ A sermon from your pastor
   ___ Watching the sessions on BTN ___ Your state Baptist paper
   ___ I attended the convention myself ___ Your daily newspaper
   ___ From other sources (please specify) _____

2. How many messengers did your church send to St. Louis? ___

3. Did your church provide financial support for its messengers?

   (0) ___ No, none
   (1) ___ Yes, partial support, staff only
   (2) ___ Yes, full support, staff only
   (3) ___ Yes, partial support for lay messengers, too
   (4) ___ Yes, full support for all messengers

4. Have you heard anything about the Peace Committee report? ___ yes ___ no
   Do you think this report will affect what happens in the convention? ___ yes ___ no
   If yes, what effects do you think it will have? _____

5. If you could have voted, which candidate would you have supported for SBC president?

   (1) ___ Adrian Rogers
   (2) ___ Richard Jackson
   (3) ___ Other _____
   (4) ___ Don't know

6. Did you attend any part of the St. Louis convention? _____ yes _____ no

> >IF YES, proceed with the final 3 questions. IF NO, you may stop here. THANK YOU.

1. What was your **most** important purpose in attending the convention?
   (1) _____ to support the conservatives.
   (2) _____ to support the moderates.
   (3) _____ to hear the mission reports and sermons.
   (4) _____ to see old friends.
   (5) _____ It's my obligation to go whenever I can.
   (6) _____ other _____

2. Which activities did you attend in St. Louis? (check all that apply)

   _____ Pastors Conference   _____ Tuesday morning   _____ Thursday morning
   _____ WMU convention   _____ Tuesday afternoon   _____ Thursday afternoon
   _____ Women in Ministry   _____ Tuesday evening   _____ seminary luncheon
   _____ SBC Forum   _____ Wednesday morning   _____ Evangelists conference
   _____ other pre-convention meeting _____ Wednesday evening _____ other related meetings

3. Overall, how would you rate this convention?

   (1) _____ better than recent years
   (2) _____ worse than recent years
   (3) _____ about the same as recent years

   Why did it seem that way? _____

A STUDY OF THE SOUTHERN BAPTIST CONVENTION

1988

Center for Religious Research
Candler School of Theology
Emory University

1. Your age _____   Your sex _____   The State where you reside _____

2. For each of the following activities, indicate whether you have been involved <u>during the last year.</u>

	No, not this year	Yes, this year
Made special efforts to attend the annual convention meeting	___	___
Encouraged people who agree with me to attend the annual convention	___	___
Tried to convince someone to change his/her mind about an issue	___	___
Attended a meeting of people concerned about the convention	___	___
Actively participated in a group concerned about the convention	___	___
Donated money to a group concerned with convention issues	___	___
Served as an officer in a group concerned with convention issues	___	___

3. Did you attend any meetings in the last year (besides the SBC) where any of these people spoke? (check all that apply)

___ Paul Pressler	___ Randall Lolley	___ Jimmy Draper	___ John Baugh
___ Paige Patterson	___ Richard Jackson	___ Adrian Rogers	___ Jerry Vines
___ Charles Stanley	___ Joel Gregory	___ Bailey Smith	___ Winfred Moore
___ other conservatives (please specify) _____			
___ other moderates (please specify) _____			

4. The controversy in the SBC has affected local churches in a variety of ways. Which of the following are true for your church? (Check all that apply)

    ___ informal discussion of the issues
    ___ special meetings to discuss the issues
    ___ more interest in the convention among members
    ___ more messengers have been sent to conventions
    ___ division among members over the issues
    ___ division between members and pastor over the issues
    ___ loss of members who disagree on SBC issues
    ___ not affected at all

5. From what sources have you heard news of the San Antonio convention? (check all that apply)

    ___ None   ___ Your daily newspaper
    ___ A report at church   ___ A sermon from your pastor
    ___ Watching the sessions on BTN   ___ Your state Baptist paper
    ___ From other sources (please specify) _____

    _____

6. How many messengers did your church send to San Antonio? _____

7. If you could have voted, which candidate would you have supported for SBC president?

    (1) ___ Jerry Vines
    (2) ___ Richard Jackson
    (3) ___ Other _____
    (4) ___ Don't know

8. Did you attend any part of the San Antonio convention?   ___ yes   ___ no

9. Has there been any event, change in policy, or other convention action during the last few years that made you especially concerned about the future direction of the convention? If so, what was it?

10. How do you feel about the future of the convention?

(1) _____ Excited.   Bible believers are continuing the process of regaining our rightful place at the helm of this great denomination.

(2) _____ Hopeful.   There are many signs of reconciliation between fundamentalists and moderates who have been fighting each other.

(3) _____ Hopeful, but sad. Dr. Rogers has led us in the right direction, but we are deeply divided.

(4) _____ Sad, but hopeful. Perhaps next year in Las Vegas the moderates can stop the fundamentalist takeover.

(5) _____ Grieving.   The convention has been taken over, and moderates must now consider other options.

11. Thinking about your church's connections to the SBC, what changes (if any) do you anticipate in the coming 10 years? For each of the following, check whether you anticipate "MORE involvement," "LESS involvement," or "about the SAME."

	MORE	LESS	SAME
Using Sunday School Board literature	___	___	___
Using denominational programs and services	___	___	___
Supporting WMU and related missions organizations	___	___	___
Attendance at routine associational and state meetings	___	___	___
Attendance at SBC annual conventions	___	___	___
Support for the Cooperative Program	___	___	___
Support for Home Missions (including Annie Armstrong offering)	___	___	___
Support for Foreign Missions (including Lottie Moon offering)	___	___	___
Inviting guest speakers from denominational schools and agencies	___	___	___
Sending youth to Baptist colleges	___	___	___
Sending youth to official SBC seminaries	___	___	___
Seeking denominational help in finding a pastor	___	___	___

12. **IF you foresee more involvement**, which of the following (if any) accounts for that change? (check all that apply)

___ the conservative redirection of the convention

___ church leaders who are more interested in the convention

___ people who have learned how important it is to be involved

___ other (please specify) _____

13. **IF you foresee less involvement** for your church in the SBC, which of the following (if any) appear likely? (check all that apply to your church)

___ seeking "dual alignment" with the SBC and other Baptists

___ support for new "alternative" institutions, but staying within the SBC

___ support for the Southern Baptist Alliance

___ selective (designated) Cooperative Program giving

___ withdrawing from the convention to become independent

___ participation in some yet-to-be-created new organization of Baptists

___ Other _____

14. **IF you foresee no change** in involvement, what accounts for that? (check all that apply)

___ The convention itself will not change very much.

___ People are used to Southern Baptist programs and would resist change.

___ Denominational loyalties are too strong for change to be possible.

___ People in the church disagree about the conservative redirection of the convention

___ Other reasons _____

THANK YOU FOR YOUR HELP

Simply place this in the enclosed reply envelope and return it to the Center for Religious Research

Notes

Preface

1. By far the best attempt at a comprehensive theory is found in J. Wilson's "The sociology of schism," *A Sociological Yearbook of Religion in Britain*, 1971: 1–20. He is limited, however, to examining historical cases.

Chapter 1. The Baptist Battle in Dallas

1. "Schism: An Overview," in Volume 13 of *The Encyclopedia of Religion*, ed. M. Eliade (New York: Macmillan, 1987), 99–102.
2. Now called the Committee on Nominations.
3. We will examine this election process in more detail in chapter 6.
4. For an overview of SBC polity, look ahead to Figure 6.1.
5. This argument is developed more fully in N. Ammerman, "North American Protestant Fundamentalism," in *Fundamentalism Observed*, ed. Martin E. Marty and R. Scott Appleby (Chicago: University of Chicago Press, 1990). See also G. Marsden, *Fundamentalism and American Culture* (New York: Oxford University Press, 1980) and my *Bible Believers: Fundamentalists in the Modern World* (New Brunswick: Rutgers University Press, 1987).

Chapter 2. From English Dissent to Southern Establishment

1. This section on early history takes its primary outline from the excellent *A History of the Baptists* (Philadelphia: Judson Press, 1950) by Robert G. Torbet, and from William Henry Brackney's *The Baptists* (New York: Greenwood Press, 1988), and Leon McBeth's *The Baptist Heritage* (Nashville: Broadman, 1987). Discussion of the English Baptists draws most heavily on M. R. Watts, *The Dissenters: From the Reformation to the French Revolution* (Oxford: Clarendon Press, 1978) and B. R. White, *The English Separatist Tradition: From the Marian Martyrs to the Pilgrim Fathers* (London: Oxford University Press, 1971). Their work has been supplemented by information from Robert A. Baker, *The Southern Baptist Convention and its People, 1607–1972* (Nashville: Broadman, 1974), and by other sources, as noted in the text.
2. Watts, *The Dissenters*, 16.
3. Quoted in White, *The English*, 129.
4. Watts (*The Dissenters*, 7–14) argues that a significant number of Dutch Anabaptists fled to England in the middle third of the sixteenth century, but were essentially wiped out under the persecutions of Queen Mary. He also argues (45–46) that it was Mennonite influence that convinced Smyth to reject predestination. The remnant of Smyth's followers in Holland eventually did join the Mennonite group. The fact that some later English dissenting groups were referred to as Anabaptist apparently only confuses the matter. See also W. G. McLoughlin, *New England Dissent, 1630–1833: The Baptists and the Separation*

of Church and State (Cambridge: Harvard University Press, 1971), 8–9, regarding the similar imprecise use of the term Anabaptist in America.

5. White, *The English*, xii.

6. See Watts, *The Dissenters*, 44, and Brackney, *The Baptists*, 4.

7. Watts, *The Dissenters*, 49.

8. Watts, *The Dissenters*, 160.

9. Brackney, *The Baptists*, 6.

10. Torbet, *A History of the Baptists*, 29–32.

11. See also McLoughlin, *New England Dissent*.

12. I use the male pronoun here to reflect the reality as it then was; in the history of the Catholic church, priests were always men. That would not always be the case for Baptists, either in their early history or their recent past. Where it is possible that a role occupant (of any sort) may be female, I will use inclusive terms, but where roles are reserved exclusively for men, I will use male terms to indicate the intentional designation of certain offices as the prerogative of men. So, for instance, fundamentalist pastors will be referred to as men, while moderate pastors will be referred to with inclusive terms. In doing this, I have tried to reflect both the reality present in the situation and my own commitment to language that allows for the presence and action of women in the world.

13. See Torbet, *A History of the Baptists*, 43–45, and Watts, *The Dissenters*, 166.

14. Watts, *The Dissenters*, 298–301.

15. McLoughlin, *New England Dissent*, 15.

16. See Neely, "Baptist Beginnings in the Middle Colonies," in *The Lord's Free People in a Free Land*, ed. W. R. Estep (Fort Worth: Southwestern Baptist Theological Seminary, 1976), 27–38, for a discussion of the character and influence of the Philadelphia Association.

17. See Lumpkin, *Baptist Foundations in the South* (Nashville: Broadman, 1961), 14–15, and McLoughlin, *New England Dissent*, 421–439.

18. H. L. McBeth, *Women in Baptist Life* (Nashville: Broadman, 1979), 43–45.

19. See D. G. Matthews, *Religion in the Old South* (Chicago: University of Chicago Press, 1977), 23–38, for an excellent account of the growth of evangelical religion on the frontier.

20. The synthesis of the "regular" traditions of places like Charleston and Philadelphia with the "separate" tradition of places like Sandy Creek never meant that the differences disappeared. Their separate emphases on "order" and "ardor" remained. See W. B. Shurden, "The Southern Baptist synthesis: Is it cracking?" *Baptist History and Heritage* 16(2)(April 1981):2–11.

21. McLoughlin, *New England Dissent*, 556.

22. Women's societies, of course, were represented by male delegates. See L. McBeth, *Women in Baptist Life*, 81.

23. J. Boles, "Evangelical Protestantism in the Old South: from religious dissent to cultural dominance." in *Religion in the South*, ed. C. R. Wilson (Jackson: University Press of Mississippi, 1985), 13–34.

24. D. C. Bruce, Jr., *And They All Sang Hallelujah: Plain-Folk Camp Meeting Religion, 1800–1845* (Knoxville: University of Tennessee Press, 1974).

25. J. W. Flynt, "The Impact of Social Factors on Southern Baptist Expansion: 1800–1914," *Baptist History and Heritage* 17(1982):21.

26. W. W. Sweet, *Religion on the American Frontier, the Baptists, 1783–1830* (New York: Henry Holt and Company, 1964), 58–76.

27. Matthews, *Religion in the Old South*, 83.

28. Boles, "Evangelical Protestantism," 26.

29. Matthews, *Religion in the Old South*, 88–97.

30. Matthews explores the multiple facets of southern religious responses to slavery in chapter 4 of *Religion in the Old South*.

31. Quoted in Torbet, *A History of the Baptists*, 291.

32. This history of the Southern Convention takes its main outlines from Baker and from W. W. Barnes, *The Southern Baptist Convention, 1845–1953* (Nashville: Broadman, 1954), along with other sources as cited in the text.

33. Flynt, "The impact of social factors."

34. J. E. Tull, "The Landmark movement: An historical and theological appraisal," *Baptist History and Heritage* 10(1)(1975):3–18, provides a good overview of the Landmark arguments, and W. M. Patterson, "The influence of Landmarkism among Baptists," *Baptist History and Heritage* 10(1)(1975):44–55, recounts their lasting influences on the Southern Baptist Convention.

35. Barnes, *The Southern Baptist Convention*, 109–113.

36. Compiled from reports contained in E. P. Alldredge, *Southern Baptist Handbook, 1932* (Nashville: The Baptist Sunday School Board, 1932).

37. In 1988, conservatives in North Carolina mounted an effort to deny seats on key committees to messengers from churches that accept alien immersion. As many Baptist churches have become more cosmopolitan, they have often changed baptism policies so as to ease membership transfers from other denominations. And from time to time, those churches are still disfellowshipped by their associations.

38. T. J. Nettles, "Southern Baptists: Regional to national transition," *Baptist History and Heritage* 16(1981):13–23.

39. Matthews, *Religion in the Old South*, 89–97.

40. S. S. Hill, *Southern Churches in Crisis* (New York: Holt, Rinehart, and Winston, 1966).

41. The most thorough examinations of the relationship between Southern Baptists and social issues are found in R. B. Spain, *At Ease in Zion: Social History of Southern Baptists, 1865–1900* (Nashville: Vanderbilt University Press, 1961) and J. L. Eighmy, *Churches in Cultural Captivity: A History of the Social Attitudes of Southern Baptists* (with revised introduction, conclusion, and bibliography by Samuel S. Hill), (Knoxville: University of Tennessee Press, 1987.)

42. Eighmy, *Churches in Cultural Captivity*, 25.

43. Quoted in Spain, *At Ease in Zion*, 21.

44. *Proceedings, 1860* of the Kentucky Baptist General Association, quoted in Spain, *At Ease in Zion*, 116.

45. Quoted in Spain, *At Ease in Zion*, 99.

46. On this period see also Barnes, *The Southern Baptist Convention*, 77–80, Baker, *The Southern Baptist Convention and its People*, 261–268, and A. B. Rutledge, *Mission to America* (Nashville: Broadman, 1969), 40ff.

47. From the SBC *Annual*, quoted in Baker, *The Southern Baptist Convention and its People*, 264.

48. J. W. Flynt, "One in the Spirit, many in the flesh: Southern evangelicals," in *Varieties of Southern Evangelicalism*, ed. D. E. Harrell, Jr. (Macon: Mercer University Press, 1981), 23–44. On the role of the mills see L. Pope, *Millhands and Preachers* (New Haven: Yale University Press, 1942).

49. See Eighmy, *Churches in Cultural Captivity*, as well as J. W. Flynt, "One in the Spirit."

50. Eighmy, *Churches in Cultural Captivity*, 77. In my reading of the history of this period, Masters seems the most openly racist among leading Southern Baptists. Among most, segregation and white superiority were assumed, and the tone is quite paternalistic. In Masters, segregation is more openly defended. He is not different in kind, but is different in emphasis. I find it ironic and somewhat disturbing, then, that Rosenberg chose Masters as her chief representative of early twentieth century Southern Baptist thought. See E. Rosenberg, *The Southern Baptists: A Subculture in Transition* (Knoxville: University of Tennessee Press, 1989), xi–xiii.

51. On the rebirth of the Sunday School Board and the regional impulses behind it, see Baker, *The Southern Baptist Convention and its People*, 273–276; and McBeth, *The Baptist Heritage*, 437–440.

52. Baker, *The Southern Baptist Convention and its People*, 294–296.

53. On the organization and proto-feminist influence of the WMU Training School, see J. W. Flynt, "Women, society and the southern church, 1900–1920" in *Religion in the South: Conference Papers*, Alabama Humanities Foundation, 1986, 52–55.

54. See Barnes, *The Southern Baptist Convention*, 134–136, and especially Baker, *The Southern Baptist Convention and its People*, 301–303.

55. J. L. Sullivan, "Polity developments in the Southern Baptist Convention (1900–1977)," *Baptist History and Heritage* 14(3)(1979):26.

56. L. McBeth, *Women in Baptist Life*. See also Barnes, *The Southern Baptist Convention*, 151–158.

57. Baker, *The Southern Baptist Convention and its People*, 289.

58. A. H. Newman, *A History of the Baptist Churches in the United States* (New York: Scribner's, 1894), 462.

Chapter 3. Organization, Growth, and Change

1. From the 1917 SBC *Annual*, quoted in W. W. Barnes, *The Southern Baptist Convention, 1845–1953* (Nashville: Broadman, 1954), 179.

2. R. A. Baker, *The Southern Baptist Convention and its People, 1607–1972* (Nashville: Broadman, 1974), 400–409, contains an excellent analysis of the organizational developments of this period. See also Barnes, *The Southern Baptist Convention*, 223–232.

3. A. Winter, "Elective affinities between religious beliefs and ideologies of managements in two eras," *American Joural of Sociology* 79(1974):1134–1150, explores the way in which even theology followed this trend toward managerial capitalism. As the economy moved from an entrepreneurial era into an era emphasizing corporate endeavor, God ceased being the remote despot and became a colleague on a team of human specialists, working together for the good of the world. Even though Southern Baptist ideology leaned heavily on cooperation in this era, modern theologies that emphasized the importance of human action were relatively unknown to them.

4. A thorough study of these organizational developments is found in B. Primer, *Protestants and American Business Methods* (Ann Arbor, Mich.: UMI Press, 1979).

5. SBC *Annual*, 1931, 44.

6. The $250 figure as the amount required per messenger had already been in place since 1888. It would remain in place for more than fifty more years, becoming an essentially meaningless criterion as inflation increased the incomes and Cooperative Program gifts of most churches above the $2,250 necessary for the maximum number of messengers. In the late 1980s, the Executive Committee discussed the possibility of change, but concluded that any change at that point would be politically impossible.

7. From E. P. Alldredge, *Southern Baptist Handbook, 1932* (Nashville: The Baptist Sunday School Board, 1932).

8. On these factors in the developing polity, see Baker, *The Southern Baptist Convention and its People*, especially 408.

9. Again, the male pronoun is used to reflect the reality that there has never been a female President, and such an event is unlikely in the foreseeable future. There have been female vice presidents; but as late as 1963, an effort was made to require all officers to be males. In that year, the seventy-fifth anniversary of the WMU, Mrs. R. L. Mathis, WMU president, was elected second vice president. The messenger who objected was ruled out of order on a technicality (*SBC Annual*, 1963, 47–95). Will Campbell's 1988 novel *The Convention* (Atlanta: Peachtree Publishers) pictures the future election of a woman and is a moving exploration of the relationship between women and power in the SBC.

10. SBC *Annual*, 1931, 97–98.

11. SBC *Annual*, 1946, 16.

12. SBC *Annual*, 1950, 24.

13. Baker, *The Southern Baptist Convention and its People*, 405, makes this point. The relationship between debate and membership has emerged in my thinking through conversations with Arthur Farnsley and Jon Gunnemann.

14. On Southern Baptists and the fundamentalist controversies, see J. J. Thompson, *Tried as by Fire: Southern Baptists and the Religious Controversies of the 1920s* (Macon: Mercer University Press, 1982), 65–82; K. K. Bailey, *Southern White Protestantism in the Twentieth Century* (Gloucester, Mass.: Peter Smith, 1968), 63–68; G. M. Marsden, *Fundamentalism and American Culture* (New York: Oxford, 1980), 165; W. B. Shurden, *Not a Silent People: Controversies That Have Shaped Southern Baptists* (Nashville: Broadman, 1972), 89–101; and

B. Primer, "The failure of southern fundamentalism," a paper presented to the Southestern Historical Association in Houston, 1980.

15. Thompson, *Tried*, 77.

16. J. J. Thompson, "A free-and-easy democracy: Southern Baptists and denominational Structure in the 1920s," *Foundations* 22(1979):43–50.

17. Thompson, *Tried*, 35.

18. Norris' role is explored by M. G. Toulouse, "A case study in schism: J. Frank Norris and the SBC," *Foundations* 4(1981):32–48.

19. Southern Baptist expansion in this and later periods is discussed in Baker, *The Southern Baptist Convention and its People*, 355–384; H. L. McBeth, "Expansion of the Southern Baptist Convention to 1951," *Baptist History and Heritage* 17(1982):32–43; and especially H. K. Neely, "The Territorial Expansion of the Southern Baptist Convention, 1894–1959," Unpublished Th.D. Dissertation, Southwestern Baptist Theological Seminary, 1963.

20. Baker, *The Southern Baptist Convention and its People*, 398, and Barnes, *The Southern Baptist Convention*, 118, give very little attention to the adoption of this statement, perhaps because it was not seen as very important by Baptists in the decades following the 1920s. Both historians place it in the context of the debates on evolution but see it as a compromise that finessed that issue. Bailey, *Southern White Protestantism*, 66, however, points out that "the price of unity was a straightforward disavowal of modernism." Shurden, *Not a Silent People*, 98–100, agrees, pointing out that motions were adopted in the following year that put the Convention on record opposing evolution and requiring employees to subscribe to a nonevolutionist reading of Genesis. These official actions appear to have calmed conservative fears, taking the wind out of SBC fundamentalists' sails.

21. Max Weber's delineation of the characteristics of bureaucracy seems especially apt here. See the essays gathered in chapter 8 of H. H. Gerth and C. W. Mills, *From Max Weber* (New York: Oxford University Press, 1946). See also Primer, *Protestants*, on the development of bureaucracy around the turn of the century in four major American denominations, and P. M. Harrison, *Authority and Power in the Free Church Tradition* (Carbondale: Southern Illinois University Press, 1959) for a somewhat later look at the American Baptist Churches. We will explore these issues of organization more fully in chapter 7.

22. Neely, "The Territorial Expansion"; also T. J. Nettles, "Southern Baptists: regional to national transition," *Baptist History and Heritage*, 16(1981):13–23. Some evidence of the effects of southern migration on the American religious scene are provided in M. A. Shibley, "The Southernization of American religion: Testing a hypothesis," a paper presented to the Association for the Sociology of Religion, 1989.

23. A. M. McClellan, *The West is Big* (Atlanta: Home Mission Board, 1953), 109–113.

24. For example, McClellan, *The West*, and C. Redford, *Spiritual Frontiers* (Atlanta: Home Mission Board, 1949).

25. W. M. Newman and P. L. Halverson, *Atlas of Religious Change in America, 1952–1971* (Washington: Glenmary, 1978).

26. J. W. Flynt, "Southern Baptists: rural to urban transition," *Baptist History and Heritage* 16(1981):24–34.

27. Ed. L. S. Barr, *The Quarterly Review: Handbook Issue,* 46(4) (1986).

28. J. C. McKinney and L. B. Bourque, "The changing south: national incorporation of a region," *American Sociological Review* 36(1971):399–412.

29. R. W. Stump, "Regional migration and religious patterns in the American South," a paper presented to the meetings of the Society for the Scientific Study of Religion, 1985.

30. S. Hill, *Southern Churches in Crisis* (New York: Holt, Rinehart, and Winston, 1966), 5.

31. J. S. Reed, *Southerners* (Chapel Hill: University of North Carolina Press, 1983), 108.

32. R. W. Stump, "Regional migration and religious commitment in the United States," *Journal for the Scientific Study of Religion* 23(1984):292–303.

33. Stump, "Regional migration and religious patterns."

34. See E. Troeltsch, *The Social Teachings of the Christian Churches* 1 (London: George Allen, 1931), 331–343; also M. Weber, "The social psychology of the world religions," in *From Max Weber,* ed. H. H. Gerth and C. W. Mills (New York: Oxford University Press, 1946), 287–288.

35. This reading of the distinctiveness of the Bible Belt is informed by a conversation with Rodney Stark.

36. Even Lutherans were affected by the region's evangelical ethos. See L. Weber, *Who are the Southern Lutherans?,* Unpublished Ph.D. dissertation, Emory University, 1989.

37. D. E. Harrell, "The South: Seedbed of sectarianism," in *Varieties of Southern Evangelicalism,* ed. D. E. Harrell (Macon: Mercer University Press, 1981), 45–57; also R. M. Anderson, *Vision of the Disinherited* (New York: Oxford University Press, 1979).

38. On the nature of denominations, see D. A. Martin, "The Denomination," *British Journal of Sociology* 13(March 1962):1–14; B. Johnson, "Church and Sect Revisited," *Journal for the Scientific Study of Religion* 10(1971):124–137; and R. Wallis, *The Road to Total Freedom* (New York: Columbia University Press, 1977), 11–18.

39. L. McSwain and W. B. Shurden, "Changing values of Southern Baptists, 1900–1980," *Baptist History and Heritage* 16(1981):45–54. For results from our survey on these practices, see chapter 4.

40. Bailey, *Southern White Protestantism,* 131.

41. D. Sapp, "Southern Baptist responses to the American economy, 1900–1980," *Baptist History and Heritage* 16(1981):3–12.

42. See G. Winter, "Religious organizations," in *The Emergent American Society* 1, ed. W. Lloyd Warner (New Haven: Yale University Press, 1967), 408–491, for a comparative report on the growth in size, centralization, and efficiency of a wide range of other denominations.

43. Compiled from the SBC *Annual* (1941) and the SBC *Annual* (1961), 369–373.

44. Eighmy, *Churches in Cultural Captivity: A History of the Social Attitudes of Southern Baptists* (Knoxville, TN: University of Tennessee Press, 1987), 179.

45. S. Hastey, "A History of the Baptist Joint Committee on Public Affairs, 1946–1971," Th.D. Dissertation, Southern Baptist Theological Seminary, 1973.

46. Eighmy, *Churches in Cultural Captivity*, 141–157.

47. P. B. Jones, "An Examination of the Statistical Growth of the SBC" in *Understanding Church Growth and Decline*, ed. Dean R. Hoge and David A. Roozen (Philadelphia: Pilgrim, 1979).

48. Newman and Halverson, *Atlas*.

49. At about the same time, a similar study by the same firm was done at the Southern Baptist Theological Seminary. It recommended the creation of the school's first real "administration," a body of persons who would have authority, at least in some matters, over the faculty. In 1958, before such an administration could be established, a struggle between the president (who wanted to implement the administration) and his faculty (who did not) resulted in the resignations of thirteen professors. McBeth gives a brief account of this in *Baptist Heritage*, 668.

50. *SBC Annual*, 1955, 229.

51. For a recent example, see F. M. White, "Letters overwhelm missionary kids," *Baptist Press*, June 29, 1988. The New England example is the experience of a colleague there in the 1970s.

52. One fundamentalist leader reminisced that after Baker James Cauthen spoke there were only two kinds of people—those who volunteered for mission service and those who felt terribly guilty for not volunteering.

53. K. P. Takayama, in "Strains, conflicts, and schisms in Protestant denominations" in *American Denominational Organization*, ed. R. P. Scherer (Pasadena: William Carey Library, 1980), 298–329, examines the relationship between internal and external strains and the ways denominations can respond. He points out that external changes often function as triggers, exacerbating inherent internal tensions. Chapters 4 and 5 will explore the way in which disagreements over values were related both to external factors and to disagreements over internal politics. In part, administrative growth in the 1950s may be seen as an effort to control the uncertain environment created by expansion. So long as the internal value concensus and communal solidarity remained high, such external chaos could be managed. What would eventually happen, as we will see in the remainder of the book, is the breakdown of both the communal solidarity and the value concensus of the denomination.

54. When we asked our 1985 survey respondents if they thought that God's involvement in creation was more important than the precise "how and when" of Genesis, 56 percent agreed or strongly agreed. The number of people willing to accept a nonliteral reading of scripture had grown to clearly out-number the literalists.

55. Elliott cites, for instance, a 1957 article in Southern Seminary's *Review and Expositor* containing similar ideas.

56. For accounts of this controversy, see Baker, *The Southern Baptist Convention and Its People*, 416, and J. C. Hefley, *The Truth in Crisis* (Dallas: Criterion, 1986), 49–51.

57. Similar conclusions from different points of view are reached by J. E. Barnhart, *The Southern Baptist Holy War* (Austin: Texas Monthly Press, 1986), 87–91; and J. C. Hefley, *The Truth in Crisis*, 44–47.

58. For example, F. D. Valentine, *A History of Southern Baptists and Race Relations, 1917–1947* (New York: Arno Press, 1980), a 1949 dissertation from Southwestern Seminary.

59. See Eighmy, *Churches in Cultural Captivity*, 189–193, and Bailey, *Southern White Protestantism*, 136–145 on progress in race relations in the 1940s and the conservative response of parishioners.

60. Eighmy, *Churches in Cultural Captivity*, 193–199, discusses responses to the Civil Rights Movement. Hefley, *The Truth*, 51–52, offers a conservative interpretation of the Sunday School Board's educational strategy. J. R. Wood, "Personal commitment and organizational constraint: Church officials and racial integration," *Sociological Analysis* 33(1972):142–151, carefully documents the stress between denominational officials and their conservative constituency and the ways in which Southern Baptist polity prevented overt action in support of the civil rights movement. These efforts by Southern Baptist leaders in favor of integration are completely ignored in Rosenberg's *The Southern Baptists*. She takes the recalcitrance of most laity to stand for the whole.

61. Quoted in Bailey, *Southern White Protestantism*, 146.

62. Baptist Church of the Covenant, in Birmingham, is an example of the former pattern, with a core of integrationists literally walking out of First Baptist Church. Oakhurst Baptist, in Decatur, Georgia, is an example of the latter pattern. Here nearly 90 percent of the congregation fled a changing neighborhood, while a remnant remained to rebuild an open church. W. Knight, *Struggle for Integrity* (Waco, Tex.: Word, 1969).

63. A useful account of the various ways in which integration happened in one community (and the various organizational responses to it) can be found in A. J. Blasi, *Segregationist Violence and Civil Rights Movements in Tuscaloosa* (Washington: University Press of America, 1980).

64. This vision of moving into a future not burdened by past sins was sometimes articulated at the highest levels of the denomination. See W. Knight, "A Future More Promising than the Past," *Home Missions* 47(December 1976):6–8.

65. Baker, *The Southern Baptist Convention and its People*, 416–417, gives a bare-bones account of this controversy. Hefley, *The Truth*, 54–58, provides more detail and a decided conservative slant. Shurden, *Not a Silent People*, 111–118, provides a more establishment view.

66. Hefley, *The Truth*, 58.

67. SBC *Annual*, 1970, "Proceedings."

68. Curtis Lee Laws first coined the term Fundamentalist in 1920 and described them as people ready "to do battle royal for the Fundamentals." He was referring especially to the controversies brewing in the Northern Baptist Convention.

69. *Southern Baptist Journal*, July-August, 1974, 6.

70. Letter from Brady Blalock, *Southern Baptist Journal*, February, 1974.

71. We will examine these institutions in more detail in chapter 6.

Chapter 4. Drawing the Battle Lines

1. On the "new evangelicals" see R. Wuthnow, *The Restructuring of American Religion* (Princeton: Princeton University Press, 1988), 185–190; J. D. Hunter, *Evangelicalism: The Coming Generation* (Chicago: University of Chicago Press, 1987); R. Quebedeaux, *The Young Evangelicals* (New York: Harper & Row, 1974).

2. See B. W. Hargrove, *The Sociology of Religion* (Chicago: Harlan Davidson, 1989), 290–291, for a discussion of the relationship between "radical" evangelicals and the modern world.

3. For details on the samples used and their representativeness, see appendix A.

4. Indeed E. Sandeen argues in *The Roots of Fundamentalism* (Chicago: University of Chicago Press, 1970) that dispensational premillennialism is the defining characteristic of fundamentalism.

5. For a discussion of the role of eschatology in the SBC controversy, see H. L. Turner, "Southern Baptist cosmogony and eschatology: mechanisms for coping with twentieth century societal stress," a paper presented to the Religious Research Association, in Chicago, 1988.

6. Details on scale construction are contained in appendix B.

7. The Peace Committee asked Baptist writers to refer to different groups in the denomination as "fundamental-conservatives" and "moderate-conservatives." Those designations may be fairly accurate for the 80 percent who fall in our middle three categories, but they fail to recognize a middle and fail to acknowledge the presence of the two self-consciously identified and self-consciously different groups at each extreme.

8. James T. Draper, Jr., *Authority: The Critical Issue for Southern Baptists* (Old Tappan, N. J.: Fleming H. Revell, 1984), 20–21.

9. From the "Firestorm Chat," a taped conversation with Dr. Gary North (Dominion Tapes, 1987).

10. "Biblical authority or inerrancy?" *SBC Today* 3(7)(November 1985):1,6.

11. R. James, *The Unfettered Word* (Waco, Tex.: Word Books, 1987).

12. D. Wilkinson, "Biblical authority key to morality, says Honeycutt," *Baptist Press*, September 12, 1985.

13. W. Ward. "The role of the Holy Spirit in relation to the authority of the Bible," in *Proceedings of the Conference on Biblical Inerrancy* (Nashville: Broadman, 1987), 478.

14. M. Blankenship, "'Biblical faith' said alternative," *Baptist Press*, February 25, 1985.

15. K. Camp, "Criswell sets limits on shared ministry," *Baptist Press*, February 21, 1986.

16. He was responding to comments by the Foreign Mission Board's William O'Brien urging North Carolina WMU members to "rise up" with an "example of Servanthood" in the face of pastors who exercise "rulerhood." Tenery called the idea of "rulerhood" a "false caricature" and voiced his concern that "WMU Women are being manipulated by the liberals in the Convention for political purposes. It is time," he said, "for local Pastors to inform the Women as to what is

being done." See "O'Brien Urges Women to Rise Up Against Pastors," *Southern Baptist Advocate* 7(2)(May 1986):13.

17. P. Cole, "Patterson suggests change for WMU," *Baptist Press*, March 8, 1988.

18. J. Sutton, "Author details rationale for SBC priesthood of believers resolution," *SBC Today* 6(5)(August 1988):6.

19. R. Land, "Pastoral leadership: authoritarian or persuasive?" in *Polarities in the Southern Baptist Convention*, ed. Fisher Humphries (New Orleans: New Orleans Baptist Theological Seminary, 1988), 79.

20. The methods by which such a small minority could pass a resolution are examined in chapter 6.

21. Camp, "Criswell sets limits."

22. Reporters Gustav Niebuhr and Gayle White noted that the decision of First Baptist Atlanta to move to the suburbs was made just one week after the congregation first heard that this was a possibility. Members were given a fourteen-page brochure outlining why the move was a good idea and asked to vote the next week on a plan conceived by their pastor and a few advisors. See G. Niebuhr and G. White, "Stanley's plan for First Baptist puts congregation at crossroads," the *Atlanta Journal and Constitution* (March 12, 1988), A-1, 18; and "First Baptist backs plan to sell property," the *Atlanta Constitution* (March 14, 1988), A-1, 7.

23. For estimates of the number of ordained Southern Baptist women and where they were serving, see S. F. Anders, "Southern Baptist Convention clergywomen and laywomen: in the eye of the storm," a paper presented to the Religious Research Association, 1988. For the story of women in Southern Baptist life, see also Anders, "Tracing past and present," in *The New Has Come*, ed. A. T. Neil and V. G. Neely (Washington: The Southern Baptist Alliance, 1989); and L. McBeth, *Women in Baptist Life*.

24. *Southern Baptist Journal* (December, 1974).

25. See E. C. Lehman, *Women Clergy* (New Brunswick: Transaction, 1985), and J. Carroll, B. Hargrove, and A. Lummis, *Women of the Cloth* (New York: Harper and Row, 1983).

26. T. B. Maston. "The Bible and Women," *The Student* 64(8)(February 1985):48.

27. G. Niebuhr, "Baptist director dies of heart attack during debate on women ministers," *The Atlanta Constitution* (October 8, 1987), A2.

28. I was present at the time of this incident and had to face the methodological question of whether to interject what I knew about the answer to that query. I determined that I would later release an abstract of my findings to Baptist Press, but would not enter the debate. However, Ms. McGhee's death interrupted the debate, and the question became moot.

29. R. Tenery, "Liturgical Dancing?????," *The Southern Baptist Advocate* 8(5)(June 1988):5.

30. "Director 'welcomes' fact-finding effort," *Baptist Press*, November 25, 1986.

31. S. Hastey, "Dunn, Neuhaus differ on role of religion in American life," *Baptist Press*, May 16, 1986.

32. Associated Press, "Stanley: God is using AIDS to punish gays," *The Atlanta Journal and Constitution* (January 18, 1986), A2.

33. M. King, "Poll: Southerners have qualms, but back right to abortion," *The Atlanta Constitution* (April 13, 1989), A1,10. A survey of Florida Baptists reported similar results to ours. See G. Warner, "Survey shows Florida Baptists agree, disagree on abortion," Florida Baptist *Witness* 106(35)(September 7, 1989):4–6.

34. While there is certainly a strong constituency among Southern Baptists for the issues of the New Christian Right, our data do not support the sort of argument made by Rosenberg, *The Southern Baptists*, ch. 6. Fundamentalist leaders had a clear conservative agenda, and they were able to put that agenda into place in the denomination's institutions; but the grassroots support for New Right causes is not nearly so monolithic as Rosenberg seems to argue.

35. J. Guth, "The Christian right revisited: partisan realignment among Southern Baptist ministers," a paper presented to the Midwest Political Science Association (April, 1985).

36. "Conservative SBC leader changes political parties," *Baptist Press*, September 30, 1988.

37. S. Collins, "Vines clarifies statements about joining non-SBC church," *Baptist Press*, November 22, 1988.

38. An enormous literature on the growth of the New Christian Right exists. It is not our purpose here to explore either the growth of that movement or all of its links to Southern Baptists. See J. L. Guth, T. G. Jelen, L. A. Kellstedt, C. E. Smidt, and K. D. Wald, "The Politics of Religion in America," *American Politics Quarterly* 16(1988):357–397, for a helpful overview of current research. The relationship between the SBC and secular politics is explored in N. T. Ammerman, "Southern Baptists and the New Christian Right," forthcoming in *Review of Religious Research*. The links between denominational and secular agendas, as well as links between SBC and NCR leadership, are explored. Among both clergy and laity, theological beliefs and attitudes toward diversity were shown to fuel support for both religious and secular (SBC and New Christian Right) agendas; but it was secular moral concerns that made the most difference in identification with the Republican party. Among clergy the ideological sources are quite strong, but among laity these variables explained relatively small amounts of the variance. Although clergy make strong connections between their religious and political concerns, the political concerns of laity are still more influenced by demographic and secular factors.

39. D. Martin, "Texas writer 'amazed' at response to brochure," *Baptist Press*, May 24, 1988.

40. E. C. Gardner, "Christian Ethics," in *The Encyclopedia of Southern Religion*, ed. Samuel S. Hill (Macon: Mercer University Press, 1984), 234.

41. J. C. Hefley, *The Truth in Crisis* (Dallas: Criterion Publications, 1986), 19–22.

42. This compares closely to responses to an identical item on the Wilkerson

and Associates survey in 1986. Forty-two percent found that statement very convincing, and 33 percent found it somewhat convincing. *SBC Today* 4(4)(July 1986):8.

43. L. C. Ingram, R. Thornton, R. Hazlewood. "Perceptions of academic freedom by professors in Southern Baptist colleges," a paper presented to the Religious Research Association (October, 1988).

44. T. Tune, "Stanley, Dilday meet face to face," *Baptist Press*, April 19, 1985.

45. M. Knox, "Draper advocates resolution of theological issues in SBC," *Baptist Press*, April 27, 1988.

46. R. G. Puckett, editor of the North Carolina *Biblical Recorder*, quoted in S. Shaw, "State editor appeals for recovery of freedom," *Baptist Press*, May 5, 1987.

47. This phrase was chosen as the title of the first book published by the Southern Baptist Alliance, ed. A. Neely, *Being Baptist Means Freedom* (Atlanta: Southern Baptist Alliance, 1988).

48. "Baptist leaders tell students about denominational heritage," *Baptist Press*, May 13, 1986.

49. These concrete differences in denominational support and activism will be explored in more detail in chapter 5.

50. See for example D. Martin, "State leadership disregarded in appointments, presidents say," *Baptist Press*, May 8, 1985.

51. T. Tune, "Stanley, Dilday meet face to face," *Baptist Press*, April 19, 1985.

52. See for example D. Martin, "Student files complaint against Texan Pressler," *Baptist Press*, September 17, 1984.

53. The bylaw read that the Committee on Boards "shall be nominated to the Convention by the Committee on Committees." The parliamentarians claimed that this placed the sole power of nomination with that body, and no nominations could come from the floor. This understanding was obviously contested. During the next year a lawsuit was brought against President Stanley, and the Executive Committee rewrote the bylaw to make clear that messengers could bring substitute nominations.

54. "Winfred Moore 'tool' of liberals, Patterson says," *Baptist Press*, May 17, 1985.

Chapter 5. *The Social Sources of Division*

1. R. W. Doherty, *The Hicksite Separation* (New Brunswick: Rutgers University Press, 1967), 16–17.

2. This view of the relationship between religion and everyday reality is perhaps most informed by P. L. Berger, *The Sacred Canopy* (Garden City, N. Y.: Doubleday Anchor, 1969). It is also informed by C. Geertz, "Religion as a Cultural System," in *The Interpretation of Cultures* (New York: Basic Books, 1973) and Max Weber's classic *The Sociology of Religion*, trans. E. Fischoff (Boston: Beacon Press, 1964).

3. H. R. Niebuhr, *The Social Sources of Denominationalism* (New York: World Publishing, 1929).

4. R. Stark and W. S. Bainbridge, in *The Future of Religion* (Berkeley, University of California Press, 1985), offer a comprehensive theory as to why these disparities exist. They argue on p. 104 that "to the extent that a religious group contains or comes to contain a number of relatively privileged members and to the extent that they can influence group policies, tension with the external world will be reduced . . . [and] there will be a growing demand among its less powerful members for more efficacious compensators for scarcity." Those "compensators" will be beliefs about otherworldly rewards that will place them in greater tension with the systems of this world and in conflict with their higher status coreligionists.

5. The concept received perhaps its most thorough research treatment in N. J. Demerath, *Social Class and American Protestantism* (Chicago: Rand McNally, 1965). The relationship between social class and religion was also examined in community studies such as L. Pope's *Millhands and Preachers* (New Haven: Yale University Press, 1942). These studies established the rough correlations between modes of religiosity and position in the community. The more subtle ways in which sectarian groups relate their members to the status order are explored in G. Schwartz, *Sect Ideologies and Social Status* (Chicago: University of Chicago Press, 1970).

Studies that directly address the question of schism include Doherty's *The Hicksite Separation*. Social class, Doherty argues, played a key role in dividing Friends, but it was not the only cause. Similar multicausal arguments are advanced about schisms in immigrant churches. See D. Vrga and F. J. Fahey, "The relationship of religious practices and beliefs to schism," *Sociological Analysis*, 31(1970):46–55; and E. H. Shin and H. Park, "An analysis of causes of schisms in ethnic churches: The case of Korean-American churches," *Sociological Analysis* 49(1988):234–248.

6. W. C. Roof and W. McKinney, *American Mainline Religion* (New Brunswick, N. J.: Rutgers University Press, 1987).

7. One significant exception might be seen in the schism in the Serbian Orthodox Church, in 1963. Here the division was not strictly ethnic (since all were Serbs), but fell along lines defined by immigrant relationships with Yugoslavia, including length of residence in the U.S. and whether immigration occurred before or after communist rule began. See D. Vrga and F. J. Fahey, "The relationship."

8. R. Wuthnow, *The Restructuring of American Religion* (Princeton: Princeton University Press, 1988).

9. Niebuhr, *Social Sources*, 31–32. For an extension of this argument, see C. Y. Glock, "The role of deprivation in the origin and evolution of religious groups," in *Religion and Social Conflict*, ed. R. Lee and M. E. Marty (New York: Oxford University Press, 1964), 24–36.

10. We asked them to tell us the occupational category of the parent who was the primary wage-earner in their family of origin. As with other tables in which occupation is a variable, those who checked "professional" or "managerial" are coded here as professional. This category contains those who might be identified

as "new class" knowledge workers, but neither our categories nor our sample size permitted separating these from other professionals. Those who checked "sales," "clerical," "technical," or "service professions" (such as nursing, social work, teaching) are coded as white collar. Those who fell into categories of skilled trades, factory work, general labor, transportation, or other service work are coded as blue collar. Farming is coded as reported, and clergy is included here as a profession. In coding the respondent's own and spouse's occupations, clergy is treated as a separate category.

11. See for example, D. C. McClelland, *The Achieving Society* (Princeton: Van Nostrand, 1961); M. Kohn, "Personality, occupation, and social stratification," in *Research in Social Stratification and Mobility*, ed. D. J. Treiman and R. V. Robinson (Greenwich, Conn.: JAI Press, 1981), 267–297; and U. Bronfenbrenner, "Socialization and social class through time and space," in *Readings in Social Psychology*, 3rd ed., ed. E. Maccoby, T. Newcomb, and E. Hartley (New York: Holt, 1958), 400–425.

12. Stark and Bainbridge, *The Future*, 103.

13. L. S. Barr, ed., *The Quarterly Review* 46(4)(1986):24.

14. In 1985, we observed that a disproportionate number of moderate leaders seemed to be wearing yellow ties. We found out later that this was no coincidence. It was planned as a way of recognizing political allies on the floor of the convention.

15. See, for example, P. Dimaggio and J. Mohr, "Cultural capital, educational attainment and marital selection," *American Journal of Sociology* 90(May 1985): 1231–1261.

16. Wuthnow, *The Restructuring*, 158.

17. Between 1939 and 1979, enrollment in theological schools in the U.S. more than tripled, from 13,000 to 44,000. See the annual reports of the Association of Theological Schools for 1941 (p.85) and 1984 (p.5).

18. T. Tune, "Stanley, Dilday meet face to face," *Baptist Press*, April 19, 1985.

19. It perhaps should be noted that Reighard's masters and doctoral degrees were earned by correspondence from the fundamentalist Luther Rice Seminary in Jacksonville, Florida. As our data would indicate, education in such schools may actually make a minister *more* conservative.

20. E. J. Daniels, with John Bos, *The Battle over the Bible among Southern Baptists* (Orlando: Christ for the World Publishers, 1985), 54. The Hollyfield survey at Southern is also cited in David O. Beale, *S.B.C. House on the Sand?* (Greenville, SC: Unusual Publications, 1985), 44–46. The original survey is reported in N. W. Hollyfield, Jr., "A Sociological Analysis of the Degrees of 'Christian Orthodoxy' Among Selected Students in the Southern Baptist Theological Seminary," unpublished Master's Thesis, Southern Baptist Theological Seminary, 1976.

21. One account of this story is found in J. Hefley, *The Truth in Crisis* (Dallas: Criterion, 1986), 63.

22. J. Guth, "The education of the Christian Right: The case of the Southern Baptist clergy," *Quarterly Review* 4(2)(Summer 1984):44–56 (and as presented

earlier to the Society for the Scientific Study of Religion, 1982) presents similar findings about the association between support for the Moral Majority and education, social class, size of church, and seminary attended.

23. The effects of age are discussed in more detail in Ammerman, "Southern Baptists and the New Christian Right."

24. My observations on northeastern Southern Baptists come from more than the thirteen cases included among our survey respondents. My husband was a Southern Baptist pastor in Connecticut and New Jersey for seven years, and we had opportunity to know and observe many of the region's Southern Baptist pastors and leaders. What I observed was that the scattered and struggling Southern Baptist churches in the northeast sought to claim a moderate evangelical identity (partly in distinction from the well-established fundamentalist sector in the region's religious economy). They were willing to accommodate many of the cognitive and lifestyle demands of this highly urbanized, secular environment, while attempting to offer an evangelical alternative to the dominant Catholic, mainline Protestant, and Jewish traditions of the region. And their position in this "marginal" location often gave them a critical eye with which to view their established southern counterparts.

25. The role of community size in predicting attitudes has been explored in a number of studies. C. S. Fischer, "The effect of urban life on traditional values," *Social Forces* 53(1975):420–432, demonstrated that community size can affect attitudes, over and above the effects of individual-level variables. N. D. Glenn and L. Hill, Jr., "Rural-urban differences in attitudes and behavior in the U.S.," *Annals of the American Academy of Political and Social Science* 429(1977):36–50, found that size of childhood community was more important than the size of one's current community. H. Whitt and H. M. Nelsen, "Residence, moral traditionalism, and tolerance of atheists," *Social Forces* 54(1975):328–340, reported a linear decrease in biblicism and traditionalism from rural folk to first generation urbanites to second generation city dwellers. Each of these studies suggests that both current and childhood community size can affect various traditional values.

Doherty, *The Hicksite Schism*, 48–49, shows that the nineteenth century Quaker schismatic group he studied was also characterized by a disproportionate rate of country-to-city migration.

26. This definition has evolved in the context of work with the group of scholars, under Martin E. Marty's direction, who are participants in "The Fundamentalism Project," under the auspices of the American Academy of Arts and Sciences. For a discussion of fundamentalism in North America that builds on that definition, see N. Ammerman, "North American Protestantist Fundamentalism," in *Fundamentalism Observed*, ed. by M. E. Marty and R. S. Appleby (Chicago: University of Chicago Press, 1990).

27. See A. Swidler, "Culture in action: Symbols and strategies," *American Sociological Review* 51(1986):273–286; and C. Geertz, *Islam Observed* (Chicago: University of Chicago Press, 1968).

28. See Marty and Appleby, *Fundamentalism Observed*, for a description of a number of such movements.

29. See Berger, *The Sacred Canopy*, 5–7, for a discussion of "modern" reli-

gion. See also R. Bellah and associates, *Habits of the Heart* (Berkeley, University of California Press, 1986).

30. T. Teepen, "Modern World's Horizons Have Been Pushed Back," *The Atlanta Constitution*, (March 28, 1989), A-15.

31. For a description of such a congregation, see N. Ammerman, *Bible Believers.*

32. The relative effects of various social factors were tested using an analysis of variance model and multiple classification analysis. The effects reported in the text are based on deviations from the mean noted in specific categories of these variables. In the analysis of variance model, amount of education had the largest effect ($b = .27$, $p < .001$), followed by region ($b = .20$, $p < .01$) and urban experience ($b = .15$, $p < .05$). Because of the number of missing cases on region, the equation was tested without that variable. The effects of education and urban experience were not substantially changed, but significance levels were strengthened. The effect of region is reduced to near zero when theology is controlled. Those on the eastern seaboard appear more tolerant of diversity largely because they are more likely to be moderate in theology.

Among clergy, income, urban experience, region, and type of education all had significant bivariate effects on acceptance of diversity. The effect of urban experience among clergy, unlike its effect among laity, is linear. Those who are first generation urban fall between rural and second generation urban on acceptance of modernity. Indeed, under some conditions (having attended a liberal seminary, for instance), clergy who have chosen to move to the city are more accepting of diversity than clergy who have lived in cities all their lives.

When these variables were tested against each other, the effect of income dropped to near zero. Type of education (whether and which seminary) had the strongest effect ($b = .31$, $p < .01$), followed by region ($b = .21$, $p < .10$), and urban experience ($b = .14$, $p < .10$). Again, because of the missing cases on the region variable, the equation was also run without that variable. The effects of the remaining three variables were largely unchanged, but the levels of significance for education and urban experience were considerably stronger. And again, when theology was included, region (and urban experience) dropped out of the equation. Among clergy, demographic variables have their primary effects in determining beliefs; and it is those beliefs that primarily determine how they respond to the modern world.

33. This is obviously a variation on the "status discontent" argument. That concept has been operationalized in such a variety of ways that consistent results are impossible to cite. See K. Wald, D. E. Owen, and S. S. Hill, Jr., "Evangelical politics and status issues," *Journal for the Scientific Study of Religion* 28(1)(1989): 1–16, for a helpful review and critique of that literature. In most forms status discontent refers to some discrepancy between one's place in the actual social order and the place one expects to occupy. My concern is not with "status" in the sense of prestige or honor in the community. Rather, it is with disjuncture between demands of one's social world and the resources with which one can meet those demands.

My argument is similar to the arguments made by Reed in *Southerners.*

He contrasts "locals" who are relatively isolated from the forces of change, with "fire-eaters" who have been exposed enough to alternative ways of life to hold their traditional southern values in a highly self-conscious (and enthusiastic) way. Both are contrasted to "new Southerners" and "cosmopolitans" who hold traditional southern values less strongly, the latter with little regional consciousness at all and the former in tandem with a heightened southern identity.

In a different way, F. Lechner, "Fundamentalism and sociocultural revitalization in America: a sociological interpretation," *Sociological Analysis* 46(1985): 243–260, also argues that fundamentalism is a uniquely modern movement, only possible once there is differentiation against which to argue for dedifferentiation.

34. J. D. Hunter, *American Evangelicalism* (New Brunswick: Rutgers University Press, 1983).

35. A summary index of denominational activity was constructed. See appendix B for more detail. Analysis of variance was used to test the relative strength of the social factors against fundamentalist beliefs and identity. For clergy, the strongest predictor was church size/location (b = .40), followed by seminary attendance (b = .20) and income (b = .17). Beliefs (b = .10) and identification (b = .02) did not have statistically significant effects. Among laity, the strongest effect was again church size/location (b = .40), followed by college attendance (b = .12). Husband's occupation (b = .11) and beliefs (b = .11) both had weak, but not statistically significant effects, with income (b = .06) and identification (b = .03) negligible in their effects once other social factors were controlled.

36. For a complete discussion of the model being tested, see appendix B. A scale of support for the fundamentalist agenda was created. The statistical model took education, region, and status variables as exogenous; beliefs, theological identification, and attitudes toward modernity as intervening; and denominational discontent as the dependent variable. Since the dependent variable was measured at interval level and the predictors were nominal-level measures (or could be meaningfully recoded as such), analysis of variance was used to test the model.

Among clergy, the strongest predictor of discontent was beliefs (b = .54), followed distantly by identification (b = .15), education (b = .15), and attitudes toward modernity (b = .11). Among laity, the pattern was similar: beliefs (b = .37), followed by identification (b = .21), education (b = .13), and attitudes toward modernity (b = .10). The clergy model explained 52 percent of the variance in discontent; the laity model explained 29 percent.

37. Wuthnow, *The Restructuring*, 217–218.

38. B. Johnson, "On church and sect," *American Sociological Review* 28(1963): 539–549, is responsible for clarifying the concept of church and sect (that Niebuhr had borrowed from Troeltsch). He, along with R. Stark and W. S. Bainbridge, "Of churches, sects, and cults: Preliminary concepts for a theory of religious movements," *Journal for the Scientific Study of Religion* 18(1979): 117–133, argued that the group's state of tension with the culture ought to be the primary defining characteristic, with other characteristics (such as social class or style of worship) seen as correlates, rather than attributes.

39. See, for example, R. Stark and W. S. Bainbridge's "Sectarian tension," *Review of Religious Research* 22(1980): 105–124.

40. See R. S. Warner, *New Wine in Old Wineskins* (Berkeley: University of California Press, 1987), 289–301.

41. R. Wallis, in *The Road to Total Freedom*, 13, defines the denomination as the religious form that is respectable and recognizes multiple religious truths. B. Johnson, "Church and sect revisited," 132–136, argues that denominations accept the rules governing voluntary associations, namely rules of civility. D. A. Martin, "The Denomination," 11–12, points to the way in which denominations also assume individualism and the freedom to choose.

Chapter 6. Mobilizing the Troops

1. On the Convention as a political entity, see A. Farnsley, "Majority Rules: The Politicization of the Southern Baptist Convention," Ph.D. dissertation, Emory University, 1990.

2. By 1989, fundamentalist preachers were receiving similar treatment. After a long and tense business session, Morris Chapman lost much of his audience for his Convention Sermon.

3. The power that rested in the hands of the SBC bureaucracy was not unlike the power wielded in another denomination based on a congregational polity, the American Baptist churches. Harrison's description in *Authority and Power in the Free Church Tradition* (Carbondale: Southern Illinois Press, 1971) is strangely prophetic of events and dynamics in the Southern church. See also R. Norsworthy, "Rationalization and reaction among Southern Baptists," a paper presented to the Religious Research Association, in Chicago, 1988.

4. M. N. Zald and M. A. Berger, "Social movements in organizations: coup d'etat, insurgency, and mass movements," *American Journal of Sociology* 83 (1978):823–861, and M. N. Zald, "Theological crucibles: social movements in and of religion," *Review of Religious Research* 23(1982):317–336.

5. Zald and Berger, "Social movements," 829. The other major focus of resource mobilization theory is the way in which a social movement falls along what Zald and Berger call "the enduring cleavages, status relationships, collective definitions, and traditions of the social system." They argue that the coincidence between a movement's issues and the "distribution of grievances" in a society will affect the perceived costs and rewards of participation. The coincidence between issues and "enduring cleavages" in the case of the Southern Baptists was seen in chapter 5.

6. The story of their meeting and initial organizing is told in J. Hefley, *The Truth in Crisis* (Dallas: Criterion Publications, 1986), 64–65.

7. Although we have interviewed a number of people who were there, their desire for anonymity remains. Only those details already made public are discussed here. For one such discussion, see J. Hefley, *The Truth in Crisis*, vol. 3 (Hannibal, MO: Hannibal Books, 1988), 14–15.

8. Zald and Berger, "Social movements," describe the processes involved in various types of movements for change in organizations. The fundamentalist movement in the Southern Baptist Convention is like a "coup" in that it involved at first a relatively small, elite, and secret group bent on creating an "unexpected

succession" in the CEO of the organization. Like a "bureaucratic insurgency," however, Southern Baptist fundamentalists had also pursued "their own concept of organizational programs [and] product development while watching over their shoulder for elite interference" (p. 839). They wanted more than mere change in leadership; they wanted to "establish their own definition of the situation [and] shift the weighting of priorities" in the entire organization (p. 838).

9. D. Martin and G. Warner, "Conservatives discuss evangelism, politics," *Baptist Press*, March 7, 1989.

10. A good example of such thinking is the analysis by E. Glenn Hinson in "SBC fundamentalists: stirring up a storm," *Christian Century* 96(July 18–25, 1979):725–727. Comparing 1970s fundamentalists to J. Frank Norris, he noted that Baptists had tired of Norris and moved on with business. "The mission spirit is so deeply imprinted on Southern Baptists that they are not likely to let concern for an ultraright 'orthodoxy' divert them for long." The *Western Recorder*, Kentucky's Baptist paper headlined the convention with the announcement that a "witch hunt" had been averted (June 20, 1979). The editor had been reassured by Rogers' assurances that he would support denominational programs, that he was not a candidate of the BFMF, and that he did not want a "witch hunt."

11. Zald and Berger, "Social movements," 855 and K. P. Takayama, "Strains, conflicts, and schisms in Protestant Denominations," in *American Denominational Organization*, ed. R. P. Scherer (Pasadena: William Carey Library, 1980), 308.

12. See especially J. Woods, *Leadership in Voluntary Organizations* (New Brunswick, N.J.: Rutgers University Press, 1981). Two earlier articles specifically address the role of congregational polity in constraining the progressivism of Southern Baptist agencies. See "Authority and controversial policy: The churches and civil rights," *American Sociological Review* 35(1970):1057–1069; and "Personal commitment and organizational constraint: church officials and racial integration," *Sociological Analysis* 33(1972):142–151.

The crucial differences between the congregation polity of the Southern Baptists and the hierarchical polity of the Roman Catholic church can be seen in their respective resources and strategies for fighting dissidents within. L. Kurtz's *The Politics of Heresy* (Berkeley: University of California Press, 1986), ch. 6, details the response of the Roman hierarchy to a modernist movement in the early twentieth century. The modernists (then the outsiders) were systematically labeled as deviant and eventually excommunicated. In the Southern Baptist case, the modernists were also labelled as deviant—despite their status as insiders.

13. P. Harrison, *Authority and Power*.

14. A classic statement of this ideology among Southern Baptists is found in former Sunday School Board chief James L. Sullivan's *Baptist Polity As I See It* (Nashville: Broadman, 1983).

15. This delegitimating of unsuspecting CEO's by a direct appeal to decision makers (in this case potential messengers) is the aspect of this social movement that looks most like a "coup." See Zald and Berger, "Social movements," 836.

16. See Wood's "Personal commitment" for a discussion of the ways in which a

congregational polity kept leaders in the SBC from leading reluctant constituents to leave behind old habits in race relations.

17. Not until the Southern Baptist Alliance was formed, in 1987, did a moderate group define itself in terms of a positive agenda. The Alliance began with freedom, but went on to include ecumenism, social justice, and the ordination of women as among the things it supported. From the numbers of supporters for those issues we have seen here, it is not surprising that the Alliance's membership remained small. The SBA will be discussed in more detail in chapter 8.

18. During the previous year's campaign, Concerned Southern Baptists of Georgia had placed a full page ad in an Atlanta Sunday newspaper. Signed by over one thousand Georgia Baptists, it urged that the "independent fundamentalist takeover" of the Convention be stopped by the election of Winfred Moore. While this ad undoubtedly reached many ordinary Southern Baptists who had paid little attention to the controversy and thought it unimportant, it is unlikely that an ad a week before the convention would result in any new messengers in Dallas.

19. "Jackson asks replacement for pre-SBC 'Baptist Hours'," *Baptist Press*, May 21, 1987.

20. Falwell's *Fundamentalist Journal* had also regularly followed happenings in the convention and ran feature articles on SBC fundamentalists Jimmy Draper (May 1985, 22–23), Adrian Rogers (July/August 1986, 59–60), Ike Reighard (June 1987, 24–26), and Jerry Vines (July/August 1989, 10, 16–18). Both the *Fundamentalist Journal* and *Christianity Today* provided news of the denomination's struggle from the fundamentalists' point of view. Moderates could count on the pages of *Christian Century* for coverage of the denomination from their point of view.

21. C. Bird, "Draper, Smith, Rogers discuss SBC on CBN," *Baptist Press*, April 4, 1985.

22. H. Parmley, "Billy Graham explains stand on Baptist vote," *Baptist Press*, June 25, 1985.

23. See J. Hefley, *The Truth in Crisis*, 176–199 for a conservative critique of Baptist Press and the state papers. An unsigned editorial in the May 1989, issue of the *Advocate* took *Baptist Press* to task for failing to report the "falsehoods" and "vitriolic" things said at a Baptists Committed symposium. It concludes "The so-called "Centrists" group doesn't really need to publish a paper. They get all the coverage they need through Baptist Press and the state papers. This is the kind of bias and unfairness that has rankled the conservatives of the Convention for a long time." (p. 3).

24. These stories are covered in the May 1983 issue, pp. 4 and 2, respectively.

25. For instance, in the ten issues preceding the proposal of a "Sanctity of Life" Sunday at the 1985 convention, the *Advocate* published at least ten editorials and news stories on abortion. See N. Ammerman, "Organizational conflict in the Southern Baptist Convention," in *Secularization and Fundamentalism Reconsidered*, ed. J. Hadden and A. Shupe (New York: Paragon, 1989).

26. This included items on new personnel and retirements, stories about missionaries, and heart-warming (and sometimes bizarre) human interest stories

(such as the efforts by motorcycle enthusiasts to convert other bikers). They also included CP budget updates, news of major bequests to institutions, and promotional pieces on new programs being developed.

27. When I began writing papers reporting on this research, I regularly supplied both the *Advocate* and *SBC Today* with copies. While the *Advocate* rarely even referred to what I had sent them, *SBC Today* regularly printed them, usually in full. Even articles originally written for a scholarly audience found their way into the magazine's pages. What always surprised me was that when I went to SBC meetings, I was recognized by people who read the paper and remembered what I had written. The readers of this paper obviously pay very close attention.

28. "Is there not a Cause?" *The Cause* (June 1989), 4.

29. G. Warner, "Lindsay says Rogers selected as candidate," *Baptist Press*, December 9, 1985.

30. The situation changed, of course, once fundamentalists had established themselves as the insiders. They then faced the challenge of retaining the commitment of people who had been willing to join them in a protest against an alien bureaucracy. That transition to power will be examined in more detail in chapter 7.

31. See Wood, *Leadership*, 82–83, for a discussion of the ease with which churches based on congregational polity may oust a pastor. See also N. Ammerman, "The civil rights movement and the clergy in a southern community," *Sociological Analysis* 41(1980):339–350, for a discussion of the resources available to pastors who became involved in the civil rights struggle. Connections to both local and national networks of support aided involvement, and Southern Baptists had neither of these.

32. We heard comments like these from numerous messengers during the convention meetings. Then in 1986, we attended convention reporting sessions in three Atlanta moderate churches and heard similar stories in each church. Many of these lay people had never before attended a convention, and the degree of disenchantment they expressed was deep indeed.

33. The only time I witnessed a comparable encounter that was initiated by a moderate was the argument between Richard Jackson and Paul Pressler during the February 1989, Executive Committee meeting. The encounter between Lynn Clayton and Paige Patterson described in chapter 4 never took on either the angry tone or the taunting crowd of the "schoolyard fights."

34. See G. Warner, "Lindsay says Rogers selected," G. Warner, "'Conservatives' rally lashes 'liberal deceit'," *Baptist Press*, January 17, 1986; M. Knox, "Rally speakers criticize teaching of 'false doctrines' in seminaries," *Baptist Press*, April 25, 1986.

35. We again used analysis of variance to test the relations among these variables. In predicting denominational activism, church size (b = .47), being clergy as compared to laity (b = .37) and support for the fundamentalist agenda (b = .20) had significant effects. In predicting political activism, being a pastor (b = .34) and denominational activism (b = .31) had the largest effects, with church size (b = .12) and support for the fundamentalists (b = .09) having smaller, but statistically sig-

nificant effects. In addition, there was a significant interaction effect between denominational activity and fundamentalist support in predicting political involvement. With denominational activity controlled, the effect of being pro-fundamentalist was strengthened, while the effect of being antifundamentalist decreased to zero. Finally, in predicting the likelihood that a respondent would go to the Dallas convention, being clergy (b = .42), political activism (b = .26), and denominational activism (b = .13) were the three significant effects.

36. Compare the messenger survey results reported in the 1985 *Annual*, 42, with 1985 figures reported in *The Quarterly Review* 46(July/August/September 1986):11.

37. Zald and Berger, "Social movements," argue based on various studies of social movements that people who are already members of similar organizations are the most likely recruits for new movements. "[B]elonging to associations and networks eases the cost of information flow and mobilization." p. 846. Denominationally active moderates certainly seem to have formed the sort of "dense associational field" that would facilitate movement organization.

38. On the decision-making difficulties experienced by the national assemblies of "congregational" denominations, see K. P. Takayama, "Formal polity and change of structure: denominational assemblies," *Sociological Analysis* 36(1975): 17–28.

39. "Proceedings," 1979 *Annual*, 45.

40. "Proceedings," 1981 *Annual*, 44–46.

41. "Proceedings," 1982 *Annual*, 49–51.

42. *SBC Today* covered the suit extensively. See esp. issues from November 1985 through March 1986.

43. See A. Farnsley, *Majority Rules*.

44. The most glaring exception to this pattern was the 1984 Convention Sermon by Southwestern Seminary president Russell Dilday. It was a blistering attack on the fundamentalist direction of the Convention and could easily be called the opening round in the "holy war" of the following year.

45. In 1987, I was able to obtain copies of all resolutions submitted to the committee and compare originals with what the committee wrote. In 1988, I was able to observe several sessions of the committee's work. My analysis is based on the official convention record, plus these observations and documents.

46. A knowledgeable fundamentalist leader was posted at the top of the only steps that gave access to the platform. He helped to control the flow of traffic, sending messages for supporters when they were needed and on occasion telling nonsupporters they could not use the platform.

47. This was covered by *Baptist Press* in M. Knox, "Flurry of convention motions creates avalanche of work," July 2, 1986.

48. An account of the Executive Committee decisions is contained in D. Martin, "Constitutional changes declined by committee," *Baptist Press*, September 20, 1985; and D. Martin, "Committee revises bylaw, declines other changes," *Baptist Press*, September 26, 1986.

49. See N. Ammerman, "Organizational conflict."

50. In 1986, for instance, the Home Mission Board responded to a 1985 reso-

lution saying essentially that they did not believe the requested activity was their job (1986 *Annual*, 175). The Sunday School Board responded to two friendly motions with detailed plans of action and explained that they did not think their consumers wanted them to follow the request of a third motion (1986 *Annual*, 194–195). The Christian Life Commission explained what they were doing to promote Sanctity of Human Life Sunday, some of which would have pleased the maker of that motion, and some of which probably would not (1986 *Annual*, 221).

51. The videotapes of the 1986 convention made clear the extent to which Stanley depended on parliamentarian Barry McCarty. At almost every juncture, even routine matters of calling for votes, McCarty was literally telling Stanley every word to say.

52. Again, the audience for these moderates was probably skewed by the absence of fundamentalists from the convention hall during many of their reports. Fundamentalists often expressed their disdain for the block of program time dominated by "the liberals." They arrived in time for the Convention Sermon and skipped the seminary and Commission reports.

Chapter 7. The Tasks of Governing

1. See M. Weber, "Characteristics of bureaucracy," in *From Max Weber*, ed. H. H. Gerth and C. W. Mills (New York: Oxford University Press, 1946), 196–204.

2. K. P. Takayama, "Administrative structures and political processes in Protestant denominations," *Publius* 4(2)(1974):5–37. See also K. P. Takayama and L. W. Cannon, "Formal polity and power distribution in American Protestant denominations," *The Sociological Quarterly* 20(1979):321–332.

3. D. A. Bolden, "Organizational characteristics of ecumenically active denominations," *Sociological Analysis* 46(1985):261–274.

4. The ecumenical efforts of the denomination, especially its "Interfaith Witness" department, are examined in R. Harmon and G. J. Sheridan, "The Southern Baptist Convention and Ecumenism" *Ecumenical Trends* 16(November 1987): 1–4. This article came after Harmon's forced resignation and just before Sheridan's dismissal.

5. P. Selznick, *TVA and the Grass Roots* (Berkeley: University of California Press, 1949).

6. The information in this and following sections comes from multiple interviews with fundamentalist leaders, trustees and committee members, and agency staff people. They include people with loyalties on both sides (and some with no loyalties except to the denomination). These are all sensitive issues and in many cases public accounts vary. The public accounts, reported in *Baptist Press* and in secular newspapers, are cited; but in most instances they are not the only source for my rendering. The remainder represents my reconstruction based on multiple sources.

7. By the late 1980s the percentage of women serving on boards had declined from nearly 15 percent a decade earlier to less than half that. See S. F. Anders, "Tracing past and present," in *The New Has Come*, ed. A. T. Neil and V. G. Neely

(Washington, DC: The Southern Baptist Alliance, 1989), 5–27. In 1987, the trustees of the Foreign Mission Board passed a resolution of regret that they were getting no women in their twenty-eight new members. See C. Bird, "Foreign Mission Board Trustees 'regret' lack of women nominees," *Baptist Press*, May 21, 1987. And from the floor of the 1989 convention, the Committee on Nominations was asked why so few women were being nominated. The chair answered that they had tried to find women and ethnics for positions, but the complicated formulas for state, local, and clergy-laity representation had hampered their efforts. His logic seemed to imply that in some or all of those categories, there were too few qualified women available.

8. On at least one occasion that meant real embarrassment when the conservative credentials of one trustee included membership in the John Birch Society, and his conservative ideology included denigration of the Rev. Martin Luther King, Jr., perceptions of "world hunger" and "peace" as communist plots, and acceptance of apartheid in South Africa. (Reported in private conversations with those in attendance at the CLC board and in M. Knox, "Southern Baptist agency drops surgeon general's AIDS report," *Baptist Press*, September 16, 1988.) These ideas were so repugnant, especially to younger fundamentalist leaders, that a 1989 move to request his resignation from the board of the Christian Life Commission was not opposed.

9. A 1986 challenge was brought against one nominee to the Executive Committee who had been a Southern Baptist ten years and who had never been to an annual meeting. See M. Knox, "Dunaway to present challenge to Executive Committee nominee," *Baptist Press*, May 16, 1987. The 1986 convention was also the first Lee Roberts had ever attended. He was the chair that year of the Committee on Nominations.

10. Since Southern Baptists are only one-third of that board, the full board refused—a fact which the Southern Baptist members made a cause celibre. See the discussion of the Baptist Joint Committee below.

11. Emotions and interest also sometimes ran low. Routine business sometimes did not command the attention of new trustees. Moderate trustees and staff people reported to us their dismay that some board members walked around the room visiting with each other during business sessions. At a Home Mission Board meeting I attended, one fundamentalist trustee read the newspaper during most of the morning business. Another left for fifteen to twenty minutes. Another leaned casually back in his chair, yawning frequently. Another left and came back with piles of copies of newspaper articles concerning national political issues, writing notes on them and passing them to various fellow members.

12. A long tradition of study in social psychology has established the power of groups to impose both norms and perceptions on minorities who might be tempted to see or do things differently. S. Asch, "Studies of independence and conformity," *Psychological Monographs* 70(9)(1956):1–70, demonstrated group effects on visual perception; and L. Festinger, S. Schachter, and K. Back, *Social Pressures in Informal Groups* (Stanford: Stanford University Press, 1950) further demonstrated the wide range of behavior that is susceptible to the definitions of others. We are perhaps most likely to go along when the others influencing us are

of higher status and perceived to have some legitimate authority. The notorious experiments by S. Milgram, reported in *Obedience to Authority* (New York: Harper, 1974) showed just how far most of us are willing to go in following orders.

The one factor moderating this process for new fundamentalist trustees was that they could assume they would eventually be the majority. So long as they were able to live in hope, anticipating that day, they could ward off the efforts of the current majority to press them toward conformity.

The effects of minority status were also seen in the eventual pressures on moderates to conform to their new superiors. A unanimous recommendation from the Home Mission Board search committee (with at least three moderate members) is strong evidence of the power of a group to define the situation and its norms.

13. See for example, D. Martin, "Breakthrough near, peace chairman says," *Baptist Press*, October 24, 1986.

14. All quotations from "Report of the Southern Baptist Convention Peace Committee," *SBC Bulletin*, first day, part II, June 16, 1987, 12–15.

15. D. Martin, "Peace committee adopts statement on diversity," *Baptist Press*, February 28, 1986.

16. D. Martin, "Six seminary presidents make reconciliation try," *Baptist Press*, October 24, 1986; and "Sherman resigns Peace Committee," *Baptist Press*, October 24, 1986.

17. S. A. Brown, "HMB staff to reaffirm BFM statement: Lewis," *Baptist Press*, June 29, 1987.

18. This new policy cost Larry Lewis the appointment of right-to-life organizer Kirk Shrewsbury. Lewis wanted Shrewsbury to head the Board's efforts on crisis pregnancy centers, but his practice of speaking in tongues made him ineligible for the post. See "Tongues vs. right to life," *SBC Today* 5(6)(October 1987):13.

19. S. A. Brown, "HMB staff to reaffirm."

20. "Politics and corridor talk," *SBC Today* 5(5)(August/September 1987):11.

21. M. Wingfield, "HMB directors approve staff reorganization," *Baptist Press*, October 13, 1988.

22. M. Wingfield, "Pastor declines HMB position; cites concerns with trustees," *Baptist Press*, February 17, 1989.

23. A. Toalston, "Missionary asked to resign; doctrinal clarity questioned," *Baptist Press*, July 7, 1988; B. Stanley, "FMB dismisses Willett for 'doctrinal ambiguity,'" *Baptist Press*, July 22, 1988. Willett circulated his own version of the story in "A Summary of the Events Leading to my Dismissal as a Foreign Missionary."

24. M. Knox, "Missionary resigns in doctrinal flap," *Baptist Press*, February 21, 1985.

25. B. Stanley, "Parks won't back Stanley; Sees threat to missions," *Baptist Press*, April 22, 1985.

26. J. U. Harwell, "Trustees override FMB staff," *SBC Today* 7(5)(August 1989):1.

27. This would appear to be more evidence of the declining significance of denominational identity and the increasing significance of "para-church" organi-

zations as the institutional infrastructure of American religion that is documented in R. Wuthnow, *The Restructuring*.

28. This is estimated from the 4.4 million adults reported enrolled in Sunday Schools in *The Quarterly Review: Southern Baptist Handbook*, 46(4)(July/August/September 1986):33.

29. See L. Wilkey, "Sunday School Board trustees postpone naming new commentary," *Baptist Press*, August 19, 1988.

30. A similar skirting of professional staff in favor of proven fundamentalist direction occurred in a 1989 decision to commission a new student ministry handbook. See K. F. Berry, "BSSB sets personnel precedent," *SBC Today* 7(7)(October 1989):1–2.

31. In particular, Elder had played a key role in preventing the reallocation of most the the Baptist Joint Committee's 1989–1990 budget.

32. "BSSB trustees turn aside attempt to fire Elder," *SBC Today* 7(6)(September 1989):1.

33. For example, D. Wilkinson, "CLC trustees reject move to narrow abortion stance," *Baptist Press*, September 19, 1986.

34. D. Wilkinson, "Larry Baker elected CLC Executive Director," *Baptist Press*, January 16, 1987.

35. Quoted in T. Fields, "CLC announces new abortion initiatives," *Baptist Press*, May 4, 1987.

36. D. Martin, "Lockard becomes 5th staffer to resign CLC," *Baptist Press*, September 23, 1988.

37. D. Martin, "CLC directors elect Land on 23–2 ballot," *Baptist Press*, September 15, 1988.

38. S. Hastey, "CLC citizenship seminar addresses national agenda," *Baptist Press*, March 18, 1988.

39. D. Martin and L. Moore, "Sanctity of life focus of CLC annual seminar," *Baptist Press*, March 31, 1989.

40. A. Hardie, "Baptist committee endorses Bork," *The Atlanta Constitution*, (September 24, 1987), A10.

41. M. Knox, "PAC pans childcare bill, praises funding process," *Baptist Press*, May 25, 1988.

42. My analysis is greatly informed here by the field work and insight of Arthur Farnsley. His discussion of the battle of the Religious Liberty Commission is contained in his *Majority Rules*.

43. J. U. Harwell, "Liberty commission dead; CLC given church-state lead." *SBC Today* 7(7)(October 1989):2.

44. A number of professors turned down other teaching jobs and pastorates during the years of controversy. They were committed both to their vocation of training ministers and to the institutions at which they served.

45. "Faculty nomination dropped; denominational politics blamed," *Baptist Press*, April 8, 1987.

46. This meeting is reported in G. White, "After 5 hours, trustees vote to retain Southwestern Baptist president Dilday," *The Atlanta Constitution* (October 18, 1989), A-12.

47. Of those on the list for concern at Southern, two had long since retired and one was dead. President Honeycutt asked the remaining ten to respond in detail to the charges leveled against them. He then asked for and got an affirmation from the trustees of the responses offered, and he mailed charges and responses to all the Baptist state paper editors. This public airing and affirmation tended to undercut the legitimacy of continued accusations against these ten.

48. Fundamentalist leaders were always careful about naming names, but ordinary folk had no such reticence. Almost any fundamentalist messenger we talked with could name at least one professor they thought should be fired.

49. B. J. Sanders, "Midwestern trustees respond to SBC Peace Committee," *Baptist Press*, April 15, 1988.

50. Technically Southern's trustees are a self-perpetuating board, electing their own successors. That fact gave many moderates hope that the Seminary might simply refuse to accept new fundamentalist trustees. However, by 1988 it was finally clear that the Board's only source of nominees was the official SBC Committee on Nominations, and that all new nominees would be elected. See "Southern moves to resolve trustee-election issue," *Baptist Press*, April 14, 1988.

51. In this way, the 1987 luncheon address was in marked contrast to his previous addresses. In 1985, he spoke of his faith in an ultimate victory that would come from the darkness and defeat of that hour. And in 1986, he urged a retreat into the catacombs so as to preserve civilization until the present Dark Age was past. He hinted that the seminary might be organizing its alumni and friends into a support network that could sustain the institution in the struggle that lay ahead. But between June of 1986 and the following June, the six seminary presidents had issued their "Glorieta statement," proclaiming their belief that the Bible is "not errant in any area of reality" and pledging to incorporate inerrancy into their institutional life.

52. D. Wilkinson, "Southern trustees show signs of harmony," *Baptist Press*, April 14, 1988.

53. That shift in language in part reflected a shift in real conversation partners. By requiring increased travel to be with church groups, trying to diffuse the controversy, the administration reduced the available time teachers had for the kind of scholarly work that would put them in conversation with their professional peers.

54. R. Lolley, "Quo Vadis, Southeastern? A Convocation Address" August 25, 1987.

55. On Southeastern events, see A. Shackleford, "Trustees name Drummond Southeastern president," *Baptist Press*, March 16, 1988; R. G. Ruckett, "Committee cautions 'troubled' seminary," *Baptist Press*, August 19, 1988; "Southeastern seminary enrollment decreases," *Baptist Press*, September 27, 1988; A. Shackleford, "Accreditation investigations occupy Southeastern trustees," *Baptist Press*, October 12, 1988; M. Knox, "Accrediting agency delays decision on Southeastern," *Baptist Press*, January 26, 1989; and M. Knox, "Southeastern trustees blame Lolley, faculty for problems," *Baptist Press*, February 23, 1989.

56. "Editorial viewpoint," 4.

Chapter 8. Southern Baptists and the Future

1. A. O. Hirschman, *Exit, Voice, and Loyalty* (Cambridge: Harvard University Press, 1970).

2. For a time I actually felt a bit like an employment bureau for dislocated Southern Baptists. Those who were most serious about exiting were looking for whatever help they could find. Because they knew about my research and knew that I was not in a Baptist institution, a series of people sought me out as a potential gatekeeper for the broader employment market.

3. See Roof and McKinney, *American Mainline Religion*, 164–177, for a summary of current "switching" patterns. While "upward" switching is not as prevalent as it perhaps once was, it is most likely among those with high levels of education and occupational prestige.

4. The rules on this are complicated. If a pastor had contributed through the "church annuity" plan, his contributions were vested from the first day of employment. That is not the case for agency employees, for whom there is usually a delay. In some cases, contributions could actually be withdrawn and invested in another plan, although matching funds paid by churches and/or state conventions could not always be converted to cash. In most instances, exiting employees would probably choose to leave investments in place, simply drawing on them at retirement.

5. R. L. Cantrell, J. F. Krile, and G. A. Donohue, "Parish autonomy: measuring denominational differences," *Journal for the Scientific Study of Religion* 22(1983):276–287. Just how complicated the question of polity has become is also discussed by J. G. Hougland and J. R. Wood in "Determinants of organizational control in local churches," *Journal for the Scientific Study of Religion* 18(1978): 132–145.

6. R. C. Liebman, J. R. Sutton, and R. Wuthnow, "Exploring the social sources of denominationalism: schisms in American Protestant denominations, 1890–1980," *American Sociological Review* 53(1988):343–352, found that size and membership in a liberal ecumenical organization were the two most powerful factors in predicting the 492 schisms they analyzed. Bigger denominations were more prone to schism, but that is counteracted by the negative effect of federation membership. In the Southern Baptist Convention, we have a very large denomination, with few ecumenical ties. It would therefore appear very prone to schism, especially as those ecumenical ties diminish. What seems likely here is that those who wish to maintain broader ties will be pushed toward the margins and perhaps out. See the discussion of the Southern Baptist Alliance below.

7. G. Niebuhr, "Southern Baptist moderates seeking to build 'resistance movement,'" *The Atlanta Journal and Constitution* (March 11, 1989), C5.

8. At the individual level, Roof and McKinney, *American Mainline Religion*, see this breakdown of the old ascriptive bases for denominationalism leading toward a "new voluntarism." At the institutional level, Wuthnow, *The Restructuring*, outlines a similar voluntarism in new networks of organizations on the religious right and the religious left that constitute, in many cases, functional substitutes for denominations.

9. J. Wilson, "The Sociology of Schism," argues that strong social control mechanisms and less individual autonomy appear to inhibit schism. However, Liebman, Sutton, and Wuthnow, "Exploring the social sources," found that polity had no effect in predicting schisms. The ability of disaffected churches to act on their own desires, regardless of polity has been examined by J. R. Wood and M. N. Zald in "Aspects of racial integration in the Methodist church: sources of resistance to organizational policy," *Social Forces* 45(1966):255–265. See also K. P. Takayama and D. G. Sachs, "Polity and decision premises: the church and the private school," *Journal for the Scientific Study of Religion* 15(1976):269–278.

10. "Southern Baptist Alliance formed to counter 'threat'," *Baptist Press*, February 13, 1987.

11. Sources for these figures are written membership reports given to the annual convocations.

12. M. Knox, "Leaders call Alliance lifeline, not scalpel," *Baptist Press*, May 18, 1987.

13. Compare the distinctions between movement and institution discussed by R. S. Warner in *New Wine in Old Wineskins* (Berkeley: University of California Press, 1987), ch. 2.

14. "Alliance, Duke explore House of Baptist Studies," *Baptist Press*, June 14, 1988.

15. The Wake Forest plan was eventually approved, pending raising funds for an endowment. President Thomas Hearn Jr. said that "while the orientation and heritage of the divinity school would be Baptist, it would be open to students and faculty members of all faiths." See "WFU OKs divinity school; seeks $15 million endowment," *Baptist Press*, April 25, 1989. They would join the Divinity School at Samford University in Birmingham as the second new university-based school. The Samford school, however, was widely viewed with suspicion among moderates. It was seen as serving the needs of conservatives more than their own.

16. M. Knox, "Alliance proceeds with seminary plans," *Baptist Press*, January 6, 1989.

17. E. Rosenberg, *The Southern Baptists*, 202, is right to observe this narrowness of vision in the early days of the Alliance, but she was wrong to assume that the narrowness would continue.

18. I had heard this story from a number of sources, but was able to confirm it myself when I chaired the Search Committee for my own church. At about the same time two other friends chaired committees in two other states, and each had the same experience of receiving 2–5 unsolicited recommendations from people they recognized as active local fundamentalists. This is also discussed in R. Coleman, "Conflict hits pastor search," *SBC Today* 6(9)(December 1988):14.

19. M. L. Steed examined the question of whether schismatic churches would eventually secede from the denomination in "Church schism and secession: A necessary sequence?" *Review of Religious Research* 27(1986):344–355. Examining Anglo-Catholic parishes in the Protestant Episcopal Church, she concluded that secession was more likely in bigger diocese and where a "pastoral" bishop was lacking. Where leaders could offer patient guidance, secession seemed less likely. It is possible that dissident Baptist churches in densely-Baptist areas may

find secession less necessary. It is also possible that sympathetic local leaders may keep some disenchanted progressives in.

20. Hirschmann, *Exit*, esp. ch. 3.

21. R. Stark and W. S. Bainbridge, *The Future of Religion*, 122–124.

Appendix A

1. See C. K. Hadaway, "Will the real Southern Baptist please stand up: methodological problems in surveying Southern Baptist congregations and members," *Review of Religious Research* 31(1989):149–161, for an extensive discussion of the problems in identifying a sample of Southern Baptists. The 1986 poll by Wilkerson and Associates (commissioned by moderates and reported in *SBC Today* 4(July 1986):8), for instance, attempted a survey of all Southern Baptists. Using random digit dialing in ten states, they identified people who said they were "Southern Baptist" and asked them a series of questions about events in the Convention. The number of blacks among their respondents (9 percent) is one clue that their identification of "Southern Baptists" may have been less than precise. Their respondents also include one third who attend church less than once a week—not a population for whom the controversy could be expected to have high salience. Indeed, when they asked about causes of disagreement in the denomination 40 to 46 percent could not offer an answer. This is comparable to the 44 percent of Florida Baptists, polled using similar methods, who said they had not heard about the controversy (from the report of the Einhorn and Lewis study, privately circulated). While such general population studies are useful tor gauging general opinion, such a high degree of ignorance of the issues would have hindered our analyses.

References

Alldredge, E. P. 1932. *Southern Baptist Handbook*. Nashville: The Baptist Sunday School Board.

———. 1943. *Southern Baptist Handbook*. Nashville: The Baptist Sunday School Board.

Ammerman, N. 1980. "The civil rights movement and the clergy in a southern community." *Sociological Analysis* 41:339–350.

———. 1987. *Bible Believers: Fundamentalists in the Modern World*. New Brunswick: Rutgers University Press.

———. 1987. "Schism: An overview." In *The Encyclopedia of Religion*, vol. 13. ed. Mircea Eliade. New York: Macmillan.

———. 1989. "Organizational conflict in the Southern Baptist Convention." In *Secularization and Fundamentalism Reconsidered*. ed. J. Hadden and A. Shupe. New York: Paragon.

———. 1990. "North American Protestant Fundamentalism." In *Fundamentalism Observed*, ed. M. E. Marty and R. S. Appleby. Chicago: University of Chicago Press.

———. forthcoming. "Southern Baptists and the New Christian Right." *Review of Religious Research*.

Anders, S. F. 1988. "Southern Baptist Convention clergywomen and laywomen: In the eye of the storm." A paper presented to the Religious Research Association.

———. 1989. "Tracing past and present." In *The New Has Come*. ed. A. T. Neil and V. G. Neely. Washington: The Southern Baptist Alliance.

Anderson, R. M. 1979. *Vision of the Disinherited*. New York: Oxford University Press.

Asch, S. 1976. "Studies of independence and conformity." *Psychological Monographs* 70(9):1–70.

Bailey, K. K. 1964. *Southern White Protestantism in the Twentieth Century*. Gloucester, Mass.: Peter Smith.

Baker, R. A. 1974. *The Southern Baptist Convention and its People, 1607–1972*. Nashville: Broadman.

Barnes, W. W. 1954. *The Southern Baptist Convention, 1845–1953*. Nashville: Broadman.

Barnette, H. 1948. "The challenge of Southern cities." *Review and Expositor* 45:423–434.

Barnhart, J. E. 1986. *The Southern Baptist Holy War*. Austin: Texas Monthly Press.

Barr, L. S., ed. 1986. *The Quarterly Review*: Handbook Issue. 46(4).

Beale, D. O. 1985. *S.B.C. House on the Sand?* Greenville, S.C.: Unusual Publications.

Bellah, R. N., R. Madsen, W. M. Sullivan, A. Swidler, and S. M. Tipton. 1986. *Habits of the Heart*. Berkeley: University of California Press.

Berger, P. L. 1969. *The Sacred Canopy*. Garden City, N.Y.: Doubleday Anchor.

Blasi, A. J. 1980. *Segregationist Violence and Civil Rights Movements in Tuscaloosa*. Washington: University Press of America.

Bolden, D. A. 1985. "Organizational characteristics of ecumenically active denominations." *Sociological Analysis* 46(3):261–274.

Boles, J. 1985. "Evangelical Protestantism in the Old South: From religious dissent to cultural dominance." In *Religion in the South*, ed. C. R. Wilson. Jackson: University Press of Mississippi.

Brackney, W. H. 1988. *The Baptists*. New York: Greenwood Press.

Bronfenbrenner, U. 1958. "Socialization and social class through time and space." In *Readings in Social Psychology*. 3d ed. Ed. E. Maccoby, T. Newcomb, and E. Hartley. New York: Holt.

Bruce, D. C., Jr. 1974. *And They All Sang Hallelujah: Plain-Folk Camp Meeting Religion, 1800–1845*. Knoxville: University of Tennessee Press.

Campbell, W. D. 1988. *The Convention*. Atlanta: Peachtree Publishers.

Cantrell, R. L., J. F. Krile, and G. A. Donohue. 1983. "Parish autonomy: Measuring denominational differences." *Journal for the Scientific Study of Religion* 22:276–287.

Carroll, J., B. Hargrove, and A. Lummis. 1983. *Women of the Cloth*. New York: Harper and Row.

Daniels, E. J., and J. Bos. 1985. *The Battle over the Bible among Southern Baptists*. Orlando: Christ for the World Publishers.

Demerath, N. J. 1965. *Social Class and American Protestantism*. Chicago: Rand McNally.

Dimaggio, P, and J. Mohr. 1985. "Cultural capital, educational attainment and marital selection." *American Journal of Sociology* 90(6):1231–1261.

Doherty, R. W. 1967. *The Hicksite Separation*. New Brunswick: Rutgers University Press.

Draper, J. T. Jr. 1984. *Authority: The Critical Issue for Southern Baptists*. Old Tappan, N.J.: Fleming H. Revell.

Edmunds, J. P. 1952. *The Southern Baptist Handbook, 1952*. Nashville: Broadman Press.

Eighmy, J. L. 1987. *Churches in Cultural Captivity: A History of the Social Attitudes of Southern Baptists* (with revised introduction, conclusion, and bibliography by S. S. Hill). Knoxville: University of Tennessee Press.

Elliott, R. H. 1961. *The Message of Genesis*. Nashville: Broadman.

Farnsley, A. 1990. "Majority rules: The politicization of the Southern Baptist Convention." Ph.D. diss., Emory University.

Festinger, L., S. Schachter, and K. Back. 1950. *Social Pressures in Informal Groups*. Stanford: Stanford University Press.

Fischer, C. S. 1975. "The effect of urban life on traditional values." *Social Forces* 53(3):420–432.

Flynt, J. W. 1981. "Southern Baptists: Rural to urban transition." *Baptist History and Heritage* 16:24–34.

———. 1981. "One in the Spirit, Many in the Flesh: Southern Evangelicals." In

Varieties of Southern Evangelicalism, ed. D. E. Harrell, Jr. Macon: Mercer University Press.

———. 1982. "The impact of social factors on Southern Baptist expansion: 1800–1914." *Baptist History and Heritage* 17:20–31.

———. 1986. "Women, society and the southern church, 1900–1920." In *Religion in the South: Conference Papers.* Alabama Humanities Foundation.

Gardner, E. C. 1984. "Christian Ethics." In *Encyclopedia of Southern Religion,* ed. S. S. Hill. Macon: Mercer University Press.

Geertz, C. 1968. *Islam Observed.* Chicago: University of Chicago Press.

———. 1973. "Religion as a cultural system." In *The Interpretation of Cultures,* New York: Basic Books.

Gerth, H. H. and C. W. Mills. 1946. *From Max Weber.* New York: Oxford University Press.

Glenn, N. D. and L. Hill, Jr. 1977. "Rural-urban differences in attitudes and behavior in the U.S." *Annals of the American Academy of Political and Social Science* 429:36–50.

Glock, C. Y. 1964. "The role of deprivation in the origin and evolution of religious groups." In *Religion and Social Conflict,* ed. R. Lee and M. E. Marty. New York: Oxford University Press.

Guth, J. 1984. "The education of the Christian Right: The case of the Southern Baptist clergy," *Quarterly Review* 4(2):44–56.

———. 1985. "The Christian Right revisited: Partisan realignment among Southern Baptist ministers." A paper presented to the Midwest Political Science Association.

Guth, J., T. G. Jelen, L. A. Kellstedt, C. E. Smidt, and K. D. Wald. 1988. "The politics of religion in America." *American Politics Quarterly* 16(3):357–397.

Hadaway, C. K. 1989. "Will the real Southern Baptist please stand up: methodological problems in surveying Southern Baptist congregations and members," *Review of Religious Research* 31(2):149–161.

Halbrooks, G. T. 1982. "Growing pains: The impact of expansion on Southern Baptists since 1942." *Baptist History and Heritage* 17:44–54.

Hargrove, B. W. 1989. *The Sociology of Religion.* Chicago: Harlan Davidson.

Harmon, G. 1963. "How to tell a Baptist from a Methodist in the South." *Harper's Magazine* 226(February):58–63.

Harmon, R., and G. J. Sheridan. 1987. "The Southern Baptist Convention and Ecumenism." *Ecumenical Trends* 16(10):1–4.

Harrell, D. E., Jr. 1981. "The South: Seedbed of sectarianism." In *Varieties of Southern Evangelicalism,* ed. D. E. Harrell, Jr. Macon: Mercer University Press.

Harrison, P. 1971 ed. *Authority and Power in the Free Church Tradition.* Carbondale: Southern Illinois Press.

Hastey, S. L. 1973. "A History of the Baptist Joint Committee on Public Affairs, 1946–1971." Th.D. diss., Southern Baptist Theological Seminary.

Hefley, J. C. 1986. *The Truth in Crisis.* Dallas: Criterion.

———. 1988. *The Truth in Crisis,* vol. 3. Hannibal, Mo.: Hannibal Books.

Henderson, S. T. 1980. "Social action in a conservative environment: The CLC and Southern Baptist churches." *Foundations* 23:245–51.

Hill, S. S. 1963. "The Southern Baptists: Need for reformulation, redirection." *Christian Century* 80:39–42.

———. 1966. *Southern Churches in Crisis*. New York: Holt, Rinehart, and Winston.

Hinson, E. G. 1979. "SBC fundamentalists: Stirring up a storm." *Christian Century* 96(24):725–727.

Hirschman, A. O. 1970. *Exit, Voice, and Loyalty*. Cambridge: Harvard University Press.

Holifield, E. B. 1976. "Three strands of Jimmy Carter's religion." *New Republic* 174(June):15–17.

Hollyfield, N. W., Jr. 1976. "A sociological analysis of the degrees of 'Christian Orthodoxy' among selected students in the Southern Baptist Theological Seminary." Unpublished Master's Thesis, Southern Baptist Theological Seminary.

Hougland, J. G., and J. R. Wood. 1978. "Determinants of organizational control in local churches." *Journal for the Scientific Study of Religion* 18:132–145.

Hudson, W. S. 1973. "The divergent careers of Southern and Northern Baptists." *Foundations* 16(April):171–83.

Hull, W. E. 1982. "Pluralism in the Southern Baptist Convention." *Review and Expositor* 79(Winter):121–46.

Hunter, J. D. 1987. *Evangelicalism: The Coming Generation*. Chicago: Chicago University Press.

———. 1983. *American Evangelism*. New Brunswick: Rutgers University Press.

Ingram, L. C., R. Thornton, and R. Hazelwood. 1988. "Perceptions of academic freedom by professors in Southern Baptist colleges." A paper presented to the Religious Research Association.

James, R. 1987. *The Unfettered Word*. Waco, Tex.: Word Books.

Johnson, B. 1963. "On church and sect." *American Sociological Review* 28:539–549.

———. 1971. "Church and Sect Revisited," *Journal for the Scientific Study of Religion* 10:124–137

Jones, P. B. 1979. "An examination of the statistical growth of the SBC." In *Understanding Church Growth and Decline*, ed. D. R. Hoge and D. A. Roozen. Philadelphia: Pilgrim Press.

Knight, W. 1969. *Struggle for Integrity*. Waco, Tex.: Word.

———. 1976. "A future more promising than the past." *Home Missions* 47(December):6–8.

Kohn, M. 1981. "Personality, occupation, and social stratification." In *Research in Social Stratification and Mobility*, ed. D. J. Treiman and R. V. Robinson. Greenwich, Conn.: JAI Press.

Kurtz, L. 1986. *The Politics of Heresy*. Berkeley: University of California Press.

Land, R. 1988. "Pastoral leadership: Authoritarian or persuasive?" In *Polarities in the Southern Baptist Convention*, ed. F. Humphries. New Orleans: New Orleans Baptist Theological Seminary.

Lechner, F. 1985. "Fundamentalism and sociocultural revitalization in America: A sociological interpretation." *Sociological Analysis* 46(2):243–260.

Lehman, E. C. 1985. *Women Clergy*. New Brunswick: Transaction.

Liebman, R. C., J. R. Sutton, and R. Wuthnow. 1988. "Exploring the social sources of denominationalism: Schisms in American Protestant denominations, 1890–1980." *American Sociological Review* 53:343–352.

Lumpkin, W. L. 1961. *Baptist Foundations in the South*. Nashville: Broadman.

Marsden, G. 1980. *Fundamentalism and American Culture*. New York: Oxford.

Martin, D. A. 1962. "The Denomination," *British Journal of Sociology* 13(March 1962):1–14.

Marty, M. E., and R. S. Appleby, eds. 1990. *Fundamentalism Observed*. Chicago: University of Chicago Press.

Maston, T. B. "The Bible and women." *The Student* 64(8):48.

Matthews, D. G. 1977. *Religion in the Old South*. Chicago: University of Chicago Press.

McBeth, L. 1979. *Women in Baptist Life*. Nashville: Broadman.

———. 1982. "Expansion of the Southern Baptist Convention to 1951." *Baptist History and Heritage* 17:32–43.

———. 1987. *The Baptist Heritage*. Nashville: Broadman.

McClellan, A. 1953. *The West is Big*. Atlanta: Home Mission Board.

McClelland, D. C. 1961. *The Achieving Society*. Princeton: Van Nostrand.

McKinney, J. C. and L. B. Bourque. 1971. "The changing south: National incorporation of a region." *American Sociological Review* 36:399–412.

McLoughlin, W. G. 1971. *New England Dissent, 1630–1833: The Baptists and the Separation of Church and State*. Cambridge: Harvard University Press.

McSwain, Larry and W. B. Shurden. 1981. "Changing values of Southern Baptists, 1900–1980." *Baptist History and Heritage* 16:45–54.

Milgram, S. 1974. *Obedience to Authority*. New York: Harper.

Moody, D. 1979. "The shaping of Southern Baptist polity." *Baptist History and Heritage* 14:2–11.

Neely, A. 1988. *Being Baptist Means Freedom*. Atlanta: Southern Baptist Alliance.

Neely, H. K., Jr. 1963. "The Territorial Expansion of the Southern Baptist Convention, 1894–1959." Unpublished Th.d. diss., Southwestern Baptist Theological Seminary.

———. 1976. "Baptist beginnings in the middle colonies." In *The Lord's Free People in a Free Land*, ed. W. R. Estep. Fort Worth: Southwestern Baptist Theological Seminary.

Nettles, T. J. 1981. "Southern Baptists: Regional to national transition." *Baptist History and Heritage* 16:13–23.

Newman, A. H. 1915. *A History of the Baptist Churches in the United States*. New York: Scribner's.

Newman, W. M. and P. L. Halverson. 1978. *Atlas of Religious Change in America, 1952–1971*. Washington: Glenmary.

Niebuhr, H. R. 1929. *The Social Sources of Denominationalism*. New York: World Publishing.

Norsworthy, R. 1988. "Rationalization and reaction among Southern Baptists." A paper presented to the Religious Research Association in Chicago.

Patterson, W. M. 1962. "The development of the Baptist successionist formula." *Foundations* 5:331–345.

———. 1975. "The influence of Landmarkism among Baptists." *Baptist History and Heritage* 10(1):44–55.

Pope, L. 1942. *Millhands and Preachers*. New Haven: Yale University Press.

Primer, B. 1979. *Protestants and American Business Methods*. Ann Arbor, Mich.: UMI Press.

———. 1980. "The failure of Southern fundamentalism." A paper presented to the Southeastern Historical Association in Houston.

Quebedeaux, R. 1974. *The Young Evangelicals*. New York: Harper & Row.

Redford, C. 1948. *Spiritual Frontiers*. Atlanta: Home Mission Board.

Reed, J. S. 1983. *Southerners*. Chapel Hill: University of North Carolina Press.

Roof, W. C., and W. McKinney. 1987. *American Mainline Religion: Its Changing Shape and Future*. New Brunswick: Rutgers University Press.

Rosenberg, E. 1989. *The Southern Baptists: A Subculture in Transition*. Knoxville: University of Tennessee Press.

Rutledge, A. B. 1969. *Mission to America*. Nashville: Broadman.

Sandeen, E. R. 1970. *The Roots of Fundamentalism*. Chicago: University of Chicago Press.

Sapp, D. 1981. "Southern Baptist responses to the American economy, 1900–1980." *Baptist History and Heritage* 16:3–12.

Schwartz, G. 1970. *Sect Ideologies and Social Status*. Chicago: University of Chicago Press.

Selznick, P. 1949. *TVA and the Grass Roots*. Berkeley: University of California Press.

Shibley, M. A. 1989. "The Southernization of American religion: Testing a hypothesis." A paper presented to the Association for the Sociology of Religion.

Shin, E. H., and H. Park. 1988. "An analysis of causes of schisms in ethnic churches: The case of Korean-American churches." *Sociological Analysis* 49(3):234–248.

Shurden, W. B. 1972. *Not a Silent People: Controversies that have Shaped Southern Baptists*. Nashville: Broadman.

———. 1981. "The inerrancy debate: A comparative study of Southern Baptist controversies." *Baptist History and Heritage* 16:12–19.

———. 1981. "The Southern Baptist synthesis: Is it cracking?" *Baptist History and Heritage* 16(2):2–11.

Southard, S. 1964. "The Southern Establishment." *Christian Century* 81:1618–1621.

Spain, R. B. 1961. *At Ease in Zion: Social History of Southern Baptists, 1865–1900*. Nashville: Vanderbilt University Press.

Stark, R., and W. S. Bainbridge. 1979. "Of churches, sects, and cults: Preliminary concepts for a theory of religious movements." *Journal for the Scientific Study of Religion* 18(2):117–133.

———. 1980. "Sectarian tension." *Review of Religious Research* 22(2):105–124.

————. 1985. *The Future of Religion*. Berkeley: University of California Press.

Steed, M. L. 1986. "Church schism and secession: A necessary sequence?" *Review of Religious Research* 27:344–355.

Stump, R. W. 1984. "Regional migration and religious commitment in the United States." *Journal for the Scientific Study of Religion* 23(3):292–303.

————. 1985. "Regional migration and religious patterns in the American South." A paper presented to the meetings of the Society for the Scientific Study of Religion in Savannah.

Sullivan, J. L. 1979. "Polity developments in the Southern Baptist Convention (1900–1977)." *Baptist History and Heritage* 14(3):22–31.

————. 1983. *Baptist Polity As I See It*. Nashville: Broadman.

Sweet, W. W. 1964. *Religion on the American Frontier, the Baptists, 1783–1830*. New York: Henry Holt and Company.

Swidler, A. 1986. "Culture in action: Symbols and strategies." *American Sociological Review* 51: 273–286.

Takayama, K. P. 1974. "Administrative structures and political processes in Protestant denominations." *Publius* 4(2):5–37.

————. 1980. "Strains, conflicts, and schisms in Protestant denominations." In *American Denominational Organization*, ed. R. P. Sherer. Pasadena: William Carey Library.

Takayama, K. P., and L. W. Cannon. 1979. "Formal polity and power distribution in American Prostestant denominations." *The Sociological Quarterly* 20: 321–332.

Takayama, K. P., and D. G. Sachs. 1976. "Polity and decision premises: The church and the private school." *Journal for the Scientific Study of Religion* 15:269–278.

Thompson, J. J. 1979. "A free-and-easy democracy: Southern Baptists and denominational structure in the 1920s." *Foundations* 22:43–50.

————. 1982. *Tried as by Fire: Southern Baptists and the Religious Controversies of the 1920s*. Macon: Mercer University Press.

Torbet, R. G. 1950. *A History of the Baptists*. Philadelphia: Judson Press.

Toulouse, M. G. 1981. "A case study in schism: J. Frank Norris and the SBC." *Foundations* 24:32–48.

Troeltsch, E. 1931. *The Social Teachings of the Christian Churches*, vol. 1. London: George Allen.

Tull, J. E. 1975. "The Landmark movement: An historical and theological appraisal." *Baptist History and Heritage* 10(1):3–18.

Turner, H. L. 1988. "Southern Baptist cosmogony and eschatology: Mechanisms for coping with twentieth-century societal stress." A paper presented to the Religious Research Association.

Valentine, F. D. 1949. *A History of Southern Baptists and Race Relations, 1917–1947*. New York: Arno Press (1980).

Vrga, D., and F. J. Fahey. 1970. "The relationship of religious practices and beliefs to schism." *Sociological Analysis* 31(1):46–55.

Wald, K., D. E. Owen, and S. S. Hill, Jr. 1989. "Evangelical politics and status issues." *Journal for the Scientific Study of Religion* 28(1):1–16.

Wallis, R. 1977. *The Road to Total Freedom.* New York: Columbia University Press.

Ward, W. 1987. "The role of the Holy Spirit in relation to the authority of the Bible." In *Proceedings of the Conference on Biblical Inerrancy.* Nashville: Broadman.

Warner, R. S. 1987. *New Wine in Old Wineskins.* Berkeley: University of California Press.

Watts, M. R. 1978. *The Dissenters: From the Reformation to the French Revolution.* Oxford: Clarendon Press.

Weber, L. 1989. "Who are the Southern Lutherans?" Ph.D. diss., Emory University.

Weber, M. 1946. "Characteristics of bureaucracy." and "The social psychology of the world religions." In *From Max Weber,* ed. H. H. Gerth and C. W. Mills, 196–204, 267–301. New York: Oxford University Press.

———. 1964. *The Sociology of Religion.* Trans. E. Fischoff. Boston: Beacon Press.

White, B. R. 1971. *The English Separatist Tradition: From the Marian Martyrs to the Pilgrim Fathers.* London: Oxford University Press.

Whitt, H. P. and H. M. Nelsen. 1975. "Residence, moral traditionalism, and tolerance of atheists." *Social Forces* 54:328–340.

Wilson, C. R., ed. 1985. *Religion in the South.* Jackson: University Press of Mississippi.

Wilson, J. 1971. "The sociology of schism." *A Sociological Yearbook of Religion in Britain,* 1–20.

Winter, A. 1974. "Elective affinities between religious beliefs and ideologies of managements in two eras." *American Journal of Sociology* 79(5):1134–1150.

Winter, G. 1967. "Religious organizations." In *The Emergent American Society,* vol. 1, ed. W. L. Warner, 408–491. New Haven: Yale University Press.

Wood, J. R. 1970. "Authority and controversial policy: The churches and civil rights." *American Sociological Review* 35:1057–1069.

———. 1972. "Personal commitment and organizational constraint: Church officials and racial integration." *Sociological Analysis* 33:142–151.

———. 1981. *Leadership in Voluntary Organizations.* New Brunswick: Rutgers University Press.

Wood, J. R., and M. N. Zald. 1966. "Aspects of racial integration in the Methodist church: Sources of resistance to organizational policy." *Social Forces* 45:255–265.

Wuthnow, R. 1988. *The Restructuring of American Religion: Society and Faith since World War II.* Princeton: Princeton University Press.

Zald, M. N. 1982. "Theological crucibles: Social movements in and of religion." *Review of Religious Research* 23(4):317–336.

Zald, M. N., and Berger, M. A. 1978. "Social movements in organizations: Coup d'etat, insurgency, and mass movements." *American Journal of Sociology* 83(4):823–861.

Index